S0-AQN-143

Great Historical Figures of Japan

Great Historical Figures of Japan

Japan Culture Institute

Edited by Murakami Hyoe and Thomas J. Harper
First printing, 1978
Published by the Japan Culture Institute
201 Park Avenue, 20, Sendagaya 1 chome, Shibuya-ku, Tokyo
Designed by Hayashi Tatsundo
Distributor: Japan Publications Trading Co., Ltd.
200 Clearbrook Road, Elmsford, N.Y. 10523, U.S.A.
P.O. Box 5030 Tokyo International, Tokyo 101-31, Japan
ISBN: 0-87040-431-8
Printed in Japan

CONTENTS

ESSAYS

CONTRIBUTORS

CHARLES S. TERRY is a free-lance translator. His works include *Contemporary Japanese Houses*, Vol. 1 and 2 (1964, 67).

G. CAMERON HURST is Associate Professor of History and East Asian Languages and Cultures, University of Kansas. He is the author of *Insei: Abdicated Sovereigns in the Politics of Late Heian Japan, 1086-1185* (1976).

ISTVÁN HALLA lectures at Eötvös Loland University in Hungary. He has recently compiled and translated an anthology, *Haiku Calendar.*

ALLAN G. GRAPARD teaches in the Department of Religious Studies, University of Colorado. His major field of study is Japanese religion, especially Kûkai.

MILDRED M. TAHARA is Associate Professor of Japanese Literature, University of Hawaii. Her *Tales of Yamato* is soon to be published.

EDWARD G. SEIDENSTICKER is Professor of Japanese, Columbia University. His complete translation of *Genji monogatari*, a ten-year project, was completed in 1976.

JEAN-RENÉ CHOLLEY is Assistant Professor of French, Aichi Prefectural University. One of his major interests is the war chronicles of medieval Japan.

MINORU SHINODA is Professor of History, University of Hawaii. He is the author of *The Founding of the Kamakura Shogunate, 1180-85* (1960).

KENNETH D. BUTLER is a consultant, and was formerly Director of the Inter-University Center for Japanese Language Studies. He has published several articles on the *Heike monogatari*.

PIER DEL CAMPANA is Professor of Literature, Sophia University. He is interested in comparative religion, especially Buddhism.

DONN F. DRAEGER is Director of the International Martial Culture Research Center. He himself has been trained in Japanese classical *bujutsu,* and is the first and only foreigner to attain the title of "Budô Kyôshi."

KENNETH A. GROSSBERG is a research fellow at the East Asian Research Center, Harvard University. His specialty is comparative political sociology.

H. PAUL VARLEY is Professor of Japanese History, Columbia University. He is the author of *The Ônin War* (1967), *Japanese Culture* (1973), and other works.

CAROLE A. RYAVEC is a research scholar and a frequent contributor to legal journals. Her particular interest is Japanese legal history, especially in the Age of War and Strife.

BILLY J. CODY is a research scholar at Tokyo University. His major interest is Ashikaga Yoshimitsu.

JOHN FREEMAN is Executive Director of the Urasenke Foundation of Hawaii and is interested in the culture of the Muromachi and Momoyama periods.

DIEGO PACHECO is Director of the 26 Martyrs Museum in Nagasaki. He is the author of *Nagasaki e no michi, Nagasaki no Tenshudô* and other works.

CHEN SHUN-CHEN is a novelist of the People's Republic of China. His works include *Ahen sensô* (*The Opium War*).

THOMAS J. HARPER is Senior Lecturer in the Department of Japanese, The Australian National University. He is interested in classical literature, especially *The Tale of Genji* and Motoori Norinaga.

JOHN W. HALL is Professor of History, Yale University. He has written many works on Japanese history, including *Tanuma Okitsugu, 1719-88: Forerunner of Modern Japan* (1955) and *Japan: Prehistory to Modern Times* (1970).

JOHN STEVENS is a lecturer at Tôhoku College of Social Welfare. He has recently completed a work on Ryôkan, *One Robe, One Bowl* (1977).

BURTON WATSON is a translator and the author of *Ssu-ma Ch'ien: Grand Historian of China* (1958), *Japanese Literature in Chinese*, 2 vols. (1975-76), and many other works.

HERBERT P. BIX is an editorial advisor and senior translator at *The Japan Interpreter.* His current research is on fascism and the state in prewar Japan.

MARIUS B. JANSEN is Professor of Japanese History, Princeton University. *Sakamoto Ryôma and the Meiji Restoration* is one of his major works; he recently published *Japan and China from War to Peace: 1894-1972* (1975).

MASAKAZU IWATA is Professor of History, Biola College. He is the author of *Ôkubo Toshimichi, the Bismarck of Japan* (1964).

WILLIAM D. HOOVER is Associate Professor of History, University of Toledo. His major interest is early Meiji Japan and he has written on Godai Tomoatsu.

GORDON M. BERGER is Associate Professor of History, University of Southern California. He has recently published *Parties out of Power in Japan, 1931-41* (1977).

MAKOTO UEDA is Professor of Japanese, Stanford University. The most recent of his works is *Modern Japanese Writers and the Nature of Literature* (1976).

PREFACE

In the pages of this book the reader will meet some of the more remarkable figures in the long and exciting pageant of Japanese history. *Great Historical Figures of Japan* is a collection of portraits of more than forty men and women – from a great yet little-known sixth-century crown prince to the late novelist and Nobel Prize winner Kawabata Yasunari – who have played crucial roles in their nation's past.

Many in the West have tended to regard Japan's history as beginning with Commodore Perry's mid-nineteenth-century mission of persuasion that opened Japan's doors to the rest of the world, but in fact it dates back two millennia. The earliest written records tell us that rule by the ancestors of the present imperial house had spread over most of the country by the fifth century A.D. This clan's ascendancy later gave rise to an unsurpassedly refined court society centered in what is now Kyoto, and produced brilliant cultural achievements. Still later, power struggles among the aristocracy led to civil wars and eventually to military control and centuries of feudal government.

The history of Japan's relations with the outside world is equally fascinating and unique. At times Japan has adopted enthusiastically the culture of the Asian continent – particularly China – deriving much of its vitality from foreign sources. At other times it has closed the nation to the outside while it assimilated these foreign imports until they matured into a culture distinctively Japanese. Then in the sixteenth century there was a great influx of European culture; but shortly thereafter this flow too was all but cut off. Prior to the Meiji Restoration Japan was rarely involved in foreign wars – there were only the series of conflicts with the nations of the Korean peninsula in ancient times, the invasions by the Mongols in the thirteenth century, and Toyotomi Hideyoshi's attempt to conquer Korea following his unification of Japan in the sixteenth century. Indeed it is one of the distinctive features of Japan's long history that the nation has hardly been touched by foreign invaders. This is due, of course, to the geographical fact that Japan is an island nation extending beyond and separated from the eastern extreme of the Asian continent; it is also one of the reasons that the unique character of Japan's history attracted so little attention among Westerners in the past.

Japan, then, has known ages of peace and effective rule as well as ages of continuous civil warfare. Periods of upheaval have produced illustrious statesmen, warriors, and religious leaders; and every age has had its share of great thinkers, writers, and artists. This book is a guide to the great men and women of every period in Japan's history.

In preparing this book for a Western audience, the editors have relied entirely on non-Japanese scholars. They include John W. Hall, Professor of History at Yale University and the author of many authoritative works on Japanese history, among them *Japan: From Prehistory to Modern Times*; Marius Jansen, Professor of History at Princeton University and a distinguished scholar of the Meiji Restoration; and Edward Seidensticker, Professor of Japanese Literature at Columbia University and a renowned translator, most recently of *The Tale of Genji.*

This collection of essays is valuable for two reasons. First, it offers readers a pleasurable way to familiarize themselves with Japanese history. While each biography is written by an authority in his or her field, the essays are by no means excessively "scholarly" or pedantic, but very accessible to the general reader. Secondly, it offers readers some answers to that oft-asked question: Just who are the Japanese? For the statesmen, artists, warriors, and thinkers who are brought to life in this book reveal in the particulars of their lives many facets of the Japanese character.

Editors' Note

The completion of any book depends on the cooperation of many individuals. The editors wish to express their deep gratitude to all who have helped make the publication of this book possible.

The Hepburn system of romanization is used for Japanese terms, which are italicized except for words included in the second edition of *Webster's New World Dictionary.*

This book was published through a grant from the Commemorative Association for the Japan World Exposition.

Legend and Political Intrigue in Ancient Japan

Shôtoku Taishi

by

CHARLES S. TERRY

According to the *Nihon shoki* (*Chronicles of Japan*),[1] in the year 592, the empress-consort Toyomike Kashikiya-hime, whose name means roughly "the princess who cooks splendid food," became the first woman to reign over Japan as *tennô.* Although she is spoken of in English as the Empress Suiko, her title in Japanese, which appears to have been first used during her reign, carries no indication of sex and is the same word that is rendered as "emperor" when its bearer is male.

It seems unlikely on the face of it that the empress was raised to her exalted status because of her culinary skills, but the sole reason offered by the *Nihon shoki,* which is the principal and almost the only documentary source for this period, is that the great ministers of the land insisted that she take the position. Why a number of possible male heirs were passed over is something of a mystery, particularly since no precedent for a reigning queen or empress existed in the entire Far East at the time. It is usually argued that she was a compromise candidate, so to speak, chosen to avoid succession quarrels that might result from the selection of any of the available princes.

Be that as it may, Suiko had unusually impressive connections. Born the daughter of the Emperor Kinmei (r. 531?-71), she was the half sister and widow of the Emperor Bidatsu (r. 571-85), the full sister of the Emperor Yômei (r. 585-87), and the half sister of the Emperor Sushun (r. 587-92). On her mother's side she was a niece of the great minister Soga no Umako (d. 626), who, as adviser to three of the emperors named and the murderer by proxy of the last, is generally considered to have been the most powerful man in the country. Most likely Suiko was made empress because Umako chose her.

Shortly after Suiko's accession, her nephew, usually called Shôtoku Taishi or Prince Shôtoku, rose to a position of special prominence. In an entry for 593, the *Nihon shoki* states, "The Imperial Prince Umayado no Toyotomimi [Shôtoku] was appointed prince imperial. He had general control of the government and was entrusted with all the details of administration." This is usually taken to mean that Shôtoku became crown prince and regent. He was not an official regent, because no such office existed at the time, but it is generally thought that he acted on behalf of the empress, who eschewed a positive role in government and politics.

Just how much effective power either the empress or her deputy had is another question entirely, and it is the key question in appraising Prince Shôtoku's career. The great majority of books on the subject say that just about everything good and decent that happened after 593 stemmed directly or indirectly from the prince's efforts. An excellent brief standard history of Japan in English states, for example, that "under the able leadership of the crown prince and regent, Shôtoku, many startling reforms were undertaken."[2] Yet Sir George Sansom warns that "the condition of Japan at the time when he came into power as regent... was scarcely such that he could in his short life have achieved all the political and social reforms and engaged in all the profound studies that are ascribed to him."[3] The sad fact, as Sansom notes, is that we have very little exact information as to what the prince actually did.

The most important sources concerning him are the *Nihon shoki* itself and the *Jôgû Shôtoku Hôô teisetsu* (abbreviated to *Hôô teisetsu* below),[4] a compilation of writings and inscriptions having to do with the prince. The former was completed in 720; the latter is of uncertain date, but contains entries that seem to antedate the *Nihon shoki.* The *Hôô teisetsu* must be used with care, because it was obviously put together for the purpose of glorifying the prince, as were several other biographical works prepared in the eighth and ninth centuries. The *Nihon shoki,* for its part, was composed partly for the purpose of demonstrating the imperial family's divine right to rule the country. It treats Soga no Umako's son and grandson as would-be usurpers of the imperial throne and appears to be biased against the whole Soga clan.

To offer a small example, in a passage quite similar to the one quoted above from the *Nihon shoki,* the *Hôô teisetsu* says, "In the time when Owarida-no-miya [Suiko] ruled the land, Kamitsumiya no Umayado no Toyotomimi [Shôtoku] and the Great Omi Shima [Soga no Umako] together assisted in governing the nation."[5] In other words, credit for managing the empress's government must be shared by Shôtoku and Soga

Shôtoku Taishi; Imperial Household Agency (Tokyo)

no Umako. The statements in the two books may have been based on different sources, but it seems improbable that the *Nihon shoki's* failure to mention Soga no Umako's role was accidental. In later passages relating specific events that occurred in Suiko's reign, the *Nihon shoki* does often say that the prince acted in conjunction with Umako.

Apart from political prejudices, many statements about Shôtoku in these two early sources are so patently mythical that one hesitates to accept anything they say about him at face value, no matter how matter-of-fact and annalistic it appears. The one conclusion that seems unshakable is that by 720, the apotheosis of Prince Shôtoku was virtually complete. Later sources, unfortunately, add much legend and little fact.

Birth, Lineage, and Names

The prince seems to have been born in 574 or thereabouts. A passage in the *Nihon shoki* immediately following the earlier quotation says: "He [Shôtoku] was the second child of the Emperor Tachibana no Toyohi

[Yômei]. The empress-consort his mother's name was the Imperial Princess Anahobe no Hashibito. The empress-consort, on the day of the dissolution of her pregnancy, went round the forbidden precinct, inspecting the different offices. When she came to the Horse Department, and had just reached the door of the stables, she was suddenly delivered of him without effort. He was able to speak as soon as he was born, and was so wise when he grew up that he could attend to the suits of ten men at once and decide them all without error. He knew beforehand what was going to happen. Moreover he learned the Inner Doctrine [Buddhism] from a Koguryŏ priest named Hyè-cha, and studied the Outer [Confucian] Classics with a doctor called Hak-ka. In both of these branches of study he became thoroughly proficient. The emperor his father loved him, and made him occupy the Upper Hall south of the Palace. Therefore he was styled the Senior Prince Kamitsumiya, Umayado no Toyotomimi."

It was suggested as early as 1905 that the story about the prince's being born at the stable door may have been inspired by the Christian account of Jesus' birth.[6] This is not impossible, because there were Nestorian Christians in China during this age, and their beliefs may have crept into Buddhist lore brought by Chinese bonzes to Japan. By the ninth century, the story had been elaborated to the extent that a priest shining with a golden light appears to the Princess Hashibito on the auspicious first day of the year, announces that he is in reality the Bodhisattva Guze Kannon (World-Saving Kannon), and persuades her to let him reside in her body for a time so as to be born a human being. This annunciation legend might be either Christian or Buddhist in origin.

Prince Shôtoku's lineage is of sufficient importance to be given in somewhat greater detail. His father, the Emperor Yômei, was the son of the Emperor Kinmei by a concubine named Kitashi-hime, who was the daughter of Soga no Iname (d. 570), Umako's father. Shôtoku's mother was a daughter of the Emperor Kinmei by a concubine named Oanegimi, who was also a daughter of Soga no Iname. Since both the prince's grandmothers were sisters of Umako, Umako was his granduncle on two scores. This probably explains why Shôtoku was chosen as crown prince over other princes with better claims to the succession. As though the relationship with Umako were not close enough, Shôtoku married Tajiko no Iratsume, a daughter of Umako.

Among the various names by which Shôtoku is known, Kamitsumiya, "Upper Palace," comes from the name of the place where he lived as a child. Umayado, "Stable Door," is traditionally said to have been inspired by the birth story, but modern scholars are inclined to believe that the legend came from the name, which may have derived from that of some place or family having a close connection with the prince. Toyotomimi, "Abundant Quick Ears," appeared in the inscription on a tapestry made in memory of the prince shortly after his death and may have been one of the names he used while still alive. The statement about his ability to listen to ten suits at once is doubtless based on this appellation. Shôtoku, "Sage-Virtue," first appears in an inscription of 706 on a metal base under the spire of the pagoda at the Hokkiji, a temple in the village of Ikaruga. In addition, the prince is often called "Great King of the Law" or "Master King of the Law" because of his efforts to propagate Buddhism.

Historical Context

Japan in the period with which we are concerned was only on the verge of becoming a full-fledged nation. Since the fourth or fifth century, the numerous small principalities of which it was composed had apparently recognized at least the spiritual primacy of a clan that resided in the Yamato area (in modern Nara Prefecture) and claimed descent from the sun goddess Amaterasu Ômikami. The head of this clan, who was later called the emperor, appears to have been regarded as a high priest capable of communicating with the gods on behalf of the world of ordinary mortals. The degree of political control he exercised is debatable, but it is almost certain that any action he took was greatly influenced, when not determined, by the chieftains of certain other great clans.

There seems to have been a loose hierarchy among the tribal groups, reflected in a system of title-surnames (*kabane*) indicating the relationship between the individual family and the sun-emperor. The most important lords were the *omi*, who traced their ancestry back through one emperor or another to the sun goddess, and the *muraji*, whose lineage was thought to spring from other deities in the Shinto pantheon. The leader of the *omi* clans was the Ôomi, or Great Omi, and the leader of the *muraji* clans was the Ômuraji, or Great Muraji (there were sometimes two men with this title). During the fifth and most of the sixth century, the Great Omi and the Great Muraji vied with each other and with the emperor for control of the central government, such as it was.

Japan had no system of writing and trailed far behind Korea and China in general cultural development. This situation was gradually changing, however, because of the arrival of numerous Korean or Chinese refugees from wars on the continent. The imperial clan, along with certain other progressive tribes, recognized the merits of the civilization these immigrants brought and organized them into corporations (*be* or *tomo*) performing various skilled tasks for their patrons. It would be no exaggeration to say that the degree to which a Japanese clan prospered in this age was proportional to its ability to acquire and exploit foreign settlers as teachers, scribes, accountants, interpreters, or craftsmen. In particular, the rise of the Soga to power in the sixth century was largely the result of their being the protectors of groups having foreign antecedents. Their closeness with immigrants from the Korean kingdom of Paekche has even led to the speculation that the Soga themselves were of Paekche descent, which may or may not be true.

In the early sixth century, Japan held a colony called Mimana (or Imna) at the southern end of the Korean peninsula, the remainder of which was divided into the kingdoms of Koguryŏ, Paekche, and Silla. The Japanese Court was consequently deeply and actively interested in Korean politics, as it had been for the previous 150 years. The history of this involvement is far too complicated to go into even briefly here, but several facts are of importance in discussing Prince Shôtoku's life. In the first place, the consolidation of the three Korean nations was gradually weakening the Japanese position on the mainland. Mimana was lost to Silla in 562 and was never regained, though successive Japanese rulers attempted by force or persuasion to recover it. Despite conflicts, all three of the Korean states maintained relations with the Japanese Court and even sent tribute from time to time, their chief aim being to gain Japanese support for their own ambitions. From the Japanese viewpoint, Korea was a source not only of wealth in the form of tribute, but also of a superior culture. It was, in fact, a filter through which the rich material and intellectual achievements of China were being transmitted, albeit not perfectly. Because of this, the Japanese had something of a love-hate complex toward the three kingdoms – a mixture of admiration on the one hand and the urge to dominate on the other.

In the mid-sixth century, the king of Paekche, seeking aid against Silla, sent the Emperor Kinmei an image of the Buddha, together with some Buddhist scriptures, religious implements, and a letter recommending the Buddhist religion. This is regarded as the official introduction of Buddhism to Japan, though the faith was already known to some extent from Korean immigrants. At the time the chief rivals for power in Japan were the Great Muraji Mononobe no Okoshi and the Great Omi Soga no Iname. Broadly speaking, the Mononobe were warriors who favored continued rule by clan heads and a belligerent policy toward Korea. The Soga were a more forward-minded group who saw their future in a stronger central government and rapid adoption of continental ways. As might have been predicted, the Mononobe opposed the new religion, whereas the Soga favored it, probably seeing in it a means of bolstering the authority of the state. The Soga were by this time well on their way to forming close marital ties with the imperial clan and must have seen little to fear from the prospect of an emperor with increased powers.

The dispute over whether or not to allow the spread of Buddhism continued, as did the political struggle of which it was but a single facet, until 587, when Okoshi's successor, Mononobe no Moriya (? -587) was defeated and his clan wiped out by Soga no Umako. Victory not only eliminated serious rivalry to Umako, but also ensured the widespread propagation of Buddhism.

That the imperial clan was in no position to resist Umako is evident from what happened next. Shortly after the war of 587, Prince Hatsusebe, brother of Shôtoku's mother and a nephew of Umako, became the Emperor Sushun, ostensibly on the advice of Kashikiya-hime. When, five years later, he showed signs of rebelling against his uncle, Umako summarily had him killed. Such was the prelude to Suiko's enthronement.

Shôtoku and Buddhism

Almost nothing is known of Prince Shôtoku's early life, though there is no dearth of stories illustrating his precocity, his devotion to his parents, and his moral rectitude. Many of the legends have a Buddhist cast that suggests the hand of pious monastic scribes. Shôtoku is presented as having powers similar to those of the Buddha or as being an incarnation of the Guze Kannon. Perhaps the most famous tale of all concerns the prince's supposed role in the battle between the Soga, whose side he was on, and the Mononobe.

According to the account in the *Nihon shoki,* at a point when Umako's forces were about to be defeated, the prince swiftly cut down a tree and made images of the (Buddhist) Four Heavenly Kings. Placing these in his topknot, he vowed that if the Soga army won, he would honor the sacred beings by building a temple and a pagoda. Umako is said to have made a similar vow at the same time. After the war, relates the text, the Shitennôji (Temple of the Four Heavenly Kings) was built in Settsu (modern Osaka), and half of Mononobe no Moriya's slaves, together with his house, were donated to the institution. Umako, we are told, carried out his vow by erecting the Hôkôji temple in Asuka, which was the capital.

The whole story may be viewed as an attempt to romanticize the founding of two well-known monasteries. The Hôkôji was indeed set up by Umako, but not primarily as a result of the battle. Modern excavations have shown that this was by far the largest and most costly of the early Japanese Buddhist monasteries. It seems to have had at least semi-official status and to have symbolized Umako's determination to implant the Buddhist faith in Japan. *Hôkô* in its name means "to cause the Buddha's Law to flourish."

The Shitennôji is another matter. Though it does appear to have been erected before the death of the empress in 628, there is no real proof that Prince Shôtoku sponsored it. Indeed, the narrative cited seems to suggest that Umako built it, since he gained possession of Moriya's property after Moriya's death.

According to the *Nihon shoki* and other sources, in 594 the empress "instructed" Prince Shôtoku and Umako to promote the prosperity of Buddhism. The *Nihon shoki* adds, "At this time, all the Omi and Muraji vied each with one another in erecting Buddhist shrines for the benefit of their lords and parents." Leaving aside the question of who instructed whom, it appears that with the Mononobe opposition in ruins, the great clans hurried to erect family temples dedicated to the memory of their forebears.

The *Hôô teisetsu* mentions seven monasteries or nunneries as having been founded by Prince Shôtoku himself. This number increases in later sources to eight, then nine, then twenty-one or more. In most cases, modern critical studies indicate that the attributions stem ultimately from the desire of the religious establishments in question to associate themselves with the prince's name. Sometimes the date of the empress's "instruction" crops up in the founding legends.

There can be little doubt of the prince's devotion to Buddhism or of his efforts to understand it and promote its spread. He began his studies under the Korean priest Hyè-cha in 595, and the *Hôô teisetsu* lists among the subjects he mastered not only Buddhist sutras, but the Chinese classics, Taoist works, astronomy, and geography. The same source goes on to say that the prince wrote seven volumes of commentaries on the *Lotus Sutra* and other Buddhist scriptures. Several versions of the commentaries have been in existence since the eighth century,[7] but opinions as to their authenticity range all the way from complete rejection to the assertion that one remaining part is written in the prince's own hand.

In 606, Shôtoku is recorded to have lectured to the empress for three days on the *Queen Śrimâlâ Sutra* (Japanese, *Shômangyô*). Later in the same year he gave lectures on the *Lotus Sutra* and pleased the empress so greatly that she awarded him a hundred hectares of rice fields in Harima Province. He gave the land to "the temple in Ikaruga," which is to say the Hôryûji.

The prince's connection with this monastery requires special comment, because the Hôryûji is the fountainhead of later worship of him.

According to the *Nihon shoki,* in 601, he began constructing a new palace for himself at Ikaruga, some sixteen kilometers from the empress's palace in Asuka. He moved into the new establishment in 605 and seemingly lived there for the rest of his life. Modern archaeologists have unearthed, under the East Precinct of the Hôryûji, remains believed to have been the Ikaruga Palace. A short distance to the southwest was a Buddhist temple, probably erected in memory of the prince's father. Called Ikarugadera or Wakakusa-garan, this was the first version of the Hôryûji.

The Ikarugadera later burned down and was replaced by the present Western Precinct of the Hôryûji. The date of the rebuilding is a matter of debate. The principal halls of the Western Precinct have long been considered representative of Buddhist architecture in the Asuka period (592-645), but there is good reason to suppose that they were not actually constructed until later. The subject is a very thorny one. Few historians argue today that the present buildings date from Shôtoku's time, but his founding of the original Ikarugadera is rarely disputed. The original temple is probably to be regarded as a family shrine of the sort the leading clans hurried to build after 594. In size, it did not compare with the Hôkôji.

Tamura Enchô, an expert on Japanese Buddhist history and biographer of Prince Shôtoku, argues that the most important sponsors of Buddhism in this period were the Soga, and that the establishment of the various clan temples represents a hierarchical grouping of the territorial magnates under Soga no Umako, whose Hôkôji was the center of a new spiritual network. After the fall of the Soga in 645, the various monasteries were forced to look to the imperial family for patronage. Hence, temple records or legends began to stress the debt of the Buddhist institutions to the Empress Suiko or Prince Shôtoku. Though Professor Tamura does not say so, this would go a long way toward explaining how the prince was sanctified so thoroughly before he had been dead a hundred years. It is symbolic that even the Hôkôji, Umako's family temple, was later said to have been founded by Shôtoku.

Shôtoku and Foreign Relations

In 600, there began a series of events that have much to do with Prince Shôtoku's later fame. First, war broke out between Silla and the states of Mimana, and a Japanese expeditionary force was sent to Mimana's aid. Silla capitulated, but once the victorious Japanese army had gone home, attacked Mimana again. Two years later a punitive force was assembled in Kyushu under the command of the Imperial Prince Kume, but was detained because of the prince's illness. When he died in early 603, his younger brother, Prince Takima, went to replace him, but owing to the death of his wife en route to Kyushu, returned without carrying out his mission. Nothing more is recorded on the subject of the expedition, which was presumably abandoned.

In the meantime, the *History of the Sui* (*Sui shu*) records the arrival of a Japanese embassy to China in 600. Japanese records do not mention this, but the reason may be that the mission failed to gain Chinese support against Silla, which had already appealed to the Chinese emperor. The Japanese effort to establish direct contact is the first recorded for more than one hundred years. During most of this time, China itself had been divided, but as of 589 it had been reunified under the Sui Dynasty (589-618), which, it might be observed, was extremely partial to Buddhism. One of the Japanese embassy's aims must have been simply to see what changes were taking place. Since the Sui emperor had designs on Koguryŏ, with which Japan was not on good terms, the Japanese rulers may have felt it a propitious time to make common cause with him.

Professor Tamura argues that Prince Shôtoku and Soga no Umako were at odds on policy toward Korea. In his opinion, Umako felt obliged to maintain a stern policy toward Silla while treating Paekche as a friendly tributary. Shôtoku, on the other hand, favored good relations with Silla because Silla was a source of cultural enlightenment. According to this theory, the appointment of imperial princes as commanding generals signified that Prince Shôtoku had acquired control of foreign affairs. The abandonment of the campaign against Silla over nothing more serious than the death of Prince Takima's wife is taken to mean that Shôtoku had been opposed to it to begin with. Tamura sees Shôtoku's decision in 601 to build the Ikaruga Palace, remote from Asuka, as resulting from his desire to be out from under Umako's domination and free to establish closer relations with Silla and ultimately China. Ikaruga, argues Tamura, afforded ready access to Naniwa (modern Osaka), the port through which missions to and from foreign countries passed, by a route different from the one used heretofore.[9]

There is nothing in the *Nihon shoki* or other sources that absolutely precludes this interpretation, but, with all deference to its ingenuity, there is precious little that supports it either. It is difficult, on the whole, to avoid the suspicion that if the compilers of the *Nihon shoki* had had the slightest inkling that Prince Shôtoku played an important role in foreign exchanges, they would have said so in no uncertain terms, rather than guard their secret. Yet the prince's name is not even mentioned in connection with the three embassies recorded during his lifetime. The idea that the initiative in importing Chinese culture was taken by a man supposed to have been a far-seeing and saintly intellectual is attractive in its own way, but it must be accepted on faith.

A second mission to the Sui Court was dispatched in 607 under the leadership of Ono no Imoko. As is widely known, the message sent from Japan opened with the words "the emperor of the country where the sun rises addresses a letter to the emperor of the country where the sun sets." It is frequently stated that Prince Shôtoku was responsible for this irreverent salutation, but again there is no proof. The letter has usually been taken as a sign that the prince insisted upon having the empress address the Chinese ruler as an equal – a point that seems rather less important now than it did a few decades back.

Though the Sui emperor was not pleased, he sent a return envoy, and when the Chinese embassy went home in 608, Ono no Imoko was sent to China again, this time with a number of Japanese students. (Actually, according to the Sui history, Ono no Imoko had been accompanied in the previous year by several tens of monks who had come to study Buddhism.) Having thus established direct ties with China, the Japanese Court proceeded in the next decades to import Chinese culture wholesale, adopting a Chinese-style government and legal system, Chinese writing, Chinese art, Chinese dress, Chinese science, and Chinese philosophy, all primarily through the medium of Buddhism. Within the next century Japan underwent a cultural transformation of astonishing proportions. Those who consider Prince Shôtoku to have dispatched the early Japanese embassies credit him with having laid the way for this achievement.

It might be noted that the *History of the Sui* gives the name of the Japanese king in phonetic transcription with characters thought by many Japanese scholars to be construable as Tarishihiko. Who this refers to is conjectural, but it seems certain that it is the name or title of a man, rather than a woman. Over and above this, surely the Sui visitors to Japan would have remarked upon the presence of a woman ruler, had they known of her existence. Speculation is that the Chinese ambassador was received not by Suiko, but by Shôtoku or Soga no Umako. The Sui source also transcribes the name of the Japanese crown prince, but the Chinese representation has not been satisfactorily related to any known Japanese name.

Shôtoku and Domestic Government

Shôtoku is usually credited with two great internal reforms, which were the establishment in 603 of a system of court ranks and the composing in 604 of a constitution.

The court ranks, known as "cap ranks" because they were distinguished by the shape and materials of the headgear assigned, numbered twelve in all and were named after six Confucian ideals, each divided into two classes. The highest rank, for example, was the Greater Virtue, while the lowest was the Lesser Knowledge. The idea behind the scheme and the titles employed came no doubt from China, but may have entered Japan by way of Korea, where all three kingdoms had already adopted similar court honors.

The purpose of the cap ranks was to replace the old system of title-surnames and clan oligarchy with a central bureaucracy appointed by the emperor. The new titles, instead of being awarded to clan leaders as such, were theoretically granted to individual persons on the basis of merit and were not hereditary. How effective the new system was is subject to doubt, but it was a noteworthy move in the direction of a Chinese-style central government.

It is of particular interest that the Soga, along with the imperial clan, were above the order of ranks. This would seem to indicate that Soga no Umako played a part in the institution of the new system. Actually, the *Nihon shoki* does not say who was responsible, but merely notes that it came into being. As in several other instances, the question of whether Prince Shôtoku conceived and carried out this measure devolves upon that of whether he actually ruled or was subject to dictation from his uncle.

The *Nihon shoki* does say that the prince himself "in person prepared for the first time laws," by which is meant the celebrated Seventeen-Article Constitution. This is a collection, not of regulations, but of political and moral precepts or exhortations based partly on Buddhism and partly on Confucianism. The general tone can be seen from the first four articles, which stress, in summary, that "harmony is to be valued," that reverence should be accorded to Buddhism, that imperial commands should be obeyed scrupulously, and that "the leading principle of the government of the people consists in decorous behaviour." Only rarely are specifics mentioned, and when they are, they sometimes suggest a later authorship.

Though the document is quoted in full in the *Nihon shoki,* there is no statement to the effect that it was promulgated as law or issued to any particular group of people. Partly because of this, the authenticity has been severely questioned, though some historians accept the work as genuine. Despite its tendency toward the abstract, it is a fairly clear statement of an ideal imperial state governed by Confucian principles and devoted to the worship of the Buddha. It might have been written by Shôtoku, or by a group of scholars working on commission from him, or by anyone with learning who favored the formation of a Chinese-style nation.

Despite the renown of Shôtoku's supposed efforts to institute good government, scholars of the Tokugawa period (1603-1867) faulted him for violation of a basic Confucian principle. Their real objection to him had to do with his Buddhist leanings, but the point on which he was attacked most tellingly was that he took no action against Soga no Umako for assassinating his lord and master, the Emperor Sushun. Modern defenders of the prince have pointed out that he was only eighteen at the time and could not have been expected to take punitive measures against his powerful uncle. Detractors, for their share, argue that if the prince was a puppet of Umako in 592, there is little reason to suppose that he did not remain a puppet the rest of his life. The *Nihon shoki* does seem to indicate that the power of the Soga continued unabated until 645, whereas the same is not evident with respect to the prince or his descendants.

Shôtoku's Later Life

Only five entries in the *Nihon shoki* mention Prince Shôtoku between 605, when he took up residence at Ikaruga, and 622, when he died. The first, for 606, has to do with his lectures, mentioned earlier. The second, for 607, says that together with the Great Omi and all the other functionaries the prince worshiped the gods of heaven and earth, apparently in response to a command from the empress. The meaning of this is not entirely clear; perhaps the empress felt that the Shinto deities were being neglected in an excess of Buddhist zeal. The third and fourth entries recount a miracle story, which need not detain us, and the fifth, for 620, relates that Shôtoku collaborated with Soga no Umako on the compilation of a national history. It is a remarkable coincidence that the last event, presented without month and date, occurred precisely one hundred years before the completion of the *Nihon shoki,* which was based in part on the history in question.

There is little here to indicate that the prince took an active part in government after 605. The assumption that he did rests ultimately on the blanket statement that he had charge of the empress's government. In terms of factual records, there is scarce reason not to suppose that he spent his later years in retirement at Ikaruga, perhaps writing his commentaries or working on the national history.

After his death, the prince was buried at a place called Shinaga, where his mother and one of his wives were also entombed. One legend has it that all three of them died on the same day, but this is probably no more than an attempt to explain their being interred at the same spot.

Postwar Reappraisals

Since the end of World War II, the Japanese imperial family has ceased to be sacrosanct, and it has been possible for historians (and others) to cast doubt on traditional views of the unbroken imperial lineage. It is no longer necessary to accept the *Nihon shoki*'s portrait of Prince Shôtoku or its rather puzzling account of the roles played by him and his aunt. Not a few writers have undertaken to reassess the prince's accomplishments downward, some going so far as to imply that he was a well-meaning cipher, if not actually the collaborator of Soga no Umako in the murder of Emperor Sushun.

One of the most imaginative theories concerning this period was set forth by the late Ôba Hiromichi in his *Asuka ôchô no higeki* (*Tragedy of the Asuka Royal Court*).[10] Ôba, a specialist on the Near East with an interest in early Japanese history, argued that Soga no Umako, having disposed of Sushun, himself became the king (*ôgimi*), but relegated the position of chief Shinto priestess to Suiko, who by virtue of being descended from the deposed dynasty could claim to be the sun goddess's heir on earth. In the process, she was given the title *tennô,* which had not previously been used in Japan and which meant in Chinese "ruler of heaven," not "ruler of the earth." Shôtoku was selected as her heir because he was a devout Buddhist and might be counted upon eventually to forsake Shinto for the foreign faith. His part in government was therefore negligible, except insofar as he agreed with his uncle.

Later, argues Ôba, Soga no Iruka (?-645), the third ruler in the Asuka (Soga) dynasty, decided to take over the title of *tennô* as well as that of king. At this point, opposition to the Soga rallied around the heirs of the earlier dynasty and overthrew the Asuka royal house. In succeeding generations, the Soga court was written out of history by presenting Umako and his progeny as the *tennô*'s ministers and ascribing Umako's more worthy policies to Prince Shôtoku.

Many will hesitate to go all the way with Ôba, but the common-sense idea that Soga no Umako, whether king or power behind the throne, performed many of the deeds attributed to his grandnephew seems likely to gain weight as time goes on. Certainly no modern reader of the sources can avoid finding Prince Shôtoku a little too good to be true.

Nevertheless, the prince will doubtless retain a place in popular historical lore. At present, his face, in a representation thought to date from the early eighth century, is probably better known in Japan than that of any other historical personage, because it appears on the Bank of Japan's ubiquitous 10,000-yen notes. Moreover, to judge from a fairly recent bibliography, some three hundred books and one thousand articles have been written about him since 1868, not to speak of one hundred or so biographies from the Tokugawa period and stories in generation after generation of primary schoolbooks.

So many legends and so few facts are known about the prince that he is useful to almost anyone. For prewar rightists, who wanted to show how enlightened, wise, and benevolent the imperial system could be, he was an ideal hero. For postwar leftists, who begrudge the imperial family the time of day, he is a perfect debunkee. For Confucianists, he can be a villain; for Buddhists, a saint; for the Bank of Japan, the personification of solidity and rectitude. For some historians at least, he is the convenient genius on whom it is possible to hang a number of innovations that might otherwise be a nuisance to explain. Specifically, for the compilers of the *Nihon shoki,* he was the logical person to credit with anything laudable Soga no Umako might have done. Whether they actually did this or not may well never be known for certain.

[NOTES]

1. The version used here is translated in W.G. Aston, *Nihongi: Chronicles of Japan from the Earliest Times to A.D. 697* (Tokyo: Charles E. Tuttle, 1972). Translations given below are all taken, with minor alternations from this work.
2. E.O. Reischauer, *Japan: The Story of a Nation* (Tuttle, 1974), p. 20.
3. George Sansom, *A History of Japan to 1334* (Tuttle, 1974), p. 51.
4. The edition used is that presented in Ienaga Saburô, *Jôgû Shôtoku Hôô teisetsu no kenkyû* (*Research on the Jôgû Shôtoku Hôô teisetsu*), revised edition (Tokyo: Sanseidô, 1951). The meaning of *teisetu* in the title is uncertain.
5. *Ibid.*, p. 253.
6. In Kume Kunitake, *Shôtoku Taishi jitsuroku* (*True Record of Shôtoku Taishi*), a pioneer study.
7. The commentaries are presented in Japanese in Nakamura Hajime, ed., *Shôtoku Taishi.* Vol. 2 of *Nihon no meicho* (*Great Books of Japan*; Tokyo: Chûô, Kôron-sha, 1970), pp. 89-405.
8. Tamura Enchô, *Shôtoku Taishi: Ikaruga-miya no arasoi* (*Prince Shôtoku: The Struggle of Ikaruga Palace*), no. 43 of Chûkô Shinsho (Chûo Kôron-sha, 1964), p. 73.
9. *Ibid.*, pp. 88-94.
10. Ôba Hiromichi, *Asuka ôchô no higeki: Soga sandai no eikô to botsuraku* (*Tragedy of the Asuka Court: The Glory and Fall of Three Soga Generations*), Kappa Books Series (Tokyo: Kôbunsha, 1977).

An Emperor who Ruled as Well as Reigned

Tenmu Tennô

by

G. Cameron Hurst

Western writers have long been fascinated by the Japanese imperial institution. They seem particularly aware of the longevity of the dynasty and the relatively weak political role of the Emperor. A good example of the way Westerners regard the Emperor can be seen in the vitriolic reactions to David Bergamini's *Japan's Imperial Conspiracy,* in which the author had the temerity to cast the present Emperor in the role of villain in the Pacific War.

Basically, both Western and Japanese scholars view the monarch in the history of Japan as weak and powerless in terms of the everyday operation of national political affairs. The Emperor is seen as a religious, or sacerdotal, figure whose basic right to reign derives from a semi-divine quality owing to reputed descent from the sun goddess. This religious function is at the crux of Japanese concepts of sovereignty and legitimacy. Political power may be, and usually is, delegated to someone else. But only a descendant of the sun goddess can occupy the position of Emperor.

This fact accounts for the longevity of the imperial institution of Japan. There is only one case of regicide in Japan (and that disputed), and very few depositions occurred. Indeed, most of those are euphemistically styled "abdications" anyway. For most of Japanese history, Emperors reigned rather than ruled, and power struggles revolved around control of the throne rather than its outright possession.

Thus, most of Japanese history is without the rich tradition of other lands where powerful kings dominate courts, carve out empires, and throw adversaries into the dungeon with reckless abandon. Likewise, bloody battles which result in the death of one king and the seizure of power by a new line of rulers are not part and parcel of the traditional Japanese

Tenmu-Jitô Ryô (graveyard at Asuka Village, Nara)

literary-historical tradition. We search in vain in Japanese history for a Great Khan or a Charlemagne, a Henry VIII or Richard III.

A few Emperors stand out in the pages of Japanese history: Go-Daigo who in the fourteenth century tried to stem the tide of warrior dominance; Kanmu who moved the capital to the new city of Heian (Kyoto); and Meiji, the "monarch for modern Japan" who reigned during the period of Japan's vigorous modernization program in the late nineteenth century. But most of these Emperors were in actuality only minor participants in the larger political process, and the actual decisions and genius behind the developments of the day were usually initiated by someone else.

In the early years of state formation in Japan, however, during both the "archaic" and "ancient" periods of the country's history, many rulers actually seemed to embody both the sacerdotal and political functions of sovereignty, to have ruled as well as reigned. They shaped the society of their day according to their will, in the manner in which we normally think of kings as operating.

One such ruler – indeed, perhaps the epitome of such a ruler – was Emperor Tenmu, fortieth in the officially recognized line of Japanese sovereigns, who vigorously pushed a policy of political centralization during his reign from 673 to 686. Not only was he unusual – by later standards – for actively ruling, but he is possibly the only Japanese sovereign in historic times to have come to the throne by wresting it away from an already enthroned Emperor. This incident, known from the era name as the Jinshin War of 672, is the most celebrated succession dispute in the history of the nation, and the last one where the participants actually resorted to force of arms. Part of Tenmu's success lay in the institution of new laws to avoid just such disputes.

Documentary evidence on Japanese history in the ancient period is sparse, and little information is available about the man Tenmu at all. Early records are not even clear as to his birth date. His older brother, Prince Naka no Ôe (later Emperor Tenji), was born in 626. In one source, Tenmu was recorded as having died at age 65; another source says he was 73. (He died in 686.) However, the former date would make Tenmu four years older than his elder brother and the latter date, twelve years older, a mathematical feat impossible even for the strongest of rulers.

So both claims must be discarded. It has been assumed by some Japanese historians that the figure 65 could simply have been a mistake for 56, a more likely figure since it would make him five years younger than Tenji. Further support for such a figure comes from the fact that a sister, Princess Hashihito, was born in the interim between the two brothers.

Such attempts at fixing a specific date appear fruitless, however, and the best we can do is simply conclude that Tenmu must have been born around 630, give or take a year or so either way. What is important is that these were years of great social and political unrest in Japan when a move to centralization of a fragmented and particularistic confederation of tribal units was underway. Tenmu is, of course, a posthumous name. As Prince Ôama, he was to be a major figure in this centralization process, but in his early formative years he witnessed considerable political turmoil and actual bloodshed which must have had a profound effect on him in later life.

Ôama was born the son of Emperor Jomei and his major consort, Ame Toyotakara Ikashi Hi Tarashihime, as she is known in her Japanese epithet. This lady succeeded her husband on the throne, however, as the second female sovereign in the annals of reliable Japanese history, and she is better known by her posthumous name, Empress Kôgyoku. Prince Ôama and his elder brother Naka no Ôe (Emperor Tenji) were the only two sovereigns in Japanese history whose parents were both ruling sovereigns.

Ôama's father, Jomei – Prince Tamura – became Emperor sometime around the time of Ôama's birth, in the first lunar month of 629. He ascended the throne in unusual circumstances. In 592, for the first time in Japanese history a female was enthroned, in order to bring to an end a long and bloody succession struggle. This was Empress Suiko, but during her reign it was actually Prince Shôtoku who held political power as Imperial Regent. Empress Suiko was simply preserving the dynastic title until Shôtoku could later be enthroned.

Unfortunately, Shôtoku predeceased the Empress, who continued to reign until her death in the third month of 628. There was thus an interregnum of some ten months between her death and Jomei's accession. The reason lies in the general indeterminacy of succession rules of Japan at the time: specifically, Suiko had no heir after Shôtoku's death. During the long mourning process for Suiko, several contenders to the throne emerged and the supporters of one contender were even put down by armed force. Ultimately, the leading courtier at the time, Soga no Emishi, prevailed and convinced the court that Prince Tamura should become Emperor. It was thus that Ôama's father Jomei came to the throne.

Jomei had already been married to Princess Takara who now became chief consort. She gave birth earlier to Prince Naka no Ôe (Ôe means "great elder brother"), and then Princess Hashihito and Ôama. Two other princes, Furuhito and Kaya, were sons of other consorts of Jomei. Four of the five children of Jomei led dramatic lives: both Naka no Ôe and Ôama came to the throne as strong ruling figures and both after coups d'état; Hashihito became involved in a scandalous relationship with her brother Naka no Ôe; and Furuhito died victim in a succession dispute.

The major source for the period, the *Nihon shoki,* gives little information at all about the reign of Jomei, so we do not know what influenced the young Ôama. There are merely records of auspicious portents, unlucky signs in the heavens, considerable comings and goings of Paekche and Silla visitors and a number of imperial progresses. But these were years of great turmoil on the continent: Silla, Paekche and Koguryŏ were engaged in a desperate struggle for control of the peninsula, and T'ang China was involved, worried about the threat of Koguryŏ attacks on her northeastern border. All these countries were sending envoys back and forth to seek allies. Ultimately, Japan was to side with Paekche while Silla and T'ang joined in a might alliance. When the dust had cleared a combined T'ang-Silla expedition eliminated Paekche and Koguryŏ and wiped out a Japanese fleet, and Silla had unified the peninsula by 668. All of this was a matter of deep concern to the Yamato Court, so that from his early days on, Ôama was well aware of continental developments.

Internally, politics at Court seem not to have been the prerogative of Ôama's father Jomei, but were rather directed by the kingmaker Soga no Emishi. The Soga clan dominated life at Court, so much so that many courtiers as well as members of the imperial clan became very uneasy about Soga dominance.

Emperor Jomei died in the tenth month of 641, and the immediate events surrounding his death were ultimately to spell the end of the Soga and must have had a powerful effect on Ôama, now perhaps in his early teens. Naka no Ôe, as heir apparent, ought to have succeeded, but at sixteen he was deemed still too young. The candidates for Emperor were two in number: Shôtoku's eldest son, Yamashiro no Ôe, who had also been a candidate at the time of Jomei's selection, and Jomei's son Furuhito, Ôama's half-brother. The Soga leaders favored Furuhito because his mother, Lady Hote no Iratsume, was Soga no Iruka's daughter.

But whichever prince was selected, trouble was sure to ensue. Tension at Court ran high. Thereupon, Ôama's mother was raised to the throne, following Suiko's precedent, to avoid possible bloodshed between the two princes and their supporters. This was Empress Kôgyoku. The imperial residence was established in Asuka at the newly-erected Itabuki Palace.

The enthronement of a female sovereign did not, however, completely prevent trouble from arising. In the new era, Emishi's son, Iruka, now gathered to himself great powers, even more than his father had enjoyed, and began, according to the official chronicle, to act in a manner little different from an imperial personage. In 643, afraid that Prince Yamashiro would ultimately come to rule instead of his favored Furuhito, Soga no Iruka forced Prince Yamashiro into revolt. The tragic prince, twice rejected as possible ruler, strangled himself in the eleventh month of that year.

This did not, however, bring about the accession of Furuhito. Rather, it was the final straw which turned courtiers against the Soga. Even Iruka's father Emishi is recorded as having been outraged at the stupidity of his son's actions. Soon there was active plotting against the Soga, led by young Prince Naka no Ôe and the courtier Nakatomi no Kamatari.

The conclusion came in the sixth month of 645 during a ceremony at the Great Hall of Audience. Kamatari and Naka no Ôe had in advance laid plans for an attack upon the Soga mainline, winning over to their side such people as Soga no Kurayamada-maro (Naka no Ôe's father-in-law) and other notables. During the ceremony the plotters cut down Soga no Iruka in front of everyone, and then other members of the clan, including Emishi, were eliminated. The coup d'état was successful, and from the sixth month of 645 the so-called Taika reform era was ushered in, led by Kamatari and Prince Naka no Ôe.

Ôama was just reaching his majority at this time, and the various struggles to which he was witness – among kingdoms, between courtier and imperial clan and between candidates for the imperial position – must have instilled in him at an early age a profound sense of insecurity for his own position and future. The move towards a more rationalized bureaucratic imperium must have been welcome to him. And indeed, he seems to have played a role during the years of the Taika reform.

The problem of dynastic stability was a recurring one in the history of the times. Faced with a newly emerging political leader in the imperial clan (Naka no Ôe) and mindful of the crisis precipitated by the premature death of Heir Apparent Shôtoku, Empress Kôgyoku immediately after the coup attempted to abdicate in favor of her son Naka no Ôe. After consultation with Kamatari, however, it was decided that both Naka no Ôe's elder half-brother Furuhito and maternal uncle Prince Karu were more appropriate candidates.

They were both duly approached but hesitated, claiming that Naka no Ôe was the proper person. Given Naka no Ôe's rather dramatic burst upon the political scene, neither prince opposed him. Furuhito in particular knew he had little support now that his Soga backers were dead, so he shaved his head to become a priest, expressing the desire to retire to Yoshino. (Ironically, this was the very same place to which Ôama was later to retire for ostensibly similar purposes, only to launch a revolt.)

Prince Karu could no longer demur, and he was duly enthroned as Emperor Kôtoku only a day later. At the same time, Naka no Ôe was named heir apparent, and he and Kamatari initiated a movement towards governmental reorganization which brought new ministers to power. But while Naka no Ôe and his co-plotters strove to carry out their reforms in the political realm, a rift developed between the young prince and his uncle the Emperor.

The reasons were both political and personal. Naka no Ôe expected to play a major role in government as had Shôtoku before him; but Shôtoku had been regent for a female sovereign and was expected to act in her place. There was no such precedent for a non-ruling male ruler, and Emperor Kôtoku resented the assumption of such rights by his young nephew.

Added to that was a galling personal problem which grew over the years of his reign. Kôtoku's consort was Princess Hashihito, the sister, as we have seen of both Naka no Ôe and Ôama. She was more crucially a uterine sibling, not a half-sister born of another mother. Under circumstances unknown to us today, a very intimate relationship developed between Naka no Ôe and his sister, and the relationship became known to the Emperor as well as the entire court. So the rift between the two grew wider: Naka no Ôe first attempted to draw away political power from the Emperor and then he even stole the Empress, an incident of shocking magnitude which Ôama certainly must have watched with considerable concern.

In fact, it is probable that the reason Naka no Ôe, clearly the most powerful imperial figure at the time, decided not to become Emperor but rather remain heir apparent until 668, was this very incestuous relationship. Marriage between uterine siblings was condemned by Japanese custom, and an earlier example in the *Nihon shoki* shows clearly that another prince was kept from accession for precisely such reasons. It may well have been that as long as their relationship continued, Naka no Ôe did not feel able to become Emperor; and it was only after the death of his sister that he at length ascended the throne.

The relationship finally reached the breaking point in 653 when Naka no Ôe tried to move the capital against Kôtoku's desires. Despite the Emperor's strong objections, the prince went to Yamato taking with him the majority of the courtiers as well as his lover, Empress Hashihito. The broken-hearted Kôtoku sent a poem to his lost consort, expressing the depths of his sorrow:

The pony which I keep,
I put shackles on
And led it not out:
Can anyone have seen
the pony which I keep?

The next year he fell ill and died, having lost both the political and personal struggle with his nephew Prince Naka no Ôe.

Again, however, Naka no Ôe avoided the succession, probably because of the publically acknowledged affair with his own sister. Instead, in a move unprecedented in Japanese history, he had his mother reascend the throne to preserve the succession for him. In this reign, she is known as Empress Saimei. There was great unrest and widespread popular opposition during this reign because of the Empress' extensive building projects. Furthermore, much attention was devoted to the outfitting of a fleet to aid Paekche in her battles on the Korean peninsula.

But for Prince Ôama, now a man in his mid-twenties and an increasingly important figure at court, the most important event must have been Naka no Ôe's treatment of Kôtoku's young heir, Prince Arima. A further source of frustration for Kôtoku had, of course, been the fact that with succession pre-empted by Naka no Ôe, his own son Prince Arima was effectively cut off from succession.

Naka no Ôe saw to it that this was permanent. Apparently worried lest someone support the prince's enthronement after his own death, Naka no Ôe had him cleverly tricked into what seemed a rebellious position. The poor prince was strangled to death, and several of his followers were executed or banished. Naka no Ôe was determined to preserve succession in his own line. The lesson was clear to Ôama, however, if we are to judge by his future actions.

Even in 661, when Saimei died, Naka no Ôe still avoided enthronement, ostensibly because of his overriding concern with preparing the fleet to aid Paekche. She died while the two were overseeing preparations in Kyushu, and Naka no Ôe did not even return with her body to the court. The throne remained empty for some seven years, the longest interregnum in Japanese history.

During the period Naka no Ôe continued to dominate government; in the *Nihon shoki* he is referred to as "the Prince Imperial," but a few times he is also called Emperor. At this time, Prince Ôama clearly emerged as a strong co-participant in the ruling process. In 664, for example, Ôama announced a newly instituted ranking system of twenty-six grades, as well as a system of designating greater and lesser clans. Most of the space in the official chronicles, however, is devoted to continental relations, clearly the most crucial issue of the day.

Naka no Ôe's sister and lover Hashihito died in 665, and in 667 was buried with Empress Saimei. The next month Naka no Ôe moved the capital to Ômi, on the shores of Lake Biwa, apparently against the wishes of much of the populace. Soon after the move of the capital, in the first month of the next year 668, Naka no Ôe ascended the throne as Emperor Tenji. Now that his incestuous affair was terminated and his sister buried, he could safely assume the imperial position. Princess Yamatohime became his consort and Ôama was made Heir Apparent, since he had long been serving essentially in that capacity anyway.

Near the end of his reign, however, Tenji, seems to have had second thoughts and turned against Ôama. This was clear in early 671 when new appointments were made, including Tenji's favorite son Prince Ôtomo as Prime Minister, the leading figure at court. The next day new regulations were promulgated; so while the *Nihon shoki* says Ôama did the promulgating, there is a note to the effect that another version attributes it to Prince Ôtomo. That there was confusion over which of the princes had Tenji's favor was certain.

In the eighth month of 671 Tenji took ill, and soon the illness became quite serious. Death appeared certain, and the fate of the realm – and of Prince Ôama – hung in the balance. Tenji called Ôama to him and explained that he was near death, offering his brother the throne. Realizing the potential seriousness of his answer, Ôama declined. Instead, he suggested that Yamatohime be made Empress and Ôtomo, Prince Regent (Presumably in conformity with the Suiko/Shôtoku and Saimei/Naka no Ôe precedents). Ôama expressed his desire to renounce the world to become a Buddhist priest. He immediately went and shaved his head. Two days later he asked, and was granted, permission to go off to Yoshino with a handful of followers.

Ôama's decision, according to the *Nihon shoki*, was taken because of a tip from Soga no Yasumaro that there was a plot by Tenji against him. Surely, Ôama needed no such prompting. He had seen his brother come to power by killing the Soga leaders, and had watched him at least twice concoct plots against other princes. Seeing the favor which Tenji now held for his son Prince Ôtomo, Ôama must have been well aware that Tenji would have used the slightest pretext to have him removed.

At any rate, Ôama made a speedy retreat from the capital to Yoshino, and Tenji took great pains to have his ministers pledge support to Ôtomo after his death. Despite Ôama's shaved head and voluntary exile, Tenji felt insecure over Ôtomo's succession. And indeed, only a scant six months after Tenji's death, the prince was to die by his own hand.

Tenji died in the twelfth month of 671. The chronicles thereupon discuss the battle for dynastic succession between Ôama and Ôtomo. They refer to Ôama as Emperor – since he was ultimately successful – and do not mention Ôtomo's accession. Later, in the modern era, Ôtomo was given that status, and he is called Emperor Kôbun in the *Dai Nihonshi* (*History of Great Japan*). But whether he actually was enthroned or not is unclear. Japanese historians on the whole tend not to regard him as a reigning sovereign. But no matter his actual position, he was in charge of the Ômi Court and desperately struggled to succeed his father. That Ôama usurped the imperial succession from him is clear.

The *Nihon shoki* records that someone at the time of Ôama's departure to Yoshino quoted the Chinese saying "give a tiger wings and let him go," a euphemism for the fact that one will later have to bear the consequences. The chronicles record that the Ômi Court – Ôtomo (or perhaps Emperor Kôbun) and his ministers – suspected a plot on Ôama's part and set up guards to cut off private supplies from his household offices. By the sixth month of 672 Ôama was convinced of a plot against him, and actively set about gathering troops and provisions to move against the Ômi Court.

On the twenty-fourth he started east for Ômi with a small band, including his consort Uno no Sarara, one of several daughters of Tenji he had married. It took a month for Ôama to arrive at the Seta bridge for a final showdown with his young nephew, and in that month his force grew considerably. Supplies and reinforcements came in from surrounding provinces, Mino and Owari in particular. Among those who joined his camp were numerous imperial princes. The *Nihon shoki* recounts a number of battles and strategic maneuvers, defections and deceptions during this month of scrambling for support.

But ultimately on the twenty-second of the seventh month, Ôama's main force arrived at the Seta bridge near the southern tip of Lake Biwa.

Prince Ôtomo and his army were drawn up on the other side: "Their banners covered the plain, the dust reached to the sky: the sound of their drums and gongs could be heard for several tens of *ri,* their ranged crossbows were discharged confusedly, and their arrows fell like rain." Ôama's troops succeeded, however, in crossing the bridge and routing the Ômi forces. Ôtomo barely escaped with his life.

But most of his generals were cut down by Ôama's troops and Ôtomo had nowhere to turn. He hid at Yamazaki and there strangled himself on the twenty-third day. He was only twenty-five years old at the time. A brief "mop-up" operation netted the arrest of most of the Ômi ministers, and Ôtomo's head was presented to Ôama. On the twenty-fifth of the eighth month, verdicts were handed down: eight ministers were executed for their part in the affair, several were banished, but a greater number of lesser nobles were all pardoned.

Ôama left "the east" and proceeded back to Yamato, where he resided in two different palaces until he built his capital at a place called Kiyomihara in Asuka. On the twenty-seventh day of the second month of the new year, 673, Ôama assumed the imperial position. His posthumous name was Tenmu ("Heavenly Valour"), an apt reminder of the manner in which he came to the throne.

Tenmu ruled for only thirteen years until his death in 686. His major consort Uno no Sarara, Tenji's daughter, became his empress, and the *Nihon shoki* claims that from the outset of his reign, she aided and gave him sage advice. (She was to succeed him as Empress Jitô, after an interregnum of several years.)

Thus Tenmu fought his way to the throne of Japan, having survived the perils of a very indeterminant succession pattern which was responsible for the premature death of many a competent prince. According to the thumbnail sketch biography in the *Nihon shoki,* Tenmu from birth "had a majestic and intelligent appearance: when he grew to manhood, he was virile and martial. He was skilled in astronomy and the art of becoming invisible." He was also shrewd and patient. He must have learned early on the prudence necessary to survive as an imperial prince, and indeed he later worried deeply about future disturbances of this kind.

The supporters of Tenmu in this struggle of course all had their own personal reasons for backing him. But historians feel that this was no simple succession dispute. The Tenmu forces included those who were in favor of continued centralization along the lines Naka no Ôe had first established in the Taika era. In his later years, Naka no Ôe had made too many concessions to the great clans, and the reform movement had lost its vigor. Certainly Tenmu lived up to the expectations of his supporters. His rule can be generally characterized by two major movements: an attempt to push vigorously on with the centralization of the state along Chinese lines and an effort to stabilize the dynasty in order to avoid the kind of bloodshed he had seen so frequently.

In the area of government Tenmu was responsible for much centralization: new ranking system, the first attempt at an administrative code to control state matters, rationalization and strengthening of the military, and a concerted effort to curtail the power of great clans by abolishing their control over all unfree persons. He also exerted great efforts to expand the influence of the Buddhist establishment in order to bolster imperial law with that of the Buddha. Yet another accomplishment creditable to the reign of Tenmu, one that survives to the present day, was the compilation of the first histories of Japan. It was at his instigation that the practice of history writing was begun, his intention being to establish the Emperor as the absolute center of all authority. And though his aim was not realized in his own lifetime, the project ultimately produced the oldest surviving histories of Japan, the *Kojiki* (*Record of Ancient Matters*) and the *Nihon shoki.*

Within the dynastic group, he tried to achieve harmony by having everyone vow to "give each other support and avoid mutual contention." And yet, the designation of his own successor was not made until late in his reign. Ultimately he and his Empress Jitô tried hard to establish the same principle that Tenji had favored when he tried to dispossess Ôama to enthrone Ôtomo: lineal primogeniture. In 681 Prince Kusakabe, his son by Empress Jitô, was made Heir Apparent and began to assist his father in affairs of state. But only two years later, another favorite son, Prince Ôtsu, also began to participate in matters of state.

Near the end of his reign, however, Tenmu made clear the direction of succession in an edict stating that all affairs of state were to be referred to his Empress and Prince Kusakabe. He was ill at the time, and in fact seems to have been bedridden for the last four months of his life. Tenmu died on the ninth day of the ninth month of 686. Jitô presided over the Court but did not succeed him, and an interregnum ensued while mourning continued. During the mourning, however, it was discovered that Prince Ôtsu plotted treason, and he was executed. Most likely, it was just another case of a plot concocted to remove a potential heir to the throne. The perpetrator was certainly Tenmu's Empress Jitô who wanted to ensure the ultimate succession of their offspring Kusakabe.

Unfortunately, Kusakabe died young and Jitô became sovereign only in order to preserve the succession for his son. At least the experience that Tenmu had gained in a lifetime of confused dynastic struggles came to some end after his death when the succession remained in his own direct line during the reign of the next seven sovereigns. From this time on, the earlier practices of fraternal succession were discredited. It is perhaps ironic that Tenmu, a dispossessed fraternal heir who usurped the throne, should be the one to end fraternal succession in order to stabilize the ancient Japanese dynasty.

[NOTES]

The information above comes from the *Nihon shoki,* Vol. 68 in *Nihon koten bungaku taikei* (Tokyo: Iwanami Shoten, 1968). All quotations come from the translation of W. G. Aston, *Nihongi: The Chronicles of Japan from the Earliest Times to A.D. 697* (London, 1956 reprint). Two other works I found useful in preparing this article are Kawasaki Tsuneyuki, *Tenmu Tennô* (Tokyo: Iwanami Shoten, 1963). and Naoki Kôjirô, *Jitô Tennô* (Tokyo: Yoshikawa Kôbunkan, 1969).

Poets of the *Man'yôshû*

Hitomaro, Okura, and Yakamochi

by

ISTVÁN HALLA

The biographies of the earliest Japanese poets are compounded of a little truth and a good deal of conjecture. The same might be said of Homer, of Ch'ü Yuan, and of all other ancient literary figures who stood on the boundary between oral tradition and the written word.

Though Kakinomoto no Hitomaro is regarded as Japan's greatest ancient poet, we have little concrete knowledge of his career. A number of literary historians have attempted to reconstruct the man from his works, but their efforts are largely imaginative. So it is with what follows, for very few hard facts are available.

It is relatively certain that Hitomaro was born not too long before or after the year 660. The first part of his surname, *kaki,* means "persimmon," and the *Shinsen shôjiroku* (*New Compilation of the Register of Families*) of 815 informs us, naively enough, that his family called itself that because a persimmon tree grew by their front gate. The Kakinomoto clan was of the same lineage as the Wani, Ono, and Kasuga families, who occupied a territory in the northeastern sector of the Yamato Plain, not far from modern Nara. During the fifth and sixth centuries, this tribal group supplied a number of imperial consorts and consequently had close familial ties with the ruling clan, but they were gradually crowded out by more powerful clans, the Soga at first, and after the Taika Reform of 645, the Nakatomi and the Abe.

Hitomaro's father was the chief Shinto priest of his clan. Shinto in the seventh century was a primitive but strong religion, containing elements of nature worship, ancestor worship, shamanism, and the sort of seasonal rites that are associated with agricultural societies. The high priest, as the clan's religious leader, recited prayers on ceremonial occasions and was

Kakinomoto no Hitomaro;
Kyoto National Museum

responsible for conveying the desires and supplications of the worshipers to the gods. His work, in short, was to turn the power of the gods on or off as needed in the interests of clan prosperity. In earlier times, the chief priest had been the most influential member of the clan.

Being born the son of a priest must have played a large part in determining Hitomaro's later life. One can imagine that as a child he not only learned children's stories, children's ditties, and folk songs from his mother, but also acquired from his father a knowledge of religious myths and song-epics. It would appear that Japanese local mythology consisted mainly of stories explaining the provenance and lineage of the various clans, passed down in word or song by chieftains and high priests. Until the eighth century, this tradition was almost entirely oral; though earlier efforts seem to have been made to record the origin and genealogy of the imperial clan, the first written annals preserved today are the *Kojiki* of 712 and the *Nihon shoki* of 720. Both works aim at demonstrating the divine right of the imperial clan to rule the nation and were intended as spiritual buttresses for a unified political state.

The highest deity in Shinto is the sun goddess, Amaterasu Ômikami, who was originally merely the ancestral deity of the imperial family, but whose glory increased with the spread of imperial authority. That the Kakinomoto clan also regarded the sun goddess as their ancestress partly explains the aura of gravity surrounding the imperial myths in Hitomaro's works.

Though he lived in an age when new literary styles were being introduced to Japan from Korea and China, Hitomaro was brought up in the native tradition. He was familiar with sacred incantations, with eulogies to the Emperor, and with shrine dances. From his childhood, he was on intimate terms with the fantastic world of folk legend and folk ballads, and his earliest poems were naturally based on these. His was a form of expression that was closely related to the oral tradition, and his collected works, *Kakinomoto no Ason Hitomaro kashû,* includes folk songs alongside his youthful creations.

Hitomaro was probably in his adolescence, perhaps fourteen or fifteen years old, when the Jinshin War of 672 took place. As a result of this conflict, the power of the Emperor was greatly increased, and that of the great provincial clans reduced accordingly. Hitherto, the Kakinomoto family had been in eclipse, but the accession of the Emperor Tenmu (r. 672-86) must have seemed to them to offer an opportunity to recoup. No doubt Hitomaro's parents held high hopes for their son, who by this time knew the ancient rituals, was skillful at composing poems, and had mastered the art of riding a horse. As it happened, he was soon presented with a chance to demonstrate his talents.

In 676, the Emperor, who wished to incorporate native art and music into the court rituals, invited men and women from the provinces who could sing or act to enter his service. Hitomaro, already known as a poet, responded to the call and became a courtier-in-waiting to the Empress (later the reigning Empress Jitô). For a young man with Hitomaro's provincial upbringing, life at the colorful imperial Court was like a world of dreams. His reverence for the imperial clan, whose members he regarded as living gods, knew no bounds.

He wrote many love poems during this period, but does not seem to have had any deep love affairs. His lyrical outpourings appear to have been inspired by beautiful court ladies whom he dared not approach.

The Emperor died in 686, and in 690 his consort, who was 45 at the time, ascended the throne with the aim of completing the great work he had done toward forming a well organized, centrally governed nation. Under the Empress's patronage, Hitomaro functioned as an official court poet, turning out numerous poems in praise or commemoration of the imperial line. No doubt his conviction that his own clan was descended from an ancient emperor caused him to approach his work with special earnestness.

In addition to the paeans and dirges and ceremonial poems he composed in his official capacity, Hitomaro wrote many works of a more personal character. Even when he sang of love or nature, however, his poems have a certain elegiac quality, as though they sprang from a profound inner sorrow.

Hitomaro's private-life is clouded by a deep mist, but he is believed to have had at least three wives, of whom two lived in the province of Yamato and one in the province of Iwami. He once fell in love with a woman he happened to meet at the marketplace in Karu, a teeming center where men and women were thrown together and many romantic liaisons began. Hitomaro carried on a clandestine affair with this damsel, but was ever fearful that too frequent meetings would lead to discovery. Though his infatuation continued unabated, he began to long for an end to the relationship. One day a messenger arrived and announced that the woman had died. Hitomaro's position prevented him from visiting her house, even though she had borne him a child. He went instead to the marketplace, where he called her name and expressed his grief in the following brief poem:

I see the messenger come
As the yellow leaves are falling.
Oh, well I remember
How on such a day we used to meet –
My wife and I! [1]

From appearances, it seems that Hitomaro loved quite a few women, but was unable to settle down very long with any of them. He is known to have abandoned a wife in the country in order to go the capital on official business, though his sadness over this parting later caused him sleepless nights.

The Empress Jitô abdicated in 697 and died in 702. Owing partly to the death of a number of princes who had served the Empress, the political trend shifted from direct control by the imperial family to behind-the-scenes control by the Fujiwara family. Under the circumstances, Hitomaro, whose great theme was personal reverence for the sovereign, came to be regarded as a nuisance, if not actually a subverter of the new regime. He himself appears to have concluded that he could no longer be of much use at Court. Although he was still only a little past forty, he gave up all hope of restoring the fortunes of the Kakinomoto clan and retired to the country to live with his aged father. Thereafter, on the occasion of the spring and fall religious celebrations, the elder Kakinomoto dispatched his son to preside over services in various outlying districts where branches of the Kakinomoto clan resided. While performing these religious duties, Hitomaro must instinctively have continued to express his deepest feelings in verse.

On a trip to the province of Iwami, he fell in love with a woman in the village of Tsunu. When he returned to Yamato, his sadness over having to leave her behind moved him to compose the following lines:

From between the trees that grow

On Takatsunu's mountain-side
In the land of Iwami
I waved my sleeve to her–
Did she see me, my dear wife?

When the time for seasonal celebrations came around again, Hitomaro set forth once more for Iwami. But the year was 706, when famine and an epidemic of smallpox swept the country, and Hitomaro himself fell ill and died en route at a place called Kamoyama. When he realized that the end was at hand, he wrote the following poem to his beloved:

All unaware, it may be,
That I lie in Kamoyama
Pillowed on a rock,
She is waiting now – my wife –
Waiting for my return.

Hitomaro was already a legendary figure in the eighth century, and by the beginning of the tenth he was referred to as the "Saint of Poetry." In the middle ages, shrines and temples were dedicated to him in various parts of the country. Such is the reverence in which he is held by his countrymen.

Yamanoue no Okura belonged to the same period as Kakinomoto no Hitomaro, but came from a very different background and produced poems of a much more personal and individualistic tone. The explorer of a new literary field, he took as his starting point the question that had concerned many Chinese poets: what is the nature of man? One obvious reason is that he was well versed in Chinese literature. Another seems to be that he himself was of unusual character, though such facts as are known concerning his life give us only a hazy and incomplete picture.

In 663 the combined military forces of Japan and the Korean kingdom of Paekche were defeated by those of China and the rival Korean state of Silla at a place called in Japanese Hakusuki-no-e, in southwest Korea. Paekche collapsed, and many of its inhabitants fled to Japan. Among them were quite a few who possessed high educational or technical qualifications and became active in Japan as teachers, lawyers, doctors, or military experts. One of these was Okura's father, a man named Okuni who entered the service of the Emperor Tenmu as a physician.

Okura, was only four years old when he was brought to Japan. Okuni, who hoped to see his son succeed in this new country, was careful to provide the boy with a good Confucian education. Okuni died in 686, but by this time Okura was twenty-six and had acquired sufficient reputation as a scholar to be included in a committee charged by the court with compiling a history of Japan. In 701 he was appointed a secretary of an official embassy to China. Not long after setting sail from Kyushu, his mission encountered a typhoon and was forced to turn back, but a second attempt in the following year was successful.

At the time relations between Japan and Korea were strained, and the embassy chose to sail directly across the East China Sea rather than risk approaching the peninsula. The voyage was very dangerous, but Okura's group reached the mouth of the Yangtze River safely and proceeded north by land to the Chinese capital in Ch'ang-an. There Okura came in direct contact with the advanced civilization of the T'ang and had an opportunity to broaden his knowledge as well as his outlook. Yet the fond memory of his home in Japan remained in his heart, as can be seen in a poem he wrote when he was about to return home.

> Come, my men, let us hasten to Yamato!
> The shore pines on Mitsu of Ôtomo
> Must wait and long for us.

After three (or perhaps six) years in China, Okura came back to Japan, where he seems to have participated in the writing of the *Nihon shoki*. This being Japan's first history in the Chinese language, the commission producing it no doubt required the services of men like Okura, who had mastered that tongue. In 716 he was appointed governor of the province of Hôki (modern Tottori Prefecture). His stay there lasted about four years, after which he returned to the capital. In 721 he became one of the first-class scholars appointed to serve as instructors to the crown prince, who in 724 was to become the Emperor Shômu (reigned until 749). Around this time, Okura compiled a collection of Japanese poems entitled *Ruijû karin* (*Classified Anthology of Verse*), which has since been lost. As an official litterateur, he had many opportunities to display his intellectual prowess by composing poems at court parties and the like.

Soon after the Emperor Shômu ascended the throne, Okura, who had worked at his side, was appointed governor of Chikuzen Province (modern Fukuoka Prefecture). Since this was the principal doorway for trade and exchange with China and Korea, Okura's continental experience made him a particularly apt choice for the post. In 728, Ôtomo no Tabito, who was also a well-known poet, was appointed head of the Dazaifu, in which capacity he had control over all Kyushu and was Okura's immediate superior. Together, Tabito and Okura gathered together fellow intellectuals and created a literary outpost in Kyushu. Almost all of Okura's known works were written while he was there.

The person who preserved Okura's literary output was Yoshida no Yoroshi, a childhood friend who around 730 was teaching medicine in

Nara. Yoshida and Okura carried on an active exchange of letters, and Okura sent his friend examples of his own poems, as well as those of Tabito and other companions in Chikuzen. After Okura's death, Yoroshi became the chief government librarian and compiled a commemorative collection of these poems, adding works of his own. This was incorporated into the fifth volume of the *Man'yôshû*. .

As a provincial governor, Okura traveled about the countryside and closely observed the life of the ordinary people. Though he was acquainted with Buddhism and Taoism, his own philosophy was based on Confucianism, as can be seen in a poem admonishing men against deserting their wives and children to become priests, or in an encomium to the Emperor's government. He was particularly concerned with the part that love plays in human life, and affection for children was one of his strongest themes. In a particularly moving work on this latter subject, he pointed out that even the Buddha, who eschewed the ties of human love, was devoted to little ones. This poem ends with a famous envoy:

What use to me
Silver, gold and jewels?
No treasure can surpass children!

While in Chikuzen, Okura was troubled by thoughts of old age. He warns that the black tresses of young maidens will in time "turn white with the frost of age," that "lusty young men, warrior-like, bearing their sword blades at their waists" will soon "totter along the road, laughed at here, and hated there." At the end, Okura sighs, "Cling as I may to life, I know no help!"

Okura returned to Nara in the seventh month of 731 and no doubt presented the customary report of his activities during his term as provincial governor. At about the same time, he gave his patron and superior, Ôtomo no Tabito, who had returned to the capital half a year earlier, a personal and poetic reflection entitled "A Dialogue on Poverty," in which he paints a poignant picture of the lot dealt out to impoverished peasants under the legal system of the time. This lament, which is Okura's most famous work, testifies to his feeling of community with the sufferers who make up the preponderance of humankind.

No fire sends up smoke
At the cooking-place,
And in the cauldron
A spider spins its web.
With not a grain to cook,
We moan like the night thrush.

In 733, Tajihi no Hironari, who had been appointed ambassador to

China, visited Okura to say farewell. The two having long been literary comrades, Okura wrote a poem wishing Hironari a safe voyage. In it, he said that he would "begrudge the time it took him to tie his sash" when Hironari's ship returned and he went to greet it. His promise was not to be fulfilled, for by 735, when Hironari returned to Nara, Okura had already been dead for more than a year.

Among the poets represented in the *Man'yôshû,* Okura is the one who dealt most eloquently with the problems and harsh realities of life. As he lay on his sickbed, not far from death, he looked back with disappointment over his career and bewailed his failure to have made a mark on his times.

Should I, a man, die in vain
With no renown – no name
Spoken of for ten thousand ages?

Perhaps Okura did not achieve the success he longed for as a government official, but he created for himself a place of undying honor in the annals of Japanese literature.

Ôtomo no Yakamochi, who as a child was introduced to Yamanoue no Okura, was born in 718 into a family that had been famous since the sixth century as the Emperor's military supporters. Yakamochi was the first son of the head of the Ôtomo clan, Tabito, who was fifty-four at the time of his birth and had been yearning many years for a male heir. The boy was consequently brought up in the Ôtomo mansion with all the care and affection that an aged father can bestow.

In 728, when Tabito was appointed head of the Dazaifu, he took Yakamochi with him to Kyushu. Tabito lost his official wife in the same year, and his younger half-sister, Sakanoue no Iratsume, came to stay with him. She was a richly talented poetess, who did not hesitate to write frankly of love and the feelings it inspires. Her influence helped form the youthful Yakamochi's poetic sensibilities.

As mentioned earlier, Tabito and Yamanoue no Okura, who was his subordinate, gathered around them a group of scholars and poets and created a literary coterie in Kyushu. According to the fifth volume of the *Man'yôshû,* in 730 Tabito invited the cultural elite of Kyushu to his official residence for a plum blossom banquet in the Chinese manner, at which the guests competed in demonstrating their literary skills. Yakamochi was thus surrounded during his adolescence by people who valued poetry and education. Small wonder that his mind turned in the same direction.

Upon returning to Nara in late 730, Tabito found the political scene greatly changed. It grieved him to see the Fujiwara clan succeeding in its effort to seize control of the government, but he died in 731, before he could be seriously affected by this development. Yakamochi, like other sons of aristocratic families, became a student in the national university. Though the loss of his father put him at a serious disadvantage in the scramble for official ranks and titles, it also gave him a degree of freedom not often enjoyed by sons of highly placed noblemen.

Important political changes resulted from an epidemic of smallpox in 737 and 738, which struck down all four of the leading Fujiwara contenders for power. In place of Fujiwara no Muchimaro (680-737), Tachibana no Moroe (? -757) became the leading minister. As Fujiwara influence plummeted, members of the imperial family and certain other old clans took control.

One result was that Yakamochi became one of the Emperor Shômu's chamberlains. This position, which was awarded on the basis of good looks and demeanor as well as intelligence, was as glamorous as a young man could hope for. Yakamochi grew closer to the Tachibana family and became friends with Moroe's eldest son Naramaro (721-57). In the tenth month of 738, when Naramaro gave a maple-viewing banquet, Yakamochi attended together with his younger brother. Until he was thirty, Yakamochi continued to hold a position in the imperial household, free of direct political responsibilities, but safely under the wing of Tachibana no Moroe and able to enjoy all the benefits of being a youthful aristocrat at a brilliant court. In 740, when Fujiwara no Hirotsugu revolted, Yakamochi accompanied the Emperor to Ise, but spent the entire time thinking of his current lover.

> Oh, night after night
> I lie in this flimsy hut
> In Kawaguchi,
> Dreaming only of my love,
> The soft, sweet touch of her sleeve! [2]

It is clear from his many love poems that Yakamochi had numerous affairs with women, as was customary among the young noblemen of his time. Young or old, men of the upper class were expected to have numerous concubines, whom they visited at their homes whenever they wished. The women were assigned the passive role of waiting until the men to whom they were betrothed chose to appear. If the man in question did not show up at reasonably frequent intervals, the woman was apt to form a new relationship. There was a fluidity about associations between the sexes that might arouse envy today.

It was the custom for approaches to prospective lovers to be made in the form of written love poems. Yakamochi, who appears to have been precocious in such matters, wrote some of his most moving poems in this genre to Sakanoue no Ôiratsume, the elder daughter of his aunt. He was about sixteen at the time. The love that blossomed between the two deepened with the years, and in the fall of 739, Ôiratsume, having made a wreath of rice ears and attached a poem to it, sent it to Yakamochi, along with the robe she had been wearing.

I wove a garland
Of early rice ears springing
From seeds I planted.
Look, my love, upon my work
And be reminded of me.[3]

Yakamochi replied to the effect that he would never tire of looking at the present. The two were married around 740, and when Yakamochi had to go with the Emperor to Ise, he poured out his sorrow over being separated from her in a moving poem. His fondness for her, however, did not prevent him from having love affairs with other beautiful women.

In 746 Yakamochi was appointed governor of Etchû (present Toyama Prefecture). Under the cloudy skies of this northern region, the tone of his poetry changed considerably. Shortly after arriving at his post, he invited his subordinates to a banquet and exchanged verses with them. Among those present was Ôtomo no Ikenushi, who excelled at writing poems in Chinese.

That winter, suffering from an illness that nearly killed him, he thought nostalgically of his birthplace and pondered over the evanescence of human life. His stay in the north lasted five years, during which he gained much as a poet from travelling around the territory under his jurisdiction. In an impressive "long poem," he depicted its scenery realistically and movingly, and described his new experiences in a fresh, lyrical style. Alone and remote from the life he had been accustomed to in Nara, he spent much of his time reading Chinese books and composing poetry, one of the results being a diary in verse. It is popularly believed that at the request of Tachibana no Moroe he compiled the *Man'yôshû* during this interval.

In 751 Yakamochi advanced in the world to the extent of being called back to his beloved Nara. There he became engaged in a continual round of banquets and parties, at which he was usually called upon to compose or recite poems. His verse was both lyrical and endowed with an elegance that evoked the color tones of a painting. The subtle beauty of his style seems to strike a middle note between the unstudied simplicity of the *Man'yôshû* and the more cerebral poetry of the *Kokinshû* (*Collection of Poetry Ancient and Modern*).

Yakamochi was shifted in 754 to military duty and later sent to Kyushu. He not only made a collection of poems by soldiers (*sakimori no uta*), but also composed a number of works of the same type, dealing with the emotions of men being taken from their homes for military duty or of women seeing their husbands off to faraway places.

Tachibana no Moroe's death in 757 left Yakamochi without a sponsor in Nara. Political power returned to the hands of the Fujiwara, and in the following year he was appointed governor of the province of Inaba (Tottori Prefecture). Once again it became necessary for him to leave the capital. At a banquet on the eve of his departure, he composed a poem in which he expressed the hope that good things would pile up like the New Year's snow in the months to come. This ironic symbolization of the coldness he felt upon leaving is the last of his known poems. It is also the last work in the twenty-volume *Man'yôshû,* which is the summation of poetic expression in ancient Japan.

Did Yakamochi actually cease to compose poetry? Probably not, though no later verses have been discovered. Having lapsed into silence at the age of forty-two, he nevertheless continued to live for another twenty-six years, during which time he led a checkered official career, marked with a certain tragic quality. As head of the ancient but declining Ôtomo clan, he was destined to undergo one ignominious transfer after another. Though he died on the twenty-eighth day of the eighth month of 785, ill fortune continued to pursue him. Before he was buried, one of his kinsmen was accused of assassinating the leading Fujiwara of the day, and the whole clan was charged with treason. Yakamochi was posthumously stripped of his honors, his property was confiscated, and his son was banished to a distant island. Only after twenty years was the family honor restored.

From the foregoing brief introduction to the lives of three great poets of the *Man'yôshû,* it is evident that none of them led a particularly happy life. As Zoltán Kodály remarked to his friend Béla Bartók, "It is the grief at the bottom of men's hearts that causes art to bloom."

(Tr. by Charles Terry)

[NOTES]

1. Unless otherwise noted, all translations are from Nippon Gakujutsu Shinkôkai, ed., *The Manyôshû* (Tokyo: Iwanami Shoten, 1940; reprint New York: Columbia University Press, 1965).
2. Translation by Charles Terry.
3. Translation by Charles Terry.

Patriarchs of Heian Buddhism

Kûkai and Saichô

by

ALLAN G. GRAPARD

"The environment changes in accordance with the functioning of the mind: if the mind is filthy, the environment will be polluted. The mind in turn is influenced by the environment: when the surroundings are quiet, the mind becomes calm. Thus, mind and environment relate to each other in an invisible manner, very much like the Tao and the Virtuous Efficiency which reside in the obscure."

These lines were written in 814 by Kûkai, one of the greatest geniuses of Japanese Buddhism, and represent a typically Japanese attitude toward man and his milieu, an attitude which was matched in Europe only in the early twentieth century by Paul Valéry in his *Regards sur le monde actuel.* Kûkai can be seen not only as the father of a new trend within Buddhism, but also as a genius who crystallized several aspects of a culture which was in the making and was to last for several centuries. Born in 774 in a small coastal village of Shikoku to a family of the local aristocracy, he was fortunate enough to receive a thorough education "à la chinoise" from his maternal uncle, the tutor of an imperial prince. It was with a solid academic background that he went to Heijô-kyô (Nara) to study at the university, probably intending to become a state official as his parents must have wished. However, it appears that the study of the Confucian classics did not satisfy him, for he quit the university and devoted himself to the study and practice of Buddhism, in which he had developed an early and serious interest. By the age of twenty-four or so, he had made up his mind as to the relative value of the different schools of thought in China and Japan, and composed a short work of philosophy, a manifesto which explained why he renounced – against the will of his entourage – a career in the administration, left society, and entered Buddhism: this is the famed *Final Truth of the Three Teachings,* in which he evaluates the virtues and shortcomings of Confucianism, Taoism, and Buddhism. Although, according to him, these teachings were all marked by sanctity, Buddhism was superior because of its universalistic aspects and because it was the only one to deal positively with suffering and its cessation. The entire work is supported by an unflagging sense of humor coupled with vast scholarship, and is unique even in comparison to works of the same nature written in China. Thus Kûkai entered the path of Buddhism with total dedication, likening himself to the "wind that nobody can stop."

This decision, the process of which can be clearly seen in his magnificent manuscript still remaining today, had tremendous consequences for the rest of Japanese history. While continuing with diligence his study of the scriptures and practicing the Law within the great silent mountains and along the rushing streams of the island of Shikoku as well as in the Kii Peninsula, he came upon a sutra which eluded his understanding and yet fascinated him: it was the *Mahâvairocana sûtra,* a late but powerful addition to the Buddhism canon, difficult indeed to approach, and even more difficult to put into practice without initiation. No masters who could give him this initiation existed in Japan, and this is why he decided to undertake in 804 the long and dangerous voyage to China, where he hoped to meet qualified teachers. Accompanying one of the Japanese embassies to the Court of the T'ang, he left his country, in a move which is typical of his courage, for the chances were great that the quest could end in death. As he himself writes:

> Disdaining our own lives and following the imperial command, playing with death, we have entered the great sea. When we were far from shore, violent winds accompanied by rain tore the sail to pieces, and the heavenly gusts broke forth, shattering the rudder. Seething waves clashed against the Milky Way, and we were afraid at dawn we should be pushed toward the Isle of Tamura, abode of cannibals, while at night we shuddered at the thought of being taken by the northern winds toward those isles occupied by men with the hearts of tigers. Our faces lashed by raging gales, we waited for the moment when, thrown into the waters, we would be swallowed up by giant turtles; closing our eyes before the terrifying billows, we watched for the moment which would throw us into the mouths of killerwhales. Thus ascending and descending at the mercy of the ocean, we drifted to the north and to the south. Having nothing to see but the emerald of the sky and of the water, we longed desperately for the white mists of valleys and mounts. We spent more than two months in such a manner; our drinking water ran out;

Kûkai; Daigoji Temple (Kyoto)

> all aboard were exhausted by the recognition of the immensity of the ocean and of the distance that separated us from the continent. What image could describe how much we have suffered, having no wings to bear us to the sky, no fins to make our way through the water? None indeed!...

This was no exaggeration: the boat's mast had indeed broken, and the ship drifted for thirty-three days, finally to drift ashore in the province of Fukien, far south from their intended destination. Since the governor of the province had never dealt with a Japanese delegation, he was, to say the least, suspicious, and detained everyone until further notice. Kûkai took up his writing brush and, in the name of the ambassador, explained the situation, expressing friendship between China and Japan and emphasizing that the ship was part of an official delegation. The governor understood and allowed the entry of all but Kûkai, for reasons which are still unclear. However, after another request from Kûkai, permission was granted and the young monk travelled to Ch'ang-an.

Aboard another ship of the same delegation was yet another scholarly monk, Saichô, who was going to China in order to meet with masters of the T'ien-t'ai School. Saichô had already been recognized by the Heian establishment and was supported by the emperor; his trip to China crowned a successful career, hence his stay was intentionally short. By comparison, Kûkai was young, hardly known outside the intellectual elite in Nara, and the objective of his voyage to China was to study for twenty years, with the humility that befitted his low rank. Kûkai and Saichô had probably never met, perhaps because of this difference in age and rank; and yet they shared a depth of spirit rarely equalled and had in common a fundamental drive to establish Buddhism in Japan. At that particular point, their interests were somewhat different, and this is why Saichô went to the center of the T'ien-t'ai whereas Kûkai went to Ch'ang-an; it is possible to see here, already, some essential differences between the two men: Saichô had a very limited, yet precise goal, and it was only by chance that he encountered other forms of Buddhism in China. Furthermore, he brought back documents which were essentially of a Buddhist nature and related to his specialty. On the other hand, Kûkai was more outgoing and curious about the general nature of Chinese civilization; his broad education and his vast talents made him a man of the world and it is quite natural that he would go to the capital. When the relationship between these two men deepened after they had met back in Japan, this difference in character was to become more and more evident.

Ch'ang-an was at the time probably the largest city of the world, with a population of more than a million, and temples of many denominations competed in beauty and height: from Zoroastrianism to Nestorianism, all schools of thought were represented, and people from everywhere filled the streets of the metropolis which marked a stop along the Silk Road. Kûkai's stay in that city was an immediate success, as he himself described it:

> One day, in the course of my calls on eminent Buddhist teachers of the capital, I happened by chance to meet the abbot of the East Pagoda Hall of the Green Dragon Temple.... As soon as he saw me he smiled with pleasure, and joyfully said, "I knew that you would come! I have been waiting for such a long time. What pleasure it gives me to look on you today at last! My life is drawing to an end, and until you came there was no one to whom I could transmit the teachings. Go without delay to the ordination altar with incense and a flower."

Indeed Kûkai was fortunate to have met the great master Hui-kuo, for he died shortly after. And there is no doubt that the essence of the meeting is faithfully reported by Kûkai, since the Chinese asked him to write the epitaph for Hui-kuo, who had been the master of three emperors: this honor could not have been bestowed upon one who was not regarded as a true disciple of the deceased master. Kûkai also met with Indian masters and learned Sanskrit from them; he had a profound relationship with Prajna, who told him: "I would like to go to Japan to transmit the Law, but my old age is an obstacle. Please take the translations I have done and take them to your country in order to save all sentient beings." In other words, Hui-kuo and the Indian masters gave Kûkai the responsibility of transmitting the essence of Buddhism to the East. This was not mere chance: Kûkai happened to be there at the right time, but he also happened to be brilliant and up to the task; for he not only studied Buddhism, but also literature and poetry (he later wrote two treatises on Chinese poetry), and was recognized as a master of China's major art, calligraphy. He also had a deep interest in technology, which he put to practice after his return to Japan. In this sense again, Kûkai and Saichô were quite different: Saichô appears to have been austere, sometimes even cold, whereas Kûkai was warm, outgoing, extremely active in all kinds of fields. These qualities no doubt had much to do with Kûkai's near deification in later centuries.

As we have already stated above, Kûkai's stay in China was supposed to last twenty years; but since he had learned what he wanted to, he decided to return to Japan after two years in order to establish Esoteric Buddhism there. So he set about collecting works of philosophy, literature, and poetry, and spent all his money doing so. To the last moment, even when his money had been exhausted, he copied some of the works himself, forgetting to eat and sleep. So great was his desire to take back as much as he could, brushes, tea and orange seeds included! Another embassy was returning to Japan; taking the opportunity, Kûkai requested to be accepted on board, and returned safely to his country in 806, some months after the death of Emperor Kanmu, the founder of Kyoto. After some time in Kyushu, he went to the capital and established himself at the temple of Takaosanji in the northern mountains. His stay in China had been fruitful beyond hope and Kûkai was soon recognized as a central figure: Saichô himself made a copy of the titles of all the texts, paintings, and objects brought back by his colleague. Kûkai rapidly gained support from the Court, becoming a friend of Emperor Saga; and, unlike Saichô, remained on excellent terms with the Buddhist schools of Nara. In 812, Kûkai performed the first Unction, a ritual of initiation into Esoteric Buddhism, which Saichô was the first to receive; from then on, the two men met whenever time allowed; Saichô borrowed scriptures; Kûkai asked help in Sanskrit; Saichô sent his top disciples to study under Kûkai. These two great men of the Heian period cooperated in order to erect firmly upon Japanese ground the pillars of Buddhism. However, their friendship began to deteriorate in 813, when Saichô asked to borrow one of the most important scriptures of Esoteric Buddhism, the *Rishushakkyô,* a commentary of the *Rishukyô* (*Adhyardhasâtika-prajnâparamita-sûtra*). To this request, Kûkai answered with a flat "no," in a rather long letter, of which some excerpts follow:

> As I opened your letter, I understood that you were asking for the *Sutra of the Ultimate Principle*.... The way of the Ultimate Principle and the writings found in the texts you are looking for are larger than Heaven and Earth; even if one were to use all the substance of this universe as an inkstick and all the water of the oceans as ink water, it would not be possible to express in minute detail the meaning of one single phrase of this text.... If you are looking for the Ultimate in terms of what can be perceived by thought, know that it is located in the very midst of any single thought of yours: there is then no need to look for it outside of yourself.... The rise and fall of Esoteric Doctrine depends solely on you and me. If the reception and the transmission of the teachings are not made properly, how will it be possible for future generations to discern what is correct and what is not?... Furthermore, the transmission of the arcane meaning of Esoteric Buddhism does not depend on written words. The transmission is direct, from mind to mind. Words are only paste and pebbles: if one relies solely on them, then the Ultimate is lost....

This must have been a terrible blow to Saichô, asked suddenly to be a serious disciple or to quit. Interestingly enough however, both men had emphasized the importance of practice in Buddhism, and particularly the practice of meditation (Zen). The last words of the preceding quotation seem indeed to come directly from the Zen tradition, and there is excellent reason to think that Esoteric Buddhism and Zen are actually very close in many ways; but this is another problem.

The relationship between Saichô and Kûkai seems to have come to an end when a disciple of Saichô's, Taihan, who had been sent to study under Kûkai, refused to go back to Saichô, who thereafter signed his letters with words such as "the rejected old master." Saichô, deeply involved in a doctrinal and institutional fight with Nara, was barely able to establish the Tendai school on Mount Hiei, and did not live to see the realization of his greatest wish, the creation of a Mahâyâna ordination platform, which was granted only after his death. Kûkai, on the other hand, had not only managed to establish his school in temples of the capital, he had also a

Shingon center within the very walls of the imperial palace, and had furthermore started to create a training center in the southern mountains, which was later known as Mount Kôya, today one of the great Buddhist centers of the world.

Tendai did develop to a tremendous degree after Saichô, but it was largely dominated by Esoteric Buddhism; in this sense it is perhaps better to speak of a complex esoteric tradition in Japan, with very few differences between the Tendai and Shingon. The Japanese tradition itself speaks of *Taimitsu* for the Tendai esoteric school and of *Tômitsu* for the Shingon school. To define their actual differences would be a difficult task, whereas it would be quite easy to establish the distinctions between "pure" Tendai doctrine and that of Shingon. This is evident in the development of *Shugendô,* for instance. Thus the claim that Mount Hiei, the center of Tendai, has been the fountainhead of Japanese Buddhism – especially during the Kamakura period – is as much due to its proximity to the capital as to doctrinal reasons. But this is a point which is open to debate, and cannot be settled without further research.

Kûkai devoted much of his energy to writing: his works amount to more than two hundred titles, most of which are discourses on the doctrine and practice of Esoteric Buddhism. Several hundred more were attributed to him during the following centuries, mostly works dealing with Shinto-Buddhist syncretism. The profundity of Kûkai's thought and the magnificence of his style can provoke nothing but awe in the mind of the reader, even in our century. His mind was of an astonishing clarity and calls to mind Pascal or Spinoza, while the structure of his debates and presentations allows comparison with Descartes. He was a philosopher and a deeply religious man; he was also a calligrapher of genius and is counted among the "Three Calligraphers" of his time, together with Emperor Saga and the scholar Tachibana no Hayanari. Even an untrained eye must recognize the beauty of his strokes, the elegance of the movement of his hand over the paper, the absolute control of space and energy. His founding of the Tôji temple, a landmark of Kyoto, is the beginning of a new era for sculpture and painting in Japan, the influence of which can be seen throughout history. Beyond his achievements as a calligrapher and as a poet, Kûkai was also a man of action and an engineer. In 821, on orders from the Court, he went back to Shikoku, his birthplace, to help create a dam for a vast reservoir called Mannôike. The work was absolutely necessary for the irrigation of the area, but the civil engineers were not successful, and the people of the country asked the government to dispatch Kûkai, whom they "regarded with the affection one has for one's parents." Kûkai directed the works and the dam was successfully built. In 825, he accomplished the same for the reservoir of Masuda in the province of Yamato. Such "Bodhisattva behavior" contributed to the creation of numerous legends throughout Japan depicting Kûkai as a master of the common people. His range of activity was indeed wide: from the common people up to the highest aristocrats of the Fujiwara family, from a song of joy after a successful prayer for rain to the most complex argument on metaphysics, he moved easily and with unmatched excellence. Even if later he was idealized to the point of becoming an archetype of the religious figure, the few documents that remain to give us an objective appreciation of his life and character are impressive. It is no wonder that proverbs such as "Kôbô does not choose his brush" (there is no bad tool to a good artisan), and "Even Kôbô misspelled," came into being. What Paul Valéry did in his work "Introduction to the Method of Leonardo da Vinci" ought to be done for Kûkai.

One more aspect of his life must be pointed out. In 828, he established, with the support of the Fujiwara, a School of Arts and Sciences, the Shugei Shuchiin, in which students regardless of birth could devote themselves to religious and secular studies. In spite of the greatness of the ideal, however, the institution did not last, and Japan had to wait some centuries more before Buddhism again became involved in popular education.

Thus we have some insight into the activity of one of Japan's greatest men, a philosopher whose practical ideal was "Integration to the Great Being," an observer of human nature so keen that he was able to discover the Unseen Buddha Nature in each and every person and then to propose a concrete path to realize it. Although he had said that "the heart-mind is nothing more than the reflection of the moon in the morning mist," he established a system of thought and practice which would surely enable man to escape the train of transmigration and reside within the Realm of the Buddha. This system was developed in his major work entitled *The Ten Residences of the Heart-mind,* which is the ultimate exposition of Kûkai's philosophy, and will – when translated – rank among the masterpieces of world thought. Only one other work in Japan can be compared to it, the *Shôbôgenzô* of Dôgen (1200-1253). To put the matter simply, Kûkai's system of thought is the most thorough analysis of the process by which a human being becomes a Buddha. Kûkai's tolerance was without limit: "Although the human vehicle (Confucianism) and the heavenly vehicle (Taoism) are but small castles, they alleviate mankind's most extreme suffering; if you compare them to transmigration, you see that all beings who adopt them have already escaped the burning house."

Or again: "Though the vehicles (of emancipation) are many and diverse, and though vertically there are differences of level, horizontally the level is always the same. He who does not understand this is like the patient who dies because he did not follow instructions in taking his medicine; he who understands this is comparable to the saint who achieves immortality by taking the drugs in the correct manner."

Kûkai's humanism was based on the possibility for all to achieve awakening and to realize the transcendent within this life: "There are highs and lows within the human heart, but none in the Buddha's world... Within our minds is the principle of the Pure Mind of Awakening"; and then he adds something which the West had learned a long time ago: "To achieve Awakening is to know truly one's own mind." Knowledge was thus a prerequisite to release, and release – or emancipation – allowed one to have a new perspective on the world: "He who lives in illusion lives in a filthy place; he who awakens finds himself in a pure place, an unspoiled space. I call this place Pure Land." Here is perhaps Kûkai's greates message: the practice of Buddhism may lead to this new perspective which results in the transformation of the space of human experience; in other words, practice is like an alchemical process in which man is transmuted into Buddha, and his world is transmuted into the Pure Land of the Buddha, a sort of paradise on earth. This view influenced Japanese culture in many ways, and lent itself to a syncretism with Shinto, which recognized the existence of the divine within the natural world. Esoteric Buddhism can thus be seen as the process of realizing immanence. Kûkai himself wrote, "if the Buddha were not to be found within the blades of grass and within the trees, there would not be any moisture in water." And he added for those who had any doubt, "truth is too close to us; that is why we fail to see it clearly."

The magical aspects of Esoteric Buddhism had only the goal of aiding man to transmute the universe, or rather to change his erroneous views concerning it, in order to see things as they are. These very same magical aspects have been the object of bitter attacks, sometimes for good reasons, and Esoteric Buddhism may appear to rely heavily on rituals which are hard to understand. But these cannot be rejected without due consideration. They were tools which helped man realize his greatness as well as his smallness, and helped him understand the order of the universe and participate in it.

Towards the end of his life, Kûkai decided to go to the southern mountains, but the Court did everything it could to keep him from doing so, even when his health had deteriorated badly. After several attempts, however, Kûkai succeeded in leaving the busy capital and going into retreat within the silence of Mount Kôya. His friends tried to convince him that such a move was dangerous and that he was needed in the "lower world," but Kûkai answered in the following terms:

> "Ah, don't you see, don't you hear? Vulture's Peak in the country of Magada is the abode of Śâkyamuni, and T'ai-shan in China is the residence of Manjuśrî, I am only what is called a *śramana,* a poor man taking the Realm of Essence as his home, in order to repay my debt to the Law.... I am without home or country, and have left my birthplace; being neither a son nor a minister, I find peace in poverty and solitude. I sustain my life by drinking from the valleys' streams at dawn, and nourish my spirit with mists in the evening; herbs and vines suffice to cover my body, leaves and bark provide my bed. Heaven grants a blue curtain, and the faithful dragon provides me with the white shades of clouds. Mountain birds chant the passing of hours while the monkeys display their agility in the branches; spring flowers and autumn chrysanthemums turn their smiling faces to me, while the moon at dawn and the winds wash filth away from my heart...."

In 835, leaving behind him a firmly established school, Kûkai passed away in the southern mountains. Later, disciples and followers did not consider him dead; they called his passing an "entrance into *samâdhi,*" a deep meditative trance in which Kûkai waits for the coming of Maitreya, the Buddha of the Future. This tradition developed to the point that statesmen in subsequent centuries would come and see the Master in his trance, and brought new clothes and offerings to the Messiah..., while the common people chanted and still chant today: "How gratifying! The Great Master is still alive on Mount Kôya!"

Thus, Kûkai became Japan's greatest saint. Known throughout the country as "the Master," he is in many ways the model of the Japanese religious figure, and the father of a most important tradition which can still be appreciated in our day.

Regent at the Peak of Aristocratic Prosperity

Fujiwara no Michinaga

by

MILDRED M. TAHARA

The Heian period is marked by the dramatic rise to power of the Fujiwara family. By the middle of the ninth century their system of "marriage politics" – in which they married their daughters to emperors and ruled through the offspring of these marriages – had proved so successful that they were able to establish permanent offices for the wielding of this power: these were the offices of Regent (*sesshô*), who ruled in place of a child emperor, and Chancellor (*kanpaku*), who ruled for an emperor who had reached his majority. From this time forward their rise must have seemed inexorable, for even their failure to produce daughters at the proper times set them back only temporarily. The Emperor Uda (867-937, r. 887-97) did not have a Fujiwara mother, and was supported by a man of extraordinary talent, the Minister of the Right Sugawara no Michizane (845-903). Yet even these men could not compete with the strength of the Fujiwara family organization. Fujiwara no Tokihira (871-909), the head of the clan, ultimately forced the Emperor to banish Michizane to Kyushu where he died in exile. The Emperor Daigo (885-930) likewise reigned for thirty-four years without a Fujiwara regent. Yet during this "Golden Age" the Fujiwara still succeeded in acquiring vast wealth – at the expense of the central government – through their manipulation of the taxation system to gain tax-free status for their own lands. Thus by the year 1000 the Fujiwara had become the most powerful and the most wealthy family in the nation. The man at the head of the clan at the peak of their prosperity was Fujiwara no Michinaga (966-1027); the story of his rise to this position of preeminence reveals a man of great talent, ruthlessness, and luck.

In 1016 Michinaga was appointed Regent when his grandson, Emperor

Go-Ichijô (1008-36, r. 1016-36) ascended the throne. In the third month of 1017 he relinquished this powerful position he had coveted for so long to his son, Yorimichi (992-1074), who was then only twenty-six. Norimichi (996-1075) and two other sons were promoted to the office of Provisional Middle Counsellor, despite the fact that they were in their early twenties and lacked experience. But the ultimate fate of Michinaga's family depended to a great extent on the women in the family. Michinaga's eldest daughter Shôshi became the consort of Emperor Ichijô and gave birth to two princes, Atsuhira and Atsuyoshi. Atsuhira later came to the throne as Emperor Go-Ichijô, and Atsuyoshi as Emperor Go-Suzaku (1009-45, r. 1036-45). Kenshi, Michinaga's second daughter, became the consort of Emperor Sanjô (976-1017, r. 1011-16). Upon the enthronement of Emperor Go-Ichijô, Michinaga held a position of absolute power. Then, by setting up Atsuyoshi as the crown prince, Michinaga made certain that his family would remain powerful in the Court even after a successor came to the throne. It was this fact more than anything else that impressed the courtiers present at the enthronement ceremony of Emperor Go-Ichijô. Other high-ranking courtiers had vied with one another to have their daughters enter the Court as concubines. However, their efforts had ended in failure. In some instances, the girl failed to produce a son; in others, even if she succeeded in bearing a male heir, the Fujiwara grandfather had died before assuming the regency. As a result, the power and influence of that particular branch of the family would decline, leaving the young prince without an influential guardian to ensure his enthronement. Michinaga alone succeeded in surpassing all of his rivals; he was able to attain a position of prestige and power heretofore undreamed of.

A year after Atsuyoshi was named crown prince, Ishi, another of Michinaga's daughters, became the consort of Emperor Go-Ichijô. Michinaga was then in the position to boast of three daughters who were either empresses or imperial consorts. He expressed his elation in the following poem:

Kono yo o ba	I cannot help but feel
Waga yo to zo omou	That the full moon
Mochizuki no	Will never wane;
Kaketaru koto mo	This world is truly
Nashi to omoeba	Mine alone.

Still another of his daughters, Kishi, became the crown princess. Kanshi, a daughter by his secondary wife Meishi, became the consort of the deposed Crown Prince Atsuakira, also known as Koichijô-in.

Having produced mothers of reigning emperors, Michinaga's family now

Fujiwara no Michinaga

had the right to be appointed Regent or Chancellor. Besides enjoying economic as well as privileged treatment in the Court, the Sesshô-Kanpaku, together with the emperor, had the right to appoint and dismiss powerful bureaucrats, thereby gaining great influence over courtiers of all ranks. Michinaga enjoyed a position far more powerful than that of any other high court noble (*kugyô*) because he had managed to get a firm grip on this exceedingly important office.

When one traces Michinaga's career back to his childhood, it is remarkable indeed that he attained such a position of power. He was truly a child of fortune. This will become clear when various events leading to his rapid rise to power are reviewed.

Michinaga was born in 966, towards the end of the reign of Emperor Murakami (946-67). His father, Kaneie (929-90), was thirty-eight at the time and not yet a high court noble. His mother, Tokihime, was the daughter of a provincial governor whose family was not particularly noteworthy. Moreover, Michinaga had two older brothers and a half brother. Therefore, as the fourth son of Kaneie, Michinaga's future did not seem very promising.

However, a series of unexpected events paved the way for the greatness Michinaga was to revel in later years. To begin with, Kaneie managed to attain a position of highest importance in the Court. As the maternal uncle of both Emperors Reizei (950-1011, r. 967-69) and En'yû (959-91, r. 969-84), he bypassed the office of Imperial Adviser to become a Middle Counsellor during Reizei's reign. Nonetheless, because he had two older brothers, Koretada and Kanemichi, he had to wait patiently for his turn to be named Regent. His rivalry with Kanemichi was especially intense. When Kanemichi, while serving as Chancellor, fell seriously ill, he applied pressure to have Fujiwara Yoritada (924-89), who was not a maternal relative of the Emperor, appointed to the post of Chancellor. As a result of this unprecedented move, Kaneie's appointment to the coveted office was delayed.

Betrayed by his older brother, Kaneie remained Minister of the Right for several more years. However, he was fortunate in that other imperial ladies, daughters of high-ranking courtiers, were unable to produce a male heir. Kaneie's daughter Chôshi was the only one who bore a prince, Iyasada, who later ascended the throne as Emperor Sanjô. Moreover, another daughter, Senshi, became the consort of Emperor En'yû and gave birth to Kanehito, the future Emperor Ichijô. Kaneie therefore had every reason to hope that the future of his family would be secure.

In 984 Emperor En'yû abdicated and Emperor Kazan (968-1008, r. 984-86) ascended the throne. The Empress Dowager Kaishi was the daughter of the late Regent Koretada. Emperor Kazan's only maternal relative of importance was a relatively low-ranking official. Thus, Yoritada remained Chancellor and Kaneie, Minister of the Right. For a time, Kaneie feared that his political ambitions would never be fulfilled. Fortunately, Crown Prince Kanehito was his grandson. All Kaneie had to do now was to force Emperor Kazan to abdicate and to encourage the enthronement of his grandson.

On the night of the twenty-second day of the sixth month of 986, Kaneie had the Emperor escorted to Gangyô-ji temple in Yamashina in Kyoto. His son Michikane (961-95) was present when Kazan took the tonsure. In the meantime, two of the imperial regalia – the Sacred Jewel and the Jewelled Sword – were removed from the private apartments of the Emperor and secretly transported to the apartments of the crown prince by two other sons, Michitaka (953-95) and Michitsuna (955-1020). When Kaneie's orders were fully carried out, Michinaga dispatched a messenger to report to Chancellor Yoritada what had happened. The entire Court was in an uproar; all available courtiers were searching frantically for the missing Emperor. Presently they were informed that he had entered the priesthood.

Emperor Ichijô came to the throne at the age of seven. As his maternal grandfather, Kaneie served as Regent. Yoritada immediately resigned as Chancellor and Kaneie's grandson Iyasada was named crown prince. Upon being appointed Regent, Kaneie wielded considerable power, lording it over all the other bureaucrats. His sons were promoted rapidly and appointed to ranks of importance, despite their youth and inexperience.

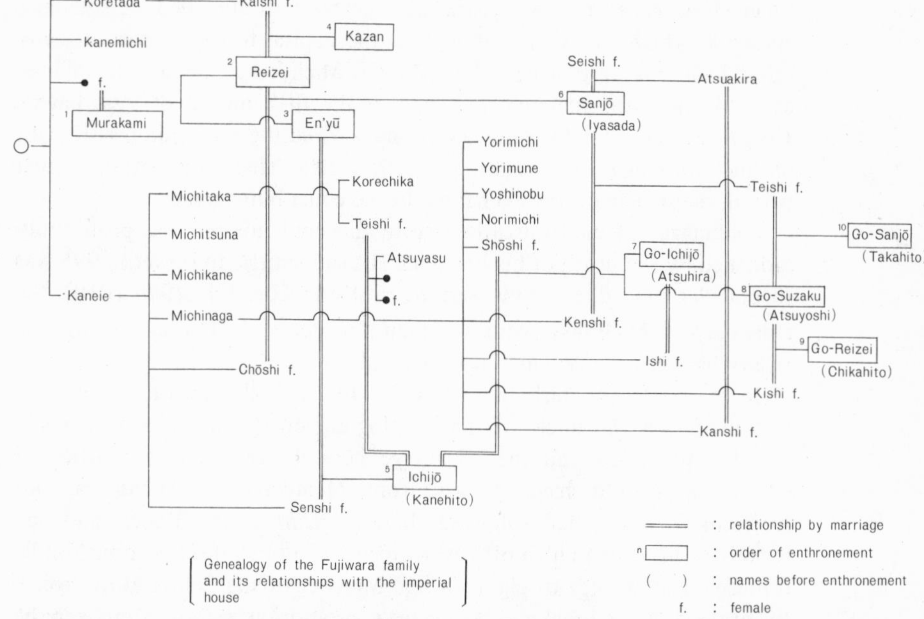

Genealogy of the Fujiwara family and its relationships with the imperial house

At the age of twenty-three, Michinaga was the tenth most important personage in Japan. His older brothers were also promoted, but being the youngest, Michinaga's rise in the bureaucracy was especially rapid. There was no fear of his being demoted as long as he did not make a serious blunder, and so he could anticipate a bright future in politics.

In the twelfth month of 987, Michinaga was married to Rinshi, the eldest daughter of Minamoto no Masanobu, the Minister of the Left. The girl's mother, Fujiwara no Bokushi, had taken a liking to Michinaga and had encouraged the match. Rinshi was then twenty-four, two years older than Michinaga, but the couple got along famously. Among their offspring were Yorimichi, Shôshi, and three other talented and attractive daughters. The daughters in particular insured the prosperity of the family. Polygamy was widely accepted and practiced among the Heian aristocrats; therefore, Michinaga took a secondary wife, Meishi. Of this union were born Yorimune, Yoshinobu, and Kanshi.

Within a period of six years after being appointed Middle Counsellor, Michinaga's father, two older brothers, and other senior courtiers of the imperial Court died. Thus, at the age of thirty, Michinaga became the head of his branch of the Fujiwara family.

Kaneie died in 990 when Michinaga was twenty-five. Shortly afterwards, Michitaka, as the father-in-law of Emperor Ichijô, was appointed

Chancellor. However, five years later he took ill and died. A smallpox epidemic which was then rampant in the capital took the lives of many other high-ranking officials of the Court. Michikane, the second in line, came down with smallpox and died in the fifth month of 995, having served as Chancellor for only seven days. While the epidemic raged, eight of the fourteen highest ranking courtiers died. Therefore, within a short period, there were dramatic changes in the court bureaucracy.

Michinaga emerged unscathed from the epidemic but was profoundly saddened by the death of his brothers. His sudden rise to power in 995 was spectacular indeed. His only serious rival was Korechika (974-1010), the eldest son of Michitaka, who was then Minister of the Center. The intense rivalry between the two men was unavoidable.

It is extremely difficult to say who had the greater advantage. Michinaga was the uncle of the reigning emperor; Korechika, his cousin. Clearly, Michinaga had the advantage here. In actuality, the office of Chancellor should have passed from Michikane to Michinaga, but Korechika's father had followed the precedent set by Kaneie and had promoted his sons to high offices. Korechika had therefore become Middle Counsellor at the age of eighteen and Minister of the Center at the age of twenty-one, thus breaking Michinaga's promotion record. Moreover, he had served as Acting Chancellor during his father's illness. Furthermore, his younger sister Teishi was the favorite of Emperor Ichijô. On the other hand, Michinaga's older sister, Senshi, was the Empress Dowager, an exceedingly powerful woman. Because Michinaga had the support of the Empress Dowager, the two men were virtually equal in power. It was left up to the Emperor, a young man of sixteen, to make the difficult choice between Michinaga and Korechika.

Exerting her strong influence, the Empress Dowager had her son appoint Michinaga Civil Examiner (*nairan*), a post which was not exactly the same as that of Chancellor but which was almost as powerful. Following the precedent set during the Engi (901-23) and Tenryaku (947-57) eras, Emperor Ichijô did not appoint a Chancellor. Michinaga continued to serve as Civil Examiner during the succeeding reign of Emperor Sanjô.

Outwardly, Michinaga had emerged victorious over his rival. Before long, he was appointed Minister of the Right, but Korechika remained Minister of the Center. Moreover, as clan chieftain, Korechika had greater power and influence. It was not Korechika's nature to leave things as they were. The eldest son of Michitaka, he had been quickly promoted, and despite his youth, he was highly talented and extremely popular. As described in *The Pillow Book,* he was a personable young man, but far from being modest, he did his best to impress senior courtiers by demonstrating that he was an efficient bureaucrat. While Korechika was a man of boundless energy, Michinaga was a man of determination and strong will. According to various anecdotes, he performed daring tasks without flinching. It is said that when his father praised the learning and accomplishments of Fujiwara no Kintô (966-1041), Michinaga, in a jealous rage, threatened to trample the young man's face. By no means was he a retiring young man.

Michinaga's personality was not in every way attractive. At times he could be ruthless and impulsive. Once, when a young courtier whom he had recommended highly failed in the civil service examination for the Ministry of Ceremonial, Michinaga had his men literally drag the proctor of the examination, a respected scholar, to his mansion. For having done this, he was severely admonished by his father. On another occasion, when the Empress Dowager was making a pilgrimage to the Ishiyamadera temple, he insulted Korechika in public, deeply shocking the members of the entourage.

An event of the first month of 996 brought to an end the intense rivalry between Michinaga and Korechika. At this time Korechika was visiting the third daughter of the late Prime Minister Tamemitsu; the Retired Emperor Kazan, who was leading a secular life, was visiting the fourth daughter. Korechika mistakenly thought that the Retired Emperor was also visiting the same woman. On the night of the sixteenth, Korechika and his brother lay in wait for the Retired Emperor and shot at him with the intention of frightening him. Guilty of this serious crime, Korechika was exiled to Kyushu and his brother to Izumo. Although they were pardoned and summoned back to the capital a year later, the two men were no longer in line for the highest office in the imperial Court and Michinaga's power was firmly established.

Without any interference from Michinaga, Korechika had damaged his own chances for a bright political future. A half year after Korechika's exile, Teishi gave birth to a princess. Three years later, she produced a son, Atsuyasu, and in 1000 she had a second son. If Korechika had not been deprived of his power, he could doubtless have risen to high office in the Court. However, the eldest son of Emperor Ichijô was born after his uncle's fall from grace; his future was therefore dark indeed. The young prince was of good character and highly educated. Nonetheless, because he did not have the necessary backing of a powerful maternal relative, he failed three times to be named crown prince and died in 1018 at the age of twenty.

The reins of power were now in Michinaga's hands. He was the most important personage in the imperial Court and was also the chieftain of the Fujiwara clan. By means of marriage politics, he did everything in his power to have the Sesshô-Kanpaku office reserved exclusively for his branch of the family, knowing that if he succeeded power and riches would naturally come to him. In 998, however, Michinaga fell seriously ill. His request that he be allowed to resign from the office of Civil Examiner was rejected. For the first time in his life he considered taking the tonsure; however, his temporary depression, heightened by a series of natural calamities, was soon dispelled.

In the eleventh month of 999, Michinaga's eldest daughter Shôshi entered the imperial palace to become a concubine of Emperor Ichijô. Accompanying her in this grand procession were over forty talented ladies-in-waiting, among whom were Murasaki Shikibu, Akazome Emon, and Izumi Shikibu. In the second month of 1000 Michinaga named Teishi – Ichijô's favorite – the Empress and Shôshi the Consort in a dramatic move which had no precedent.

In 1008 Shôshi, who had replaced Teishi in Ichijô's affections, gave birth to Prince Atsuhira. Fortune had indeed smiled on Michinaga, for all his efforts would have been in vain if his daughter had failed to produce a son. In the following year, Prince Atsuyoshi was born. Michinaga's joy was beyond description now that he was the grandfather of two princes. In her diary, Murasaki Shikibu gives us glimpses of this great statesman as a doting grandfather.

Upon the demise of Emperor Ichijô in 1011, Emperor Sanjô ascended the throne. He, like his predecessor, was a nephew of Michinaga, but the two men had never been close. Moreover, Emperor Sanjô was already in his mid-thirties at the time of his enthronement. He and Seishi, the daughter of the late Fujiwara no Naritoki, had had six children. The Emperor had been antagonistic toward Michinaga even before coming to the throne and resented being looked upon as a mere bridge to the next reign.

The four years of Emperor Sanjô's reign were painful and bitter for Michinaga. However sure Michinaga was of his power in the bureaucracy, he avoided an open confrontation with the reigning emperor.

Michinaga maneuvered behind the scene to have his second daughter Kenshi become Imperial Consort, but soon afterwards Emperor Sanjô decided to recognize formally his beloved Seishi, the mother of his children, as his Empress. On the very day Seishi was to be named Empress, Michinaga had his daughter make a grand entrance into the imperial palace, knowing full well that the courtiers would be obliged to gather at the ceremony he had planned. As a result, Seishi's ceremony was a truly dismal event. Not a single high court noble of importance went to offer his congratulations at the residence of the newly-named Empress. Thereafter, it became impossible for the Emperor and Michinaga to be reconciled.

Shortly afterwards, Emperor Sanjô fell seriously ill and lost his eyesight. Michinaga demanded the Emperor's abdication, arguing that he could no longer effectively conduct the business of the government and perform his duties in the Court. Reluctantly Emperor Sanjô relinquished the throne to Crown Prince Atsuhira, who came to the throne as Emperor Go-Ichijô.

At long last Michinaga, the grandfather of the nine-year-old emperor, was named Regent. He was then fifty-one. For twenty years he had wielded considerable power in the imperial Court. Moreover, his family was now firmly established as the maternal relatives of both reigning and future emperors. It was enough for him to become Regent in name only, and after serving as Regent for only a year and two months, he appointed his son Yorimichi to the office.

Who would be Emperor Go-Ichijô's successor? This problem occupied Michinaga's mind at this time. At the time of Emperor Sanjô's abdication, it was agreed that Atsuakira, who was not Michinaga's grandson, would be named crown prince. Michinaga covertly applied pressure on Atsuakira, making the young prince's position a very uncomfortable one. The most powerful man in Japan, Michinaga was simply waiting for a chance to replace Atsuakira with his grandson. When the courtiers realized that the crown prince was the object of Michinaga's resentment, they abandoned him. Not very popular to begin with, the crown prince soon found himself with no strong supporter. As was expected, in the fifth month of 1017, less than three months after his father's death, Atsuakira announced to Michinaga his intention to step down as crown prince.

Michinaga moved quickly. He made his way to the palace of the crown prince with the Regent Yorimichi. On the following day, he summoned the high court nobles and set the date for the ceremony in which his grandson Atsuyoshi would be named crown prince. With all available courtiers assisting in the preparations, the ceremony, held two days later, was truly magnificent.

Successful in setting up his grandson as the crown prince, Michinaga was assured of having him become the next emperor. After naming his daughter Ishi Empress, he could boast of having three daughters who were empresses or consorts. He also had his daughter Kishi named crown princess.

Michinaga's health began to deteriorate and in 1019 he took the tonsure, even though he continued to give orders regarding various official matters. Having known worldly success, he began to prepare for the life after death and devoted himself wholeheartedly to the construction of the Hôjôji temple which was splendid in every detail. The Amida Buddha in the Phoenix Hall of Byôdôin in Uji, built by Yorimichi, is impressive even today, but the nine images of Amida Buddha enshrined in the Hôjôji temple were surely beyond description. Moreover, the Amida Hall was just one of more than ten halls in the temple complex.

Under Yorimichi, the Chancellor, the courtiers helped to recruit laborers and gather materials for the building of this temple. On the fourteenth day of the seventh month of 1022, a memorial service of great magnitude and unsurpassed extravagance was held. Present at the ceremony were the emperor and empress, the crown prince, the great empress dowager and the empress dowager – all of them children and grandchildren of Michinaga.

In the Amida Hall Michinaga intoned the Nenbutsu daily, contemplating his future life in the Buddhist paradise. Then, on the fourth day of the twelfth month of 1027, he breathed his last as the voices of those gathered about him recited the Nenbutsu. He was sixty-two years of age.

Michinaga is closely associated with an age of glory which flourished nearly 1000 years ago. However, it is extremely difficult to determine the actual extent of his power, for he held the office of Regent for only a little over a year and was never appointed Chancellor. Nonetheless, the political system of the Heian period was still based on the *ritsuryô* codes in effect since the Nara period (710-94). According to the codes, the emperor had absolute power. Therefore, the Fujiwara Regent or Chancellor came close to being as powerful as the sovereign.

That which sets Michinaga apart from all the earlier Sesshô-Kanpaku is the fact that he actually put into practice the principle that he who rules the imperial Court rules over the entire land, and even went as far as to have three of his daughters become imperial consorts. He was further fortunate in the fact that the girls were so productive. Other courtiers had daughters who had become imperial consorts and concubines but with less fortunate results. Some of the women failed to bear sons. Even when a girl did produce a son, the girl's father passed away, leaving the young prince with no important personage to champion his cause. In this respect, Michinaga's daughters had an advantage over their rivals. Michinaga had become the most powerful man in the realm by the time of Emperor Go-Ichijô.

In the imperial Court, Michinaga overwhelmed and outshone all other high court nobles. It was no wonder that leading bureaucrats turned to him for advice, even after he took the tonsure. During Michinaga's lifetime, the aristocratic society enjoyed a stability never known before. Supported and encouraged by the great wealth of the Fujiwara family, art and literature flourished. This was the age that produced both *The Tale of Genji* and *The Pillow Book.* The sensibility and exquisite taste of the aristocrats have been transmitted down through the ages. Michinaga thus might also be considered a patron of art and literature.

The outwardly stable Sesshô-Kanpaku system was transmitted directly to Yorimichi. Related maternally to the Emperors Go-Ichijô, Go-Suzaku and Go-Reizei (1025-68, r. 1045-68), Yorimichi served in the capacity of Regent or Chancellor for fifty years. This had been made possible as a result of the strategic moves made by his father. Nonetheless, rapid changes were taking place underneath the thin veneer of stability.

In 1036 when Emperor Go-Suzaku ascended the throne, his eldest son Chikahito was named crown prince. Kishi, the mother of the crown prince, was Michinaga's daughter. Until her death soon after the birth of the prince, the position of Michinaga's family had been unshakable.

Emperor Go-Suzaku had a second son, Takahito, whose mother was Princess Teishi, the daughter of Emperor Sanjô. Yorimichi realized that if Takahito were allowed to come to the throne, his family would be deprived of their prominent position. Yorimichi and his brothers, Norimichi and Yorimune, vied with one another to set their daughters up as imperial consorts. Unfortunately, none of the girls were able to produce sons. Yorimichi fought desperately to keep Princess Teishi from entering the Court, but his efforts were in vain. At the time of Emperor Go-Reizei's enthronement, Takahito, later ascending the throne as Emperor Go-Sanjô, was named crown prince. Thus, Yorimichi's family lost altogether their position as maternal relatives of a reigning emperor.

The system of marriage politics, perfected during Michinaga's lifetime, was destroyed in the next generation. Nevertheless, Michinaga emerges as a shining figure in history, a symbol of the heights to which Heian culture soared when the Sesshô-Kanpaku system was at its most powerful.

Eminent Women Writers of the Court

Murasaki Shikibu and Sei Shônagon

by

EDWARD G. SEIDENSTICKER

Asked to name a few women who have been prominent in Japanese politics, people who know a little about Japanese history would think of Hôjô Masako, the wife of the first Kamakura shogun. And who next? It might be remembered that there were empresses, regnant and not consort at an earlier time, and that one or two of them became somewhat notorious; but they are known by Chinese names which look very much alike and have faded one into another. There are no genuinely scarlet empresses and wicked dowagers as in other lands. For most respondents the list would begin with Hôjô Masako and end with her as well. She is described in the table of contents for this book as "the woman of power behind the Bakufu," or something of the sort, and there are no others at all like her.

We are informed by the realistic fiction of the Heian period that there were strong, determined ladies who engaged men in political combat and more than held their own, but most of us would be hard put to say who these ladies might have been in real life. Even if the expanse of history were extended down to yesterday, it would be hard to think of a Japanese equivalent for Queen Victoria or Eleanor Roosevelt. There has not been much place in Japanese political history for women. It may, indeed, be unique among political histories for their absence.

If the subject were changed to literary history, few people who know a little about Japan would have much difficulty naming a dozen or so prominent women. It would not be surprising, indeed, if the list of the finest Japanese writers of prose, from the beginnings down to yesterday, were to begin with two lady writers, both from the Heian period, Murasaki Shikibu of *The Tale of Genji* and Sei Shônagon of *The Pillow Book.* If the

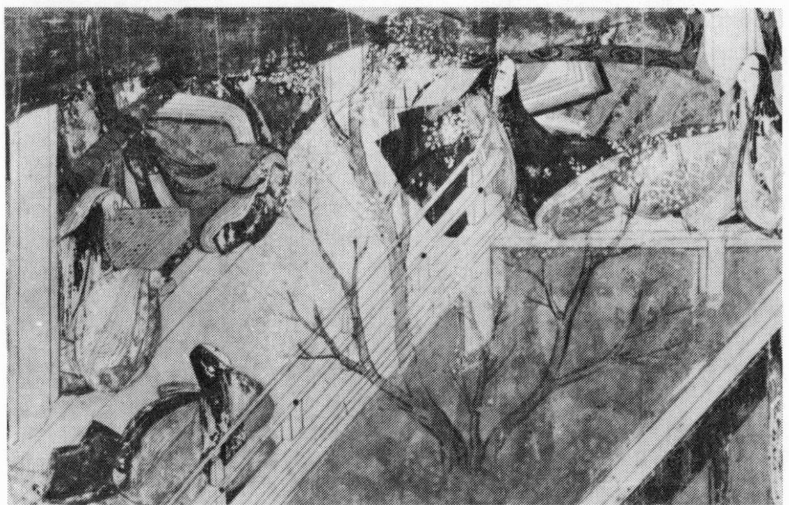

Genji monogatari emaki, "Takekawa" II (National Treasure); The Tokugawa Reimeikai Foundation (Tokyo)

list was chronological, it would probably not begin with ladies, but upon reaching the Heian period it would have trouble *not* including them.

The frequency of feminine names on almost anyone's list of literary eminences might give the impression that Japanese literature has been more womanish, in the sense of being a woman's pursuit, than in fact it has been. That numbers of extraordinarily gifted women should appear as the literature was having one of its finest days is certainly a happening not common in the literary history of the world. Even in the literary history of Japan, however, it happened only once.

The finest talents of the Nara period were turned to poetry, and there were some women among them, but the finest poets were men. Of the "Six Eminent Poets" (*Rokkasen*) of early Heian, some of them, in fact, not so very eminent, only one was a woman. Most of the prose romances preceding *The Tale of Genji* are either anonymous or of doubtful attribution, but most scholars would hold that the art of romancing was chiefly masculine.

Then, suddenly, in the years before and after the Christian millennium, women emerged dominant, and the great ones among them were Murasaki Shikibu and Sei Shônagon. In poetry women continued to be prominent until the courtly tradition itself came upon bad days. In prose their contribution was ever slighter through the middle ages, the Kamakura and Muromachi periods, and in the Tokugawa period it becomes almost as difficult to find eminent women writers as eminent women politicians. In the modern period women writers have had a somewhat better time of it, although it is hard to repress a feeling that women have their prominence in the literary histories because a truly modern country must have women writers, and Japan is a truly modern country.

In the longer perspective of history, then, the period when court ladies were doing what was best in Japanese literature is a limited one, less than a hundred years, from the last half of the tenth century into the first half of the eleventh. It is also one of the most brilliant periods in the history of Japanese literature. In prose literature, indeed, it may be the one period when Japanese literature was the very best in the world. In the popular Japanese view of Japanese history, the late seventeenth century demands attention as another uncommonly fine day for literature, but the prose literature, at least, has a narrow and somewhat parochial look about it. Then there is the modern period. The Japanese have done very well, especially in the novel; but it will take a while yet for reputations to sort themselves out, for some writers to become immortal and others to fade away.

The indisputably fine period was that half century and more in mid-Heian. Women were among the more interesting poets of the period, and many would say that Izumi Shikibu, a woman, was the most original of them all. In prose women were completely dominant. Murasaki Shikibu was the greatest of innovators in the art of prose fiction, Sei Shônagon the great pioneer in the art of "following the brush," of the discursive lyrical essay, at which the Japanese have been uncommonly good over the centuries, and of which they have been uncommonly fond.

Murasaki Shikibu was in a sense the less Japanese of the two, for her imagination was essentially dramatic, making its points and conveying its meanings through the mediation of character. Sei Shônagon preferred the more direct lyrical means, describing immediately what interested or amused or moved her. There they were side by side, in any event, the two recognized masters of prose in the day that was perhaps the finest of all for Japanese literature, and they were both women.

A rich variety of theories has been offered to explain this unique period of womanly superiority. We are told, for instance, that women were more flexible and adventuresome than men, and less willing to admit and bow down to the Chinese influences that were considered properly intellectual and academic. It is argued, further, that the two great historical phenomena mentioned above, the scarcity of strikingly successful lady politicians and the abundance of eminent lady writers, are related. Because there was not a great deal that an ambitious and able lady could do in politics, the theory would have it, such ladies sought to make their mark in letters. Yet if the ladies had not been remarkably talented in the first place, they would not have fitted themselves into the circumstances, however favorable these might have been; and so the best explanation, perhaps, is that it was largely an accident. The geniuses who made the most of the occasion happened to be women and not men.

We do not know much about either of our two. We do not even know their names. The names of ladies in the topmost reaches of courtly society, empresses and mothers of crown princes and the like, are recorded in the genealogies, but in the lower levels of the aristocracy anonymity prevails. Both came from the second level, that of courtiers who could not hope to rise to the highest posts in the capital but might be in charge of provincial governments. It was this second level, that of the provincial governor, that did the most for the literature of the day. The grand ladies on high thought literature important, and numbers of them were competent enough poets, but it was on a slightly lower level that they searched for a more brilliant sort of literary talent with which to grace their retinues. Once in the grand retinues, literary ladies were often contemptuous of their own origins. In *The Tale of Genji* Murasaki Shikibu does not have many kind words for provincial governors. They tend to be boors and buffoons – despite the fact that her own father was one.

We do not know when either of the two ladies was born, though there can be little doubt that Sei Shônagon was the older by perhaps ten or fifteen years. There is scholarly agreement at least as to probabilities, and it holds that Sei Shônagon was born in the seventh decade of the tenth century and Murasaki Shikibu in the eighth. We have recently passed the two millennials. In terms of pedigree it might be argued that Sei Shônagon was born to a slightly loftier position, for her family, the Kiyohara, was an offshoot of the royal family. She could trace her ancestry back a dozen generations in the paternal line to an emperor. Murasaki Shikibu was born to a place somewhat nearer the real seats of power. She belonged to a cadet branch of the Fujiwara family, which did not seek to displace the royal family but ruled in its name through a large part of the Heian period. She had a common paternal ancestor six generations back with Fujiwara no Michinaga, in whose day the Fujiwara hegemony was at its grandest and most secure.

Both ladies were from literary families. Sei Shônagon's father was one of the "five poets of the Pear Court" to whom was entrusted the editing of the second royally commissioned anthology of poetry. He and Murasaki Shikibu's great grandfather were on the list of "thirty-six eminent poets" that prevailed in the Heian period. Both ladies were themselves lyric poets, and *The Tale of Genji* contains as many original poems as some of the official anthologies; but neither was thought in her own time, or has been in the centuries since, a particularly distinguished practitioner of the art of formal verse.

It may be that their indifferent success with the thirty-one-syllable lyric, which everyone was expected to write and which was so surrounded by comfortable rules and tests that almost anyone could produce a harmless example, was itself a mark of distinction. They were interested in forms which required more daring and which allowed more room for originality. One of her translators once remarked that Sei Shônagon was the finest poet of her day. He did not mean the sort of thing that might have found for her a place on lists of thirty-six poets. He meant that she put great sensitivity to the uses of freer forms.

The great and crucial time for both ladies came with invitation to court service. Again a period of ten or fifteen years separated them. Sei Shônagon was at Court in the last decade of the tenth centry, Murasaki Shikibu in the first decade of the eleventh. They were in the service of two Fujiwara empresses, both consorts of the Emperor Ichijô. Freedom from the most vicious sort of harem politics puts the Japanese Court in happy contrast to the courts of many other Asian countries, but ladies were very important all the same in political maneuvering and conspiring. It was through their daughters that ambitious statesmen in the upper ranks of the Fujiwara clan sought to control the royal house. A Fujiwara would be married to an emperor, and the next royal generation would be dependent upon a Fujiwara grandfather. In *The Tale of Genji* are vivid glimpses of how the system worked. Though not a Fujiwara, Genji uses Fujiwara methods. He dotes upon his royal grandchildren, and it is quite clear that he is more important to them than is their paternal grandfather, a retired emperor.

Sei Shônagon was in the service of the Empress Teishi, Murasaki Shikibu of Empress Shôshi. They were first cousins, daughters of Fujiwara brothers. Important Fujiwaras became chancellors and regents, but there was no fixed procedure by which they succeeded one another. Though the most powerful and glorious positions were a monopoly of the senior branch, several members of that branch might be in savage competition for a vacancy. In the late tenth century the husband of another important literary lady, the *Kagerô* or "gossamer" diarist, was able to assert himself with sufficient force that all subsequent Fujiwara regents and chancellors were his direct descendants, but there was fierce family squabbling before Michinaga emerged dominant in the next generation.

The two empresses, Teishi and Shôshi, were their fathers' principal weapons through it all. Teishi, whom Sei Shônagon adored, is in historical perspective a sad little figure. For a time her father was the greatest statesman in the land, and the future seemed to belong to him and his family, and then he died, and his heirs were not able to hold their own against the capable and ruthless Michinaga. Their branch of the family went into permanent eclipse. In 1000 the Empress herself died, not much beyond girlhood.

Shôshi, on the other hand, lived to a very old age, and there were no eclipses for Michinaga's branch of the family. She was the mother of two emperors. All the honors and emoluments of grand dowagerhood were hers. She has been likened to Queen Victoria, and the comparison is not at all pointless if it is meant to emphasize that she was the most respected old lady of them all – though her influence upon practical politics must have been very slight compared to Victoria's.

Sei Shônagon probably started to write her *Pillow Book* after her debut at Court. A passage towards the end says very clearly that she did, but it is of doubtful authenticity. She continued to write through her years at Court, apparently, and after. Eminent scholars believe that the little miscellanies, the lists of pleasant things and unpleasant and the like, were the beginning of *The Pillow Book.* It is generally believed that Murasaki Shikibu began writing *The Tale of Genji* in the early years of her widowhood, years immediately preceding her court debut, and that she too went on writing through the court years and perhaps after. The debate over which parts of *The Tale of Genji* were written first has been complex and inconclusive, but it is not unlikely that they were the first episodes about that other Murasaki, presently to become the great love of the hero's life in the *Genji* itself.

The one lady was in the service of an empress whom she adored and whose great day was a fleeting one. The other lady did not, perhaps, have quite the same intense affection for her empress, but they seem to have been close, for Murasaki Shikibu tells us in her diary that she was the Empress's tutor in Chinese poetry; and the Empress had a long and prosperous career. It would have been very much in keeping with the circumstances in which the ladies found themselves if the older one, Sei Shônagon, had been the pessimist, writing darkly of the bleakness and evanescence of it all, and Murasaki Shikibu the buoyant optimist.

In fact it is the reverse. For all the sadness of her empress's career and for all its merits as illustration of the grand Buddhist principle of evanescence and emptiness, Sei Shônagon is perhaps among eminent Japanese writers the one who most unconditionally delights in the moment as it comes, and asks of it nothing more than that it be sufficient unto itself. Among the delights of *The Pillow Book* is that its author has so little sense of history. The past is old and fusty, and the future – well, of that, who can say? What is important is the present moment. We may ask of it that it be perfect in all its details, but we may not ask that it tell us the why and the whither. Acceptance of the present is what the reader must delight in if he is to become a devotee of Sei Shônagon and her *Pillow Book.*

Not everyone thinks it a reasonable and proper attitude. There is a kind of "liberal" critic and historian, indeed, who thinks it irresponsible. For him Sei Shônagon becomes a reactionary and an advocate of feudalism, one of those ineluctable stages in history which must be got through that something better may come into being. Sei Shônagon becomes a feudal remnant, without the perspicuity to see how rotten the old order is, or the canniness to see that people's courts will one day come along. Murasaki Shikibu, the pessimist, filled with misgivings about the old order, becomes by contrast a sort of prophet of the people's democracies. It is a way of looking at things that does not have much to do with literary judgments – since it is possible for a very good work of literature to be unapologetically reactionary. As social and intellectual history, however, it is not merely silly. Sei Shônagon *was* very pleased with the privileges to which she was born and promoted, and if that makes her an enemy of the people, there is not a great deal that can be done to change her. For those prepared to accept it, her delight in the moment is a delight.

Even for those who find them charming, it is possible to make too much of her worldliness and materialism, as when, for instance, she remarks upon how important it is that priests be handsome. The esoteric Buddhism of the Heian Court made much of ceremony and art as intermediaries between the worshiper and mysteries beyond the grasp of the rational faculty. If priests were other than handsome, therefore, a ceremony of the highest importance was flawed. Yet it remains true that for Sei Shônagon the passing moment was the thing. One does not go to her for social criticism or trenchant theory. One goes to her, rather, for a description of what fun it all was – and, with proper acceptance, one has it all over again, the fun of almost a millennium ago.

Given complete security in the entourage of an eminently successful empress, and all the reflected glory which such a position must have provided, Murasaki Shikibu might well have been the satisfied, optimistic one. Yet *The Tale of Genji* is a pessimistic book. Murasaki Shikibu may not have looked ahead to the people's republics, exactly, but she had a deep sense of the inadequacies of her day and its institutions. Indeed the past was as much with her as the present. If for Sei Shônagon the past lacked all the qualities that make for esteem and admiration and enjoyment, for Murasaki Shikibu it was a constant and overwhelming presence.

The first two-thirds or so of *The Tale of Genji* describe the life and loves of the prince who, as he approaches middle life, becomes the most powerful statesman in the realm. Perhaps the two most important things about him, for the artistic purposes of his creator, are that he is a prince of the blood and not a member of Murasaki Shikibu's own Fujiwara family, and that his life may be considered to lie some distance in the past. A nostalgic, retrospective, antiquarian mood hangs over the whole of the tale, and what it tells us is that the great days, when a prince of the blood might manage an ideal state, is in the past. The present, or the imagined day which provides Murasaki Shikibu's vantage point, is a lesser day, and the diminished action of the thirteen chapters that remain after Genji's disappearance from the scene tell us that we may expect the decline to continue.

Indeed it is an absolute, metaphysical decline. The Buddhist notion of evanescence appealed so strongly to the Japanese as to make one wonder whether it was not with them in some vague, misty form before the introduction of Buddhism. It runs all through Japanese literature, and it is never absent through the enormous length of the *Genji.* A strain of Buddhist thought which had wide currency in the Heian period held that Buddhism itself was not immune from the operations of the law of evanescence – in effect, that the law itself was the one immutable thing. There would come a time when the Buddhist law would weaken and fade, and the chronology was fairly precise, with the twilight of the law to come in the mid-Heian period, not long after the writing of the *Genji.* A sense of *Mappô*, of the last day of the law, intensifies the sense of decline that makes the *Genji* such a pessimistic book.

There is a sense in which the two works, *The Pillow Book* and *The Tale of Genji,* are similar. It would be wrong to think of the *Genji* as a bleak and despairing work. The sense of evanescence which so pervades it does not produce in the characters an immediate sense of hopelessness. The beauty of the passing moment is made perfect by an awareness that it must pass. Perfect love is possible, the *Genji* seems to tell us, because it cannot last, and so the mood of the *Genji* is of sweet, sad acceptance, and not of despair.

Yet the awareness of the present moment is very different for Murasaki Shikibu and for Sei Shônagon. Murasaki Shikibu is always aware of the moments that have gone and of the moments that are to come, and the awareness makes her a pessimist. For Sei Shônagon the past is fusty and the future is a matter of speculation, which is not very interesting. It would not be possible to call her an optimist as the word refers to an awareness of the future; but to describe her view of the present it would be hard to think of a better word.

No one knows whether the two ladies met. It does not seem likely, since imperial consorts lived in almost complete seclusion from one another, and since Teishi was already dead before Murasaki Shikibu entered Shôshi's service. There is no notice of Murasaki Shikibu in Sei Shônagon's writing, although it seems scarcely possible that word of the other lady's growing reputation should not have reached her, provided that she was still alive to receive it. Murasaki Shikibu's diary, covering a year and some months of her court service, contains a very uncomplimentary reference to Sei Shônagon, accusing her of self-satisfaction and shoddy craftsmanship. It is in a part of the diary which dangles in curious chronological isolation, and in which Murasaki Shikibu gives her opinions of other court ladies too. The other prominent literary lady among them, Izumi Shikibu, fares perhaps even less well than Sei Shônagon, and ladies who produced scarcely anything of note come off fairly well. So it seems likely that Murasaki Shikibu was concerned with literary reputation, and had not met Sei Shônagon in person. She recognized a genuine rival when she saw one, and took her shots.

Almost nothing is known about the last years of either lady. Tradition has it that Sei Shônagon lived a sad and impoverished old age, alone with her memories, but her early life and the tone of her writings are such that moralists would wish her to have such an old age, and would wish to invent one for her whether she had it or not. There are reasons for believing that she married after her time at Court and had a time in the provinces. In dwelling upon the pleasure she took in the passing moment, it is easy to make *The Pillow Book* seem like a more joyous document than it is. There is certainly nothing in it that might seem to imitate the tragedy of Sei Shônagon's empress, but there are sober passages all the same. It has been argued persuasively that they were the last passages written, and that, in contrast with the happy, slap-dash quality of the little miscellanies, they suggest an aging author, and one for whom the good times are over. It may be so; but we do not know how long Sei Shônagon lived, or when she died.

There is documentary evidence that Murasaki Shikibu did not leave court service immediately after 1010, when her diary ends. If, as most scholars think to be the case, *The Tale of Genji* was begun in the years after she was widowed and before she went to Court, then not quite a decade elapsed before she broke off her diary; and a decade is not much time for such a long work, especially at the hands of a court lady who had to busy herself with other things, such as lecturing an empress upon Chinese poetry. The sections of the *Genji* which treat of Genji's later years, moreover, and those which follow upon his death, suggest a writer who has seen a great deal of life, and learned to accept it. There is a gradual withdrawal from society, indeed, which suggests an aging recluse. If Murasaki Shikibu lived into the years when tragedy comes into Genji's life, and one wants to think that the power with which the tragedy is described is based upon experience, then she lived at least a half century, and died no earlier than the third decade of the eleventh century. Although we know nothing about her last years and death, we may visit a spot in the northern environs of Kyoto that is said to be her grave, and no one has yet demonstrated beyond doubt that it is not.

The accepted view of Japanese literary history is that mid-Heian was among its finest times, and Sei Shônagon and Murasaki Shikibu would head every school child's list of its finest writers. It is one of those matters in which the foreign view may in some measure differ from the Japanese. The foreigner would not be likely to come up with other ladies or gentlemen to put at the top of his list, but the distance between number one and number two might seem so considerable as to give the list an uneven or incongruous look. To the Japanese the two ladies seem like towering peaks rising from the highest uplands of Japanese literature. To the foreigner it may well seem that one of them is indeed a towering peak, but that the other is a pleasant enough hill, not really of the same eminence at all.

Murasaki Shikibu is surely one of the finest writers of prose fiction the human race has produced. Because she was so far in advance of the others, it may be, indeed, that she was the most remarkable genius of them all. She did something that no one had done before her, not in her part of the world, not in any other, and something that no one was to do again for a very long time. The *Genji* is such a rich and complex fabric that any number of strands, historical, social, religious, metaphysical, can be isolated from it. Most of all, however, it is what it is before such abstractions, concrete representation of believable individual life. There are several hundred characters and perhaps fifty or sixty major characters, and each of them has strong, credible individuality. It is, in other words, a novel, having as its irreducible essence the concrete humanity on which the realistic psychological novel is based. It is a most remarkable achievement. The great English novels of the nineteenth century had the eighteenth-century novel behind them and Shakespeare behind that. There was very little in Japanese literature of the tenth century or Chinese literature of any century to prepare the way for Murasaki Shikibu. She may have been influenced by Chinese historical writing, which certainly was very good, but to move from the figures of history when they are doing things for the history books to figures of fiction when they are doing things for their own quiet enjoyment required a great leap of the imagination. A person of the most extraordinary talent, and in the final analysis it seems accidental that she was a woman, saw a possibility which no one had seen before, and pursued it with triumphant success.

It may be that the greatest literary figures do not have successors, wherever they are in time and place. They stand in isolation, solitary peaks. (Shakespeare is an exception to everything.) Certainly Murasaki Shikibu had no real successors. She had imitators, but they missed what is most important in her work, the humanity. In modern times, under the influence of the West, there came a sudden burst of interest in the realistic novel, and Murasaki Shikibu was noticed as someone who had a very long time ago done what was deemed necessary for the future; but in the near millennium between there were not many who were able to isolate and identify the really important thing in her work, although her popularity never waned, and there were none at all who set about recreating it. A great deal of prose narrative was written, and a great deal of it was fiction, but it tended strongly towards exaggerated plot, and caricature or cartoon rather than character.

They may seem to the outsider an ill-matched pair, the two great ladies of Heian prose, one of gigantic proportions, the other very charming but also very petite. It is hard, at first, to think of *The Pillow Book,* there beside *The Tale of Genji,* as other than a miniature, and its author as other than a minor talent. Yet there is a way in which Sei Shônagon is historically the more important of the two. It is possible for a figure to be very great and yet by virtue of unique greatness to stand outside of history, and for another figure, less extraordinary, to be at the head of a very important tributary to an important and continuing stream.

In pre-modern times the Japanese valued lyric verse far more highly than prose narrative. It was considered a worthy endeavor for the most dignified and important of personages, and prose narrative was for women and children. Even when not writing formal verse, people who wrote well had a high regard for the lyrical mode. The lyrical essay was esteemed above the romance, and if *The Tale of Genji* stands in grand isolation, with no genuine and worthy successors down almost to our own day, *The Pillow Book* stands near the head of a tradition of "following the brush" that has been continuous. Indeed it might be said that if the lyrical discursive mode of expression has been the main stream of Japanese prose literature, then its two great fountainheads are the tenth-century *Tales of*

Ise, a collection of little anecdotes centered upon thirty-one-syllable poems, and *The Pillow Book,* a collection of little prose lyrics, some of them very beautiful.

It may be, too, that *The Pillow Book* must be read in the original if it is to be properly judged, whereas *The Tale of Genji* passes language barriers in fairly good condition. *The Pillow Book* is the better written of the two. *The Tale of Genji* is in sum very great, but in detail it can be careless and even somewhat sloppy. Only a very daring translator would venture to imitate the carelessness, and so in translation the two tend to take on a similar appearance of stylistic competence, or at least not of marked incompetence. *The Pillow Book* is recommended to the student of classical Japanese as a model of careful, precise, evocative prose. *The Tale of Genji* may be recommended as many things, but not that.

Advocates of cultural exchange and international understanding often fall into what may be called the cosmopolitan fallacy. They assume that everything is grist for their mill, and that what proves recalcitrant is unworthy. That which does not transcend barriers of nation and language with complete distinction becomes merely parochial. Yet there unquestionably is a great deal of very good writing that is to be appreciated fully only in its own language. (Let anyone who does not believe it have a look at translations of *Alice in Wonderland* into Japanese, or, I should think, any other language.) Perhaps we can go a step farther and say that it is not proper to rank important authors against one another except in their own languages. It may be that Murasaki Shikibu will always seem to the foreigner considerably the greater of the two great Heian ladies; but when they are read in their own language some diminution in the gap between them is to be observed.

The Rise and Fall of a Great Military Clan

Taira no Kiyomori

by

JEAN-RENÉ CHOLLEY

Most historians agree that the major historical event of the twelfth century in Japan was the collapse of the monopoly of power held by the Court-based Fujiwara aristocracy in Kyoto, and the appearance of a new political and social system now called feudalism. Until then, all the key positions of the administration had been occupied by members of the Fujiwara clan, the real masters of the country under the nominal authority of an emperor who more often than not was merely a child, and in many instances the son-in-law of the head of an influential branch of the clan. They could thus reign as regents and dictate their will to the infant sovereign, but, simple and effective as it was, this way of seizing and holding power had a serious built-in defect. None of the decision-making Fujiwara nobles could leave Kyoto, the center of their power, lest some rival take their place in one of the countless conspiracies of the time. Neither could they delegate their authority, for no one of good birth and no talented man would ever dream of leaving town and living in virtual exile in some remote province; many poems testify that the most hideous sanction that could be taken against a disgraced high functionary was to send him away as governor of a "barbarous" Azuma or Kyushu province, far from the source of culture and fortune.

The inevitable result of such a situation was the almost complete neglect in which the provinces were left, and this was precisely the undoing of the Fujiwara.

The very people whom they had evicted from the Court had no choice but to settle in these provinces and carve fiefs out of them, where they sought to be as independent and powerful as possible. Among the numerous warrior families who thus established themselves far from the center of

Taira no Kiyomori; Rokuharamitsuji Temple (Kyoto)

power, two were destined to rise and to rule Japan as supreme masters. The Minamoto, or Genji, had control over the eight eastern provinces in the Kantô, and they felt that they had every right to claim their share in the government of the nation, for they counted in their numbers direct descendants of the Emperor Seiwa who had ruled only two hundred and some years earlier. The Taira, or Heike, were in a somewhat less favorable position at the beginning: they had settled in Ise Province and they were openly treated as country boors, for none of them was even allowed at Court until one Tadamori, a talented poet and an able Minister of Justice, succeeded in winning Emperor Shirakawa's favor. Needless to say, the Taira also felt strongly that Japan should be theirs by right, for they were related to Emperor Kanmu, who had reigned a mere three hundred years earlier.

By the middle of the twelfth century, these two clans were rivals but not yet in open hostility. Then a palace intrigue set them against each other during the civil war of Hôgen (1156) which ended in a Taira victory and the strengthening of their authority. Three years later, the Genji tried to attack them in the civil war of Heiji, but were once again vanquished, and the clash created a web of deep hatreds that disappeared only thirty years and many battles later with the extermination of the last of the Heike.

Taira no Tadamori, who had done so much for his family, found himself one day with a son who was to become the most renowned of the Heike. One can surmise Tadamori's slight bafflement when he found out that he was going to be a father, for some strange rumors were afloat concerning his son's birth, if one is to believe the *Tales of the Heike.* There was first a theory that the boy was a reincarnation of a renowned monk, the High Priest of the Tendai sect Jie, who had died in 985. Book VI, chapter 10 of the *Heike* gives yet another amusing version: the year when the child was born the ex-Emperor Shirakawa was visiting one of his favorite concubines, the Lady of Gion, who lived near a temple; and one particularly dark and rainy night he saw a luminous being whose raised arm seemed to hold a fiercely blazing mace. Frightened out of his wits, the ex-Emperor summoned Tadamori who was then an officer of the North Guard, and ordered him to kill the horrible thing. Tadamori decided instead to catch it alive, and when the "ghost" was apprehended, it turned out to be nothing more than a sixty-year-old monk on his way to light the lamps in the nearby temple. The ex-Emperor much admired Tadamori's courage and wisdom in not slaying the apparition outright, and as a reward he gave him the Lady of Gion, who was already carrying his child. Shirakawa was prepared to take care of the infant if it was a girl, but as the lady gave birth to a boy, he decided that Tadamori should consider him as his son. This boy had a habit of crying and howling during the night, and when the ex-Emperor heard of it, he wrote a poem:

Even if he cries at night,
Let Tadamori take care of him.
For the day will come
When he blossoms out
In pure prosperity.

And this is the reason the boy was given the name Kiyomori ("pure prosperity"). Probably thanks to his imperial blood, Kiyomori followed a very rapid *cursus honorum* that brought him to the post of Lieutenant in the Military Guard at the age of twelve, and at eighteen he was elevated to the much-envied Fourth Rank in the Court. He then seized ever greater powers for himself until he became all powerful after the Heiji war: he was absolute master of Kyoto and of the Palace, for he had succeeded in eliminating all his opponents, and neither the reigning Emperor, still a child, nor the Retired Emperor could do anything against his will. He had no longer any reason to conceal his ambitions, and he started rooting out the Fujiwara from the offices they had held for centuries; when he took the title of Prime Minister and President of the Supreme Council of the Empire in 1167, he put himself in a position of unchallenged power until the day of his death. He had followed the time-honored practice of the Fujiwara by marrying one of his daughters to an emperor, and when she bore a son, he forced his son-in-law to abdicate in favor of the prince, then only a few months old. Members of his family held all the important posts in the government and the provinces, and for a time not even the Genji dared contest his authority. Kiyomori and the Taira had then reached the height of fortune and glory, but as the *Tales of the Heike* reminds the reader, "the haughty do not last long, just like a dream in a spring night." The Heike had nowhere to go now but down, in accordance with the Buddhistic philosophy that perfection is in itself the first step toward decline and death.

There are of course political reasons for the ultimate extinction of the Taira a few years after they had obtained complete mastery of Japan, but it might be interesting to pause here and examine one cause of their defeat that is seldom noticed, or at any rate never pointed out in history books. It concerns Kiyomori himself, who after an illness in 1168 had shaved his head and become a monk, nominally at least. The Minister-Monk, as he was known thereafter, had a passion for women as great as for power, and one exceptionally pretty woman happened to be the origin of a great many Taira disasters. Lady Tokiwa, a maid of honour to the wife of Emperor Konoe, had been chosen from among one thousand other contenders as the most beautiful woman in Japan, and she had been given as a concubine to Minamoto no Yoshitomo, one of Kiyomori's most stubborn adversaries in the Heiji war. She had had three sons by him, and after his death in 1160, she had to flee with her children to a hidden village in the countryside. Furious that he could not discover her, Kiyomori had her mother arrested, whereupon she immediately surrendered herself and appeared at Rokuhara, Kiyomori's palace. As soon as he saw her, Kiyomori forgot every idea he might have entertained of torture by fire or water, and, as the *Chronicle of Yoshitsune* (Book I, chapter 1) relates, "he thought that if only she would submit to him, even if her three sons turned out one day to be enemies of the empire and his family, he would be willing to spare their lives." He sent her innumerable love letters which she refused even to open until she was made to understand in no uncertain terms that there was no lack of finely sharpened swords for the necks of Yoshitomo's children. This very subtle piece of courtship was not lost on Tokiwa who decided to save her sons from certain death: they were put away in monasteries, and although Kiyomori had a dark impression that the third boy was a little too smart for his liking, he forgot all about it in a few days. He certainly had his mind on more pressing business. This act of humanity, so out of character for Kiyomori, was perhaps the most grievous mistake in his life. For Tokiwa's last son was none other than the four-year-old Ushiwaka who was later take the name Minamoto no Yoshitsune and became by far the best commander any Japanese army has ever known. His deeds of valour are indeed such that, after his elder brother Yoritomo had him killed in 1189, the people refused to believe that he was dead and legend has him escape through Hokkaido to Mongolia where he began another brilliant military career under the name of Genghis Khan. The legend seems a trifle farfetched, but what Yoshitsune did in Japan is real enough: he soon began to "retrieve the honour of the Genji," and in a series of splendidly planned battles culminating in the Dan no Ura victory of 1185, he dealt the final blow to the Taira whose name was forever wiped from Japanese history.

Kiyomori died four years before this calamity and thus was spared the sight of his family being literally exterminated at the hands of the child he had taken so much trouble to spare, but it is one of those fine ironies of history that the founder of the clan's fortune was at the same time its destroyer because of his overfondness for women. The sad sigh of the chroniclers commenting on the vanity of worldly pursuits could not be better applied than to Kiyomori: "Alas, how miserable is the fate of heroes! Indeed what should be avoided and feared, if not woman?"

The same comment was made some six centuries later when the Edo merchants and townsmen developed their own literature and merrily spent their time lampooning the great figures of their country in seventeen-syllable comical verses called *senryû.* Kiyomori was so tempting a target for their wit that scores of these *senryû* relate his life and doings in a highly particular way. One of the more restrained sums up the tragedy of the Heike in a few terse words:

That Kiyomori, a widow with a bitter aftertaste he grabbed.
(*Shûi,* 7)

Still, while he was enjoying Tokiwa's company, Kiyomori had no idea that the beginning of the end had come. He was busy trying to get rid of the ex-Emperor who was at the center of a small coterie of unsatisfied nobles and monks conspiring against him day in and day out. He succeeded in banishing the ex-Emperor far from the Court, but the monks, especially those living in Nara, were not impressed in the least. In their eyes, he had committed the blunder of showing partiality to the notorious warrior-monks of Mount Hiei who had taken his side and whom the Nara monks hated with a vengeance. Just as the Genji were beginning to grow restless in the provinces, a strange monk stepped onto the scene and precipitated the action. He was Mongaku, the hero of the celebrated Japanese film *Jigokumon,* and, brandishing an old skull which he claimed to be Yoshitomo's, he first incited Yoritomo to rebel, and then he had the idea to go to the ex-Emperor from whom he extracted a decree declaring the Heike enemies of the empire and ordering the Genji to destroy them. Revolt was now a lawful duty and the Minamoto assembled at once a powerful army to attack their rivals. The Heike sent against them some seventy thousand picture-book cavalrymen who kept asking themselves just why on earth they had to go a-fighting, and whose generals were at their best only in military parades. Before they could engage in battle with the Genji, they were frightened into screaming panic by a flock of birds suddenly leaving a marsh, and they fled for their lives in a state of utter confusion that provided one of the most humorous episodes of the *Tales of the Heike.*

Mad with rage, Kiyomori found a last an opportunity to take vicarious revenge. The Nara monks had been teasing him for a long time, and he entrusted his fifth son Shigehira, another operetta general, with the task of teaching them a lasting lesson. Attacking in the midst of a tempest during a dark winter night, Shigehira asked for torches so that he might at least know where he was, but his men mistook this for an order to burn down everything standing on the ground. They had some excuse, for the words spoken by their commander were not very clear; according to Book V of the *Heike* ("The Burning of Nara"), Shigehira merely directed his troops to "light fires." The result was appalling: more than three thousand men were burned alive, and the most venerable monasteries in the town were completely destroyed, along with priceless art treasures and an eighth-century statue of Vairocana. Kiyomori was highly pleased with this act of fine warfare, but his petty revenge had wrought upon the Buddhist Law a catastrophe unrivalled in China or India, as the *Heike* laments in the final lines of the episode.

The Minister-Monk could not however enjoy his last triumph for long. Precisely at the time when alarming news was coming from the eastern and northern provinces where the Genji were growing bolder by the day, Kiyomori fell sick on the twenty-seventh day of the second lunar month of 1181. Nobody knew what ailed him, but many people suspected that the fires of hell were on his body as a punishment for the burning of Vairocana's image, for his illness was no ordinary one. The *Tales of the Heike* (Book VI, "The Death of the Monk") gives a vivid account of it: "His body radiated a heat similar to that of a burning fire. Those who approached within ten yards of the place where he was lying could not bear the heat .... Water was poured on him, but it began to simmer and in an instant it was boiling .... When water touched him, it took fire so that a cloud of black smoke filled the rooms and twists of flames crept into the air." There seems to be a bit of hyperbole in this account, but it bears testimony to the frightening end he must have had and to the astonished awe of those who watched him in his death throes. Many centuries later, the *senryû* authors also tried to express their wonder at what no doubt was a very rare sight:

When he enters his bath, the Monk says "pssssssh!"
(*Shûi,* 6.2)

Some authors even, remembering Kiyomori's reputation as a philanderer, have him clamouring for his favorite delicacy to the very last moment:

The Monk shouts: "Bring chilled women, chilled women!"
(*Shûi*, 6.7)

In fact, he was approached only by his wife, and he found enough strength to tell her that he wanted neither a funeral service nor mourning, only a reasonable last gift: if somebody would chop off Yoritomo's head and have it planted on a spike in front of his grave, he would be happy enough on his way to hell. His fever grew steadily worse until on the fourth day of the second intercalary month he fell from the water-covered plank he had been laid on, suffered a final convulsion and perished in his sixty-fourth year.

It was a fitting end for a man whose life, temper, and doings had known no measure. In his days, he had seen his family rise from obscurity to eminence, and he himself had worked, lied, and killed his way to a position of such absolute power as nobody had ever enjoyed before him; then, carried away by the excesses of his reckless nature, he had proceeded to sow the seeds of some of the greatest turmoils that took place on the soil of Japan. When he left his country, he knew that all he had built was soon to disappear, and this knowledge may have played not a small part in the fiery fever that took him away.

It is no wonder that Kiyomori and his shadow dominate over half of the *Tales of the Heike,* for his life is a perfect illustration of the Buddhistic phrase on which the text is built, "the prosperous must fall." If politics and philandering had left him time to become acquainted with the philosophy of his religion after he became a monk, he might have taken solace in the thought that even his rivals, the Genji, would necessarily take the first step on the road to decline and extinction as soon as they took his place, which is just what happened.

Meanwhile, "this man who over the whole empire of Japan had spread the glory of his name and imposed his power, his body reduced to fleeting smoke, had vanished into the sky of the capital, and his ashes, hardly more lasting, mixed with the sand of the beach, had returned to earth" (Book VI).

Victory in Battle and Family Tragedy

Minamoto no Yoritomo and Yoshitsune

by

MINORU SHINODA

No story in all of Japanese history is better known than that of the brothers Yoritomo and Yoshitsune who flourished in the twelfth century. No story has been romanticized as much as this story in which the brothers, reunited after many years of enforced separation, combine their talents in a wide-ranging, five-year war to help their own clan, the Minamoto (or Genji), to destroy their bitter rivals, the Taira (also known as the Heike, Heishi, and Heiji), and to catapult the Minamoto to a position of political preeminence in the country – only to have, in the very flush of victory, a falling out between them, with the one relentlessly pursuing the other to the bitter end.

The story actually hangs on the barest of historical threads. But because it contained the elements of a stirring war tale as well as the pathos of a tragic drama, the storyteller and the dramatist have stepped in to provide what the historian has not been able to do. The result has been the addition to the story of a vast amount of detail, for the most part imaginary and improvised, and greatly outweighing the factual. Moreover, the overwhelming tendency in this literature has been to cast the younger brother in the role of the hero, the hero who is later misunderstood, unappreciated, and unjustly persecuted, and the older brother in the role of the villain.

Although the story begins in the middle of the twelfth century, one must see it, if one is to savor something of the impact of the story on the Japanese mind, against the larger background of: (1) the rise of the provincial warrior class and the decline of the ancient court nobility; and (2) the long and bitter rivalry between the Taira and the Minamoto clans. The first to emerge as a power in the provinces were the Taira. The time was the ninth and tenth centuries. The place was the rugged frontier country of northern and eastern Japan.

But the Taira were soon to be challenged by the Minamoto. This was in the eleventh century when Taira no Tadatsune, a power in Musashi in eastern Japan, sought to extend his control into a neighboring territory. The imperial Court sent two expeditions against him, the second under Minamoto no Yorinobu who successfully suppressed Tadatsune.

Yorinobu's victory provided the first great impetus for the beginning of Minamoto influence in the east and subsequently in the north. A few years after the suppression of Tadatsune, Yorinobu's son Yoriyoshi became governor of Sagami, the province destined to become the site of the first military government in Japan that was established by a direct descendant of Yorinobu and Yoriyoshi some one hundred fifty years later.

In the north two wars in the latter half of the eleventh century were to establish the Minamoto as a great local power. These were the Nine Years' War and the Three Years' War which began in 1051 and 1083 respectively. In the former Yoriyoshi and his son Yoshiie, commissioned by the imperial Court, successfully put down a defiant local lord. In the latter, Yoshiie, who had succeeded his father as chieftain of the clan, was sent by the Court to suppress another rebellious local lord. What is significant about these campaigns in the rugged mountains of northern Honshu against a hardy race of northerners, who themselves had earned a reputation as warriors in generations of fighting with the Ainu, is that the bond between Minamoto leaders and their followers was greatly strengthened, and the reputation of the Minamoto as warriors reached new heights. The Court showered father and son with honors and offices while landowners commended their lands to them. The latter movement became so pronounced that the very Court which had honored them began in 1091 to prohibit the practice of land commendation to Yoshiie.

But the Taira, as they gave way to the Minamoto in the north and in the east, were building the basis for a resurgence in western Japan in the area around Ise and along the Inland Sea. In the tenth century, Taira no Korehira became governor of Ise. With Masamori, Korehira's grandson, Taira influence reached into Inaba on the Japan Sea and to both sides of the Inland Sea as far west as Bizen and Sanuki. Early in the eleventh century the Taira were challenged in this region by the Minamoto. Yoshichika, one of the sons of the famed Yoshiie, had defied the Court and had committed excesses during his governorship of a province in Kyushu, for which he had been exiled to the island of Oki in the Japan Sea. When he escaped to Izumo and seized power there, the imperial Court sent Masamori to subdue him in 1107. Thus the Taira successfully met a

Minamoto no Yoritomo; Jingoji Temple (Kyoto)

Minamoto challenge in the west just as, nearly a hundred years earlier in the east, Minamoto no Yorinobu had succeeded in checking the ambitions of Taira no Tadatsune.

In the first half of the twelfth century, Masamori's son Tadamori was to rise to even greater heights than his father. By accomplishing the feat of subduing piracy in the Inland Sea and by gaining control of shipping and commerce on this ancient waterway, Tadamori became a power in western Japan and a favorite at the Court. In fact, with Tadamori, Taira influence at the Court was to increase so rapidly as to rival that of the Minamoto, who, through their alliance with the Fujiwara, had earlier entrenched themselves in the capital.

But it was Kiyomori, Tadamori's son, who was to raise the Taira to the pinnacle of power and glory. In this development Kiyomori was greatly aided by the fortuitous occurrence of two brief military encounters in Kyoto from which he was to emerge as the undisputed political master of the country. The first, the Hôgen War of 1156, was an imperial succession dispute in which the factions sought the assistance of warrior groups from the provinces. The significance of this move on the part of the Court cannot be overemphasized, for it meant, first of all, that the important question of who was to succeed to the throne was being determined by the power of the provincial warrior. It also meant that after the resolution of the dispute, the provincial warrior would no longer be content to serve merely as servant, lackey, and body guard to the court noble and that he would demand instead a greater share in running the government. And this is precisely what happened. Kiyomori, who emerged the victor, astutely channeled the rewards of victory to himself and to his clan, to the exclusion of his other partners in the war. Among the latter was a Minamoto: this was Yoshitomo, great-grandson of Yoshiie and the father of Yoritomo and the yet unborn Yoshitsune, who in his resentment toward his former partner conspired to overthrow him. The result was the Heiji uprising of 1159-60 which proved to be disastrous to the Minamoto cause. Yoshitomo's two eldest sons as well as Yoshitomo himself lost their lives, the latter at the hands of a treacherous retainer. Kiyomori again emerged the winner. He proceeded immediately to drive out the Minamoto from the capital and to take measures to establish and assure Taira rule in the country for generations to come.

It is at this juncture, the end of the Heiji uprising, that the Yoritomo-Yoshitsune story really begins, the first phase covering the twenty-year period up to the commencement of the Genpei war in 1180. It is a period which has produced very little factual information about the brothers, especially about the younger brother who was but an infant at the conclusion of the Heiji uprising. It is not surprising therefore that the period has given birth to some of the more imaginative and fanciful aspects of the Yoshitsune legend – the legend, for example, that he, as a young boy of seven, learned swordsmanship and agility from a long-nosed goblin (*tengu*) who inhabited the forests.

The first problem facing the victorious Kiyomori in 1160 was the disposition of Yoshitomo's sons. Of nine sons six had survived the recent wars. Yoritomo, the third son, was at age fourteen the oldest, as well as being heir to the chieftainship of the Minamoto clan. Yoshitsune, the ninth son, was the youngest, being scarcely a year old. Since all were young – the last three being infants – they posed no immediate threat to Taira security. However, given the bitterness of the rivalry between the two clans and the temper of the times, it is surprising that Kiyomori did not take harsher – even extreme – measures against the boys. Instead, for some inexplicable reason, he chose to spare their lives and to banish them to different parts of the country in the custody of loyal Heike retainers or to have them brought up in the quiet, pacifist environment of a Buddhist monastery. Accordingly, he sent Yoritomo to Izu in eastern Japan as a ward of one of the trusted members of the Heike, the Hôjô family. Yoshitsune was permitted to remain with his mother until he was six or seven when he was transferred to a Buddhist temple in Kurama, a few miles north of Kyoto.

Kiyomori's compassion and leniency, somewhat uncharacteristic of the chieftain of a warrior clan, has given rise to one of the first of many myths which have grown up around the Yoritomo-Yoshitsune story. This is the view that Tokiwa, Yoshitsune's mother who was a lady-in-waiting renowned for her beauty, consented to become Kiyomori's mistress in exchange for the lives of her sons. If indeed the two had entered into such an arrangement, the relationship did not last very long, for we find Tokiwa, shortly after the Heiji uprising, becoming the wife of a member of the Fujiwara family.

But while this story attempts to explain why Yoshitsune's life was spared, it does not offer any explanation as to why Yoritomo, the next chieftain of the Minamoto and potentially the more dangerous of the two, was also spared. Here too it is interesting to note that it was a woman who interceded in Yoritomo's behalf and who persuaded Kiyomori to take the lesser of the two measures. That woman, who was probably a complete stranger to Yoritomo, was Kiyomori's stepmother. That a supposedly cold and calculating clan chieftain chose to be persuaded by women, even in matters as grave as those of life and death, point to the important role women played in medieval Japan in teaching their warrior-husbands, warrior-brothers, and warrior-sons a sense of restraint and respect for their fellow men, whether kin or not, whether friend or foe.

It should be pointed out at this time that although Yoritomo and Yoshitsune were brothers, they had different mothers. They were, in other words, only half-brothers. Yoritomo's mother was the daughter of a Shinto priest. Yoshitsune's mother, as already explained, was the beauteous Tokiwa, a lady-in-waiting. As half-brothers they were brought up in different households, and, given the wide difference in their ages, they could not have been very close. This helps to explain, at least in part, their later estrangement.

For Yoshitsune the period from his transfer from Kyoto to Kurama at the age of six or seven until his joining Yoritomo in eastern Japan some thirteen or fourteen years later is the least known period of his life. But, by the same token, it is the most elaborately embroidered period of his life. It would seem that later generations, realizing the lack of adequate information about the adolescence of their hero, felt compelled to invent one befitting a young warrior destined for greatness.

In this regard, Kurama in the neighborhood of Kyoto and Hiraizumi in northern Japan, the two places where Yoshitsune was to spend these years, were ideal for the cultivation and growth of myths. Kurama is a heavily wooded valley, the sunlight barely shining through the leaves and branches of the tall cryptomeria trees. It was the very sort of place which might attract hermits and breed supernatural beings – like the *tengu* – with whom Yoshitsune is supposed to have cavorted. Hiraizumi, likewise, had an aura of mystery about it, mainly because it was so far removed from the capital and few knew anything about the place, except that it was a splendid city being built in the image of Kyoto by Fujiwara no Hidehira, the powerful lord of the region.

Four legendary or semi-legendary episodes highlight this phase of Yoshitsune's life. The first concerns Yoshitsune's friendship with Benkei, the burly, powerfully-built monk, who had a most unorthodox way of expressing his piety, which was to rob one thousand persons of their swords and to donate them to the church. For this purpose he had posted himself on the Gojô bridge which was on one of the busier east-to-west thoroughfares in Kyoto. The prospective one thousandth victim to come along was none other than Yoshitsune, still a mere lad of about ten or eleven. What an acolyte from a suburban temple was doing in the big city at night has never been satisfactorily explained, but the story goes on to say that far from meekly surrendering his sword, Yoshitsune challenged and eventually humiliated the astonished Benkei with his swordsmanship and his incredible agility. Thereupon, the monk vowed to be the lad's retainer and to serve him loyally to the end. This celebrated incident at the Gojô bridge has become the basis of numerous songs and dances.

The second occurrence of significance in this phase was the chance discovery by Yoshitsune of his true identity through a genealogy kept at the Kurama temple. It was then that he resolved to confront the Taira someday so that he might avenge his father's death. To do so, however, he would have to abandon his training for the Buddhist priesthood – which he would gladly do – and to escape from the watchful eyes of his wardens. As a matter of fact, it has never been clearly established whether his wardens had ever strictly enforced the condition that Yoshitsune should be trained for the priesthood, for neither the war tales nor the plays portray Yoshitsune at Kurama as a novice with shaven head and appropriate religious garb. In any event, he succeeded in escaping from Kurama in 1174, although not without help from an itinerant merchant, and he made his way north to Ôshû where he was warmly received and given asylum by Fujiwara no Hidehira. This was the third important event of this phase. Enroute to Ôshû, Yoshitsune paused briefly at a place called Kagami to conduct a *genbuku*, or "coming-of-age ceremony," which he performed himself and which constituted the fourth significant happening of the initial phase. Needless to say, such a ceremony was normally administered by an adult to a youth who had attained his majority. This unusual episode illustrates Yoshitsune's sense of independence and his impatience with the niceties of tradition. More importantly, it shows the essentially lonely and isolated character of his life. Yoshitsune's inability in his later life to get along with his superiors and his colleagues may have been due to the fact that as a youth he had been denied the chance to grow up in a normal way with his brothers, other members of his family, and friends. Except for Benkei – and Benkei was many years his senior – the only companions Yoshitsune seems to have had were the sprites of the forests of Kurama.

In contrast to the many myths which developed around the life of Yoshitsune, there is hardly an episode in Yoritomo's early life that bears any resemblance to a myth or a legend. Perhaps the only event suggesting that Yoritomo was endowed with qualities approaching the legendary concerned his amorous life. This was his success in persuading Masako, his warden's daughter, to elope with him on the eve of her marriage to another. The incident further illustrates Yoritomo's powers of persuasion, for he was successful also in winning her father's blessing for the union and, tacitly, his political freedom as well. Later, when Yoritomo raised his standard of revolt, his father-in-law and, until lately, his warden was, not surprisingly, among the first to declare for him.

The crucial period in the development of the Yoritomo-Yoshitsune story is the second phase consisting of the war years between 1180 and 1185. It begins with a tearful, highly emotional reunion of the brothers at an encampment in eastern Japan and ends five years later in their bitter, irreconciliable separation. There are those who say that the so-called "reunion" in 1180 never actually took place. They point to the fact that Yoshitsune's rise to fame and notoriety occurred in the late stages of the war when the fighting had shifted to western Japan and that Yoritomo, on the other hand, had never ventured out of eastern Japan throughout the five years of the war. When it is also remembered that Yoritomo later was to refuse to give an audience to Yoshitsune, one might well surmise that the two never met face to face.

If, on the other hand, Yoshitsune had made the long journey from northern Japan to offer his support to the Genji cause, and the brothers had met at Kisegawa in the east, there are very few references subsequently to Yoshitsune's activities in eastern Japan. There is, however, one episode in the early stages of the war that bears repeating, for it shows the contrasting nature of their personalities and seems to portend what is to happen later to their relationship. At a ceremony honoring carpenters who were about to begin the construction of a shrine in Kamakura, Yoshitsune had balked at performing the lowly service of leading one of the horses to be presented to the carpenters. Only after a reprimand and a second command from Yoritomo did Yoshitsune finally perform this duty in which all the leading vassals, most of them much older than he, had participated.

It was not until 1183 that the first opportunity for Yoshitsune to demonstrate his military talents was to present itself – and it was to come from rather unexpected quarters. Minamoto no Yoshinaka, a cousin who had become a power in north-central Japan between 1180 and 1183, had defeated a Taira army which had been sent against him, and on the momentum of that victory he had emerged from his mountainous homeland and had raced into Kyoto. There, decisions of state were being made by the crafty ex-Emperor Go-Shirakawa whose method of enhancing the Court's position was to play the Taira against the Minamoto, or one Minamoto against another. Until Yoshinaka's sudden appearance in Kyoto, the ex-Emperor had favored the Taira and had given them the mandate to pursue and chastise the Minamoto who were regarded as rebels. Now that a Minamoto and his thirty thousand troops were in the capital and the Taira leadership had fled the city, taking with them the boy-Emperor Antoku and his Taira mother, the ex-Emperor conferred on Yoshinaka the commission of shogun and gave him a mandate to pursue and punish the Taira. Go-Shirakawa had also hoped in this way to rid the city of Yoshinaka and his unruly troops.

But Yoshinaka's real aim was to dispute the leadership of the Minamoto clan. To achieve this, he would have to hold and defend Kyoto against a possible attack from Yoritomo, the nominal head of the Minamoto clan. To this end, Yoshinaka succeeded in obtaining a second mandate from the ex-Emperor which named Yoritomo a rebel and authorized Yoshinaka to proceed against him.

Thus the stage was set for Yoshitsune's first important military assignment. On orders from Yoritomo, Yoshitsune and another brother Noriyori were given joint command of an army in order to try and dislodge Yoshinaka from Kyoto. In this regard it is interesting to note that Yoritomo seems to have had reservations about his youngest brother from the very beginning, deciding not to give him full and exclusive command of the troops. Despite this restriction, Yoshitsune managed to carry out the assignment almost single-handedly. Employing daring and swift maneuvers, he penetrated Kyoto's defenses and forced his cousin to flee toward Lake Biwa where further escape was cut off by Noriyori's army. At Awazu, Yoshinaka met his death, only two weeks after he had become shogun and with only one faithful follower at his side.

Yoshitsune's second assignment was carried out in an even more spectacular manner than the first, and it came only seventeen days after his troops had entered Kyoto. This was the attack on Ichinotani, a Taira stronghold in Settsu Province not very far from Kyoto. In this attack Yoshitsune led seventy of his troops down a precipitous mountain path thought to be impossible of descent and completely surprised and routed the enemy.

At this point, one would suppose that the victorious Genji would press their advantage and pursue the disorganized Heike. But, instead, Yoritomo restrained his armies, bringing the Minamoto offensive in western Japan, which had only begun, to a virtual standstill. It was six months after Ichinotani before another Genji army was to leave Kamakura for the west, and an entire year before another major Minamoto victory was to be achieved. There were two reasons for Yoritomo's cautious strategy. One was the nature of the geography of western Japan which is dominated by the waters of the Inland Sea. To fight effectively in such a region would require boats, in addition to horses, and men experienced in naval warfare, neither of which the land-based Genji from eastern Japan possessed. The Heike, on the other hand, were at home on the sea, in particular on the waters of the Inland Sea where they had risen to power and fame. Thus at Ichinotani the Genji were superior so long as the battle was a contest on land, but as soon as the battle changed to a naval contest – the Heike having taken to their boats to flee to Yashima on Shikoku island – the Genji, without boats and experienced seamen, were virtually immobilized. It was just such knowledge which prompted the astute Yoritomo to stop the Minamoto offensive for the time being in order to prepare to fight a very different kind of campaign.

The second reason for mometarily slowing down the western campaign was the appearance for the first time of a rift between Yoshitsune and his fellow commanders on the one hand, and between Yoshitsune and Yoritomo on the other. The most serious disagreement was between Yoshitsune and Kajiwara Kagetoki, a fellow officer, over the question of strategy and tactics to be used in the forthcoming naval campaign to Shikoku. Yoshitsune's unwillingness to compromise and his threats to "do it alone" if his colleagues refused to yield compelled Yoritomo, in the interest of maintaining unity and harmony among Genji commanders, to remove Yoshitsune from the field and to order him back to Kyoto. At the same time, and to further aggravate the deteriorating relationship between the brothers, Yoritomo named Noriyori as commander of the Genji forces in the west.

But the event which most seriously damaged the relationship between the brothers was the conferment by the imperial Court of two offices on Yoshitsune without the prior knowledge and approval of Yoritomo. One was the rank of Junior Lieutenant of the Outer Palace Guards and the other, the vice presidency of the Imperial Police.

The furor caused in Kamakura by this incident must be seen against the feudal background of the times. For Yoritomo to retain his position as lord over his vassals, he could not afford to have the latter accepting offices and honors without his knowledge or approval. It was also the vassal's obligation to his lord to seek his master's approval before accepting any honors. Thus, Yoshitsune, in accepting honors from the imperial Court without the approval of his lord, had violated a cardinal rule of vassalage. Moreover, Yoshitsune was not an ordinary vassal – he was a vassal of the blood, one of four living sons of the former chieftain of the Minamoto who could claim the leadership of the clan. Thus, Yoritomo was understandably concerned when Yoshitsune accepted the honors without the courtesy of consulting him.

On the other hand, it must be said for Yoshitsune that he was convinced that his brother was deliberately slighting him. Yoshitsune had carried out every one of his assignments from his brother with distinction. Yet Yoritomo had not recommended him for a Court appointment. Noriyori, an older brother with whom he had shared joint command of the Genji armies earlier, had been recommended for and had subsequently received a governorship. So had half a dozen other vassals of non-Minamoto lineage, none of whom seemed on the record to be as deserving as Yoshitsune.

The alienation of the brothers might have continued indefinitely, and Yoshitsune might never have become the great hero he turned out to be, were it not for the almost complete lack of progress of the western campaign under Noriyori. He had left Kamakura in the eighth month of 1184 with instructions to get to Kyushu, but after reaching the western tip of Honshu in the tenth month, he could not cross the narrow channel. Other problems plagued the Genji armies to such an extent that Yoritomo decided, in sheer desperation, to restore Yoshitsune into his good graces – at least in outward appearance – and to reassign him to the western front.

Exactly when this decision was made is not clear, but Yoshitsune appeared at the port of embarkation in Settsu in the middle of the second month of 1185, armed with the proper authorization from the imperial Court which had been issued at Yoritomo's request. From that point on, the Genpei war moved swiftly to a conclusion. Two days after his embarkation, notwithstanding a storm and further disagreements with his fellow commanders, Yoshitsune succeeded in destroying the Taira headquarters at Yashima and in forcing the enemy, including the Emperor Antoku and his entourage, to flee by boat toward the west.

The first confrontation, another naval encounter, was to come at Dan no Ura at the far western end of the Inland Sea. The date was the twenty-fourth day of the third month of 1185, less than five weeks after Yashima. By early afternoon of the same day the Genji had achieved a spectacular victory, and once again it was Yoshitsune who emerged the hero. While Yoshitsune's role in the victory was considerable, so was Yoritomo's in masterminding the war from behind the lines. It was Yoritomo who had persuaded many former Taira adherents in western Japan to join the Minamoto and to contribute boats and provisions to the cause. Thus, it was that Yoshitsune had at his command a total of 840 boats, which was 300 more than the Heike could assemble for Dan no Ura. Yoshitsune's failure to appreciate the contributions made by his brother and his fellow vassals toward his victories at Yashima and Dan no Ura was a major factor in the worsening relations between the brothers.

And thus the victory over the Taira widened rather than narrowed the rift between the brothers. The victory seemed to make Yoshitsune even more headstrong and arrogant than ever, causing sub-commanders like Kagetoki to plead with Yoritomo to relieve them of their duty to work under Yoshitsune. The imperial Court further aggravated the relationship by sending a congratulatory message to Yoshitsune first and then to Yoritomo.

The second phase comes to an abrupt but not a wholly unexpected ending at Koshigoe on the outskirts of Kamakura where Yoshitsune had come with a number of prisoners of war to turn over to Yoritomo. But Yoritomo refused to see him. Moreover, Yoritomo refused to permit Yoshitsune to enter Kamakura. Yoshitsune waited at Koshigoe for nearly ten days, hoping that his brother would change his mind. When this appeared unlikely Yoshitsune wrote a letter, the now classic "Letter from Koshigoe," pleading his case. It is clear from the letter that Yoshitsune was not the least remorseful nor apologetic, declaring among other things that he had expected to be honored for his "prodigious deeds," and that his acceptance of offices and titles from the imperial Court was an honor to the house of Minamoto. Despite his eloquence there was no reply from his brother. Instead Yoshitsune was dropped from the ranks of the Genji when he was dispossessed of twenty-four estates which had been given to him earlier, and any hopes of a reconciliation disappeared.

The story enters its third and final phase with Yoshitsune becoming a fugitive and Yoritomo the relentless hunter. Although Yoshitsune succeeded in eluding capture and in reaching the friendly confines of northern Japan, whose powerful lord – Fujiwara no Hidehira – had once before given him asylum, the odds were overwhelmingly against him. Moreover, in 1187 Hidehira passed away, leaving Yoshitsune in extreme doubt as to his immediate future.

The end came in the spring of 1189 when Yasuhira, Hidehira's successor and ostensibly Yoshitsune's friend and protector, succumbed to pressures applied by Yoritomo and the imperial Court and sent a force of several hundred warriors against Yoshitsune. Unable to cope with the situation, Yoshitsune took his own life, after killing his wife and infant daughter. And thus, in this tragic manner, the Yoritomo-Yoshitsune story comes to an end.

But the hero worshipper, refusing to see his hero die as a quarry in such ignominious circumstances, has added a fourth phase. This is the legend which says that Yoshitsune escaped to the continent and emerged as the great Genghis Khan, consolidating the tribes of Mongolia and leading his mighty armies deep into Inner Asia and into Eastern Europe. Although this legend does not make the hero immortal, it does have him die a hero's death in some far-away, unknown battlefield.

Woman of Power Behind the Kamakura Bakufu

Hôjô Masako

by

KENNETH D. BUTLER

Hôjô Masako (1157-1225), wife of the first Kamakura Shogun Minamoto no Yoritomo, mother of the second and third Shoguns, and daughter of Hôjô Tokimasa, the first Hôjô Regent, was one of the most powerful and influential women the male-dominated society of pre-modern Japan ever produced. Depending on one's viewpoint, she is also either one of the most tragic or one of the most Machiavellian figures in Japanese history.

After the triumph of Yoritomo in establishing the military government in Kamakura and bringing the warrior groups of Japan under his sway, Masako's personal life centered on the Minamoto clan began to disintegrate around her. First there was a cooling of her relations with Yoritomo as a result of his excessive attentions to his mistress which began even before the final Genpei battles of 1185. Then in 1197 Masako's eldest daughter Ôhime died at the age of twenty, having lapsed into a melancholic illness after her husband was killed by her father Yoritomo. Next Yoritomo himself died under suspicious circumstances at the age of fifty-three in 1199. His death was followed six months later by the death at seventeen of Masako's second daughter. Yoritomo was succeeded as shogun by his eldest son Yoriie, aged eighteen, who was killed five years later in 1204 at the instigation of Masako's father Tokimasa. Masako's second son Sanetomo became shogun in 1203, at the age of twelve, and this gave rise to the institution of regent for the young shogun, a position which was first filled by Tokimasa. Sanetomo lasted somewhat longer than Yoriie, but in 1219 at the age of twenty-seven he also was killed, purportedly by the son of Yoriie, who in turn was killed by Masako's younger brother, the second Regent Hôjô Yoshitoki.

With the death of Sanetomo, Yoritomo's line came to an end, and the position of shogun was filled by an infant of the Kujô Fujiwara family sent to Kamakura at Masako's request. The position of regent was filled by Hôjô Yasutoki, son of Yoshitoki and nephew of Masako, who was assisted by Hôjô Tokifusa, Masako's younger brother. At this point the Kamakura government came under the complete dominance of the Hôjô, and members of this family continued to rule Japan in the name of the extinct Minamoto until their decline more than a century later.

Viewed in the tragic sense, Masako's life after Yoritomo achieved prominence was a continuous series of personal calamities in which she witnessed the successive deaths of her husband and children and the final extinction of the Minamoto line. The majority of the entries concerning Masako in the *Azuma kagami,* the semi-official chronicle of the Kamakura government compiled in the late thirteenth century, picture her as alternately praying for the continued health and prosperity of her husband and children at shrines and temples in both Kamakura and Kyoto, overcome with inconsolable grief at the death of members of her family, or plotting and scheming in various attempts to assure the safety and succession to the position of shogun of her sons who still remained.

The *Shôkyûki,* a minor military chronicle of the period, relates that at the death of Ôhime in 1197 Masako was so overcome with grief that she was determined to follow Ôhime in death, and was only dissuaded at the last moment by Yoritomo. Similarly, after Yoritomo's death in 1199, she is pictured as determined to kill herself and follow him in death, but reconsiders only after thinking of her responsibilities to her remaining children.

Masako was evidently disappointed by her eldest son Yoriie who after becoming Shogun gave himself over, according to the *Azuma kagami,* to excessive indulgences, among them an almost insatiable addiction to kick-ball, a favorite pastime of the period. When Yoriie suddenly became ill, Masako is reported to have easily acquiesced to replacing him with her second son Sanetomo. This was not accomplished without some effort, however, since Hiki Yoshikazu, father of Yoriie's wife felt that the office of shogun should go to Yoriie's infant son Ichiman. The *Azuma kagami* records that Masako overheard her son Yoriie and his father-in-law plotting to kill Sanetomo and informed Tokimasa, who had Hiki and Yoriie's infant son Ichiman killed.

Here the plot begins to thicken, since after contriving the death of her grandson Ichiman, we find Masako pitted against her own father Tokimasa in a struggle over replacing Sanetomo with a collateral member of the Minamoto, who was the husband of Tokimasa's daughter by his second

Hôjô Masako; An'yôin Temple
(Kamakura, Kanagawa Prefecture)

wife Makiko. The accounts of this affair have a suspicious ring to them, since one would not expect Tokimasa to put aside the fortunes of the Hôjô family as regents to the young Sanetomo in favor of an outsider of mature age and sufficient pedigree to claim legitimacy in the Minamoto succession. But Tokimasa's second wife Makiko is reported to have been almost as strong of will as Masako herself, and to have held decisive influence over Tokimasa at this time. At any rate, the upshot of the attempt to do away with Sanetomo was that Masako immediately called upon her brother Yoshitoki to oppose their father and Tokimasa was subsequently forced to retire to Izu and no longer took a direct part in the affairs of Kamakura.

The final development in this long list of consanguineous slaughter was the defeat of Sanetomo in 1219. Yoriie's second son Kugyô (by a different mother than Ichiman) who was under the care of his grandmother Masako, was made the adopted son of Sanetomo in 1206. But then in 1213 he was forced to take Buddhist vows by Masako, and was sent to Kyoto in the care of a priest at the Onjôji. With the death of the head of the Tsurugaoka Shrine in Kamakura in 1217, Kugyô was brought back to Kamakura at the age of seventeen to become head of this shrine, again at the instigation of Masako. There are no reliable historical sources which give the details of what Masako's intentions were in returning Kugyô to Kamakura. But the records do relate that in 1219 when Sanetomo was paying a ceremonial visit to the Tsurugaoka Shrine, he was attacked and killed by Kugyô. Kugyô was then immediately tracked down and killed by Masako's brother, the Hôjô Regent Yoshitoki. The third son of Yoriie, Senjumaru, had previously committed suicide in Kyoto at the age of fourteen when a plot against the Hôjô in which he had been involved was discovered. So with the death first of Sanetomo, who had no children, and of Kugyô, the remaining son of Yoriie, all children resulting from the marriage of Masako and Yoritomo were dead.

If we assume that Masako's objectives were first, last, and always to assure the continuation of the Minamoto line, then we would have to acknowledge that as of 1219 all was a total failure, that her lifetime of political machinations in the cause of her husband and sons had come to nil, and that she indeed was a most tragic figure.

But following the death of Sanetomo, Masako wasted little time in bemoaning her fate. Rather she set about immediately putting the finishing touches to the organizational machinery of the Kamakura government which would assure the continued dominance of her own family, the Hôjô, for more than a century to come.

In the previous year, 1218, Masako, at age sixty-two, had gone to Kyoto, ostensibly to pray for the good health of Sanetomo, but actually to make arrangements for an imperial prince to be selected as the successor to Sanetomo as shogun. Masako previously had chosen Sanetomo's wife in Kyoto, with the aid of Kyô no Tsubone (Fujiwara no Kaneko), the wet nurse of Emperor Go-Toba who had risen to a position of such dominance over Go-Toba that she controlled all appointments to Court office. Since Sanetomo's marriage had produced no children, this gave Masako the pretext to suggest to Kyô no Tsubone that a child of Go-Toba be sent to succeed Sanetomo, and Kyô no Tsubone agreed to send Prince Yorihito, a son of Go-Toba whom she personally had raised. Jien, the author of the *Gukanshô,* makes reference in his work to the meetings in Kyoto between Masako and Kyô no Tsubone and implies that the women now controlled all of Japan. Other sources refer to Masako and Kyô no Tsubone as "the two women politicians of east and west," and there is little doubt that in the year 1218 they were two of the most powerful figures in Japan. Masako obviously hoped that if an imperial prince were sent to Kamakura as shogun, this would give the Hôjô, as regents, added influence over the Court. It is interesting that she was pursuing this plan during the year before Sanetomo was killed, when, at the age of only twenty-six, he supposedly had expectations of continuing as shogun for many years to come.

At the time Sanetomo was killed in 1219, the promised imperial prince had not yet been sent to Kamakura. But immediately after Sanetomo's funeral Masako dispatched Nikaidô Yukimitsu to Go-Toba with a formal written request that either Prince Yorihito or another son of Go-Toba be

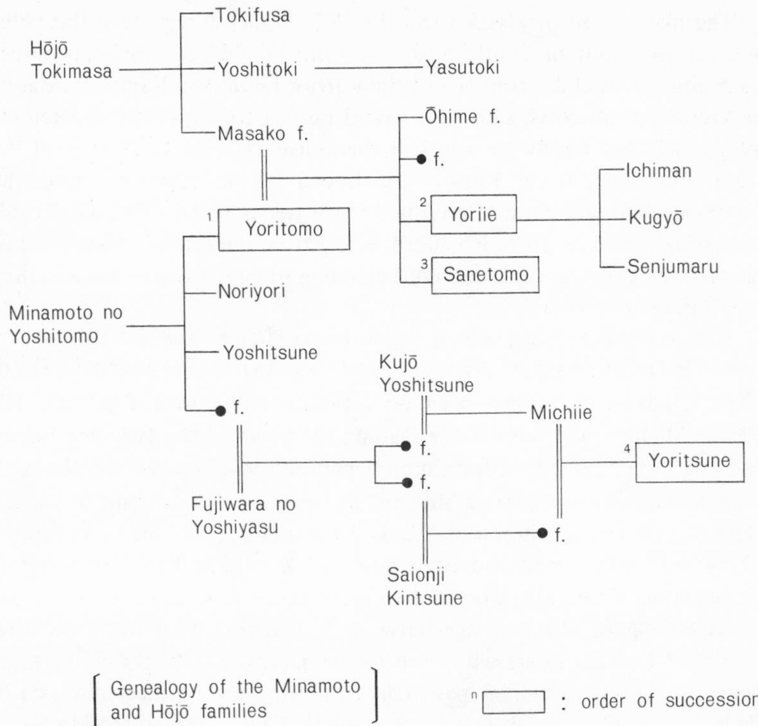

sent to Kamakura immediately to be invested as shogun. Go-Toba, who no doubt already was having thoughts of attacking Kamakura, gave an evasive reply, saying that the time was not yet ripe for such an action. Then the following month Go-Toba sent a messenger to Kamakura demanding the abolition of land stewards appointed to two manors which he had given to his mistress Iga no Tsubone.

Masako, who now was single-handedly directing the Kamakura government, refused even to consider Go-Toba's demand, since the appointment of land stewards was central to Kamakura's system of control of the warriors. Dismissals without cause would undermine the very basis of feudal rule. After consulting with her advisers, Masako dispatched her brother Tokifusa to Kyoto with a thousand troops to notify Go-Toba that his demand would not be met, and to reiterate her request for one of his sons to be made shogun. Go-Toba, in his turn, still procrastinated, and after some discussion back and forth, it was agreed that instead of an imperial prince, a two-year-old son of Fujiwara no Michiie, grandson of Kujô Kanezane, would be sent to Kamakura.

The major need of Masako and the Hôjô family as regents at this point was for an infant or youthful shogun who would be completely under their control. A child from one of the warrior families in Kamakura was to be avoided at all costs, since this would immediately give rise to attempts by the selected family to establish themselves as regents in place of the Hôjô. Therefore, while Masako had hoped for an imperial prince, the Fujiwara child was perhaps even better for her purposes. With Go-Toba's increasingly defiant attitude towards Kamakura, the idea of making one of his sons shogun was undoubtedly beginning to appeal less to Masako than it had the year before.

Yoritsune, the infant son of Fujiwara no Michiie was also very appropriate in another sense. As mentioned, he was the great-grandchild of Kujô Kanezane, who had been on intimate terms with Yoritomo. His father, Michiie, was one of the leading members of the Fujiwara family and could be counted on for close cooperation with Masako and the Hôjô regents once his son became shogun. But even more important to Masako were lineage relationships which linked the infant Yoritsune to Yoritomo. Yoritomo's sister, who had been raised in Kyoto, had married a certain Fujiwara no Yoshiyasu, who rose to prominence in Kyoto after Yoritomo became shogun. The marriage between Yoshiyasu and Yoritomo's sister produced two daughters who, true to the accepted practices of the time, were used as matrimonial pawns in furthering the political interests of their father. One daughter was married to Kujô Kanezane's eldest son, Yoshitsune, at Yoritomo's urgings, and became the mother of Michiie. Therefore, Michiie's son Yoritsune, the infant candidate for shogun, was the great-grandson of Yoritomo's sister. But not only was the link to Yoritomo valid through Yoritsune's paternal lineage, his mother, Michiie's wife, was the daughter of Saionji Kintsune, who had married the other daughter of Yoshiyasu and Yoritomo's sister. Michiie's wife was therefore his own first cousin, and thus on the maternal side as well there was a direct link going back to the fateful union between Yoshiyasu and Yoritomo's sister. It is almost as though Yoritsune had been expressly created with just the right degree of qualifications in anticipation of the extinction of Yoritomo's direct line. His claims to a family connection with the Minamoto were just strong enough to make him plausible to the Kamakura warrior families as a successor to Sanetomo. But being based as they were on maternal links through families of the Kyoto nobility, Yoritsune's claims were not of a type which would pose a military threat to the Hôjô, as they would have if he had been the product of a marriage with one of the Kamakura warrior families. And not only was there no military threat involved, Yoritsune's position as son of Michiie and grandson of Saionji Kintsune promised to provide Masako and the Hôjô regents with direct ties to two of the most powerful families in Kyoto, who would be useful in assuring that the wishes of the Hôjô would be faithfully followed by the imperial Court.

Yoritsune arrived in Kamakura as the Shogun-designate in the seventh month of 1219 and was duly placed under the care of Masako. For the next two years Masako, along with her brother the Regent Yoshitoki, continued to take an active part in directing the Kamakura government. Then on the nineteenth day of the fifth month of 1221 word arrived in Kamakura from Yoritsune's grandfather, Saionji Kintsune, that Go-Toba had declared the Hôjô outlaws against the throne and had ordered all warriors of Japan to attack and destroy them. Masako immediately assembled all of the Hôjô retainers in Kamakura and in a passionate speech urged a direct attack on Kyoto. She exhorted the assembled warriors to act together as one in avenging the slander cast on the Minamoto name by Go-Toba's edict branding the Hôjô as outlaws. And, according to some accounts of her famous speech, she stated that if any of the warriors had thoughts of joining the imperial forces, they should kill her first, since her existence would have come to naught.

Her exhortations had the desired effect and it was decided that Yoshitoki's son Yasutoki would immediately lead the Kamakura forces in an attack on Kyoto. Yasutoki's army met little real resistance, and in less than a month the attempt by Go-Toba to reassert imperial authority was crushed. Go-Toba was banished from Kyoto and the manors of his supporters were confiscated to be distributed as rewards to the meritorious warriors of Kamakura. The records indicate that Masako directly supervised the division of over three thousand confiscated manors, personally deciding the appointments of land stewards and constables through which the rights to the lands were conveyed.

With the defeat of Go-Toba the Hôjô family led by Masako reached their zenith. Yoshitoki, regent since 1205, died in 1224 at the age of sixty-two. But Masako immediately appointed his son Yasutoki as Regent for the young Shogun Yoritsune, and designated her remaining brother Tokifusa as his assistant. The sons of these two were sent to Kyoto to act as Kamakura's representatives in the capital, and with this the structure of the Hôjô regency which Masako had labored for throughout her life was finally perfected.

One last threat to Masako's grand design appeared when Yoshitoki's wife attempted to enlist the aid of the powerful Miura family in establishing her father's family, the Iga, as regents in place of the Hôjô. But Masako, true to her indomitable spirit, personally confronted Miura

Yoshimura and challenged him to state his intentions. Such was the imposing presence of Masako that Yoshimura immediately declared his renewed support of the Hôjô, and the conspiracy collapsed. Following this, in one of her last major acts before her death, Masako personally ordered the banishment from Kamakura of the warriors who had taken part in the Iga conspiracy. This effectively removed all opposition to the Hôjô regents in Kamakura, and with Kyoto also firmly under their dominance, Masako was free to die at the age of sixty-nine in 1225, secure in the knowledge that the Hôjô family was now firmly established.

After Masako's death, the Hôjô continued to follow the policies and procedures she had taken such pains to establish. When the Shogun Yoritsune reached an age in 1244 where he might be thought capable of asserting his independent will, he was sent back to Kyoto and replaced as shogun by his young son Yoritsugu. Then in 1252 Yoritsugu was in turn dismissed, to be replaced this time by an imperial prince. From this point on the pattern was continued, and representatives of the Hôjô continued to provide firm, but on the whole just, rule of Japan until well into the fourteenth century, when accumulated problems resulting from the Mongol invasions and a general decline in the caliber of the Hôjô rulers created conditions which allowed their dominance finally to be successfully challenged.

Any attempt to evaluate Masako's motives and objectives throughout the forty-five years from the time Yoritomo first raised the Minamoto battle flag in the name of the warriors of the east in 1180 to her death in 1225 is greatly inhibited by the fact that the major source for the period, the *Azuma kagami,* is unreliable as an objective historical account. It was not compiled until late in the thirteenth century, at least one hundred years after the events of 1180 it purports to relate in its opening pages. Also, since it was compiled under the direction of the Hôjô as a semi-official history of the Hôjô regency, care is taken not to include any materials derogatory to the Hôjô. As indicated earlier, Masako is portrayed as the model Confucian wife, striving always to further the interests of her husband and sons, and overwhelmed by grief at their successive deaths. But when we consider the actual events of the period as they unfolded, this picture of Masako as the faithful wife and mother begins to become somewhat clouded.

The actions of Masako, as distinguished from the sentiments attributed to her, show that from beginning to end she was always at pains to assure that no matter what happened to the Minamoto, her own family the Hôjô would emerge supreme. One would hesitate to go so far as to suggest that right from the first Masako, together with her father Tokimasa, set out with ruthless determination to utilize Yoritomo's position as legitimate heir to the illustrious Minamoto name to establish the doninance of the Hôjô, regardless of the costs in terms of destruction of members of the Minamoto clan or even the deaths of the children she herself had mothered. Still, in effect this is exactly what occured.

Viewed in terms of the mores of the times, it is not at all unusual that Masako would give primacy to the fortunes of the Hôjô. The records of the period are filled with plots and intrigues attributable to the practice of families seeking matrimonial alliances for their daughters which would advance the interest of the maternal group. In most cases, the primary loyalties of a daughter remained to her own parents, even after being given in marriage to another family.

Before Masako married Yoritomo, who had been banished to the care of Hôjô Tokimasa in Izu after the defeat of his father by the Heike in 1159, she had been betrothed by Tokimasa to a local Heike official in Izu, Yamagi Kanetaka. The *Genpei seisuiki,* a variant of the *Heike monogatari,* relates that Masako had previously fallen in love with Yoritomo, and after being sent to be the wife of Kanetaka she fled his house in central Izu and took refuge with Yoritomo near the present Atami. It is difficult to believe that in an age in which matrimonial alliances were the major means of establishing relationships among warriors, Tokimasa would allow his valuable daughter to go against his wishes. Viewed with an awareness of subsequent events, it seems likely that although originally having betrothed Masako to a representative of the Heike, Tokimasa came to feel that the Minamoto name would be of more value to him than that of the Heike in expanding his influence in Izu, and hopefully the entire eastern warrior region. At any rate, the relationship between Masako and Yoritomo was allowed to develop, and the opening section of the *Azuma kagami,* in describing Yoritomo's receipt of Prince Mochihito's rescript calling upon the Minamoto of the east to rise up against the Heike in 1180, takes care to establish that Hôjô Tokimasa was second only to Yoritomo as the outstanding warrior in the east. After receiving this rescript Yoritomo's first act was to send Tokimasa with a force to attack the unfortunate Yamagi Kanetaka and dispatch his head forthwith, under the banner of the overthrow of the Heike. This seems to have been one of those rare cases in which public duty and personal interest happily coincided.

The legitimacy of the claim of the Hôjô to direct the Kamakura government in the name of the Minamoto rested solely on Masako's position as Yoritomo's wife. In the *Azuma kagami,* therefore, Yoritomo is not presented in terms which would detract from the luster of the

Minamoto name itself, but his own personal actions are related in such a way that doubt is cast on his character to a sufficient degree that his sudden death does not call forth our sympathies to any great extent. A preponderance of the entries in the *Azuma kagami* concerning Yoritomo portray him as fulfilling ceremonial and symbolic functions befitting his position as leader of the Minamoto and founder of the Kamakura government. Care is also taken to show that the system of warrior ties and feudal relationships which formed the basis of the Kamakura government was created directly by Yoritomo as the chief of all the warrior clans.

But at the same time other entries are included which depict the character of Yoritomo in a rather unfavorable light. He is shown to have been somewhat cowardly in his relations with his mistress, always fearful of the wrath of his strong-willed wife should she discover his indescretions. Effort is also devoted to establishing that the deaths of Yoritomo's brothers, Yoshitsune and Noriyori, and his uncle Yukiie, as well as assorted other warriors of the period who conceivably might have had some claim to succession to the Minamoto name, were due solely to the suspicious and vindictive nature of Yoritomo himself.

Yoriie, Yoritomo's eldest son and his successor as Shogun, is depicted in the *Azuma kagami* in Chinese historical fashion as a despotic ruler who lost the mandate of heaven through his wanton indulgences and lack of concern for his subjects. Specific care is taken to contrast him with Masako's nephew Hôjô Yasutoki, the later Regent, who goes to Izu to relieve the suffering of the people at a time of poor harvests while Yoriie remains in Kamakura playing kick-ball with his cronies. So while the *Azuma kagami* neglects to mention that Yoriie was killed at the orders of Masako's father Tokimasa (as is made explicit in the *Gukanshô* and other sources) the warriors of the time seem to have accepted his death with little protest, especially since there was another Minamoto in the direct line, Sanetomo, available to take his place.

When it came time for Sanetomo to depart this world, however, the Minamoto vs. Minamoto ploy again appears, with Yoriie's son Kugyô acting as the agent. This then provides the pretext for the Hôjô to wipe out Kugyô in all good conscience, thereby bringing the Minamoto line to an end, while maintaining their own legitimacy to continue to rule under the banner of the Minamoto name.

In viewing Masako's life one is impressed by the single-mindedness of purpose she displayed throughout her forty-five years of daily machinations on behalf of her family. The problem of her true intentions towards Yoritomo and her sons becomes of secondary importance when we realize that of all the major actors in the drama of the founding of the Kamakura system of feudal rule, Masako alone played a leading role in every event crucial to its establishment. Yoritomo, Tokimasa, and a host of other characters all fell by the wayside at various points, but Masako always remained. If there is any single person deserving of the title of "founder" of the Kamakura government it is Masako. Although she never personally led the warriors in battle and always operated from a position of assumed deference to her male colleagues who held the titular power, she was ever ready to provide the spirit of direction and relentless dedication to objectives which made the Kamakura feudal system a success. She fully deserves to be remembered as the "Nun Shogun" of Kamakura, the name by which she was known in the later years of her life.

Innovators of Kamakura Buddhism

Shinran and Nichiren

by

PIER DEL CAMPANA

The Kamakura period (1185-1333) was an age in which a society formerly under the control of the aristocracy was transformed by the rising warrior classes. It was also an age in which a new form of Buddhism – now known as Kamakura Buddhism – emerged, which was to penetrate even to the lower levels of society. The aristocracy had put their faith in a form of Buddhism with strong magical elements. But the patriarchs of the new Buddhism – Hônen, Shinran, Nichiren, Dôgen – all of whom emerged from the degenerate sects of the Buddhism of the nobility, criticized the older sects and strove, often under considerable pressure and repression, to establish their own systems of thought. In this short essay I cannot discuss all of these developments. What follows is but a sketch of the life and thought of the two patriarchs whose influence remains strong in present-day Japan – Shinran and Nichiren.

SHINRAN

The scarcity of documentary evidence precludes any detailed reconstruction of Shinran's life. He was born in 1173. We know that he came from a secondary branch of the Fujiwara family, and that his father, Hino Arinori, was in the service of the Empress Dowager.

When the boy reached the age of nine (1181) he entered Buddhist orders. The *Shinran denne* (*The Illustrated Life of Shinran*) written by Kakunyo (1270-1351), Shinran's great-grandchild and the third Abbot of the Honganji, states that the boy was entrusted to the care of Jien, the learned monk who was four times appointed to the position of Tendai Abbot. Later on we learn that the young monk resided at Enryakuji, the center of the Tendai sect, where he held the office of *Dôsô*, a monk whose

Shinran; Honganji Temple (Kyoto)

duty was to practice the form of meditation called "*jôgyô-zanmai*." This practice consisted in continuously circumambulating a statue or image of Amida Buddha, ceaselessly repeating the deity's name.

Shinran remained in this office until 1201. By that time he was twenty-nine and it had become clear to him that the teachings of Tendai Buddhism were not sufficient to bring him to enlightenment and salvation. What the concrete reason was for his dissatisfaction is not clear. We only know that at this time Shinran decided to make a hundred-day retreat at the Rokkakudô, a famous Buddhist chapel in Kyoto, hoping to find there a solution to his problems. The prevailing theory is that Shinran was having difficulties with his vow of celibacy. To confirm this opinion we have the tradition that on the ninety-fifth day of his retreat Shinran saw a vision in which the Bodhisattva Kannon appeared to him and presented to him a poem saying: "If a follower of the Buddha, because of past karma, must unite with a woman (thus breaking his vow of celibacy), the Bodhisattva Kannon himself will take the body of a princess and become his wife and please him for his entire life, and at the time of death will lead him to rebirth in paradise." At the end of the vision Shinran was instructed to preach this way of salvation to all men.

After this vision Shinran did not complete his retreat. Having decided not to return to Mount Hiei, he instead visited Hônen (1133-1212) for a hundred days at his hermitage in Yoshimizu, where he preached the doctrine of salvation through faith in Amida and the recitation of the Nenbutsu (the chant "Praise to Amida Buddha"). From that time on Shinran professed to be a disciple of Hônen. In Hônen's doctrine he found the peace he had looked for but had not found at Mount Hiei. From his later writings we also gather that during this time he studied thoroughly the scriptures and commentaries of the Pure Land tradition.

This peaceful period of study and recitation of the Nenbutsu lasted only six years. In the second month of 1207 the Court in Kyoto issued an edict banning the Pure Land sect. Hônen, the founder and head of the sect, was exiled and with him were exiled many of his disciples including Shinran. Before leaving for exile he was officially defrocked by the authorities and was given the lay name of Fujii Yoshizane.

It is not certain when Shinran married. Some scholars have advanced the theory that he was married very early after his conversion to the Amidist faith, and have even suggested that he had more than one wife. What we can gather from the documents is that he was married to a woman by the name of Eshin-ni, the daughter of a provincial official who probably had property in the province of Echigo (present Niigata Prefecture). Some scholars are of the opinion that Shinran met Eshin-ni during his period of exile, since Echigo was the place of his exile.

In 1211 the Court repealed the ban on the Pure Land sect and pardoned Hônen and his disciples. Hônen returned to Kyoto where he died shortly afterwards. The death of his master was perhaps one of the reasons why Shinran did not go back to the capital, but remained instead in eastern Japan. In 1214 we find him established in the province of Hitachi (present Ibaraki Prefecture) where he preached his faith to the farming population of that region with considerable success, judging from the number of his followers listed in the documents.

Probably around the year 1235 Shinran left the Kantô area for Kyoto, and here too we do not know the reasons for his change of residence. Probably his departure was motivated by a ban issued in that same year by the Kamakura government against followers of the Pure Land doctrine. His years in the east were also years of intellectual activity. During this period he wrote his most detailed exposition of his doctrines, the work now known as the *Kyôgyôshinshô*. His personal copy is still extant, and from it we see that he kept adding notes and corrections to the book until almost the end of his life.

Even after his return to Kyoto, Shinran did not loose contact with his followers in the Kantô. He wrote to them answering their questions and sending them doctrinal works. Some of these were copies he himself had made of works written by others, and others were his own works. Most of these writings are in simple language, very different from the scholarly style of the *Kyôgyôshinshô*. They are written in a style adapted to *"inaka no hitobito"* – country folk – as he used to call them affectionately.

We still have about forty letters written to various people, his *Hymns on the Pure Land,* the *Seven Patriarchs of the Jôdo School*, and many other essays and works intended for the instruction and the edification of the followers of the Nenbutsu.

In Kyoto, Shinran lived with his daughter, Kakushin-ni. In his last years he had to endure one of the hardest trials of his life, betrayal by his own son Jishin, who almost succeeded in destroying the community Shinran had left in the Kantô and had helped from afar for more than thirty years.

Until his last days Shinran continued to preach the mercy of Amida and salvation through faith. He died in his ninetieth year, on the twenty-eighth day of the eleventh month of 1262.

Shinran's doctrine may be summarized as follows: Amida vowed that after his enlightenment all his followers would be saved provided they had faith in him and recited his name. The fact that he has attained supreme enlightenment is proof that men can be saved through faith in him. On the other hand, men are so corrupt that they cannot merit salvation and rebirth in the Pure Land through their own efforts. No matter how much a person practices austerities and performs good deeds, he cannot save himself; salvation comes only through faith in Amida.

Moreover, Shinran maintains that even this act of faith cannot be elicited by man, but is Amida's gift. The profession of faith "Praise to Amida Buddha! " is not a meritorious act, but only the result of, and the expression of our gratitude for, the gift of Amida.

This being so, any action man performs, any effort he exerts not only is of no use in obtaining salvation, but can even be an obstacle to the gift of faith and rebirth in the Pure Land. In one of his letters Shinran expresses this concept in the paradoxical statement: "the right way to plan our salvation is precisely not to plan at all." Man must entrust his salvation entirely to Amida's mercy and have faith in him alone.

But the most paradoxical pronouncement by Shinran is that at the beginning of the third chapter of the *Tannishô* (*Essay Lamenting Differences of Views*), a collection of Shinran's sayings compiled by his disciple Yuien: "If even a virtuous person is reborn in the Pure Land, how much more so an evil one." These words can surely be misleading and in fact have often been interpreted in the wrong way both by Shinran's followers and by his opponents. However, they also express in a terse and incisive way the essence of his doctrine.

It is true that his words could be interpreted as a complete denial of the value of morality and even an incitement to a sinful life, since the evil person becomes the object of Amida's mercy. But then one could say the same about Christ's words: "I did not come to call the virtuous but the sinners."

Shinran never said that it was right to do evil knowingly and willingly. To his disciples who misbehaved so as to become more deserving objects of Amida's mercy, he answered with his usual terseness: "Just because we have the medicine, it does not follow that we should drink the poison." What Shinran said was that salvation and rebirth in the Pure Land are above the power of man and that the only way to achieve salvation is, on the one hand to recognize and admit our sinfulness and helplessness, and on the other to expect everything from the Other Power, the merciful power of Amida.

For Shinran, then, an evil person is one who has experienced his own sinfulness and has understood that only Amida can save him, and therefore entrusts himself entirely to Amida. A good person, on the contrary, is one who does not even suspect the depth of his own misery, and is convinced that he can achieve rebirth in the Pure Land through his own efforts. Of course his efforts are doomed to failure, although in the end Amida's mercy will reach him too, and free him from the illusion of his self-sufficiency.

Much has been said and written about Shinran's attitude to the present world and human society. In a letter probably written in 1252 Shinran speaks of the need to detest the world and abandon the ways of the world: "There is a sign to be seen in those who for years have recited the Nenbutsu with the desire to be reborn in the Pure Land. This sign is that they have changed their former ways of thinking, and that they are charitable to their fellow believers. It is the sign that they detest the world." But Shinran never advocated a flight from the world or a monastic life. Quite the contrary: he himself married and fathered children, and thus abolished the traditional distinction between the clergy and the laity. Of himself he said that he was neither a monk nor a layman, but called himself a "*tokunin,*" one whose hair was not as long as that of a layman, but neither closely shaved as that of a monk.

What one did in life and how he made a livelihood did not matter in terms of salvation: "It makes no difference if one lives by casting nets or fishing in the rivers and seas, if one makes a living by hunting beasts or birds in the fields and mountains, or if he spends his life trading or working in the fields." What did matter, however, was faith and gratitude towards Amida, a faith and gratitude that, if truly present in one's heart, would surely appear in his peaceful and charitable behavior.

He had the same detached attitude toward the civil and political authorities. There are those who consider him a sort of revolutionary leader, siding with the oppressed and fighting against those in power. Others see him as an ecclesiastical conservative. Both views make little sense, for they are based more on preconceived ideological positions than on solid documentation.

In some of his writings Shinran uses severe and even angry words towards the authorities who exiled and persecuted Hônen and his disciples in 1207. He was also adamant against asking or even accepting help from the civil authorities in his missionary work, and instructed his disciples to take the same stance in the matter: the gift of Amida could not be obtained through the help of the state. But even in times of persecution he never incited his disciples to revolt: if they could not preach the doctrine in one place they should leave and go elsewhere. A day would come when the mercy of Amida would reach even those who now refused it. In the meantime the missionary should not hate his persecutors but rather recite the Nenbutsu for their conversion. We can say that once his religious independence was assured and his missionary work was no longer hindered, Shinran did not concern himself with the authorities or political events. He was solely concerned with religious values: all else had no relevance to the only thing that mattered, rebirth in Amida's Paradise.

Yet it must also be acknowledged that Shinran's religious principles could have been revolutionary had they been applied to the social and political dimensions of human life. The fact that all men are equally sinful and equally dependent on Amida's mercy for their salvation; the community of faith in Amida in which the mercy of the Buddha is to be manifested in mutual respect and charity; the principle that Amida is the only saviour and that among the believers there should not be any other religious authority: all these ideas are potentially capable of changing the social and political thinking of those who accept them and live by them. One cannot help regretting that they were – on the whole – never fully accepted in Japanese society.

NICHIREN

Of all the patriarchs of Kamakura Buddhism, Nichiren is the only one who did not belong to the nobility. Far from being ashamed of his origins, he styled himself a "*sendara ga ko,*" a child born to a family of the *candâla* caste, the lowest caste in Indian society. In fact he was born in the second month of 1222 in the fishing village of Kominato on the east coast of the province of Awa, present-day Chiba Prefecture.

In 1233 he was brought by his father to a Buddhist monastery on Mount Kiyozumi not far from his birthplace where, in 1237, at the age of fifteen, he entered Buddhist orders. Although the Kiyozumi monastery belonged to the Tendai sect, the doctrine Nichiren learned during his novitiate was not pure Tendai doctrine but one tinged with many esoteric elements. This was not an uncommon thing at that time, as the Tendai sect has always tended to incorporate doctrines and practices from other schools.

This eclectic religious and intellectual attitude, however, did not satisfy Nichiren's desire for clarity. It was not simply intellectual and scholastic clarity he was looking for; perhaps even more, he felt the need for a clear doctrine of salvation for those living in an age of corruption. It was for this reason that in 1238 he asked for and obtained permission to spend some time in Kamakura where he studied Amidism and the doctrine of the Pure Land under the guidance of a renowned master of that school. He remained in Kamakura for more than a year and from his later writings we can see that he acquired a thorough knowledge of the Nenbutsu doctrine. At the same time he convinced himself that Amidism was not the true Buddhism that could save the people of the Latter Days of the Law.

The young monk went back to Kiyozumi, but he did not remain there long. In 1243 he left again, this time to visit all the major Buddhist centers of the country. He first went to Mount Hiei, the cradle of the Tendai sect in Japan. He then moved to Kyoto where he studied the Sôtô and Rinzai branches of Zen, and then went to Nara where he studied the older sects, especially the Ritsu sect which at that time had experienced a considerable revival in Japan. Finally he visited Mount Kôya, the headquarters of Shingon.

Nichiren's scholastic journey lasted ten years. In the early spring of 1253 he was on his way back to Kiyozumi where he arrived in the fourth month. According to tradition he spent seven days in seclusion before he presented himself to the monastic community assembled in the great hall of the temple. Then, in front of the Abbot and all of his fellow monks, he declared solemnly that the only true Buddhism was the doctrine of the *Lotus Sutra,* and that all other forms and schools of Buddhism should be rejected as heretical. His blunt declaration was a tremendous shock to the monks and also to the feudal administrator who was present in the hall when Nichiren spoke.

The result was that Nichiren was expelled from the community and

Nichiren; Honmonji Temple (Tokyo)

actually had to escape during the night to avoid physical harm. He spent the following years in Kamakura where he engaged in missionary activities, practicing his famous "*tsuji seppô,*" preaching on streetcorners of the city.

His preaching method was always the same: an attack against other forms of Buddhism followed by a strong exhortation to embrace the doctrine of the *Lotus Sutra.* In Nichiren's approach there was no room for compromise or accommodation. He attracted many followers with this method, but inevitably made many enemies.

During these years Nichiren reflected more and more deeply on the religious as well as the social and political situation of the country. It was a time of war and upheaval, and even though relative calm had followed the so-called Shôkyû Disturbance of 1221, there still were conflicts among the various factions, and even among the various branches of the Hôjô family, the ruling regents of Kamakura. Moreover, records of the time report a succession of epidemics, floods, earthquakes, and other natural calamities.

Nichiren saw in all these frightful events the fulfilment of the prophesies contained in the sutras: plagues and calamities will certainly afflict the country that rejects the doctrine of the Buddha. It was, then, because Japan had abandoned the true doctrine of the *Lotus Sutra* and had chosen instead to follow the false doctrines of other sects that her people suffered.

In 1260 Nichiren completed a short treatise which he called *Risshô ankoku ron* (*On the Establishment of the True Doctrine and the Security of the Country*) and presented it to the authorities in the summer of that same year. In it he quoted the sutras and their prophesies and showed their fulfilment in events that had occured in Japan. Finally he exhorted the government to return to the true doctrine of the *Lotus* and ban all other sects, especially the Pure Land sect, which according to Nichiren was the one most responsible for the ruin of the country.

The reaction to the *Risshô ankoku ron* was immediate. The hut where Nichiren lived was attacked and burnt down and he himself barely escaped being killed. The following year the authorities arrested him and exiled him to the Izu Peninsula, in the present Shizuoka Prefecture.

He was pardoned in 1263, and as soon as he reached Kamakura he not only resumed his preaching of the *Lotus* but intensified his attacks on the other sects. Listing all the calamities prophesied in the sutras, Nichiren remarked that only two of them had not yet been fulfilled: invasion from a foreign country and internal strife. He stated that these would also afflict Japan if the government continued to disregard his warnings. In 1268 envoys from the Mongol dynasty in China arrived in Japan and brought a message demanding that Japan become a tributary country to that dynasty.

On hearing the news of the arrival of the envoys Nichiren made several copies of the *Risshô ankoku ron* and sent them again to the government and to the heads of the major temples in Kamakura. He pointed out that his prophesies had come true and that therefore his request should be granted to make the doctrine of the *Lotus* the only religion of Japan.

This time the government tried to ignore Nichiren and his petition, but he was not easy to ignore, especially since he was constantly challenging the other Buddhist leaders to public debates. Finally he so irked the authorities that he was arrested and sentenced to exile on the Island of Sado. His guard and escort, one of his fiercest opponents, was authorized to behead him en route if he deemed this necessary. Miraculously he escaped execution and arrived in Sado in the eleventh month of 1271.

Nichiren remained in exile until the spring of 1274 and during this time he wrote two of his major works: the *Kaimoku shô* (*The Opening of the Eyes*) and the *Kanjin honzon shô* (*On Seeing in One's Own Heart the Supreme Object of Veneration*). In 1274 Nichiren's friends in Kamakura were able to obtain a pardon for their master and he returned to that city in the fifth month. In the meantime the attitude of the government toward Nichiren had grown more conciliatory. The threat of the Mongol invasion had increased and the fact that Nichiren had predicted it made people regard him with fear if not respect. Upon his arrival he was summoned by some senior officials and asked what he thought of the possibility of an actual Mongol invasion. Nichiren answered that it would occur soon, and then passed immediately to his old requests. This time the government had no intention of taking severe measures against him, but neither was it ready to comply with his demands. Indeed it was precisely at this time that the authorities had asked all Shingon temples in the country to offer special prayers and services to avert a Mongol invasion.

On hearing this Nichiren was disgusted and disheartened at what he considered the blindness of the rulers of the country. In his opinion the prayers of Shingon monks could only worsen the situation. He decided that it made no sense to remain in Kamakura, and, accepting the offer of one of his followers, he retired to a hermitage on Mount Minobu, in the present Yamanashi Prefecture. There he spent his last years instructing his disciples, and there he wrote the last of his major works, *Senji shô* (*On Discerning the Times*), and *Hôon shô* (*On Repaying Indebtedness*).

In the autumn of 1282 his health grew so bad that he accepted the invitation of one of his disciples and came to Ikegami (now a part of Tokyo) where he died on the thirteenth of the tenth month.

Nichiren is not admired by Japanese intellectuals. He was intolerant and incapable of compromise, a fault of which he himself was well aware. In a letter written to one of his disciples in 1282, a few months before his death, he says: "Well, I am certainly the most intractable person of all Japan...."

Another common criticism made against him as a thinker is that he changed his doctrinal position over the years, and therefore does not offer a unified doctrinal system, as, for instance, Shinran does.

And then of course he is blamed for something which in all justice is not his fault: that his thought was used by certain nationalists who were active during the imperialist era of Japan.

However, Nichiren's personality and doctrine can be better understood if one analyzes them from an impartial point of view, even though one may still conclude that one dislikes both the man and his thought.

Unlike Shinran and other leaders of Kamakura Buddhism, Nichiren could not afford to be indifferent to the world and events around him. The reason for this is – to my mind – mostly doctrinal, in the sense that the doctrine of Nichiren is above all a philosophy, or rather a theology of history. In this he is unique in Japanese Buddhism. For him religious ideals were inseparable from society and had to be realized in society.

Salvation could not be achieved only at the level of individual meditation, because, first, no individual exists by himself, and secondly, because a living being can only realize itself through action and not by mere spiritual activity. Hence the necessity for Nichiren to deal with social and even political realities.

The civil and political authorities thus could not escape the responsibility of building a society reflecting the ideals of Buddhism. In this Nichiren reversed the idea, traditionally accepted in Japan, that the Buddhist institution was a tool of the government, and that its purpose was to ensure the welfare of the country. For Nichiren precisely the opposite was true: the raison d'être of the government and of social institutions was the building of a society that could be called a Buddha Land. The Pure Land to which Amidists looked forward after death was, for Nichiren, to be achieved in this world.

In such a view there is great danger of intolerance, for when social and political reality must reflect a religious ideal, little room is left for a democratic approach.

From this point of view we can also understand why Nichiren changed his posture in response to changing circumstances. Nichiren's basic idea remained the same, but since it was living idea and not a conceptual one, there was the need for growth and for continuous redefinition of its practical consequences. In other words, Nichiren's basic conceptions had to be redefined in terms of the circumstances under which they were to be realized.

The logic that we find in the thought of Nichiren is not the sort of logic we find in Shinran's religious system, where all concepts are finished and formed once and for all. The logic we must look for in Nichiren is the logic of a living organism which must react and adapt itself to the contingencies of time and space.

In this characteristic of Nichiren's thought and personality we discover what is meant by those who describe him as the most Japanese of Japanese Buddhists.

Brigand or Patriot?

Kusunoki Masashige

by

DONN F. DRAEGER

In the last decades of the Kamakura period (1185-1333) there appeared in Japan a superbly professional *bujin* (classical warrior) whose dynamic lifestyle has indelibly colored Japanese legend and history. This heroic figure is Kusunoki Masashige (1294?-1336), formidable man who in the minds of most Japanese of subsequent ages sets the standard against which all Japanese fighting men are to be judged. Though historical evidence concerning Kusunoki's life is extremely limited and we are aware that much of what is written or said about him is embellished fiction, the authentic information we do have indisputably shows him to be the greatest hero of his time. He emerges as a charismatic leader and a man for whom compromise with the enemy was abhorrent. Kusunoki typifies the modest but necessarily forceful nature of the battle-tested warrior who is whole-heartedly dedicated to and completely secure in his skill at arms. On the other hand, and this is what sets Kusunoki apart from others who may have been equally skilful and dauntless, he was an extremely sensitive man and genuinely compassionate. He could shed a tear for others, as is seen in his deep concern for the welfare of his family and his fighting men. He was likewise a man of great honor and integrity, both toward his sovereign and the Japanese people as a whole.

Kusunoki served as a warrior in an age of violence and exploitation that accompanied the breakdown of the *shôen* (demesne) system. Added to the almost constant turmoil in which there was little rest for either sword or horse was a succession dispute between two opposing imperial lines. The Bakufu (military government), in the meantime, relentlessly sought to retain its *de facto* rule over the country. The recourse to martial force that followed was a natural attempt to settle an intensely complex and vexing situation. That Kusunoki lost his life at an early age in this process was perhaps inevitable; moreover, it was almost kind, for it made him immortal. Kusunoki chose to die by *seppuku* (self immolation), the accepted and expected practice for warriors who found themselves in dire circumstances. That act of bravery made him indestructible, and his inspiring spirit survives today.

From the age of fifteen Kusunoki underwent training as a student-acolyte at a Shingon Buddhist monastery in Yamato Province. At this temple the youngster allegedly displayed an insatiable interest in Chinese tomes on martial strategy and tactics. Still earlier Kusunoki had been given the childhood name of Tamon and was, at that time, consecrated to Bishamonten (Kubera or Vaiśravana), the Buddhist Regent of the North, a deity of wealth and war. Tamon is an alternate name for Bishamonten, who was the patron deity of warriors, and children who were consecrated to this deity were expected to become professional warriors.

We have no evidence that the young Kusunoki engaged in classical *bujutsu* (martial arts) training at this Shingon temple, but it is reasonable to assume that in his mid-teens Kusunoki was initiated into the art of swordsmanship (*kenjutsu*). It was common for teenage lads who aspired to the warrior's profession to seek the guidance of some competent swordsman for training with the *tachi* (a long, curved, single-edged sword) which was, in Kamakura times, the warrior's principal weapon in close combat. Unfortunately, the first known documentation of the various schools of martial arts appears only in the fifteenth century and thus it is not yet possible to describe the precise technical nature of the *bujutsu* that Kusunoki studied. Future research on the origins of these schools may one day clarify this interesting aspect of Japanese institutional history. But it is well established that after he obtained a balanced education – *bun* (civil) and *bu* (martial) – Kusunoki was, in his adult years, a successful middle-ranking estate holder in Kawachi Province. His competence in administrative and martial matters secured his lands and commanded the respect of others.

It would be wrong to interpret the influence of early education upon Kusunoki's behavior as a warrior solely in terms of his training in martial skills. His actions were of course conditioned by martial training, but the nature and direction of these actions were guided by ideology, in particular that of loyalty to imperial authority. Kusunoki maintained steadfastly the traditional Confucian virtues of respect for his forefathers and love for posterity, and had a deep sense of responsibility toward both. Respect for ancestors and love for posterity on a family basis is *kô* (filial piety), while on a national basis it is *chû* (loyalty to the sovereign).

Kusunoki Masashige
(Imperial Palace Outer Gardens, Tokyo)

Loyalty and filial piety are inseparable from each other, and the relationship expressed as *chû kô ippon* (absolute oneness of *chû* and *kô*) was held up as a fundamental principle of national life. Japanese of this period also distinguished between state and government. The state was an irreducible spiritual entity with the sovereign at its center. The government was merely a medium between the sovereign and his subjects, a changeable extention of his divine existence, created by the sovereign in order to fulfill his wishes for his subjects. Whereas the state was sacred, government was not. If government transgressed upon the state, dissatisfaction could be openly displayed and action taken against the government without fear of committing a moral transgression. Thus, in Kusunoki's view, when the Bakufu began acting on its own initiative, ignoring the dictates of the sovereign Go-Daigo, the government was guilty of an immoral act; it was the inescapable duty of loyalists like himself to take corrective action, even to the extent of force of arms, in order to uphold the principle of oneness of loyalty and filial piety (*chû kô ippon*).

Various constructions have been put upon the character of Kusunoki in his early years as a warrior. There is a tendency to paint him an outlaw (*akutô*) who followed in the footsteps of his reputedly rowdyish father. The elder Kusunoki had been dubbed (mischievously perhaps), "Kusunoki, the Lay Priest of Kawachi," and his chief activity is said to have been raiding nearby properties not his own. To what extent this same practice was followed by young Kusunoki is not known, but it is probably fair to accept the accusation that Kusunoki did conduct or partake in raids. There is speculation that he headed a small band of bandit-like followers and that he preferred to operate independently of major families and their causes; but such is as yet only speculation. Some references found in early historical literature, however, are not defamatory. The *Masukagami* (*Pellucid Mirror*) describes Kusunoki as a man "bold and stalwart by nature." Kusunoki's early local reputation may well have derived from his participation in combative raids. But until all the facts are known, it seems extreme to brand Kusunoki a "swashbuckler," "bandit," or an "outrageous samurai." Kusunoki was certainly a confident, daring, and aggressive warrior, for such are the minimal requirements for any successful man at arms. Yet though he was formidable in the foray, Kusunoki was no brash fighter! His comprehension of natural phenomena and the workings of men's minds was acute, and this made him a shrewd and careful strategist and a canny tactician. For Kusunoki the final objective of battle was simply to force the enemy to submit; to gain peace, the use of force was required, and in this Kusunoki proved himself a master.

It was not long after he had attained a local reputation as a formidable fighter that Kusunoki demonstrated to the nation his unfaltering courage, combative tenacity, strategic cunning, and tactical audacity. This opportunity came in connection with the loyalist movement that fought to restore the Emperor Go-Daigo (1287-1339; r. 1318-39) to the throne. Go-Daigo was of the junior imperial line and a legitimate claimant to the throne. Soon after his accession this stubborn man's insistence that the sovereign should not only reign but also rule greatly irked the Hôjô Bakufu. Go-Daigo's ambitions coincided with a time when the Bakufu was in serious economic difficulty and was fast losing the political support of the great military families for reasons of its corrupt and unjust administration. Thus, when a plot to subvert the hegemony of the Bakufu was uncovered in which Go-Daigo appeared to be involved, the crafty Emperor was forced to quit the capital city of Kyoto (1331). He took refuge in a bastion of warrior-monks (*sôhei*) located atop Mount Kasagi a short distance from Nara. It was at this critical juncture that Kusunoki formed an alliance with Go-Daigo that was greatly to aid the return of this Emperor to the throne (1333).

The alliance between Go-Daigo and Kusunoki owes more to Kusunoki's loyalty to the imperial cause than to a similarity of personal motives, for the selfless sincerity with which Kusunoki supported Go-Daigo's cause contrasts sharply with the decidedly selfish interests of Go-Daigo. Go-Daigo needed a catalyst in order to realize his designs for imperial control of the nation. He cleverly chose Kusunoki as that catalyst at a time when the Hôjô administration was in a precarious situation. Go-Daigo, being a man of considerable tenacity and an opportunist *per excellence,* did not miss this splendid chance to overthrow the Hôjô.

At this point in history, then, there arose a conflict between the *de jure* ruler, the Emperor Go-Daigo, and the *de facto* rulers, the Hôjô Bakufu, whose authority theoretically depended upon imperial sanction.

Beyond a doubt Go-Daigo realized that if he could but swing Kusunoki over to his side, there was little chance that a man of Kusunoki's moral mettle would ever betray him. Moreover, Go-Daigo had no standing army of his own save some scattered bands of warrior-monks and a few friends. He had even less in the way of popular support. He could not hope to recruit the martial leadership or the military strength necessary to destroy the Hôjô. Thus, equally important in Go-Daigo's choice of Kusunoki was the fact that he commanded a devoted following of disciplined and competent fighting men. This then was the situation as Go-Daigo must have seen it. With proper timing and the support of an intensely loyal and highly competent military force, he stood a chance of defeating the Hôjô and seizing power for himself. Being a resolute man with a strong sense of self-confidence, he elected to take that chance.

Go-Daigo's precipitant departure from Kyoto (1331) to take refuge among the warrior-monks of Mount Kasagi only temporarily delayed the Bakufu's dogged pursuit. He was soon captured and sent into exile to a remote island in the Oki group (1332). It was at this time that the Emperor's implicit trust in Kusunoki proved to be well grounded. Later in that same year Kusunoki gained tactical advantage over the Bakufu in the rugged Yamato-Kawachi area where, by means of guerrilla raids, he kept constant pressure upon government troops operating there. It is in these and subsequent military actions that Kusunoki demonstrated the high level of moral and martial excellence which mark him a supremely successful warrior. But the full story of his exploits and the final outcome of the succession issue is too long to tell in a short essay; one can only summarize some of the cataclysmic events that led to Kusunoki's death.

The Bakufu, under constant harassment by Kusunoki's men, found Kusunoki here, there, everywhere, but nowhere. He was the elusive leader of well-disciplined fighting men who fought with great *esprit de corps.*

Kusunoki's men operated in small, highly mobile units. Always, after causing havoc in Bakufu ranks, these units managed to disappear as quickly as they had come. It became clear to Bakufu officials that there could be no settlement of the issue of imperial succession until Kusunoki was exterminated. An all-out campaign against Kusunoki, their most respected and troublesome enemy, was ordered. This forced the Bakufu to withdraw substantial numbers of troops from outlying areas. Martially minded loyalists read this mustering of troops as an admission of the Bakufu's inability to cope with Kusunoki, and their opinion had a damaging effect on the already fading image of the Bakufu. It provided positive opportunities for those provincial military families who long, but silently, had hoped to overthrow the corrupt and martially incompetent regime of the Hôjô at Kamakura. Now sufficiently emboldened by Kusunoki's successes, they rose against the Bakufu. Fighting men from many areas of Japan rallied to Go-Daigo's loyalist cause. Kusunoki and his men continued to be a phantom force for the Bakufu military commanders.

Kusunoki was fighting in terrain that he knew well. He depended on ruses and strategems to canalize the Bakufu troops and to lead them in vain pursuit of his phantom forces. He expressed his hope for a less destructive solution to the conflict. He took calculated risks in the form of tactics designed to wear down, tire, and discourage the enemy from further action, rather than those which would produce butchery. "Losses" in Kusunoki's tactical positions have been called "failures" by some historians, but in many cases these may have been well planned and precisely executed submissions based on the wish to avoid needless loss of life, and the need to gain time by means of delaying tactics. In every case the Bakufu's "gain" slowed their combative momentum as they strove to consolidate and occupy the position they had just seized. The case of Akasaka, one of Kusunoki's fortified positions, is a splendid example in which its "loss" (1331) and "recapture" (1332), followed by still another "loss" (1333) to Bakufu forces served well the ends of Kusunoki's overall strategical scheme. Again in a showdown engagement near Kyoto (1333), three thousand Bakufu troops were led into a tactical mistake, a virtual trap. They became involved in a difficult river-crossing operation believing themselves to be in final pursuit of Kusunoki. But Kusunoki proved to be a phantom once again. He quickly outflanked them and then mauled them without mercy. After discovering their plight the Bakufu commanders attempted to break off the costly and futile engagement. This Kusunoki permitted, though they fled in great disorder.

Though the initiative was often in Kusunoki's hands he did not always elect to follow up his advantage; he was content to underscore his psychological edge and hoped that his enemy's discouragement would exceed their martial ardor. Historians who criticize the "failure" of Kusunoki to take up pursuit of the fleeing Bakufu forces after the river-crossing fiasco near Kyoto ignore Kusunoki's martial acumen. He had neither the number of men nor sufficient supplies to sustain effective pursuit and mop-up actions. Furthermore, Kusunoki understood well the tactical rule of the minimal engagement ratio, in which the attacker (in this case Kusunoki's forces) must have a three-to-one advantage in manpower. At Chihaya, when Kusunoki's forces were on the defensive, Kusunoki would demonstrate the maximum limit of the engagement ratio. There, under his superior leadership and on terrain he had chosen and prepared for combat, Kusunoki's men extended that ratio to one-hundred-to-one.

In the early months of 1333 the Bakufu was determined to launch a surprise attack against Kusunoki, who was secure at his fortified position at Chihaya. Chihaya lay in the western foothills of Mount Kongô, some one thousand meters above the Kawachi plains. There the Bakufu found Kusunoki well prepared for their most determined onslaught. Very quickly the Bakufu's drive bogged down as Kusunoki masterfully canalized them at every turn. They advanced, but at a slow rate of speed and through areas that Kusunoki's men had prepared well in advance; delaying actions fought elsewhere had bought precious time. Enfilade and interdiction tactics reduced Bakufu troop strength on the lower slopes leading to Chihaya, thus gaining still more time for the defense of the innermost areas of Kusunoki's fortress. Here, on this perimeter, Kusunoki systematically compassed the total ruin of the Bakufu attackers. Chihaya never fell.

As the Bakufu troops moved slowly upward, perhaps they never fully realized that the ground they were "gaining" was leading them to their final defeat. They came upon increasing difficulties. Log-fall ambuscades crushed unlucky victims under tons of wood. Deep camouflaged pits with sharpened bamboo stakes lining their bottoms impaled the falling bodies of careless troopers. Rock, boiling water, and fusilades that could not be avoided took additional heavy tolls of Bakufu ranks. Bakufu bowmen found themselves unable to deliver vital covering and supporting fire; Kusunoki's men had erected thick unpenetrable brush screens that conveniently deflected or stopped arrows in flight. Nevertheless, the Bakufu men inched their way slowly upward until they reached the walls of Kusunoki's sanctuary. There were seeming breaches in Chihaya's walls, but these soon proved to be keys to horror, humiliation, and hell. On one occasion, as Bakufu troops were in the act of scaling Chihaya's walls, Kusunoki demonstrated his utter contempt for his enemy. Bakufu stalwarts who clung perilously to the walls were suddenly met by a cascade of foul-smelling liquid. Kusunoki, months earlier, had ordered the collection of his men's fecal matter in large wooden vats for the purpose of slopping the fetid mixture down upon any attackers who might attempt to climb Chihaya's walls. The foul and rancid stench of the fecal slurry filled the air, drenched the bodies and armor of the attackers, and denied them secure purchase of foot or hand. The Bakufu men that had been caught in this revolting predicament hastily abandoned their mission, while those who stood by waiting their turn to make the climb had no further stomach for such action.

News of Kusunoki's valiant stand at Chihaya reached the exiled Emperor Go-Daigo through a loyalist agent who travelled to Oki in a fishing boat. Encouraged by this turn of events, the crafty Emperor escaped from his island prison and set up a rival Court in Hôki Province on the main island of Honshu. When Ashikaga Takauji, the general sent by the Bakufu to destroy Go-Daigo's forces, turned against the Bakufu in support of Go-Daigo (1333), the Emperor was once again able to establish himself as the reigning sovereign at Kyoto. Loyalist forces captured Kamakura in that same year.

Go-Daigo's administration proved to be a total failure. His vacillation and interference in departments of government reached ridiculous limits and a great deal of dissatisfaction was generated throughout the country. Thereafter, remaining units of the Hôjô armies managed to recapture Kamakura (1335), but their success was short lived. Ashikaga, moving against Go-Daigo's wishes, drove the Hôjô from Kamakura and secured the area. With such effective power at his command, Ashikaga named himself *Sei-i Tai Shôgun* and disregarded Go-Daigo's order to return to Kyoto. Nitta Yoshisada, the loyalist general sent by Go-Daigo to "chastise" Ashikaga, met with a smarting defeat near Mount Fuji at the hands of the cunning Ashikaga. In retaliation Ashikaga then marched on the city of Kyoto. There were sizeable defections in the loyalist camp, and many fighting men followed Ashikaga's banner. Quite naturally Kusunoki made a desperate, but unsuccessful, attempt to check Ashikaga, who finally gained Kyoto as his prize (1336). Go-Daigo was obliged to flee, this time to Mount Hiei where he took refuge among the Tendai warrior-monks. Within a few days Nitta and Kusunoki rallied the loyalist forces and drove Ashikaga to the west. Before making his decampment, however, Ashikaga managed to obtain a commission from the sovereign of the senior imperial line who had been named Go-Daigo's successor. That paper provided

Ashikaga with a façade of legitimacy inasmuch as he was then under the orders of a former emperor to "chastise" Nitta, and could not be declared a rebel (*chôteki*) against the imperial Court. Ashikaga fled to Kyushu. By spring he had regrouped and expanded his forces and was moving with speed against the loyalists. Events now moved at a rapid pace, leading to the ultimate death of Kusunoki.

The forceful and undisguised approach of Ashikaga's forces caused a fearful Court to order a full-scale stand against Ashikaga at the Minato River estuary where it flows into the Inland Sea. Nitta, in full command, was already encamped there when Kusunoki, in Kyoto, warned the Court that such a stand would lead to disaster. He offered an alternative plan in which Go-Daigo was to flee to Mount Hiei and abandon the capital to Ashikaga. Thereafter, once Ashikaga's lines were overextended, Kusunoki was confident that he could cut and disconnect enemy units by guerilla raids, and deal with them in his own time and in his own inimitable way. The Court, with Go-Daigo's support, refused to accept Kusunoki's advice. Because he believed that it was his duty to support imperial policy despite its deficiencies, and not wishing to offend his sovereign, Kusunoki bid farewell to his family and proceeded to the appointed and fateful battleground.

At the Minato River estuary the loyalists established a defense line from Wada no Misaki to the Ikuta River. It was a hot, humid day on which was fought the seven-hour battle that saw the loyalist cause broken beyond repair. As Kusunoki had predicted, Ashikaga's forces were well prepared and numerically overwhelming. They struck by land and sea routes in a splendidly coordinated attack. Nitta was scheduled to fight the seaborne invaders, while Kusunoki, his back to the dry bed of the Minato River, would engage the land forces. While Nitta was undergoing a terrible mauling from a frontally deployed enemy unit, he also perceived a threat to the rear of his position. Nitta thereupon hastily withdrew from his assigned sector of responsibility. This unscheduled maneuver left Kusunoki's troops fully exposed to a furious flanking attack which led to their eventual encirclement and complete isolation.

Nitta's sudden withdrawal had undermined Kusunoki's tactical position, but not his loyalty. He, too, might have made a desperate attempt at withdrawal, but his honor would not allow retreat without intolerable shame. Instead, he chose to accept his lot in the spirit of *seishi o chôetsu* (transcending thoughts about life or death). Kusunoki, without demur, attempted courageously to defend the gross tactical blunder of his superior Nitta. By evening Kusunoki's forces were all but decimated. He himself had sustained multiple wounds. As his life's blood drained slowly away, in order to avoid the humiliating shame of capture, Kusunoki ordered mass *seppuku* among all survivors. Both Kusunoki and his younger brother Masasue died by their own hands. Therewith, the full meaning of the respectful message of acceptance that Kusunoki allegedly delivered to Emperor Go-Daigo some four years earlier came clear. It foretold correctly the future of the loyalist cause: ".... as long as you hear that Masashige still lives, be confident that your sacred cause will prevail."

Insurgent Warrior to Supreme Hegemon

Ashikaga Takauji and Yoshimitsu

by

KENNETH A. GROSSBERG

The Shogunates of Ashikaga Takauji (1305-58) and Ashikaga Yoshimitsu (1358-1408) marked the beginning and end of an era in Japanese history known as the Nanbokuchô (1336-92), the Age of Northern and Southern Courts. This was a period of civil war which ended with the exclusion of the imperial Court from real power until the nineteenth century, and which resulted in the concomitant rise to national ascendancy of the military houses (*buke*). The period got its name from the rivalry between two lines of the imperial family, the Northern Court in Kyoto which was the instrument of Ashikaga Takauji and his descendants, and the Southern Court whose standard bearer, Emperor Go-Daigo (1288-1339), had been ousted from power by that selfsame Takauji. Takauji was the first of fifteen Ashikaga shoguns, and on the surface he and his grandson Yoshimitsu would seem to have little in common other than that they were of the same family and occupied the same office. The military government (Bakufu) that Takauji founded in 1336 was transformed during the Nanbokuchô period until there remained hardly any superficial resemblance between the office of shogun as it had been under him and as it was to become under Yoshimitsu. Ashikaga family traits do, nonetheless, give one a sense of continuity concerning at least some of the qualities displayed by the two men in their official and personal lives. Both were shrewd manipulators of men, although Takauji did so as a boisterous provincial warlord and Yoshimitsu did so as a subtle urban prince. Both were pious by the standards of the time, and showed their devotion in a public and theatrical manner by becoming the great temple builders and benefactors of their dynasty. Both loved the performing arts and patronized them enthusiastically. Both were considered effective leaders by their contemporaries, although of very different stamps. Both broke with the restricting bonds of precedent, although Takauji thought he was not and Yoshimitsu tried to convince others that he was not doing so. Here the similarities end, and a vivid contrast between the two in style, politics, and personality remains dominant. Let us examine their lives and careers separately in order to clarify the differences.

Who was Takauji and why is he important in the history of his times? The Ashikaga family was a samurai clan of high lineage which traced its ancestry back to the founder of the Kamakura Bakufu, Minamoto no Yoritomo. As senior Minamoto stock, the Ashikaga had long cherished the dream of once again ruling the empire, and nursed that ambition from their home province in the Kantô. The *Nantaiheiki* by Imagawa Ryôshun, an apologetic work written to clear both the author's reputation and that of his Ashikaga overlords, records a story of some relevance. It tells us that Minamoto no Yoshiie (1039-1106) left a will in which he predicted the rise of the Ashikaga to preeminence in the seventh generation following his own. That seventh generation was Ashikaga Ietoki (1283-1317), a depressive type who failed to fulfill the prophecy in his own lifetime, and so he extended the mandate in his own will by foretelling Ashikaga ascendancy within three more generations. After writing this testament, Ietoki took his own life for having failed his ancestors. The third generation of which he spoke, as it turned out, was Takauji. While the prophecy alone would not have won the empire for the Ashikaga, it no doubt made them more willing to seek the mantle of power when the opportunity arose. That chance came when Emperor Go-Daigo raised his banner against the Hôjô regents who ruled the military houses from their Bakufu in Kamakura. Takauji threw in his lot with Go-Daigo's imperial restoration in the hope that the Emperor would appoint him shogun, an office which he coveted as the key to Ashikaga success. When the Emperor showed no inclination to do so, after some soul-searching during which time Takauji retired to a monastery in Kamakura, he turned against his former ally and forced Go-Daigo to seek refuge in the mountains of Yoshino south of the capital. Takauji then placed Emperor Kômyô (r. 1337-48) of the Northern (senior) imperial line on the throne as his puppet sovereign, and was rewarded with the shogunal title that in his mind went so far toward fulfilling Yoshiie's prophecy.

By the time Takauji received the title in 1338, he already had the skeleton of a government operating in Kyoto. In 1336, he and his brother Tadayoshi (1306-52) promulgated the *Kenmu Formulary* (*Kenmu shikimoku*) which became the basic statement of principles for their

Ashikaga Takauji; Collection of Moriya Yoshitaka (Kyoto)

Bakufu. The document consisted of seventeen articles which: exhorted thrift; prohibited boisterous behavior, lawlessness, and the commandeering of private homes; ordered the return of vacant lots in Kyoto to their original owners; called for efforts to revive the moneylenders and mutual aid societies; demanded the proper selection of *shugo* (provincial military governors appointed by the shogun); prohibited women and priests from meddling in government; ordered strict selection and supervision of officials; prohibited bribery and gift giving; called for proper selection of the shogun's bodyguard; emphasized the importance of decorum, and of rewarding upright and loyal men; affirmed the need to give special attention to petitions of poor vassals; underscored the need for careful examination of suits brought by temples and shrines, and ordered prompt and careful action in all suits. The *Kenmu Formulary* was actually just a listing of moral guideposts for the new regime, and a way of highlighting the Ashikaga Bakufu's virtues as opposed to the excesses of Go-Daigo's brief imperial restoration. And its contents reflected Tadayoshi's views more than Takauji's, since Tadayoshi was in charge of those magistrates who drafted the document. Takauji, on the other hand, controlled the three important bureaus of the Board of Retainers (*samuraidokoro*), the Administrative Board (*mandokoro*), and the Office of Awards (*onshôgata*). Through these three organs the shogun exercised his authority as commander-in-chief of all samurai and as supreme benefactor who dispensed awards of land and offices to loyal retainers. Takauji exploited this power as a modern politician does the patronage system, to gain allies and supporters. He sought such allies among the local warlords of the Kinai region around Kyoto, and gave them free rein to seize crops and lands belonging to the estates of temple, shrine, and *kuge* (aristocratic) proprietors. Unlike this free-wheeling generalissimo, his brother Tadayoshi was intent on protecting those original estate proprietors from such inroads, which had been greatly accelerated by Takauji's wholesale award-granting practices.

In fact, generosity was one of Takauji's three great virtues, according to the Zen prelate Musô Soseki (1275-1351), whose opinions on this subject are recorded in the *Baishôron*. The three virtues which he identified were courage in battle, benevolence and compassion toward friend and foe alike, and an unstinting liberality. Prodigality seems to have been a hereditary trait of the Ashikaga, for while Takauji practiced his munificence toward retainers, his grandson Yoshimitsu gave evidence of it by building palaces for himself and for the reigning emperor. Both Takauji and Yoshimitsu became patrons of the Buddhist establishments as well. For Takauji, generosity took the form of erecting a temple and a pagoda in each province to ensure the peace of the nation, a policy which was conceived in 1337 and carried out between 1342 and 1350. Takauji also built the great Tenryûji monastery on the recommendation of his beloved sage Musô Soseki, to commemorate Go-Daigo's death.

Takauji's expressions of piety and benevolence did not, however, prevent him from also behaving in character as a samurai conqueror. His war with Go-Daigo's loyalist supporters became a triangular contest involving him against his own brother Tadayoshi. Tadayoshi briefly seized the upper hand after a power struggle between him and Takauji's steward Kô no Moronao burst into open hostility in 1342, but his persistent advocacy of temple, shrine, and original *shôen* proprietors lost for him the support of *shugo* whom he had once been able to count in his camp. Takauji's virtue of generosity (at others' expense) paid off handsomely by gaining him allies among the rising class of samurai warlords. When Tadayoshi was poisoned in Kamakura in 1352, the fratricidal aspect of the Nanbokuchô civil war, as far as the Ashikaga clan was concerned, was brought to an end. Not until Yoshimitsu's Shogunate would the two imperial lines be nominally reconciled, however, and by that time the Bakufu would have absorbed all vestiges of Court authority into its organization. But Takauji's simple, straightforward way of dealing with retainers and his liberal use of confiscated property accomplished Ietoki's prophecy by the time he died in 1358. Long before Yoshimitsu built a palace in Kyoto's Muromachi quarter which gave the Ashikaga regime the new name of Muromachi Bakufu, the Ashikaga had indeed become Japan's national government.

In his personal tastes, Takauji had displayed some of the preferences which became trademarks of the Ashikaga shoguns. He was an avid fan of *dengaku* plays, so much so that Tadayoshi once chided him for neglecting his official duties on account of his mania for theatricals. Tadayoshi suggested that if he liked them so much, he should set aside one day a month for such performances, and Takauji acted on the advice, thus beginning the family's reputation as great patrons of the performing and visual arts. If there is any single bond which ties together all of the Ashikaga shoguns, it is their passion for such diversions, and it remains perhaps the most salient similarity between Takauji, the warlord chieftain, and his grandson Yoshimitsu, the Shogun autocrat.

Yoshimitsu was the first Ashikaga shogun to have been raised in a style befitting a royal princeling, and although the civil war between the Bakufu's supporters and the Southern Court continued, he received the protection and solicitude of many different powerful members of the Bakufu. Born in the mansion of the Ise family, who were to become hereditary stewards of the Administrative Board after Yoshimitsu reached adulthood, the shogunal heir-apparent was sheltered by the Akamatsu *shugo* in Harima Province during the Ashikaga's last brief ouster from Kyoto by the armies of the Southern Court. After returning to Kyoto, Yoshimitsu became the ward of the new shogunal regent and Bakufu plenipotentiary, Hosokawa Yoriyuki (1329-92). Yoriyuki exercised the responsibilities of shogunal guardian diligently, and saw to it that the child received all the respect due him. In the meantime, Yoshimitsu's supporters waited impatiently for him to grow up and assume the mantle of power, and rivals of the Ashikaga hoped that such a day would never come.

Yoshimitsu's breeding was different from that of previous Ashikaga shoguns in that he was constantly surrounded by the very best that his society offered in terms of both physical comforts and cultural advantages, and more particularly as he grew to adulthood he was drawn ever more deeply into the world of the imperial Court, with its special preoccupations and *kuge* customs. His life as a courtier – as one who possessed official *kuge* rank – began in 1373 when he was sixteen years old, and under Yoriyuki's watchful eye he rose rapidly in the Court hierarchy. Not only was he the first shogun to attain the office of *Dajôdaijin,* but he was also the first to take a wife from a *kuge* family, the Hino. The Hino would in the future provide the most famous of all shogunal consorts, Yoshimasa's wife Tomiko, and their influence in the capital was in no small way due to this repeated selection of their daughters as brides for Ashikaga heirs.

In keeping with his new majesty as a kingly shogun, Yoshimitsu built himself a new palace in the Muromachi section of Kyoto, on the site of a former palace of a retired emperor which had been destroyed by fire. This Muromachi "Palace of Flowers" was a major undertaking, with water drawn from the Kamo River to fill a large man-made pond on the palace grounds, and a profusion of flowers of the four seasons planted in the garden which gave the new residence its name. The Muromachi palace gave Yoshimitsu the appropriate setting in which to play his role of prince-shogun and man of *virtú*. While never neglecting his official responsibilities, he was also an enthusiastic participant and dignitary at *kuge* banquets and entertainments, including concerts, *kemari* (football), *waka* and *renga* poetry contests, and cock fighting. Yoshimitsu was an uncommonly astute ruler who understood the value of symbols in legitimizing his unique position in the Bakufu and the nation, and his new palace was a concrete manifestation of the drive to legitimate an Ashikaga autocracy.

During the first decade after he dismissed Hosokawa Yoriyuki as his Chief Minister (*kanrei*) and began to make his own political decisions, his primary task was to subdue the powerful *shugo* and to make his Bakufu the undisputed center of all decision-making. In pursuing this goal, he undertook a series of excursions and pilgrimages during the 1380s to various parts of the country to demonstrate his personal power far from the capital. He traveled to Suruga Province to view Mount Fuji and to pacify the Kantô region, and to Miyajima in Aki Province to lord it over the provinces of western Japan and their *shugo,* such as the Ôuchi. He visited the Kasuga shrine in Nara, and Mount Kôya to conciliate the monks there to his regime (many of whom had supported Go-Daigo's Southern Court) and to intimidate other die-hard imperial loyalists in that region. Unlike his grandfather Takauji, who was forced to flee Kyoto more than once and whose only travels were on military campaigns, almost all of Yoshimitsu's separations from the capital took the form of triumphal shogunal progresses. The Muromachi Bakufu had come far during the half-century since its founding, and another symbolic milestone was reached in

1392 when the Southern Emperor Go-Kameyama handed over the three sacred treasures of the imperial house to the Northern Emperor Go-Komatsu, bringing to an end the war between the Courts.

In 1393, following the unification of the Courts, Yoshimitsu made his first visit to the Ise shrine to strengthen the impression of national unity under his rule which had gradually come into being as a result of his policies. With the Southern Court effectively eliminated as a threat, Yoshimitsu was now free to visit the shrine whenever he wished, and he made ten more such trips to Ise before he died. The subjugation of the powerful Yamana *shugo*'s revolt in 1391 left him even more latitude to travel at will throughout Japan. In 1394 he paid visits to the Kôfukuji temple and the Hie shrine, and in later years he made many excursions to Kitano, Iwashimizu, Ise, Kasuga, and Mount Kôya. On these trips he was invariably escorted by a retinue of relatives, vassals, and servants, and with the increasing political stabilization from the 1390s on, he was able to reap more pleasure from such outings, freed as they were from political necessity.

Yoshimitsu the innovator, the Shogun who was always at least one step ahead of both his admirers and his adversaries, surprised everyone in 1394 when, at the age of thirty-seven, he resigned as Shogun in favor of his nine-year-old eldest son Yoshimochi (1386-1428), and took the title *Dajôdaijin* for himself. A year later he shocked everyone a second time by announcing his intention to abandon all worldly titles to become a monk. The fact that Yoshimitsu did so when he was still only thirty-eight years old and at the height of his power left many in the government puzzled. It soon became apparent that he had no intention of surrendering real power, and unlike his grandfather's retreat, his decision was not motivated by either mental anguish or indecision. In the meantime many members of his entourage – both *kuge* and samurai – followed his example by shaving their own heads and taking holy orders as well.

Like his grandfather, Yoshimitsu was a great believer in the material manifestations of Ashikaga piety, and so he built temples in Nara, Kyoto, and on Mount Hiei. In them he imitated the Court custom of having prayers recited by high-ranking monks of various sects for one week beginning on the eighth day of the first month to ensure the peace of the country and the successful harvest of the five grains. Yoshimitsu observed scrupulously the precedents which had been established by retired emperors, as if to force the public mind to view his own rule in a similarly exalted light. His most ambitious project as far as the religious institutions of the country were concerned, was his organization of the Gozan ("five mountains") system of Zen monasteries. This consisted of parallel hierarchies of ranked

Zen temples in Kyoto and Kamakura. One of the Kyoto Gozan temples, the Tenryûji, had been built by Takauji on the advice of Musô Soseki. Yoshimitsu's decision to organize the Gozan temples was also influenced by a high-ranking Rinzai Zen prelate, Gidô Shûshin (1325-88), who was a disciple of Musô's. Dear to Yoshimitsu's heart was the construction of the Shôkokuji temple (1383), which involved the wholesale displacement of both rich and poor who lived on its proposed site adjoining the shogun's Muromachi palace. Yoshimitsu went so far as to rearrange the Gozan hierarchy so that his favorite temple could be counted in its ranks. His patronage of the Zen establishment, his pretensions in aping the ways of retired emperors, and his passion for palace construction merged after he took the tonsure in his decision to build a retreat for himself northwest of Kyoto. In 1397 construction began on his new Kitayama villa, where he pursued the life of a retired emperor-monk while retaining all power in his hands. He moved into the new compound in 1399 and gave his former Muromachi palace to his son Yoshimochi. All government activity moved with him, and remained there until his death in 1408. As he had done in his former palace, he gathered all of his favorites and subordinates around him to serve him in the new quarters.

From about this time, the system of three *kanrei* (Shiba, Hosokawa, Hatakeyama) and seven *tônin* families (Yamana, Isshiki, Toki, Akamatsu, Kyôgoku, Uesugi, and Ise) which formed the nucleus of Bakufu power from then on, was fixed. But Yoshimitsu was not yet dead, and as he had used other *shugo* to crush the power of the Yamana clan in 1391, so in 1399 he used their collective might to defeat the Ôuchi. He even enlisted the services of the Rinzai Zen priest Zekkai Chûshin (1336-1405) to try to coax Ôuchi Yoshihiro back to Kyoto in hopes of avoiding a military clash, showing that he was neither bloodthirsty nor intemperate in the use of the resources available to him. When Yoshihiro refused to capitulate and decided instead to fight to the bitter end, Yoshimitsu then did not hesitate to launch a combined Bakufu army of some thirty thousand samurai against him at Sakai.

Free of rivals at last, Yoshimitsu was now able to turn his attention to foreign policy, and he entered into formal diplomatic and trade relations with the Ming empire, from whose sovereign he received the tributary title of "King of Japan." It was a fitting compliment to the Shogun who had no major failures to his credit, and who had finally fulfilled Takauji's cherished dream of an Ashikaga dynasty holding sway over the entire country.

Preeminent Patron of Higashiyama Culture

Ashikaga Yoshimasa

by

H. PAUL VARLEY

The age of Ashikaga Yoshimasa (1436-90) was both the worst of times and the best of times. Elevated to the headship of the Ashikaga shogunal house in 1443 at the callow age of seven, Yoshimasa presided over the affairs of the Muromachi Bakufu in the decades leading to the great civil war of Ônin (1467-77), which plunged Japan into a century of disunion known as the Age of the Country at War (*sengoku jidai*). Throughout his years as Shogun (1449-73), Yoshimasa demonstrated – at least so far as the records show – an almost total incapacity or unwillingness to deal with the deterioration of Bakufu administration. On the contrary, he seems to have given himself over largely to extravagance and pleasure, while remaining callously indifferent to the suffering and decline of others. Here, for example, is a description from *The Chronicle of Ônin* of preparations for a flower-viewing excursion that Yoshimasa led in the ninth month of 1466 on the very eve of the Ônin holocaust:

> A feast of a thousand delicacies was prepared.... The Shogun's attendants were supplied with eating sticks of gold, while other guests received sticks carved from scented wood and inlaid with precious metals. People ran about madly preparing their costumes. So great was the expense, they were forced to put all their holdings in pawn and to sell their valuables. Taxes were levied on people in the provinces and collection of the land and household taxes was pressed. Farmer and landlord suffered dreadfully. Without the means to continue planting and harvesting, they abandoned their fields and turned to begging and lived in misery on whatever their hands and feet could bring them. Most of the hamlets and villages throughout the country reverted to uncultivated fields.[1]

Yet, despite the appalling downward course of events in government during the middle and late fifteenth century, it was also a time of splendid cultural and artistic achievement. Known as the Higashiyama epoch after the location of Yoshimasa's retreat in the Eastern Hills of Kyoto, it witnessed a remarkable efflorescence in such fields as Japanese literary scholarship (*wagaku*), the culture of tea, monochrome ink painting (*sumi-e*), linked-verse poetry (*renga*), and landscape gardening. At the center of Higashiyama culture stood Yoshimasa, recognized as unchallengeably its foremost patron and sponsor. Such recognition has given Yoshimasa a Janus-headed image in Japansee history: stigmatized as a futile if not scandalously negligent shogun, he is also seen as a connoisseur of the arts and an arbiter of taste who stands perhaps supreme among all of Japan's rulers – both royal and non-royal – as a leader of cultural life.

This two-fold perception of Yoshimasa as a disastrously bad ruler but a sublime patron of the arts may be essentially true, but the fact is that we have so little detailed information about his life and behavior that we are not likely ever to know him well or be able to evaluate him fully as a historical personage. If anything, Yoshimasa seems to have been a solitary and lonely figure, surrounded by people who wished to dominate and exploit him and buffeted by the forces of conflict and disunion that increasingly engulfed the country in his time.

One way to approach Yoshimasa is to view him as an end product of measures first taken by his grandfather, the third Ashikaga Shogun, Yoshimitsu (1358-1408), to transform the Shogunate into a feudal kingship. Under Yoshimitsu the Ashikaga Bakufu achieved its greatest influence as a governing body, but nevertheless rested on a precarious balance of power between the shogun and a group of regional barons known to historians as *shugo-daimyô* (constable-daimyo). The centrifugal pulls of such a power balance were great and led eventually, in Yoshimasa's time, to the nearly total destruction of the Ashikaga ruling system during the Ônin War and its aftermath.

Yoshimitsu sought to mould the office of Shogun into a feudal kingship by various means, the most important of which was the merger of the *bu* (military) and *bun* (cultural) aspects of rule. In his quest for *bun,* Yoshimitsu assumed the role of patron of all the arts – including both those traditionally associated with the *kuge* or courtier class and those, such as the *nô* theatre and *renga,* that had emerged from at least partly plebeian sources in the Muromachi period. Yoshimitsu also styled himself not only as warrior chieftain but also as courtier. While advancing steadily to the highest ranks and offices of the court hierarchy,[2] he

Ashikaga Yoshimasa;
Tokyo National Museum

took as his wife a member of the aristocratic Hino family[3] and disported himself in the grandest *kuge* manner. Toward the end of his life, Yoshimitsu even built a palatial retreat in the Kitayama or Northern Hills suburbs of Kyoto, where he lived very much like an *in* or retired emperor (and, in addition, symbolized in his person the Kitayama epoch of cultural flowering).[4]

By Yoshimasa's age, the process of acquiring *bun* and thereby transforming the shogun into a feudal king had, in one sense, admirably succeeded. For the shogun seemed, by every criterion, to be more unassailably "legitimate" as a ruler of all classes, including the *kuge*; and in the elegance of his role at the center of Kyoto life, he rivalled even the emperor. On the other hand, the ever greater intrusion of the shogun into the softer realms of Kyoto society and life seriously threatened to undermine his role as military leader (that is, the possessor of *bu*). With few exceptions, the Ashikaga shoguns before Yoshimasa were personally forceful rulers. But it seemed inevitable that one day a Yoshimasa, who so adored the arts and the cultivated life and cared not at all for the way of the bow and the horse, would come along. And when he did, it became apparent that the Ashikaga Bakufu had been structured for rule by a strong-willed shogun and had few institutional checks against the exploitation of a weak one.

Yoshimasa's father, Yoshinori (1394-1441), was a harsh and cruel man who tried to maintain the Bakufu's balance of power with the constable-daimyo by means of suppression that were at times draconian. Such suppression led in 1441 to Yoshinori's assassination by Akamatsu Mitsusuke (1381-1441), a constable who had various personal grievances against the shogun but who may also have acted in concert with other disgruntled constables. At any rate, the sudden death of Yoshinori resulted in the appointment of his seven-year-old son, Yoshikatsu (1434-43), as Shogun; and when Yoshikatsu died of illness two years later, he was in turn succeeded by his brother, Yoshimasa.

Much of Yoshimasa's life is a record of domination by others, including blood relatives, concubines, his wife, and ministers at the Bakufu Court. In the years immediately after his succession to the Ashikaga headship, Yoshimasa was especially influenced by his mother, Hino Shigeko (1411-63). A second major force in Yoshimasa's early life was Ise Sadachika (1417-73), a member of family that played two key roles in Ashikaga and Bakufu affairs. First, the Ise were the chief managers of Bakufu finances through the office, which they hereditarily held, of head of the Administrative Board (*mandokoro*); and second, as traditional authorities on warrior etiquette and custom, the Ise were entrusted with the responsibility for educating future Ashikaga shoguns. Yoshimasa, in fact, was largely raised in Sadachika's household. If we are to believe the contemporary chronicles, the experience must have been devastatingly harmful. For in an age of "bad ministers" (at least as portrayed in the chronicles) Sadachika is presented to us as the most corrupt and venal of all on the stage of events leading to the Ônin War. Appointed to the headship of the Administrative Board in 1460, he was frequently at Yoshimasa's side during these years. Although the war may have been inevitable because of its larger historical origins, Sadachika – ever scheming to gain advantage from the endless conflicts and plottings that swirled around the Bakufu in the immediate prewar years – was certainly one of its leading instigators.

In the 1450s Yoshimasa came under the sway of a nefarious trio of people dubbed by anonymous satirists of the time as the "three *ma*" or "three devils" from the fact that each had the phonetic element "*ma*" in his or her name. The three were: a concubine, Imamairi-no-Tsubone (also called simply O-Ima); an in-law, Karasuma Suketô; and a sychophantic minister, Arima Mochiie. Little is known about Suketô and Mochiie, but O-Ima appears to have presented a major threat to the Hino in their carefully cultivated ties with the Ashikaga. In 1455 Yoshimasa married Hino Tomiko (1440-96), but his affections openly remained with O-Ima. For the Hino, the most critical purpose was to produce an heir to the Shogunate. Yet even when a son of Tomiko's died shortly after birth in

1459, that fiercely determined woman took clever advantage of such an ostensibly adverse turn of events by accusing O-Ima of casting a spell over the infant. The charge was accepted as true even by Yoshimasa, who ordered O-Ima's exile to a distant island, where she was soon put to death by Tomiko's agents.

The origins of the Ônin War so complex as to defy easy generalizations. Yet, in addition to the failure of leadership in the Bakufu, we may take particular note, first, of unrest and disorder among the peasantry and, second, of the growing inability of the constable-daimyo as a class to maintain order and control in their territorial domains. The peasant unrest of the fifteenth century stemmed chiefly from excessive feudal pressures placed upon the country's agrarian base, especially in the central provinces. Increasingly restricted in its range of authority as a governing body, the Ashikaga Bakufu was forced to make ever greater demands in the form of feudal rents upon those lands that were nearest and most accessible. At the same time the Bakufu sought additional revenue through the taxation of pawn brokers, who in their turn derived some of their largest profits from usurious loans to peasants. This vicious cycle of exploitation of the peasantry finally exploded into uprisings (*doikki*), which gained steadily in scope and intensity from the outbreak of the first one in 1428. Complicating the social character of these peasant uprisings was the fact that in many, if not most, cases they were actually led by members of the *bushi* or warrior class.

The constable-daimyo declined and vanished from the stage of history in the late fifteenth century essentially because they could not establish permanent governance over their sizable domains of two or more provinces (the Yamana family, at one time, held as many as eleven provinces). Having asserted their original control over these domains – from above and usually as outsiders – during the civil wars of the fourteenth century, the constable-daimyo were constantly plagued by inadequate and often unreliable bases of direct revenue from land. In addition, they were obliged to deal with powerful – and frequently recalcitrant – local magnates whom they sought to make their hereditary vassals. The decline of constable-daimyo houses from about the mid-fifteenth century on typically assumed the form of the succession dispute in which leading vassals took the sides of contenders for the office of constable. When disputes over succession erupted in the 1450s within two of the most powerful constable-daimyo houses, the Hatakeyama and Shiba, the ceaseless contention they spawned eventually became a major factor in the outbreak of the Ônin War.

Yoshimasa's behavior in the years leading to the Ônin War has contributed probably more than anything else to the bad press he has received in history. For example, despite grievous suffering on the part of the people owing to a series of natural disasters, Yoshimasa insisted on embarking upon several lavish building and renovation projects. including the erection at great cost of a new mansion for his mother, Hino Shigeko, and the refurbishing of the shogunal palace, known as the Hana-no-Gosho or "Palace of Flowers." So blatant was Yoshimasa's profligacy in undertaking these projects at a time of stress and uncertainty that they elicited a rare imperial rebuke in the form of a poem by Emperor Go-Hanazono (1419-70):

> The suffering people struggle for ferns on Mount Shouyang
> While everywhere their ovens are banked, and their bamboo
> doors shut.
> It is spring and the second month; yet there is no joy
> in verse.
> For whom are the colors of the land bursting forth? [5]

Yoshimasa, along with his wife Tomiko, also sponsored a spectacular round of social and ceremonial events during these years even as the distant rumblings of war began. Among them were a grand, three-day performance of *nô* at Tadasugawara in the spring of 1464 and a flower-viewing excursion to Kachô-zan in the outskirts of Kyoto during the third month of 1465 that was described by a diarist in attendance as possessing "a splendor that was breathtaking to behold."[6]

The proximate cause of the Ônin War was a succession dispute within the shogunal house itself. It will be recalled that Tomiko's first son died in infancy in 1459, an occurrence that provided her with the opportunity to dispose of her chief rival, the concubine O-Ima. The years passed and in 1464 Yoshimasa, still without a male heir and proclaiming his desire to unburden himself of the responsibilities of the Shogunate, persuaded his younger brother, Yoshimi (1439-91), to become his appointed successor even though to do so Yoshimi, a Buddhist priest, was obliged to shed his holy robes. Within a year after this appointment, Tomiko gave birth to a second son, Yoshihisa (1465-89). Determined to have her issue become shogun, Tomiko enlisted the backing of the great western chieftain, Yamana Sôzen (1404-73). Yoshimi, meanwhile, received the support of Hosokawa Katsumoto (1430-73) who, at a time of decline in the fortunes of the Hatakeyama and Shiba, was head of the only house – the Hosokawa – of the three constable-daimyo houses entitled to provide candidates for the key Bakufu office of Chief Minister (*kanrei*) that was still united and strong. The lines were thus drawn for the Ônin War, which began early in 1467. Because of the location of its camp in Kyoto to the west of the Bakufu's offices, Yamana's side became known as the Western Army; Hosokawa and his supporters, on the other hand, were called the Eastern Army.

Yoshimasa appears at the last moment to have made a genuine personal effort to stave off war by declaring to both Hosokawa and Yamana in the early days of 1467 that whoever began fighting first would be declared a rebel. But once the conflict got underway, the Shogun assumed a largely passive role. Critics, seizing on certain accounts in the chronicles, picture Yoshimasa as drinking and carousing his way through the Ônin War. But if one wishes to be fair at all, it must be observed that there was very little he could have done. Of all the civil wars in Japanese history, this one, as it was actually fought in Kyoto during the decade 1467-77, seemed to have possessed a unique insanity of purpose. Its greater causes, adumbrated above, were certainly real enough. But, once begun, the war was perpetuated by a frenzied urge on the part of its belligerents to continue fighting, no matter how obscure the original goals of such fighting might become. One of the greatest ironies of the war, for example, was that in the tortuous twistings and turnings of its course the Hosokawa, who had originally backed the candidacy for shogun of Yoshimi, embraced the cause of Yoshihisa, whereas the Yamana shifted their support from Yoshihisa to Yoshimi!

The issue of succession to the Shogunate was, in fact, finally decided by Yoshimasa himself, who simply transferred it to Yoshihisa in 1473, the same year that both of the leading generals of the war – Hosokawa Katsumoto and Yamana Sôzen – died. Perhaps this was the ultimate irony of the Ônin War: that the only thing ostensibly "settled" by it, the shogunal succession dispute, was accomplished by the most seemingly effete and indecisive of its major actors.

The Ônin War came to an end when the last armies withdrew from Kyoto in 1477. But although the fighting thus ceased in the capital, it continued on in the provinces, drawing Japan into the century of the Country at War. For Yoshimasa, the war's end inaugurated a distinct new phase of his life in which, on the one hand, he seems to have sought greater personal freedom from the domination of others than he had ever enjoyed before and, on the other hand, devoted his efforts to what became his greatest project, the building of his Higashiyama retreat.

For years Yoshimasa's chief dominator had been his wife, Tomiko, whose voice probably exceeded his in Bakufu circles and who had accumulated enormous wealth through the imposition of levies on travel barriers (*sekisho*) in the capital region. Even during the war Yoshimasa had attempted to escape from her tentacles by moving from their Muromachi mansion to a separate residence; and when Tomiko and Yoshihisa, after a fire at the Muromachi mansion, joined him at this new residence, he decamped to another. Yoshimasa's great desire was to build an estate, much like Yoshimitsu's Kitayama residence, to which he could retire in tranquility and pursue his interest in the arts. He had been thinking about the project and considering sites for years, and in 1482 he finally had work begun at the location of a former Pure Land Temple in Higashiyama. Upon completion of the main residential building (*tsune-no-gosho*) in 1483, Yoshimasa moved to Higashiyama and resided there until his death in 1490.

The Higashiyama epoch of cultural history is probably best regarded as the last half of the fifteenth century. Yet one might argue that its strongest and most distinctive characteristics are to be found especially in the decade or so following the Ônin War – a briefer period in which Yoshimasa, known as the Lord of Higashiyama (Higashiyama-dono), inspired an even greater flourishing of the arts through his tireless pursuit of beauty in the construction of his new estate.

In addition to levying the constables for funds to build the Higashiyama estate, Yoshimasa dispatched *kawaramono* (literally, "people of the riverbeds")[7] to temples and estates as far away as Nara to commandeer unusual rocks and trees for his landscaping. In many ways the landscape garden epitomized the values of Higashiyama culture. Regrettably, Yoshimasa's original gardens at Higashiyama have long been obliterated by time and we have little way of knowing how close they may have been to the present gardens – splendid in themselves – that were constructed during the Tokugawa period. But we do know that Yoshimasa, like Yoshimitsu before him, was much inspired by the gardens first built at the Saihôji temple in southwestern Kyoto in the early fourteenth century by the Zen priest Musô Soseki. Yoshimasa, an insatiable garden visitor, is said to have gone to Saihôji in each season of the year to study the changing aspects of its landscaping. We may imagine that he was particularly impressed with that portion of the Saihôji gardens that was a *kare-sansui* or "withered landscape," for the most distinctive aesthetic value of the Higashiyama epoch was that of the monochromatic or "withered." In painting it was exemplified by the Sung Chinese style ink work of Sesshû (1420-1506) and in gardens by the severely simple sand and rock arrangement at the Ryôanji temple, whose construction is traditionally attributed to Hosokawa Katsumoto.

Of the buildings that made up Yoshimasa's Higashiyama estate, only the Ginkakuji (Silver Pavilion) and Tôgudô (Hall of Eastern Yearning)[8] remain. For us today, the Ginkakuji stands as the supreme symbol of the

Higashiyama epoch of cultural history. Weathered over half a millenium of time, it is a wonderful visual reminder of the *kare* aesthetic; and in its construction it is an invaluable example of the new and more intimate *shoin* form of domestic architecture[9] that developed in mid-Muromachi times.

One of the rooms in the Tôgudô – a room called Dôjinsai – was traditionally thought to have been a birthplace, so to speak, of the tea ceremony (*cha-no-yu*). Although recent research has disproved that the Dôjinsai was exclusively designed as a tea room (*chashitsu*),[10] its builder – Yoshimasa – undoubtedly played some role in the creation of *cha-no-yu* in the Higashiyama epoch through his close association with the *dôbôshû,* men of cultural taste and connoisseurship who served the Bakufu. For of equal if not greater importance than the actual ceremony itself was the development of a setting for *cha-no-yu,* a setting based, structurally, on the new forms of *shoin* architecture and, in terms of decoration, on tastes in pottery, painting, and the like that had been refined since Kitayama times through the handling of imported objects of art and craft (*karamono*) from China. And it was in this area of decoration and connoisseurship of art that the *dôbôshû* (the most famous of whom were members in three generations of the same family: Nôami, 1397-1471; Geiami, 1431-85; and Sôami, d. 1525) are particularly remembered.

In addition to the aesthetic of the monochromatic and the withered, Higashiyama culture was permeated with an intense nostalgia and yearning for the past. The past that Yoshimasa and his contemporaries yearned for, however, was not precisely a historic time but rather a fictionalized age of the Heian court at its zenith, particularly as portrayed in *Genji monogatari.* This nostalgia for the past was especially intensified by the destruction wrought in Kyoto during the Ônin War and, in the postwar years, brought a strong wave of popularity to such *wagaku* scholars as Ichijô Kanera (1402-81), who was much in demand for lecturing on *Kokinshû, Ise monogatari, Genji monogatari*, and other masterpieces of Heian literature.

A particularly significant phenomenon of culture during the Higashiyama epoch was its spread outward from Kyoto into the provinces. Military leaders were zealous in seeking to have scholars like Ichijô Kanera visit their provincial seats, and *renga* masters such as Sôgi (1421-1502) devoted their lives to journeying about the country. Yoshimasa himself had no particular interest in or concern for the provinces that we know of; but, as the grand patron of the arts and a symbol of the connoisseurship of the age, he set standards that were thereafter followed by people everywhere. A dismal failure as military leader, he had by his death in 1490 fulfilled perhaps beyond all expectations the promise inherent in the assumption by the Ashikaga a century earlier of leadership also in the *bun* aspect of kingly rule.

[NOTES]

1. H. Paul Varley, *The Ônin War* (New York: Columbia University Press, 1967), p. 141.
2. He received the junior first rank (*ju-ichi-i*) in 1380 and the high office of *daijô daijin* in 1394.
3. A sublineage of the northern branch of the Fujiwara family.
4. The Kitayama cultural epoch may be thought of as roughly coterminus with the period from Yoshimitsu's accession to the office of Shogun in 1368 until his death in 1408.
5. Varley, *The Ônin War*, p. 118.
6. *Ibid.*, p. 119.
7. *Kawaramono* were people on the lowest level of the social scale who lived in the region of the Kamo River in Kyoto. They were employed in the construction of gardens and, in the later Muromachi period, also became garden designers. Yoshimasa was particularly fond of the *kawaramono* Zen'ami.
8. The title of this hall refers to the concept of those who "yearn in the east for rebirth in Amida's western paradise." Its selection was one indication of Yoshimasa's deep devotion to Pure Land Buddhism.
9. Some of the principal elements of *shoin* architecture are *tatami, shôji,* the *toko-no-ma* or alcove, asymmetrical shelves (*chigaidana*), and the built-in *shoin* writing desk.
10. The room was intended chiefly for Buddhist practices.

Daimyo in an Age of Strife

Takeda Shingen

by

CAROLE A. RYAVEC

> Things fall apart; the centre cannot hold;
> Mere anarchy is loosed upon the world.
> The blood-dimmed tide is loosed, and everywhere
> The ceremony of innocence is drowned.
>
> from *The Second Coming*
> by W.B. Yeats

The Country at War: 1467-1568

For the most part of a century after the Ônin War of 1467 to 1477, the whole of Japan was disturbed by continual military struggles waged by samurai competing for autonomous territorial control. The contention led to such chaos that conflict arose at every level of society; peasants rose against landlords, soldiers against generals, and warlords challenged their neighbors. Daimyo who derived authority from the Ashikaga Bakufu, the nominal government, led armies in the environs of Kyoto, vying to control the Bakufu. After the death in 1490 of the Shogun, Ashikaga Yoshimasa, famous for patronizing the *nô* and leading an aesthetic movement from his Silver Pavilion, succeeding shoguns fell under the power of these warlords. As government organization broke down, a measure of self-government became more evident throughout the country. Near the capital at Kyoto, peasants successfully resisted taxation by unifying in strong village organizations. Sake and rice merchants banded together to rebuild the blighted capital and resist military depredation. Leaders of the most famous of the salvationist Buddhist sects, the Ikkô Church, were powerful enough to overthrow the provincial constable of Kaga, on the Japan Sea coast, around 1486, and maintained an autonomous territorial government until 1576. Thus peasants, merchants, and other non-military groups rallied to grasp control over their own affairs as the great daimyo loosened their grasp on the countryside in an attempt to hold their own in the old order.

However, the real victors to emerge from the political chaos were the eastern warlords who took advantage of the conflict in the west to develop their own military and civilian political organizations at home. The new leaders were the Warlords of the Age of Strife (*sengoku daimyô*), who marked history with dramatic exploits and daring military encounters. They fought to control new territories, and they forged a new social order in the lands they conquered. From the end of the Ônin War, the warlords pressed the countryside samurai into service, and stretched their control over agriculture and commerce. Among the dozen or so heroes in this dramatic period, it was Takeda Shingen of Kai Province who proved himself to be the warlord's warlord.

Kai Province, modern Yamanashi Prefecture, was a perfect setting for Takeda's reorganization of material resources in the construction of a war machine. Lying just west of the Great Plain of the Kantô, the rice production center of eastern Japan, it was not of primary economic or military importance to other warlords. A traveler coming due west from modern Tokyo enters the Kai area at its northeastern edge to face a basin cut by rushing rivers emanating from the northern mountain range. Some four thousand square kilometers of the Kai basin seem telescoped into the Japan Alps, eighty kilometers across the basin to the west, and Mount Fuji, fifty kilometers to the south. During the early half of the sixteenth century, the Takeda family chiefs, hereditary provincial constables, forced the petty samurai landlords of this region to submit to their political authority. Shingen, who came to head the Takeda house in 1541, succeeded to a province well pacified, but subject, like most of the country, to famine and hardship wrought by natural disasters. His finesse as a civil governor matches the record to Hôjô Sôun, the first of the innovative eastern warlords, in providing relief for agrarian distress. And his fame on the battlefield, made over some thirty continual years of warfare, provides tales of classic strategy and brilliance in the gamesmanship of war.

The Emerging Order: Maintaining the Home Front

The warlords shaped a new order by forging a direct link to all groups within their territories, to all military men, merchants, artisans, and peasants. To accomplish this, they placed strict controls on agricultural administration, since rice was still at the core of Japan's economy. Rice

Takeda Shingen; Seikeiin Temple (Kôya, Wakayama Prefecture)

production areas had become independent of the old capital-centered estate control by the early 1500s. However, agriculture was under the control of local samurai landlords who employed labor and material resources just as manorial lords of Frankish Europe had lived on the labor of peasants and artisans. Takeda Shingen was one of a handful of warlords who issued proclamations of a new legal order to break the hold of these petty landlords. In absorbing one right after another, Takeda tried to reduce the once stubbornly independent samurai of his realm to officers of his own administration.

In Kai Province, the Takeda family had managed to hold the constable title throughout the unstable post-Ônin War period until final defeat in 1582. The strategy of juggling alliances within Kai to maintain political leadership from 1498 to 1541 was a microscale model of conflict which expanded to intra-territorial warfare from the time of Hôjô Sôun's invasion of Kai in 1501. One reason that Kai was able to withstand outside incursions so stoutly was Takeda's earlier success in political manipulation of the samurai of Kai. The most powerful of these landlords ruled fertile rice producing areas along the river system running from northern Kai to join in the Fuji River, southeast of Kôfu, the provincial capital. Since the Heian period, Kôfu had been the communication link between Kyoto and the western rice producing estates of the province. Only after the Ônin War did the Takeda begin to take these areas under their direct control.

From the twelfth century, it had been the constable's task to act on behalf of the Kamakura Bakufu (1185-1333), the central military government, in such duties as registering samurai vassals for military service and arresting felons. Gradually the constables expanded their powers. From 1336 to 1392, a long battle was waged between the imperial Court and the Muromachi Bakufu, which deposed the Emperor and established a rival Northern Court. The military government granted taxation rights to provincial constables, specifically for commissariat purposes, but the Takeda for their part were not about to give up the taxes when the war was over. The wealth derived from taxation and from expansion of administration rights over rice production estates provided constables with an advantage at the local level when government disintegrated into free-for-all contention after the Ônin War.

Takeda's offensive on Shinano dates from the 1520s. Shingen's father, Nobutora, escalated his attack during the thirties, and Shingen continued the campaign into the early 1560s. The purpose of the northern campaign was to bring the numerous samurai leaders of Shinano under Takeda control. Their independence would have been a constant threat to Shingen if he had attempted to confront the western warlords in an early move toward Kyoto. The first step of attaining Shingen's dream to conquer all of Japan was securing the northern front of his small mountainous province. Then he could move to the south. Since direct passage between Kai and Kyoto was blocked by the southern Alps at Kai's western border, the established line of transportation was to move southeast through the Mount Fuji lakes area to Suruga Bay. From Suruga one could travel west by land or sea to Kyoto. Constant battles brought one samurai band after another into the Takeda war machine. Since the border between Kai and Shinano is a range of towering peaks, known as the "Switzerland of Japan" the rhythm of battle became attuned to the melting snows. Political gatherings and religious rituals were performed throughout the snowbound winters, and military strategy was tested in the spring.

At the core of wintertime planning was organizing supplies for the spring offensive. Shingen's commissary was famous as the birthplace of many a Tokugawa period merchant house. With a fifty-thousand-man standing army, about one quarter of which was cavalry, the government

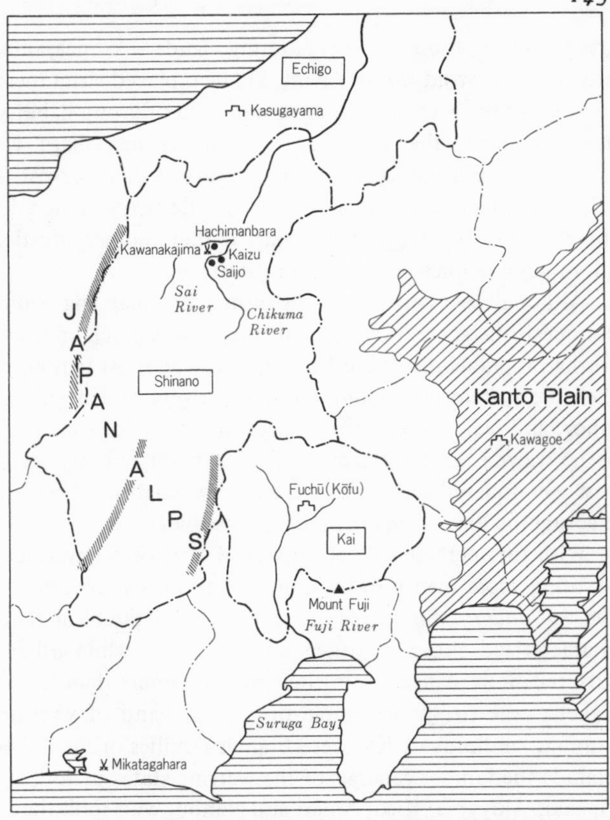

was faced with constant financial and logistic problems. The financial problems were met in the manner governments tend most to depend upon, by increased taxation. Shingen maintained his retainers' loyalty by assigning them to administer lands with set production. In return for the income from those lands, the retainers supplied appropriate military service. Shingen devised ad hoc taxes of all types, and levied residence taxes directly upon peasants to increase his income and to avoid dealing with the old rice rent system in the hands of local landlords. He placed toll levies upon devotees coming to the shrines at Mount Fuji, and made large demands for provisions from wealthy landlords. For his skill in public administration he was praised by other warlords, and all indications confirm that the strength of the Takeda war machine rested as much upon his civil policy as his military strategy.

In spite of his success at home, the technology of the age was not advanced enough to provide for everyone. The peasants still suffered from famine in bad years. Shingen's residence taxes were two to four times greater than those of neighboring lands. As peasants fled to other provinces to avoid tax payment, Shingen placed strict measures on villages to account for taxes according to a system of group liability. In retaliation, at least once, the inhabitants of an entire village went off to the mountains, refusing to turn over any part of their harvest. This occurred in 1551, when peasants of Tsuru district fled from a new levy imposed for the Shinano campaign. They burned their homes and fields, abandoning all, more in helplessness than in protest.

Although peasants bore the brunt of financing Shingen's dream of conquest, the general level of cultivation was much improved by the public works programs instituted by Shingen. The most famous of these works is the dike system built along the major rivers of central Kai. He used local labor, and waived taxes for villages in return for construction service, just as he waived taxes for samurai in return for military service. Old forts in newly-conquered territories were also reconstructed with the intention of meeting the local needs as much as possible.

With the increased fiscal activity of territorial government, Shingen had to bring more men into his administration. His government organization, the *kashindan,* was formed in the same hierarchical feudal pattern that characterized those of other warlords. But while other warlords often suffered more danger from their own retainers than from outside armies, Takeda was firmly in charge of a loyal band of warriors. Many of the samurai landlords of Kai were branch families of the Takeda house. These include the famous generals of the warring states period, Ogasawara, Isawa, Itagaki, Akiyama, Kiso, Amari and Nanbu, who took their names from the localities where they settled. Most of these houses remained loyal to the Takeda for four hundred years after the split into branch houses in the twelfth century. Outsiders were also welcomed into the government. Priests, scholars, poets, strategists, and storytellers all came to Kôfu to act as the warlord's council. Although the story may be apocryphal, one remark by Shingen about his government expresses concisely the reason for his success. When explaining to his retainers that he did not need to build new forts in Kai he said, "The people are my castles, my stone barriers, and my moats. We show compassion for our allies, and vengeance for our enemies."

Warlords and War

Rapid technical developments in crafts and arts were enthusiastically sponsored by warlords during the sixteenth century in order to line the coffers of their treasuries. Even today, the area which Takeda governed is well known for fine craftsmanship in leather and metal, materials utilized in medieval armour. The most important technical development of the age was the mastery of firearms manufacture. This discovery, since it portended the equalization of access to military technology, was suppressed by the Tokugawa, just as they suppressed opportunities for social mobility common during the sixteenth century. They froze the class structure and granted the samurai class privileges tied to its exclusive control of martial arts.

The contenders in the Age of Strife (*sengoku jidai*) had placed no restrictions on techniques of warfare. Even before the introduction of guns on the battlefield, rules were made only to be broken. One island battlefield named Kawanakajima is famous for a series of confrontations manipulated by Takeda Shingen to trap his most bitter rival, Uesugi Kenshin of Echigo Province. Kenshin had decided almost simultaneously upon a strategy of national conquest. The moment was ripe for a confrontation of the eastern warlords. The victor would surely move on to the west to assume hegemony. One clash with Kenshin at Kawanakajima, which took place on the tenth day of the ninth lunar month of 1561, is now remembered as one of the three most decisive battles of the age. The other two battles, at Kawagoe Fort in 1546, and Itsukushima in 1555, determined the ruling warlords of the entire eastern and western regions respectively. History books regard the events surrounding Kawanakajima from a different perspective, since it was the bloodiest battle in Japanese military history. Ordinarily, generals succeeded in bringing new territories under their power with minimum casualties. Kawanakajima was an outstanding exception. One military chronicle relates that more than eight thousand soldiers died in this single encounter. Shingen met his rival Kenshin at this same island several times before and after 1561, but no battle approached this one in its level of destruction. If it had, the warlords' strategic warfare would have led to total annihilation of both sides. Kenshin of Echigo headed some eight thousand men. Shingen of Kai brought about eight thousand with his vanguard and held twelve thousand more men as a rearguard force. Of these thirty thousand participants, the losses are estimated at thirty-four hundred men of the Echigo army, and forty-six hundred men of Shingen's side. Losses such as this, forty percent of Kenshin's army, can in no way be justified by the strategic importance of the battle. These encounters at the same battlefield came to symbolize war when the entire country was embroiled in war. In addition to the tremendous loss of life, the 1561 battle is of particular interest because it was conducted by the leading military strategists of the day.

In the early summer of 1561, Kenshin, who had just attained the highest position of the eastern military government, the post of *Kantô*

Kanrei, returned to his own castle, Kasugayama. Without rest, he mustered his troops and set off for Shinano Province. The army camped at Mount Saijo, about four kilometers south of Kawanakajima. Three kilometers to the east was Shingen's new fort, Kaizu, to which he had sent all generals assigned to northern Shinano Province. Fort Kaizu was strategically located to control the main thoroughfare through the province. Protected at three sides by mountain ranges, it was open only at the northwest, facing the Chikuma River. Kenshin's fort at Mount Saijo, west of Kaizu, was also on the eastern bank of the westward-winding Chikuma River.

On the morning of the tenth day of the ninth lunar month, the armies of Kenshin and Shingen met at Hachimanbara, near the convergence of the Chikuma and Sai Rivers. Our only reliable record provides little information about the events. We know that Shingen's younger brother Nobushige died in battle, and that several of Kenshin's generals were killed. Actually, we know the details of the story only from the myth it had become by the early seventeenth century, some forty years after the event. The *Kôyô gunkan,* a military chronicle of popular history, is our main source. Despite the tendency of its compilers to exaggeration of "body counts," the gist of the narrative is consistent with authenticated facts.

On the night before battle, Kenshin had been able to observe Shingen's fort from the peak of Mount Saijo. He saw a sudden increase in activity. He surmised from the deployment of horses and men, and from the unceasing smoke signals that Shingen was about to make a move. This was the sign that Kenshin had awaited in his twenty day encampment at Saijo. The next morning Kenshin secretly led his men across the Chikuma River to Hachimanbara, at the center of Kawanakajima. Shingen's army had not even noticed that its enemy had left camp until the whole force of the Echigo army appeared in a moment, bearing down upon them out of the heavy river fog at dawn. Shingen's vanguard was shattered. Just as it faced absolute defeat, with Shingen and his son Yoshinobu both wounded, twelve thousand Kai rearguard soldiers arrived to save their general. The alleged author of the *Kôyô gunkan* chronicle is Kôsaka Danjô, the leader of the rearguard forces and lifelong companion of Shingen.

The majority of the thirty-four hundred of the Echigo army who were killed were overtaken and slaughtered as they fled the battlefield. Many drowned in the rapids of the Sai River. But the encounter at Kawanakajima was a total victory for Kenshin. Neither side was incapacitated, and Kenshin led his army to the Kantô two months later. The following month, Shingen clashed again with Kenshin while invading a province to the northeast of Kai.

Tradition has it that the 1561 clash was the fourth of a five-round battle between the great generals. Although the earliest encounter took place in 1553, we have no recorded comment by the participants themselves until the time of the final fight in 1564. Actually, there are documents that predate this, but these consist solely of thank you notes from Kenshin and Shingen to their retainers for heads taken in battle. The notes look suspiciously like form letters bearing the generals' seals. "I thank you," Shingen wrote again and again, "for *x* number of heads taken on *y* date at *z* battle. It was terrific. Keep up the good work." These notes tell us little of the personalities of the contenders. Uesugi Kenshin, in preparation for the 1564 battle, visited a shrine in the environs of his fort and made an offering. This prayer, offered in the hope of receiving divine assistance for victory, is a list of Takeda Shingen's misdeeds. Written in simple vernacular script, it gives us a glimpse of Kenshin's attitude toward his rival. He lists seven categories of wrongdoing. He charged that Shingen had been remiss in overseeing religious ceremony and had assigned secular authorities to supervise temples and shrines when he invaded Shinano Province. Some of Kenshin's charges go beyond simple indictment of Shingen's impious action. "Now that Shingen has destroyed Shinano's temples and shrines, and exiles their attendents, who could possibly revere the authority of the gods if they allow his continued victory? " This threat to divinity, demanding that it act in order to preserve its believers' faith, is reminiscent of the early Greek idea of the relationship between human and divine.

The gods of Japan were controllers of the natural forces acting on some location. They are linked even now to the agricultural cycles discovered with civilization. The meaning of religion for the peasant, just like that for the Athenian, was performance of ritual. Japanese divinities of the medieval period were a potpourri of Shinto *kami* and Buddhist *bodhisattva* with interchangeable identities and powers. While villagers held festivals in honor of agricultural deities, warlords and other samurai supported and worshipped gods who could provide succor in battle. The most famous of these gods is Hachiman, the War God. The Minamoto, a great samurai family who established the first military government at Kamakura appealed to its protection. Support of religious institutions was one of the fundamental duties of local samurai landlords. The fact that all but one of the charges against Shingen cite his failure to support established ritual shows that character of one major form of medieval religious practice, the cyclical ritual of agrarian society.

Kenshin was a devout Buddhist, and remained single throughout his life. Luis Frois, the Jesuit missionary who lived in Japan from 1564 to

1587, wrote that Shingen too had taken the tonsure and led a priestly life. It may be true that Shingen liked monastic trappings, but his heart was bound to affairs of state. He could never have given up the hunt, the battle, or the romance for a purely religious life. His attitude toward religion was divided into matters of personal faith and political policy. Religion, in the form of Zen and Confucian training, was essential to prepare the samurai to be a good soldier and public administrator. In the form of ritual, it was essential to control the peasants of governed territories. Shingen was basically conservative, hoping to preserve at least the religious aspect of the medieval order. Oda Nobunaga, who conquered all Japan a decade after Shingen's death, was an iconoclast, never hesitating to crush the Buddhist temples which opposed him with brutal force. Under Nobunaga's protection the Jesuits were able to continue their missionary work. One wonders what would have been the fate of the foreigners at the hands of a less ruthless, but equally ambitious, warlord. If Shingen had lived but a few years longer? .... the historian may ask the question, but his early death at fifty-three left only a few contenders in the arena where the course of history was decided.

Takeda Shingen: The Man and his Age

People are bound to history, and history to them.

from *Notes from a Native Son*
by James Baldwin

Takeda Shingen was born in 1521, the first son of Takeda Nobutora's principal wife. Although little is known of his childhood, his appearance on the political scene upon his coming of age in 1536 was so dramatic that his character and life are fairly well documented from that time. As a child he was shunned by his overbearing father, and once it became clear to him that a younger brother might be selected by Nobutora as his successor, Shingen took action. In 1541, in league with a group of dissatisfied retainers, he ousted his father and exiled him to Suruga, lying just south of Kai. After taking the reins of government, he stepped up the pace of his war machine on the provincial and "foreign" fronts. His career thereafter was recorded with fear and admiration, in degrees only a great military leader can command. His rivalry with Uesugi Kenshin, his relationships with numerous women, and his passion for poetry and calligraphy became legends during his lifetime. When he died in 1573, the powerful eastern warlords who had faced the Kai daimyo in battle joined in mourning his untimely death. It is said that Uesugi Kenshin prohibited samurai of his castletown in Echigo from hearing music for three days. A rival of more recent date, the man destined to fulfil Shingen's ambitions to rule all Japan, Tokugawa Ieyasu, joined in lamenting Takeda's death.

He praised Shingen as a fine archer and soldier. From the man who had just been soundly defeated at Mikatagahara in Tôtômi Province by Shingen, the praise reflects a sense of military comradery among the warlords. By the 1570s, their number had dwindled considerably. At Mikatagahara, the last of the major daimyo faced their rivals. Oda Nobunaga, Tokugawa Ieyasu and Takeda Shingen joined battle. Shingen defeated the two allies, and was pressing a new attack on Ieyasu at Hamamatsu Castle when he died.

Shingen's reputation with women, as with weapons, matched his father's. His two principal wives, Lady Uesugi and Lady Sanjô, and three mistresses, Ladies Yugawa, Suwa, and Nezu, were far outnumbered by the ladies whom he knew equally intimately, but to whom he was tied less formally. It is probable that the Lord of Kai had at least twenty or thirty such mistresses. He admitted paternity of seven sons and five daughters, and the maternity of several is not recorded. The system of "marriage alliance" has been used in the twentieth century to guarantee financial stability and efficient transfer of capital among the elite. Medieval warlords used the system for another purpose. Interested solely in strengthening the bonds of military and political alliances, the warlords traded sisters and daughters off in the hopes of creating familial ties to bind otherwise unstable relationships. In 1553, at the age of thirteen, Shingen was affianced by his father to the daughter of the Uesugi castellan of Kawagoe, the fortress which had held sway over all of eastern Japan during the late fifteenth century. Ten years later the rising star among the eastern warlords, Hôjô Ujiyasu (1515-71), defeated Uesugi in an attack on Kawagoe. Later, Shingen lost no time in arranging the marriage of one of his daughters to Ujiyasu's son, Ujimasa (1538-90).

Not long after his first wife died, Shingen held his coming of age ceremony in Kai. Many of the leading courtiers of Kyoto elite society came to offer felicitations. The celebration of coming of age dates from the Nara period, when boys between the ages of twelve and sixteen first wore adult formal apparel, shaved their hair and donned caps signifying rank in the aristocracy. They were given a new personal name, and one Chinese character of that name was granted by a godfather-style protector who held high rank at Court. In the middle ages the ceremony was conducted by samurai as well, for they had come to hold a plethora of courtly titles during the medieval period. By the sixteenth century, courtiers from Kyoto had to seek protection from powerful warlords in the provinces. Sanjô Kinyori, retired *Dainagon,* was one of the illustrious members of Shingen's ceremonial party. It was then that the boy changed his childhood name Tarô for his adult name Harunobu, having been granted the first character, *haru,* by the Shogun himself, Ashikaga Yoshiharu. Many years later, Harunobu took the Buddhist name Shingen by which he is now known. Along with his name, he received titles and ranks of the nominal central government. He was appointed to lower fifth rank, minor grade, and received the title of Honorary Governor of Shinano Province.

Shingen went one step further in taking on the accouterments of elite society. It seems that Sanjô Kinyori brought along his beautiful and talented daughter when he arrived to offer his congratulations to the young Takeda. Sanjô was one of the few intimates of the next Shogun Ashikaga Yoshiteru (1536-65). One of his daughters was married to Hosokawa Harumoto, and another to the Chief Abbot of the Buddhist stronghold at Honganji. The opportunity for an alliance with Sanjô was not missed by the Takeda. The elegant Lady Sanjô and Takeda Shingen were soon married. It is said that Lady Sanjô was extremely influential in transforming her provincial husband, "the monkey from Kai," into the literate cultivated gentleman he wanted so much to become. During the following years, as he juggled war and poetry contests, she was his most helpful advisor. Her family's political connections also served Shingen well throughout his career.

No matter how essential Lady Sanjô was in his strategy to conquer all of Japan, Shingen was obviously not worried about risking her jealous wrath in establishing one mistress after another at his capital. The popular histories of the age often contrast Lady Sanjô's strong will with the sweetness and simplicity of Lady Nezu, the astonishing beauty of Lady Yugawa, and the young and tragic Lady Suwa. The story of Shingen's relationship with Lady Suwa is very much in keeping with Shingen's character and the morality of the age.

In 1542 Shingen entered Suwa district aided by retainers of the local samurai leader, Suwa Yorishige. Yorishige, caught in a pincer attack, retreated to a fortress in his district. Shingen pretended to conclude a peace agreement with Yorishige, and invited him to Kai's capital, Fuchû. There, after marrying Yorishige's daughter, he forced the hapless Suwa to commit ritual suicide. Suwa district was divided, with half of the territory granted to Shingen's generals and half to Takatô Yoritsugu. Later Yoritsugu became disgruntled, unsatisfied with his portion, and rebelled against the Takeda. Shingen responded by supporting the successor of Suwa Yorishige in battle against his old retainer, and regained control of the entire district. While her father and brother suffered at the whim of

Shingen's political strategy, the young Lady Suwa lived at the capital facing the jealousy of three higher-ranking women. But years later, when her son Katsuyori succeeded Shingen in 1573, her position was instantly reversed. She displaced even Lady Sanjô from the seat of house politics.

Due to the highly political nature of marriage throughout Japanese history, it has been considered normal for men (and, in the early period, for women as well) to seek love from other relationships. Shingen was not atypical in this respect. During the medieval period, at the palaces of the Muromachi Bakufu Shogun, warlords found affection from young men as well. Men, in the company of men, developed patronage relationships. Temple acolytes, dancers, singers, *nô* performers, all found favor with lords in the advancement of their arts. It was in the Age of Strife, that *bushidô*, "the Way of the Samurai," came to stress preparedness for death above all other warrior virtues. Homosexual love was one expression of the tie between such men who had committed themselves to death. There are many examples of lifelong friendships founded upon this tie.

At twenty two, Shingen took the son of a prosperous cultivator into his service. The boy, then only sixteen, was the lover and constant companion of Shingen throughout his life. Some twenty years after their friendship commenced, this man, Kôsaka Danjô, commanded the rearguard forces which saved Shingen at Kawanakajima in 1561.

Although the deeds of his personal life are impressive enough in themselves, the full range of Takeda Shingen's life and character fit an image of a medieval man in search of the future. Shingen was a great politician, who understood that people formed government. His death in 1573 deprived the country of the one leader with credentials in the old order who had an acute appreciation of the needs of the new social order.

Unifiers of Japan

Nobunaga, Hideyoshi, and Ieyasu

by

BILLY J. CODY

In the Muromachi period (1338-1573), the constable lords (*shugo daimyô*) of the several provinces found it necessary to live in Kyoto in order to protect their interests in the capital and to participate in the central government. For this reason they entrusted the administration of their domains to deputies called *shugo dai* who actually resided in the provinces. These deputies and other leading vassals of the constable created their own military organizations and formed alliances among themselves as well as with other military families in their area, enabling them to increase their power at the expense of their lord who was away in Kyoto. Deputies and powerful local warriors competed with one another to strengthen their own positions and weakened the power of the constable family. Activities of this sort reached a tumultuous level at the time of the Ônin War (1467-77).

The Ônin conflict drew the constable lords into a quagmire of contention that led to wholesale war on the provincial level, and to even greater opportunities for their deputies and other warriors living on the land to expand their bases of power. The inauguration of the Ônin battles gave rise to a century of war called the *sengoku jidai* or "The Age of the Country at War." Many vassals emerged from this warfare far stronger than did their lords, and whenever possible, they sought to overthrow them.

The action of overthrowing one's lord and taking his place is called *gekokujô.* Oda Nobunaga was a master of *gekokujô*. His family was a low ranking branch of the Oda clan whose higher ranking members held the position of deputy to the Shiba family. Nobunaga trod the path of *gekokujô* from this obscure origin to become the greatest lord in the land.

Overthrowing one's lord, however, did not constitute a denial of the

Oda Nobunaga; Chôkôji Temple(Toyota, Aichi Prefecture)

concept of a hierarchical system or the lord-vassal relationship. Having successfully attained the position of lord, the newly risen daimyo had to maintain himself and prevent his own retainers from overthrowing him. Confronted with this problem, Nobunaga sought a remedy in the political and moral concepts of Confucianism. In particular, it was the Neo-Confucian ideal of absolute subordination of the vassal to his lord that he tried to instill in his followers. This is symbolized in his strict prohibition of his vassals' sleeping with their feet pointing in the direction of Nobunaga. Nobunaga's ability to force his vassals to accept this kind of autocratic domination, however, was due far more to the persuasiveness of real military power than it was to the allure of abstract ideals.

Oda Nobunaga was born in central Japan in 1534 at Nagoya castle in the province of Owari. Today Nagoya is one of Japan's foremost cities but at that time its population was quite small, and the castle of Nobunaga's family could hardly be called large. Indeed, compared to the castles belonging to the Oda clan, the size of Nagoya castle indicates that the strength of Nobunaga's family was so slight that they were unlikely to have played a major role even in the affairs of the clan.

It was only in the lifetime of Nobunaga's father, Nobuhide, that the family began its drive to prominence. Nobuhide was one of the very few in

Owari who was able to resist the pressure of strong and influential warriors from the surrounding provinces, such as Matsudaira Kiyoyasu of Mikawa, Imagawa Yoshimoto of Suruga, and Saitô Dôsan of Mino. Nobuhide further extended his power base when he overthrew Oda Toshisada who was head of the Oda clan and deputy for the Shiba family. From that time on he set his sights on becoming something more than just the strongest member of the Oda clan, and strove to carve out as much new territory as he could. He incorporated as many warriors as possible into his own organization, suppressed decisively any signs of internal resistance to his authority, and came to administer two-thirds of Owari when he died of illness in 1549.

Seizing the opportunity offered by Nobuhide's death, malcontent warriors of the Oda clan mounted a vigorous attack on the fifteen-year-old Nobunaga who had succeeded to his father's position. Contrary to the expectations of his attackers, he resisted them skillfully, and destroyed the Oda families living in Matsuda and Fukada. The degree of hostility felt by these members of the clan toward Nobunaga is demonstrated by the fact that they enlisted the aid of their traditional enemy, Imagawa Yoshimoto, in their attack on him. Indeed it appears that Imagawa encouraged this assault on Nobunaga. Had Nobunaga been defeated with his aid, there is little doubt that Imagawa would have incorporated the Oda territory into that of his own, or at the very least would have been able to influence internal matters there considerably.

In 1554 Nobunaga followed up his victory with an offense against Oda Hironobu who was the adopted son of Toshisada and an ally of Imagawa; he defeated Hironobu and forced him to commit ritual suicide. He then plotted and carried out the murder of his uncle Nobumitsu. Nobumitsu was sympathetic to Nobunaga's ambitions, cooperated extensively with him, and had been one of Nobunaga's major commanders in the campaign against Hironobu, but Nobunaga feared his power more than he valued his services and had him killed.

The deepest tragedy that occurred within Nobunaga's family grew out of the fear and jealousy he had of his younger brother, Nobuyuki. The vassals of the family held Nobuyuki in high esteem. This alone would have been enough to invite Nobunaga's distrust, but in addition their mother, who was excessively fond of Nobuyuki, plotted to make him head of the family. The chances of such a plot succeeding were good, for there were many Oda followers who chafed under the heavy hand of Nobunaga; but before any of these plans could bear fruit, Nobunaga counterattacked in 1556.

Though Nobuyuki's popularity with the retainers of the family continued unabated, he himself strove to avoid any association with a second attempt at rebellion. This was not sufficient to satisfy Nobunaga, however, and in the following year he sent a message to Nobuyuki saying, "I have been taken with a sudden illness and my life is imperilled; come to me so that I can turn over to you headship of the family." Receiving this, Nobuyuki vacated his own castle, was captured by Nobunaga's forces, and was compelled to take his life by ritual suicide.

Nobuhiro, an older brother by a different mother, fearing the same fate, submitted unconditionally to Nobunaga. In 1560 Nobunaga attacked and killed Nobukata, the sole remaining Oda who could endanger him. By the age of twenty-seven he had consolidated his rule over Owari and eliminated any threats to that rule from within the family.

Having pacified Owari, Nobunaga immediately set about defending his domain from incursions by rivals in neighboring provinces. A confrontation with Imagawa Yoshimoto who had formented such devastating dissention within his clan was not long in coming, and Nobunaga put in motion various plans to entrap and injure him.

In one such plan, a follower of Imagawa by the name of Tobe Shinzaemon played the starring role. He reported in detail to Imagawa on matters in Owari, and Nobunaga, knowing of this, decided to turn this to his own advantage. He had his secretary practice duplicating Shinzaemon's writing for more than a year, and then had him forge a letter, the contents of which indicated that Shinzaemon had betrayed Imagawa and gone over to Nobunaga. Thinking this letter genuine, Imagawa ordered the beheading of the hapless Shinzaemon.

Nobunaga, on the basis on his own intelligence, knew that Imagawa's forces lacked strong organization, and that if he could kill Imagawa, he could deal a lethal blow to his army. Nobunaga calculated that this would cause the followers of Imagawa to quarrel over the appointment of his successor and destroy their effectiveness as a fighting force. Hence, ruses were devised to disrupt and impair Imagawa's ability to gather intelligence. After seriously deceiving him by means of such strategems, Imagawa was lured into entering Owari quite unprepared for the adversary who awaited him.

Nobunaga at this time had at his command no more than three or four thousand troops, but he trapped the force of twenty-five thousand led by Imagawa in a surprise attack on their camp at Okehazama. While the enemy celebrated an earlier victory with food and drink, and were confused by a sudden thunder storm, Nobunaga struck from behind one of the ridges that formed the gorge. On Nobunaga's instructions, his soldiers made for Imagawa whose head they took. His death marked not only the end of his dreams of taking the capital, but also the beginning of the rapid decline of his family as Nobunaga had foreseen.

The success achieved on the battlefield of Okehazama greatly raised the prestige of Nobunaga, and it is clear that from this time he sought to unify the country under his own rule, a goal that had been the ideal of so many warrior lords of the Sengoku period. Chief among the steps that Nobunaga took to realize this goal was the military pact that he concluded with Tokugawa Ieyasu, who heretofore had been one of Imagawa's rear-vassals and had distinguished himself in the invasion of Owari. They agreed to divide the country into two spheres of influence that left Oda free to rule west of Owari and Tokugawa to rule the east. Both pledged to refrain from attacking the other. This pact lasted until the death of Nobunaga twenty years later, and was never broken, a singularly remarkable achievement considering the treachery of the age.

The alliance held great significance for Nobunaga in that it was a highly effective shield that protected him from attacks of powerful families who dominated areas to the east of him. In particular, he was able to avoid making an enemy of the powerful Takeda Shingen, whose favor he gained gradually by honoring him with rare and precious gifts. Shingen himself harbored the ambition of uniting the country and ultimately had to confront Nobunaga's power, but because he was locked into a deadly struggle with the Hôjô and Uesugi families, he welcomed these overtures from Nobunaga.

In 1565 Nobunaga brought about the marriage of his niece to Takeda Katsuyori, the son of Shingen, but because she died immediately after giving birth to a son, it was agreed in 1567 that Shingen's daughter would marry Nobunaga's heir, Nobutada. Alliances based on marriage were a common political device of the time, but their purpose went well beyond the normal limits of political policy. Wives were military hostages, and were utilized to implement military objectives. Nobunaga pledged his younger sister, O-Ichi no Kata, to Asai Nagamasa whose family dominated Ômi Province, one of the two provinces, that stood between Owari and Kyoto. This measure was directed in large part against the Saitô family who controlled the province of Mino that lay between the domains of Oda and Asai. In this way, Nobunaga cut the Saitô off from the rear before he carried out their destruction in the following year, 1567. He annexed their territory and was then in a fine position to march on the capital.

The efficacy of alliances based on marriage, however, was extremely temporary, for in general they were responses to specific needs, such as the protection of a domain from invasion or the acquisition of military aid. When they no longer filled these particular needs, they were dissolved,

Tokugawa Ieyasu (left) and Toyotomi Hideyoshi; Kôdaiji Temple (Kyoto)

and the union involving O-Ichi no Kata was no exception to this rule. Ultimately, there was no alternative to the use of naked military might.

The number of troops at the command of Nobunaga, compared to those available to such foes as Imagawa, Takeda, and Uesugi, was relatively small. But in spite of the superior numbers of his enemies, Nobunaga was for the most part successful against them. The primary reason for this was that he introduced new tactics and new weapons.

One of the most important innovations Nobunaga made in combat was the use of tight formations of troops in order to maximize the effectiveness of the long lance. The length of the lance used by Japanese armies before the time of Nobunaga was generally about fourteen feet. Each lancer brandished his weapon in all directions, which required that he keep a distance of sixty feet between him and his fellow soldiers on all four sides. He thrust his lance at any enemy who entered this space. Hence, lancers lined up in formation presented large gaps. Lancers were highly skilled, and acquiring the necessary proficiency was arduous and difficult for the non-specialist.

Nobunaga altered the traditional alignment of lancers by forming them into tight lines that thrust their weapons to the front and rear. He equipped them with lances that were either eighteen or twenty-one feet in length. These tightly formed lancers were highly lethal in dealing with any enemy who entered the area in front of their weapons, and were far more effective than their earlier counterparts. What is more, even relatively inexperienced and poorly trained personnel, namely peasants, could learn these lance techniques and use them well.

Nobunaga also used troops armed with guns and utilized fully their destructive power. Tradition has it that guns first came to Japan via the Portuguese who arrived at the small island of Tanegashima in southern

Japan in 1543. The guns of this age were matchlocks fired after inserting powder and slug into the front of the barrel, and consequently loading was time-consuming and delayed the process of firing a second shot. For this reason, guns were chiefly used in surprise attacks.

Nobunaga's use of the gun went well beyond its employment in surprise attacks, and was a devastating innovation. He arranged his troops armed with guns in alternating rows that fired in rotation. After the first line fired and was bending down to reload, a second and third was firing or preparing to fire. This permitted him to maintain a continuous barrage that was formidable. Nobunaga's use of this technique at the battle of Nagashino where he crushed Takeda Katsuyori is particularly well known.

Oda also improved on previous uses of guns in Japan when he utilized them in his attack from the sea on Ishiyama Honganji, a fortress temple surrounded by ramparts and moats near present day Osaka. He mounted cannon on armoured ships. Japanese ships before this time easily caught fire, but Nobunaga adopted the practice of covering large wooden ships with iron plate.

In this fashion Nobunaga introduced the use of new tactics and weapons in Japan, but even more important than this was his realization that warfare was entering a new age. Previously, individual soldier had fought individual soldier, but combat had now entered the age of confrontations between massive groups. For this new form of military operation, skilled and charismatic commanders were indispensable. An extremely important factor in the success of Oda was his ability to attract to his standard and command the loyalty of such fine generals as Toyotomi Hideyoshi, Shibata Katsuie, and Akechi Mitsuhide.

Warriors, especially those from the east, generally came from military organizations comprised of varying numbers of small family units and their vassals. Thus the individual groups, despite their acknowledgement of the authority of the same lord, aggressively competed for power among themselves. This was especially true of those warriors comprising the forces of the Takeda and Imagawa families. Depending on whether or not they thought it to be in their own interest, vassals would either fight for their lord, remain neutral, or fight against him. Inevitably, military success was dependent on the degree to which these individual units felt that they could steal a march on their rivals. Often it was easier to organize masterless warriors and members of robber bands than former vassals.

The situation in Owari was ripe for the organization of groups that stood outside the traditional network of warrior relationships. The social order in Owari was breaking down and changing due to the many years of warfare within the Oda clan. Many vassals had lost their lords and become masterless warriors who managed to live by robbery and extortion. This was possible in Owari because it straddled the transportation route between eastern and western Japan. Nobunaga's leading general, Toyotomi Hideyoshi, himself of humble origin, was particularly successful in organizing these bands.

Hideyoshi's association with outcast elements served Nobunaga well as was demonstrated in Nobunaga's last battle with the Saitô family over control of Mino Province. Between the domains of the Oda and the Saitô flowed the tempestuous Kiso River, and victory would go to whichever side first crossed the river and built a fort. The fort was necessary to protect the soldiers as they crossed the river, an enterprise that was physically taxing and time-consuming. Hideyoshi collected the lumber needed to construct the fort, but rather than cross the river at the point where the two armies were poised, he crossed at a ford and came down the other side. Within three days, while a third of his men held off the Saitô army, the rest of them transported the lumber and built the fort. Had his troops been of the traditional type, they would have refused to haul the lumber and build the fort. They would have insisted, instead, on fighting the enemy directly. Had they done so, their chances of succeeding would have been slim.

Shibata Katsuie also contributed greatly to the successful completion of Nobunaga's undertakings. He was originally a vassal of Nobuyuki, Nobunaga's younger brother, but at the time of the plot involving Nobuyuki, Katsuie informed Nobunaga of its details. From this time on he was highly trusted by Nobunaga. Though it was originally Nobunaga's idea to use the longer lances that played a large role in the battle against Oda clan members in 1554, it was Katsuie who actually commanded the troops.

In addition to Hideyoshi and Katsuie, Akechi Mitsuhide rendered great service to Nobunaga, though he was far more successful in the political sphere than in the military. Mitsuhide's political maneuvering paved the way for Nobunaga's entry into the capital.

The military leader bent on unifying the country would naturally feel compelled to control the capital. Kyoto had been the administrative and economic center of Japan since 794. To the Japanese people of the time, the importance of Kyoto as the seat of political authority and the home of the emperor from whom political legitimacy flowed was of vast significance. In spite of the fact that central political authority collapsed with the waning of the power of the shogun and the concomitant increase of warfare among provincial barons, the idea of one central political authority in Japan never died. In order to give his authority legitimacy, the man who would unite the country had to control the capital.

The justification for Nobunaga's entry into Kyoto had its origin in the events that led to the assassination of the thirteenth Ashikaga shogun, Yoshiteru, in 1565. Members of the Miyoshi clan and Matsunaga Hisahide murdered Yoshiteru and at the same time attempted to kill his younger brother, Yoshiaki. Hosokawa Fujitaka saved Yoshiaki but he was no match for the assassins, and Yoshiaki was forced into exile. He wandered in poverty and distress through the provinces adjacent to Kyoto until Asakura Yoshikage of Echizen Province came to his aid.

Nobunaga, cognizant of the significance of Yoshiaki's plight, invited him to newly conquered Mino, and agreed to assist Yoshiaki in becoming shogun. He accompanied Yoshiaki to Kyoto, cast down Ashikaga Yoshihide who had been installed as fourteenth shogun by the assassins of Yoshiteru, and established Yoshiaki in his place. Akechi Mitsuhide conducted the negotiations between Yoshiaki and Nobunaga. Mitsuhide was a retainer of the Asakura and a close friend of Hosokawa Fujitaka who brought Yoshiaki to Nobunaga.

Oda drove the Miyoshi from Kyoto and subdued Matsunaga. He then requested that the Court grant Yoshiaki the title of shogun and went on to set up a government in which he acted as the shogun's agent. The Court cooperated extensively with Nobunaga for so far as it was concerned anyone who restored the lands of the imperial family and of the aristocrats, was to be welcomed, and Nobunaga promised to do just that. In addition, contrary to the opinion of many, his troops were well disciplined and left the capital in peace. Nobunaga's offer of assistance must have been received favorably by Yoshiaki, since he lacked completely the resources to make himself shogun. Hence, the relationship among the three parties – the Court, the shogun, and Nobunaga – promised to promote the interests of all.

Yoshiaki dreamed of the restoration of the glory of his ancestors, however, and actively endeavored to escape the role of puppet. It was inevitable that the fragile dreams of Yoshiaki would collide with the realities of Nobunaga's power.

In 1569, a year after Yoshiaki became Shogun, he clashed with Nobunaga over the question of pacifying Shikoku, one of Japan's four main islands. Nobunaga wanted to bring this area under his control as the next step in his process of unifying the country, but Yoshiaki wanted to delegate this responsibility to the Môri family, one of the most powerful families in western Japan. Were they to succeed, Yoshiaki could look to them to balance the power of Nobunaga and thereby achieve a greater degree of independence.

The Court was disturbed at the prospect of a breach between Yoshiaki and Nobunaga, and dispatched imperial emissaries several times in 1570 to soothe the latter. Nobunaga seized this opportunity to deliver an ultimatum to Yoshiaki. There were five demands in this ultimatum, the substance of which was that the shogun refrain from issuing directives without the permission of Nobunaga, and that Nobunaga was to be authorized to issue orders in the shogun's name without first securing Yoshiaki's permission. Since there was no hope of the Môri coming to his aid, Yoshiaki had no choice but to submit to this humiliation, and was frozen out of participation in the very government that bore his name.

Yoshiaki did not accept this fate passively, but instead plotted rebellion. He turned first to the Asakura family which had sheltered him when he was driven from Kyoto. They answered his call, and together with Oda's brother-in-law, Asai Nagamasa, drove Nobunaga from Kyoto. While Hideyoshi protected him at the rear, Nobunaga retreated to Mino, barely escaping annihilation. Later Tokugawa Ieyasu joined him, and their two armies took the offense against Asakura and Asai with some success. They were unable to exterminate them, however, and this encouraged Nobunaga's other foes to rise up against him.

Chief among Oda's enemies and one of the most dangerous was the temple citadel of Ishiyama Honganji, the back of which was protected by the sea. It was extremely difficult to attack for it was built on marshy ground and could easily be supplied by sea should it be subjected to a seige. Its greatest strength, however, was its defenders, who were adherents of a new and popular form of Buddhism that imbued them with deep religious fervor. Adherents of this new faith from throughout the country came to the aid of the Honganji whenever it was threatened, and it had long defied the greatest warriors of the era.

Rebellions of peasants who professed this religion and acknowledged the authority of the Ishiyama Honganji were called *Ikkô-ikki.* Nobunaga had been harassed by the sect for many years and fought ruthlessly against them. They resisted fiercely and were so successful that they were able to immobilize Akechi Mitsuhide's offensive in northern Japan, and kill Nobunaga's younger brother, Nobuoki, at Nagashima in Ise Province.

The Ishiyama Honganji enjoyed a very close relationship with the Takeda family. The wife of Kennyo, head of the temple, was the younger sister of Takeda Shingen's wife, and this was but one manifestation of the relationship. The Takeda family joined the war against Nobunaga as did the militant and powerful temple on Mount Hiei, the Enryakuji, which overlooked Kyoto.

The allied armies of Asai and Asakura fled to the Enryakuji upon their defeat by Nobunaga and Ieyasu, and then launched a counterattack with the aid of the temple's obstreperous warrior-monks. Nobunaga responded with a vigorous attack of his own, and put this ancient and famous temple to the torch. Those soldiers, priests, and children who sought to flee the savage flames were caught and beheaded. This broke the power of the great temple which had intimidated the capital for centuries, but it further inflamed the resolve of the anti-Nobunaga groups.

The unexpected death of Takeda Shingen in 1573 brought relief from a powerful enemy and a brief respite for the forces of Nobunaga, whose strength was failing from fighting battle after battle. Not only did the morale of the Takeda army plunge with the loss of their outstanding leader, but along with this, Nobunaga was able at long last to destroy Asakura and Asai. This permitted him to concentrate his attention on dealing with the Honganji.

In the ninth month of 1574 Nobunaga finally suppressed the Ikkô-ikki rebellion of Nagashima and in the tenth month of the next year he conquered the Ishiyama Honganji itself. In the meantime he had also put down an Ikkô-ikki uprising in Echizen, and had defeated Takeda Katsuyori in the battle referred to earlier. 1576 was a year of peace for Nobunaga and he set about building a magnificent castle. In 1577 Hideyoshi subdued Harima Province and Akechi delivered the province of Tanba into the hands of Nobunaga, but it was not long before he began to suffer reverses in his attempts to bring western Japan under his domination.

The Môri family stubbornly resisted Nobunaga's advance into their sphere of influence, and in 1582 stalled Hideyoshi's offensive, and then began to press him severely. Nobunaga himself was preparing to lead a huge army to the relief of Hideyoshi when he was treacherously attacked in Kyoto's Honnôji temple by Akechi Mitsuhide. Here ended Nobunaga's drive to unite the sixty-six provinces of Japan, and though his enterprise was interrupted by death, twenty-six provinces were clearly in his hands.

Nobunaga died as he had lived, in cruelty and betrayal, and to this day his name conjures up these images. He burned the Enryakuji and its inhabitants, slaughtered those who surrendered to him, and freely utilized starvation tactics during seiges. In his campaign against the Nagashima Ikkô-ikki he shot those who fled the fortress and burned to death the twenty thousand who did not. It is said that he exterminated over forty-thousand persons in his campaign against the Ikkô-ikki in Echizen, and thousands more lost their lives resisting him. Even in an age infamous for its carnage, Nobunaga's actions stand out vividly and are a severe judgment of his character.

Not only were his measures extreme and excessive, they often endangered the implementation of his own goals. They may even have led directly to his death. Though Akechi Mitsuhide's actual motives for betraying Nobunaga may never be fully known, certainly revenge was no small factor. He had sent his mother-in-law to Nobunaga's enemies as hostage, and when Nobunaga annihilated them, she had not been spared. Akechi was not the only follower of Nobunaga to see his services repaid with disappointment and despair. Even the great Tokugawa Ieyasu whose good will was vital to the interests of Nobunaga lost a son to him. Ieyasu's son, Nobuyasu, married Nobunaga's daughter only to die because Nobunaga feared him as a rival to his own far less competent son Nobutada.

In his defense it should be noted that many of his measures were in response to the nature of his adversaries, and in keeping with the climate of the times. Enryakuji temple had defied the civilian and military leaders of the country for centuries, and Nobunaga's methods, while extreme, may have been the only way to deal with it. The vehemence with which he campaigned against the partisans of the Ishiyama Honganji was partly in reaction to the tenacity with which they fought him, and partly out of revenge for the death of his brother. His purpose was not the extermination of their religion, but only its political and military role. The death of Tokugawa Nobuyasu was necessary to the protection of the Oda family in the next generation.

Nobunaga was a highly innovative and skilled tactician. He displayed a generous attitude toward Christianity and deep interest in things foreign. His patronage of the arts was lavish and produced a rich harvest. And while Nobunaga's character can be interpreted in various ways, there is no disputing his significance as a figure in Japanese history. This significance lies in the political, social, and economic policies he developed and implemented, and these are of two sorts.

The first is Nobunaga's political policy regarding trade and transportation. Central to this was his policy of *rakuichi rakuza* or open markets and free trade. He freed merchants from having to seek the protection of aristocrats, temples and shrines, and permitted them to conduct business without membership in monopolistic guilds as had been the case for centuries. This encouraged the development of commercial enterprises which made important advances under relatively free market conditions.

Nobunaga also promoted the stabilization of currency. Previously, both high quality coins minted in China and coins of poor shape and quality minted privately in Japan had circulated in the markets. What is more, the Japanese coins were of various grades, which complicated the process of assigning exchange ratios. This caused confusion in the market place and disturbed business activity. Nobunaga decided to rectify this situation by establishing a strict and fixed rate of exchange that was determined according to whether the coins were Japanese or Chinese. At the same time he minted coins, which marked the first time since 958 that a public authority issued currency.

In addition Nobunaga removed the toll barriers on roads which had been erected by aristocrats, temples, and shrines to make up for the income they had lost when the warrior class usurped their manors. There were places where toll barriers were so numerous that they were only 500 feet apart. All this greatly increased the expense of transporting goods and impaired economic activity.

No less significant than Nobunaga's trade policies was his policy regarding agricultural villages. In the territories he controlled, he implemented the *kenchi* system, a kind of cadastral survey that indicated ownership, tenancy, size, quality, and yield of the land. When compared to that carried out later on a national scale by Hideyoshi, Nobunaga's survey was extremely primitive. Yet this step marked an important stage in the rationalization of land use and the rights to its produce, and brought an end to the ancient *shôen* system.

In conjunction with this policy, Nobunaga maintained that his followers held land at his discretion, and that he had the final right to dispose of it as he wished. Warriors could no longer hold rights to particular pieces of land and could be moved from area to area as their lord pleased. The idea of divorcing a warrior from the land he inherited was unthinkable in the early part of Nobunaga's life, but by the time of his death it was already in practice and came into common use under Hideyoshi and Ieyasu.

Cadastral surveys and the collection of swords from the peasants are closely associated with the policies of Hideyoshi, and though the latter was his own innovation, this measure too was inspired by Nobunaga. He ordered Shibata Katsuie to implement a sword hunt in Echizen Province in 1576. At the very least the separation of farmer and warrior and the establishment of the class system of the Tokugawa period find their roots here.

Nobunaga's dream of unifying Japan was interrupted at midpoint, but his ideas lived on and were developed by Hideyoshi and Ieyasu. It was Oda Nobunaga who blazed the trail that led to the prosperity of the Momoyama and Tokugawa periods, and it is this which marks his lasting contribution to the development of the Japanese nation and secures his place in history.

Tea Master in a Time of War

Sen no Rikyû

by

JOHN FREEMAN

Sen no Rikyû is well known to scholars of the Muromachi period as the synthesizer of *chadô,* literally the "Way of Tea," but more commonly known as the "tea ceremony." However, the "tea ceremony" itself constitutes only a portion of the Way of Tea as Rikyû conceived it. To Rikyû the Way of Tea was a way of life, an almost religious pursuit which drew its philosophical bases from many sources: Taoism, Confucianism, Zen Buddhism, and even Christianity. In its early stages *chadô* developed mainly at the hands of Zen monks. It was Sen no Rikyû who realized the full potential of tea as a way of life for people of all levels of society, from merchants to aristocrats.

Sen no Rikyû was born in the city of Sakai, which was the main commercial center of the Muromachi period and one of the most powerful cities as well. He who was destined to be the leader of the world of tea, was born Tanaka Yoshirô, son of Tanaka Yohei, a merchant who owned and operated warehouses. Extant records of this period are few, however it is believed that the Tanaka family was quite wealthy. Sakai was probably the most important city in sixteenth-century Japan due to its trade with China. Such commercial cities were removed from the direct control of both feudal and religious power, and as a result enjoyed a degree of political autonomy. Sakai was ruled by a citizen's council and provided its own military protection. It was in this atmosphere that Rikyû grew up, and the merchants of the city who were accomplished in tea were thus quite influential. The strength and individualism of Rikyû's personality no doubt reflect this influence.

Rikyû's grandfather, Sen'ami, was an official cultural advisor to the eighth Ashikaga Shogun, Yoshimasa. Rikyû seems not to have used his family name Tanaka, but took the name "Sen" from his grandfather's name, probably because of his interest in cultural pursuits rather than in business. In most records his name is recorded as Sen Sôeki or Sen no Rikyû. Until his early twenties, when Rikyû left the city of Sakai to study under Takeno Jô-ô, he had been using the name Yoshirô. From this point on the name Sôeki appears in various diary entries of tea gatherings, and this signature is still preserved in some of his writings. How the name Sôeki originated is not clear. It may have been given him at the time of his tonsure as a lay priest, or merely as a recognition of his progress in Zen. Many Zen monks took names beginning with the character "Sô," and there is little doubt that the use of this character by men of tea evolved from Zen practice. At a very young age he entered the world of tea as a follower of Kitamuki Dôchin, who had studied the elegant Chinese style of tea as developed by Nôami in the Higashiyama period.

It is not known who devised the name Rikyû, and there are numerous theories as to why the name was chosen. Most theories focus on the year 1585 (Rikyû was by then sixty-four years old), when Hideyoshi served tea in the imperial palace. Hideyoshi had petitioned the Emperor in 1584 to allow him to present tea. He was to use his own treasured utensils, and the petition also included the name Sôeki. However it appears that protocol of the period demanded that Sôeki could not enter the imperial palace with a common name that had no official status. The Emperor Ôgimachi's approval of Hideyoshi's petition includes the title "Rikyû Koji" thus permitting Sôeki to serve tea. "Koji" was a title given to Zen priests who have attained enlightenment. The name Rikyû seems to connote the unimportance of fame and wealth, a fitting name to accompany his title. One theory states that this name and title were used only for this occasion, but it is the name by which he would come to be known to people in all sectors of Japanese society. Other theories date the name of Rikyû earlier, but most extant records and letters refer to the mid-1580s.

The first record of Sen no Rikyû and his association with tea is in the *Matsuya kaiki,* records kept by three generations of the Matsuya family of Nara, in an entry for the thirteenth day of the second month of 1537; he was only sixteen years old at the time. We know too that at this time Rikyû took Zen training at the Daitokuji complex of Rinzai Zen temples. When he was nineteen, in the eventful year 1540, his father Yohei died, he took the names Sôeki and Hôsensai, and he entered the training of Takeno Jô-ô, the supreme man of tea at that time.

From this time forward we see the development of the blend of styles that marks Rikyû's individual taste in tea. The training he had received under his early teacher Dôchin was in the elegant Ashikaga style,

Sen no Rikyû; Urasenke Foundation of Kyoto (or Konnichian)

characterized by the fine wares of China and the refined *shoin* style of architecture. His new teacher Jô-ô advocated the use of simple, unpretentious implements and the *sôan,* or "grass hut" style of tea room. Rikyû's genius lay in his talent for combining the rough and the refined, the ostentatious and the understated, the aristocratic and the common. At a time when the warrior class was rising to the peak of its power and the merchant class had come to wield considerable economic power, Rikyû developed a style of tea through which these men could display their wealth and power without having to import treasures from China. As with so many of the monuments of Japanese culture, Rikyû's style skilfully assimilated elements from abroad and transformed them into something truly Japanese.

Something of the nature of his innovations may be seen in a few illustrations. Before the time of Rikyû, tea was mostly a pastime for the upper strata of society, and social distinctions were very important. Hence the basin holding the water to purify the guest who entered the room for tea was placed at such a height that bending was unnecessary and their extravagant kimono would not be soiled. Rikyû introduced a style of stone basin that could only be reached by crouching – a humbling posture that brings the participant closer to nature. It must have taken considerable daring to try such a variation with a "noble" guest invited for tea; daring, because the physical lowering of the body for anyone of higher social position was considered demeaning.

This same characteristic is evident in the *nijiriguchi,* the small crawl-in entrance to the tearoom that is only two-and-a-half feet square. Until Rikyû's time this entrance was used only by the retainers of a lord or those of low status. The lord, of course, entered the room in a standing position in keeping with his social status. Rikyû, however, made the *nijiriguchi* the *only* guest entrance to the room. To enter a room in this manner is a truly humbling experience. No matter what social position or rank a guest possessed he had to shed it and leave it in the outer world. This act of metamorphosis brought the guest into the pure unadulterated equality of tea. Rikyû himself felt that the world of tea should stand apart from political and social entanglements. This could only be achieved by one who possessed courage and innovative talent to challenge the norms of society.

Rikyû's renown came to the attention of numerous men of power. Oda Nobunaga, who came to control the free city in the late 1560s, was well aware that Sakai was an important source of supplies for his war campaigns. Sakai was also the place where Christian missionaries landed to spread their religion, which Nobunaga favored owing to his bitter opposition to the Buddhist establishments that threatened his power. Nobunaga became very interested in the Way of Tea as handed down by Jô-ô to such famous merchant families and men of tea as Imai Sôkyû, Tsuda Sôkyû, and Sen no Rikyû. It is interesting to note that the Tsuda family were also members of the council which governed the city of Sakai, and probably other council members were also men of tea. However, it was Rikyû whom he favored most. In 1575 Rikyû was made Nobunaga's personal tea master. He attained this supreme position in tea at the age of fifty-four.

The importance of the Way of Tea amongst the warrior class at this time is illustrated in Nobunaga's practice of presenting tea utensils as rewards for valor. Many of these utensils were requisitioned from Sakai, and the retainer who was charged with this duty was Kinoshita Tôkichirô, later to be known as Toyotomi Hideyoshi, who in this capacity became acquainted with important men of tea. During Nobunaga's many military campaigns Hideyoshi steadily rose in rank until his lord was killed.

It is said that when Nobunaga was killed in the fire of Honnôji temple on the second day of the sixth month of 1582 thirty-six famous tea utensils of the earlier Higashiyama culture were also destroyed. It is interesting to note, too, that Akechi Mitsuhide, whose short-lived revolution eliminated Nobunaga, was also well versed in tea. However, when he was about to die at Hideyoshi's hand, he handed over his tea utensils willingly so they at least would survive.

Toyotomi Hideyoshi finally gained supreme control at the end of the Muromachi period. He had become acquainted with the Way of Tea through his service as retainer to Nobunaga; and to the same three masters with whom Nobunaga had studied Hideyoshi granted fiefs of 3,000 *koku,* and he made Rikyû his personal tea master.

Hideyoshi himself was a strong personality who had also challenged the former strict rules of class nobility and rose from peasant to military ruler of the country in a short span of time. Hideyoshi came from quite a different background from Rikyû. It is true he had a garish golden tearoom; but there must also have been a part of Hideyoshi's nature that was in tune with Rikyû's simpler taste; and under Rikyû this taste was nurtured. It was in 1578 that, in recognition of his achievements,Hideyoshi was given the rare privilege of serving tea to Nobunaga. Hideyoshi may have met Rikyû well before this time through his acquaintances in tea in Sakai, but there is no boubt that the strong relationship between these two men developed through Nobunaga.

Not too long after, an interesting letter was written by Hideyoshi to Rikyû which is still preserved in the Nagahama Hachimangû shrine on the east shore of Lake Biwa. The content of the letter is of little importance, but the greeting is. The letter begins "Lord Sôeki," a title usually reserved for the aristocrats or high-ranking officials, and is thus indicative of the high regard in which Rikyû was held by Hideyoshi. Hideyoshi came to power in 1582, and Rikyû was appointed his personal tea master in the fifth month of 1583. An unusual bond developed between them.

Hideyoshi's strong likes and dislikes are well-known. He built a golden tearoom with all gold utensils, but he also possessed the simple rough wares and had tea in grass huts. In one service of tea Hideyoshi was offended by the host, Yamanoue Sôji, over a trivial matter, and had him permanently exiled after removing his nose. Such was the temperament of Rikyû's lord. In his response to this temperament we see an interesting aspect of Rikyû's personality. For instance, when the priest Kokei of the Daitokuji, a long-time friend and Zen teacher of Rikyû, was exiled by Hideyoshi, Rikyû held a farewell tea gathering for him. Rikyû possessed one of his master's treasured scrolls, written by one of the most respected calligraphers of the time, and he used this scroll at the farewell tea gathering for Kokei. This act could have cost him his life. However, Rikyû took the chance.

The strong personalities of Hideyoshi and Rikyû were pitted against each other during most of their relationship, because Hideyoshi first became interested in tea as a means to personal and political ends, whereas Rikyû was more interested in the spiritual aspect of tea.

Rikyû used the Way of Tea to bring people together in harmony, but Hideyoshi – though he may have been able to appreciate this fact – used his tea master for other purposes as well. Most of his generals had been instructed in tea, and the small tea gatherings provided an excellent means for Hideyoshi to convey messages to them through Rikyû. As a consequence, Rikyû attained a position of importance among Hideyoshi's retainers as well as with the lord himself. Moreover, many of the materials of war were procured through the merchants of Sakai, and this also served to strengthen the importance of Rikyû.

Something of a climax in the relationship between Hideyoshi and Rikyû was reached in 1587. In the first month of that year the Great Osaka Tea Gathering was held at Osaka castle, which Hideyoshi had built four years earlier. In the past small gatherings had been the rule, but this event was on a grand scale. Feudal lords were invited and tea was served by various tea masters; Rikyû was in charge. This trend was carried a step further in the tenth month of the same year at the Great Kitano Tea Gathering in Kyoto. It was a most impressive event, again with Rikyû in charge. In this case anyone was allowed to set up a stall or hut for serving tea. Eight hundred people from all walks of life, from everywhere in the country came. Everyone was welcome, but the atmosphere was one of simplicity. No one was to go beyond his means to serve tea because this was opposed to the spirit of tea. Rikyû had in effect liberated tea from the ancient chains of social structure; for the first time tea was made available to every class of Japanese society.

Rikyû had gained Hideyoshi's respect as well as his confidence, but this in turn made him subject to the jealousy of others. Rikyû's personality was such that he resisted those opposing him, and this trait might have been the very seed of the rift that developed between Hideyoshi and Rikyû. Early in 1591 he was ordered to commit ritual disembowelment by his lord. The reasons behind the incident are unclear; the theories are numerous. These range from Rikyû's planning to poison Hideyoshi with a bowl of tea to his refusal to give his daughter to his lord. Few records remain. However, the incident may well have been generated by a simple wooden statue. In 1589 the priest Kokei had been pardoned by Hideyoshi through Rikyû's intervention and had returned to his position as Abbot of one of the Daitokuji temples. He asked Rikyû for help in raising funds for repairs to the temple, and the main gate was rebuilt through Rikyû's generosity. As a token of gratitude, a wooden statue in the likeness of Rikyû was to be placed in the upper part of the gate. This meant that Hideyoshi and other lords and aristocrats would have to walk beneath the statue of Rikyû. Even more insulting than this, however, was the style in which the statue was carved. It was common practice for wooden statues of enlightened or venerated figures to be placed in the upper part of such gates, however, they were invariably depicted in a crosslegged position after the fashion of the Buddha. Rikyû's statue depicted him in a standing position. Hideyoshi could be cruel in his whims, as when he cut off the nose of Yamanoue Sôji and banished him for a trifling breach of etiquette. The statue incident was probably the climax of many occasions when the strong personalities of lord and teacher-servant clashed. The head of the statue was removed and displayed at a bridge on the day Rikyû died. It was later returned to the family and is presently in the possession of Sen Sôshitsu, fifteenth generation descendant of Sen no Rikyû.

It is impossible to delineate all of the factors that might have contributed to Hideyoshi's decision. Hideyoshi was planning to relinquish his title as military ruler, and several contending factions developed around Hideyoshi's sons and other relatives. Since Rikyû's influence might have swayed Hideyoshi's decision in this matter, he may have earned the wrath of other men of power. Rikyû seems too to have opposed Hideyoshi's plan to conquer Ming China, and some of his anger at being refused free passage through Korea may have been directed at Rikyû. Then again, Hideyoshi may have associated Rikyû with the threat of Christianity. Rikyû dedicated tea in a Christian mass, as we know from João Rodrigues' *História da igreja do Japão.* Of Rikyû's select group of seven disciples more than half were known to be Christians, one of whom was banished to the Philippines. Some of Hideyoshi's military staff members were also converts. Through tea, Rikyû had influence with these Christian lords, and Christian elements remain a part of tea. Rikyû always tried to remain apart from the political dealings of his lord, but Hideyoshi's fanatic desire for supremacy, in one way or another, brought about the death of the leader of the world of tea.

It is impossible in a brief essay to deal with every aspect of the life and work of so important a figure. His aesthetics, his influence upon present-day culture, his relationship to other important cultural figures – all deserve special treatment. In time, however, Rikyû may become as well known in the West as he is in Japan; for now, four centuries later, we find his descendants emulating Rikyû in promoting the Way of Tea, this time on an international scale. Such efforts will inevitably enhance Rikyû's reputation, for as Benjamin Franklin has said in another context, "whoever learns about his deeds remembers longest the man who did them."

Fate of a Christian Daimyo

Takayama Ukon

by

DIEGO PACHECO

In the summer of 1587 Toyotomi Hideyoshi was at the peak of his career. In a brilliant campaign he had obtained the submission of the whole of Kyushu and was now encamped in a pine grove at Hakozaki, near the city of Hakata. There he planned the reconstruction of that city and divided out the conquered territories among his allies. It was there also that on the night of 24 July he placed his red seal on an edict which would later have far-reaching effects on the history of Japan, for this proscription of Christianity was the foundation of all the other decrees which would eventually terminate in the Era of the Closed Country (*sakoku jidai*). On that same night Hideyoshi took drastic steps against a man on account of his Christian faith – a man who had always served him loyally and who up to that time had been bound to the ruler by ties of personal friendship.

The man was Justo Takayama Ukon, daimyo of Akashi, and he calmly declined to obey the order of Hideyoshi and all that he represented. The paths followed by the two men now abruptly diverged; the two men would later renew contact, but the spiritual gap between them would ever increase. This was not the first confrontation with authority in which Takayama Ukon had risked his life and career, for in a remarkable way the three great generals who brought about the unification of Japan in the sixteenth century had all felt the need at different times to confront Ukon with a decisive choice. On all three occasions Ukon followed the dictates of his own conscience; in a society which was rapidly veering toward servile submission to a central authority, Ukon chose the path of personal liberty.

Takayama Ukon was born in 1552, the year in which St. Francis Xavier

Takayama Ukon (Takatsuki, Osaka)

died; his death took place in 1615, only a few months after Tokugawa Ieyasu had expelled the Christian missionaries from Japan. Ukon therefore witnessed practically the whole period of missionary endeavor during the so-called Christian Century of Japan. At times in this period other men perhaps played more important roles that he did, but no other person occupied such an enduring and crucial place in the history of the Japanese church. His first feat of arms took place when he was sixteen years old and was in the service of Yoshiaki, the last of the Ashikaga shoguns; only a few months after Ukon's death, Hideyori, son and heir of Hideyoshi, perished in the flames of Osaka Castle. Brought up in the last years of the Era of Civil Wars (*sengoku jidai*), Ukon was to experience at first hand the turbulent but stimulating Azuchi-Momoyama age; he withdrew from the scene when the Tokugawa regime consolidated its central power. Takayama Ukon not only witnessed but also took part in this era of political dynamism, violence, and, at the same time, refined artistic taste and searching for authentic human values. Almost from the very beginning of his career he was under the undeniable influence of men of forceful personality; but he chose to follow his own path, although this independent course of action would inevitably bring him into open conflict with these same men.

Throughout Ukon's rich and complex life it is possible to discern three basic roles which must be studied and understood to gain a genuine insight into this controversial figure. These are his roles as a political and military leader, as an accomplished master of the tea ceremony, and as an outstanding Christian apostle. In his infancy and childhood the first role occupied all his energies; he was, above all, a samurai. His father, Takayama Hida no Kami, was lord of the small castle at Sawa in the Yamato mountains to the south of Nara. His father had few retainers and was not wealthy, but he was closely connected by bonds of service and family with one of the outstanding warriors of the time. And it was through Wada Koremasa that the Takayama, father and son, came into contact with Ashikaga Yoshiaki and with the Shogun's champion, Oda Nobunaga. This last contact was of great importance because it was through Nobunaga that Ukon was able to obtain military and political power.

Ukon was baptized a Christian in Sawa Castle in 1563 when he was eleven years old. Only three years earlier Gaspar Vilela, a Portuguese missionary, had finally managed to begin work in Miyako, present-day Kyoto; Buddhist opposition had brought about his expulsion from the capital, but Vilela was both a tough and dedicated personality and he established himself in the nearby city of Sakai where he continued to engage in apostolic work. Ukon's father was a fervent Buddhist and decided to put an end to the activities of the bothersome foreigner by inviting him to defend his doctrines in public debate. Vilela was unable to accept the challenge, but his place was taken by an engaging character, Brother Lorenzo, a half-blind former *biwahôshi,* or wandering minstrel, who had been converted to Christianity in Yamaguchi by Xavier himself. Ukon's father and his companions were won over by Lorenzo's eloquent exposition of the Christian faith, and shortly afterwards the Takayama family was baptized in Sawa Castle; Hida no Kami received the baptismal name of Dario, while Ukon, his eldest son, was thenceforth to be known as Justo.

But there was then little opportunity for extended religious instruction, for central Japan was embroiled in wars and Wada Koremasa was killed in an ambush while in the service of Nobunaga. The Takayama family thereupon became the vassals of his successor, Wada Korenaga, lord of the castle at Takatsuki, which occupied a strategic position between Kyoto and Osaka and was located in the territory of the powerful daimyo Araki Murashige. Only a year after the death of his friend and protector Wada Koremasa, Ukon went through the traumatic experience of saving his own life at the cost of the life of his immediate lord. A completely different character from his father, Wada Korenaga was jealous of the prestige enjoyed by the Takayama and decided to eliminate the family. The plot reached the ears of the intended victims, who thereupon conferred with Araki Murashige and were given permission to act in their own defense. On the night of 12 April 1573 Korenaga and fifteen retainers were gathered in the dining hall in Takatsuki Castle. The two Takayama and their followers arrived, and in the midst of the ensuing festivities Korenaga attacked Ukon. The latter, however, had been forewarned and he not only defended himself ably but managed to wound Korenaga, who thereupon fled from the scene. The castle was burned down and Korenaga died a few days later. Ukon was seriously wounded in the fighting. Oda Nobunaga transferred the fief of Takatsuki to Dario, but the old warrior had had enough; wishing to devote his remaining days to religious and charitable works, he soon entrusted the territory to his son. As a result, Takayama Ukon began his political career at the age of twenty-one.

Ukon's supervision of the rebuilding of the castle revealed his military talent, while his administration of the fief showed that he was a wise and able leader, and glowing references to him are found in contemporary Jesuit letters written back to Europe. Both Nobunaga and Araki expressed their appreciation of his qualities, and by the time Ukon was twenty-five years of age a brilliant career seemed assured. The somewhat Machiavellian character Araki Murashige was more of a politician than a warrior. He was ambitious for power, and yet at the same time he displayed a deep appreciation for the aesthetic ideals of the tea ceremony. It is quite possible that Ukon came to enjoy the tea ceremony in sessions held in Araki's castle; certainly it was there that he first met the great tea master, Sen no Rikyû, one of the men who was to exert a deep influence on him. But as already noted, Takatsuki was located between Kyoto and Osaka, and so Ukon occupied territory lying between Nobunaga's and Araki's strongholds. When Araki rose up against Nobunaga in 1578 in an attempt to wrest supreme power for himself, Ukon, as both samurai and Christian, was faced with the first great test of his life.

Ukon had advised Araki not to side with Nobunaga's rivals, and as token of his sincerity he had handed over his sister and her son as hostages. But Araki had finally decided on war and Ukon, as his vassal, was obliged to follow him. But Nobunaga had shrewdly realized just how much Ukon's faith meant for the young warrior. The ruler therefore turned his attention to the missionaries stationed in central Japan and sent the most famous of them, the Italian Organtino Soldi, to Takatsuki with a message in which he threatened to execute the missionaries and destroy the churches in his domains unless Ukon handed over his castle. On his part Organtino also applied pressure, declaring that Ukon could not support Araki with a good conscience as the war initiated by the latter was not just. But there were also strong and suasive reasons on the other side – Ukon's honor as a samurai, his father's resolute resistance to surrendering the castle, and the danger to which the hostages would be exposed. Ukon wished to follow the voice of his conscience and this inclined him to open the gates of the castle. At the same time he realized the grave consequences of this action, and he spent hours in agonized prayer seeking a solution to the problem.

Ukon finally hit on a solution which he believed would not violate the code of samurai behavior. Having shaved his head as a sign of retirement from the world, he presented himself before Nobunaga without weapons or companions so that the ruler could do with him what he wished. The results of this gesture exceeded all his expectations. Now able to enter Takatsuki without difficulty, Nobunaga pardoned Ukon and his retainers and, once the campaign had been successfully concluded, not only restored to Ukon his former territory but also increased the size of his fief. Further, Araki did not harm the hostages. There was, however, a deeper result which was not immediately visible: the crisis had brought about a change in Ukon and had freed him from all fear and ambition. Thenceforth Ukon was a new man. Historians would later debate whether his decision had been the wisest course of action to take, but Ukon had sacrificed everything for his religious beliefs and knew that his faith was the only thing that could not be taken away from him. In the future he would live for his faith alone.

From the human point of view, the following four years were the most rewarding period in Ukon's life. Many of his vassals were converted to Christianity; he received the Jesuit Visitor Alessandro Valignano at Takatsuki as an honored guest; he collaborated in the founding of a seminary at Azuchi, Nobunaga's new city on the banks of Lake Biwa; he advised Nobunaga in the arrangements for the famous parade in Kyoto at which the Emperor himself was present; his circle of friends grew steadily. But on 21 June 1582 Nobunaga was assassinated at Honnôji in the capital; the traitor, Akechi Mitsuhide, tried to win Ukon over to his cause, but Ukon, then in Takatsuki, was not persuaded by his promises. He set out to do battle against Akechi and played an important role in the fighting at Yamazaki. From that time on Ukon's fate was inextricably linked to Toyotomi Hideyoshi, who in masterly fashion declared himself protector of the young Sanbôshi (Hidenobu), Nobunaga's grandson, and thus took over supreme power. In his dealings with Hideyoshi, Ukon never hesitated to show that his Christian faith came first in his life. During Nobunaga's funeral ceremony, organized by Hideyoshi, Ukon conspicuously remained in his place when it was his turn to offer incense at the Buddhist altar. Hideyoshi studiously pretended not to notice the incident.

Later, in the battle of Shizugatake, Ukon experienced the bitterness of defeat; he himself was wounded in the fighting and he lost many retainers. But Hideyoshi continued to show his favor and once more his revenues were increased. There followed years of strenuous activity, and the campaigns in which he took part in Hideyoshi's service would be enough to fill the life of any one man. He continued to practice the tea ceremony and was already considered one of the most outstanding disciples of Sen no Rikyû. He sometimes met in the tea room with just two companions – Hideyoshi and Rikyû. Various of his friends received baptism – Kuroda Yoshitaka, Gamô Ujisato, Makimura Chôbei – under his influence and persuasion. The territory of Takatsuki could be considered practically a Christian fief and Ukon used his position to aid the propagation of Christianity in other regions of the country. When Hideyoshi, following the example of Nobunaga, offered a site in his new castle at Osaka for the former Azuchi Seminary, then located in Takatsuki, Ukon assumed responsibility for its construction. He also paid the expenses involved in transferring the beautiful church of Okayama all the way to Osaka. The daimyo, the Christian, and the aesthete – all three basic roles of his life were now in complete harmony. He followed a path of personal self-fulfillment, honor, and progress in virtue. In writing of this period, the missionary Gregorio de Cespedes attributes to Hideyoshi the eulogy: "No one else can possibly emulate Ukon's great purity of life."

In 1585 Hideyoshi reshuffled the fiefs under his sway and transferred Ukon from Takatsuki to Akashi. The new territory bordered the Inland Sea and its annual revenues amounted to 60,000 *koku,* but Ukon was not given the opportunity to settle there for long. Following the invasion of Shikoku and the campaigns against the Negoro monks at Kii, Ukon looked forward to a period of peace and rest, but just at that time emissaries visited Hideyoshi at Osaka and asked him to intervene in Kyushu. Yet another man to talk with Hideyoshi in his newly constructed castle at Osaka was Gaspar Coelho, the superior of the Jesuit missionaries, and his visit marked the height of Ukon's material prosperity and also perhaps the turning point in his fortunes. Coelho was a fervent, possibly naive, man and his self-confidence prompted him to meddle in political affairs. As a result he had adopted a policy which would lead to the petition he presented to Hideyoshi on 4 May 1586, asking the ruler to intervene in Kyushu and put down the Shimazu clan; for his part, Coelho promised to use his influence in support of Hideyoshi.

At the end of that year the advance armies commanded by Hashiba Hidenaga and Kuroda Yoshitaka invaded Kyushu. In the following spring Hideyoshi, who had just received the title of *Kanpaku,* went down to

Kyushu in person with the rest of his army. Ukon was a member of his personal guard and accompanied the ruler throughout the campaign. Once the operations were over, Hideyoshi set up camp in the Hachiman shrine in Hakozaki, and there he planned the reconstruction of Hakata and the distribution of the newly won territories among his allies. An optimistic Coelho sailed from Nagasaki to Hakata in his decorated ship to offer his congratulations to the ruler on his successful campaign. Ukon had already warned the missionary that he feared there might be a change in the fortunes of the Japanese church and had suggested that it might be prudent to present the handsome ship to Hideyoshi as a gift. But Coelho had ignored both the warning and the suggestion, and by the time he was awakened from his dreams at dawn on 25 July it was too late to remedy matters.

It is said that the messenger who carried Hideyoshi's ultimatum to Ukon on the same night was none other than Sen no Rikyû, who at that period was one of the ruler's most trusted advisers. The message contained a command and a question: if Ukon wished to continue in the service of the *Kanpaku,* he must abandon his Christian faith; and why had he so encouraged Christianity among his vassals in Takatsuki? This time Ukon had no need to ask the advice of Organtino, much less of Coelho, or to ponder for long on the reply which Rikyû, most likely secretly approving of its contents, carried back to Hideyoshi. The reply was simple: Ukon was willing to obey the ruler in everything that concerned his status as a vassal, but he would not abandon his faith; as regards his work of evangelizing his former retainers, he considered this to have been his most outstanding achievement. On the following day, while an agitated Coelho vainly searched for somebody to intercede for him, Ukon serenely bade farewell to his friends and left Hakozaki. He was now an exile, a man enjoying no civil rights in Japanese society; but at the same time he was also a man who was truly liberated. He was soon to be found in the company of Organtino on the small island of Shôdoshima in the domains of Augustin Konishi Yukinaga, whom they helped to overcome a crisis of faith brought about by Hideyoshi's decree. When Konishi received a large territory in Kyushu as fief, Ukon went down to Kyushu again and took the opportunity of meeting Coelho in the small town of Kazusa in the Shimabara Peninsula. His purpose was not to complain or criticize what had happened but to discuss the future of the church in Japan. He then retired to the Jesuit novitiate in Arie to spend some days in prayer. Now that his political and military ambitions had come to nothing. his religious fervor increased and he even began to consider the possibility of entering the religious life. For some years he hesitated about taking this step, but Valignano settled his doubts once and for all by showing him where his vocation lay. Even Hideyoshi unintentionally helped to indicate his future mission when he entrusted Ukon to the care of Maeda Toshiie, daimyo of Kaga.

In 1592 Hideyoshi summoned Ukon to Nagoya Castle in Hizen, where the ruler had set up his headquarters for the invasion of Korea; only shortly before, his only son, Tsurumatsu, had died, and he had ordered Rikyû to commit suicide. The meeting between Hideyoshi and Ukon was an interesting one; the ruler did not return to Ukon his former territories or his rank as daimyo, but he re-admitted him into his close circle of friends for the tea ceremony and other pastimes. On his part Ukon showed no trace of resentment and accepted the friendship that was offered to him, at the same time continuing to practice his religion openly. He invited the missionaries at Nagasaki to go to Nagoya and look after the spiritual needs of the Christian samurai, and when the opportunity presented itself, he himself went to Nagasaki to bid farewell to Valignano, who was returning to Macao. According to Luis Frois, the contemporary Jesuit chronicler, Ukon's favorite pastime at this time was the tea ceremony, and among his guests at these sessions was sometimes to be found Tokugawa Ieyasu, the powerful lord of the eight Kantô provinces.

Ukon spent the next few years occupied in intense apostolic activity in Osaka and Kyoto, and the years 1595 and 1596 witnessed a notable expansion of Christianity in these two centers, especially among the young samurai and sons of the great lords. Among those baptized were Oda Hidenobu, grandson of Nobunaga; Hachisuka Iemasa, daimyo of Awa; and various others. This surge of Christian activity brought Ukon into confrontation with the monk Seyakuin Zensô, Hideyoshi's physician and adviser. The ruler was now in an obvious state of decline; the war with Korea had been a disastrous failure and he had condemned to death Hidetsugu, his nephew and heir. The renewed confrontation with Christianity culminated in the deaths of the twenty-six Martyrs on their crosses at Nagasaki on 5 February 1597. Ukon's name had headed the first list of Christians drawn up in Kyoto and Osaka, but the governor, Ishida Mitsunari, wishing to avoid open persecution as much as he could, had crossed out Ukon's name and shortened the list to a minimum. On this occasion Ukon went to bid farewell to his lord, Maeda Toshiie, and as a parting gift presented him with a valuable tea bowl.

A year later Hideyoshi was dead. Ukon returned to Maeda's domain and there in Kanazawa he spent sixteen fruitful years. The new daimyo, Maeda Toshinaga, was his personal friend – even, in some respects, his disciple – and he allowed Ukon to work freely; had it not been for fear of Tokugawa Ieyasu, it is possible that Toshinaga himself would have become a

Christian. In these favorable circumstances Ukon was able partially to rebuild his family fortunes. He received an income of 40,000 *koku* and his daughter was married to Yokoyama Yasuharu, son of Maeda's principal governor. Ukon himself was one of Maeda's leading vassals and advisers, and he served his lord loyally. In 1600 he served in the war under Maeda's banner but with scant success; he left proof of his military skill, however, in the reconstruction of the daimyo's castle residence at Takaoka. Using the artistic name Minaminobô, Ukon continued his activity as tea master and formed a school at Kanazawa. Some of his former retainers and other Christian exiles, such as Naitô Tokuan and Ukita Kyûkan, took refuge in his lands in Noto Peninsula, where Ukon had built two churches; from 1604 a Jesuit priest and brother resided permanently in the church, also built by Ukon, in Kanazawa. These were years of serene spiritual progress. It is quite possible that the Portuguese missionary João Rodrigues, "The Interpreter," had this particular period in mind when he notes in his fine chapter on the tea ceremony that Ukon used to withdraw to the tea room and there was accustomed "to stay a long time in intense and silent prayer."

Rodrigues' remark seems to indicate something more than an advanced spiritual life. The three fundamental roles of Ukon's life – the man of power, aesthete, and Christian – were combined in harmony, and there in the confined space of the tea room he was at peace with himself and enjoyed an inner freedom. His serenity was never more to be disturbed, even when, for example, within the space of a few months in 1608 he lost his mother, eldest son and daughter-in-law. But the increasing Christian activity of Ukon had not escaped the notice of Ieyasu, and when the ruler ordered the expulsion of the missionaries in 1614 he paid special attention to this Christian community, exiling its leaders Ukon and Naitô Tokuan along with their families. Other outstanding members of this church were condemned to hard labor in the region of Tsugaru. Ukon's friend and protector, Maeda Toshinaga, had retired from active life and had been succeeded by his younger brother Toshitsune, who was married to a daughter of Tokugawa Hidetada. Toshitsune never really understood Ukon and feared that, on receiving the edict ordering him into exile, mostly likely to be followed by the death sentence, Ukon would take up arms to defend himself. So Toshitsune prepared for fighting, but Ukon hastened to put his mind at rest by sending a message that gave evidence of the evolution of his ideal of a gentleman warrior. The message read, "I do not strive for my salvation with weapons but with patience and humility, in accordance with the doctrine of Jesus Christ which I profess." He further sent the daimyo sixty bars of gold as a gift, "because this year I will not be able to repay with my services the emoluments that I have received." He also presented to his old friend Toshinaga, living in retirement, a valuable tea utensil; for himself, he took with him a small tea utensil that had been made by his master, Sen no Rikyû.

The road to exile was hard. Ukon was accompanied by his wife, daughter, and five grandchildren, and was obliged to cross snow-covered mountains. There were long delays filled with uncertainty. He spent some months in Nagasaki, where he made a spiritual retreat under the direction of the Jesuit Pedro Morejon and collected religious books for future reading. Finally, on 8 November 1614 he sailed from the nearby port of Fukuda in an old ship along with the expelled missionaries. Their destination was Manila. It is related that when news of Ukon's expulsion reached his old friend Hosokawa Tadaoki, daimyo of Kokura, he exclaimed, "Minaminobô has now placed his seal on his life's achievements." Coming from Hosokawa, this praise is significant because, although a personal friend of the missionaries, he had turned persecutor out of fear of Ieyasu.

Ukon was greeted as a hero in Manila, and the Governor, Don Juan de Silva, wished to provide him with an income for the support of his family. But Ukon declined the offer, for he was no longer in a position to offer his services in exchange for the income. There were also other reasons which were not at that time apparent. Perhaps Ukon did not wish to serve a foreign lord. But in any case there was no longer any reason why he should continue the public life that he had led in Japan, and he could now devote himself completely to spiritual matters. After so many years of wars and persecutions, he could now enjoy peace and quiet. With his final sacrifice Ukon had obtained complete inner freedom and had reached the goal of self-liberation. Forty days after reaching Manila, he fell ill and on 5 February (3 February according to some reports) 1615 he gave up his soul in peace at the age of sixty-three. His last words to his grandchildren were an exhortation to stand firm in their Christian faith.

A year later Ieyasu died in Suruga. At the time of his death he was the lord of Japan, but not even Tokugawa Ieyasu had been able to curb the spiritual freedom of Justo Takayama Ukon.

Creators of a New Literature

Saikaku, Bashô, and Chikamatsu

by

CHEN' SHUN-CHEN

The Genroku era (1688-1703), comparatively short though it was, saw a flourishing of the arts that gives it particular importance in Japanese history. Most notably, in the field of literature it witnessed three of the greatest writers in Japanese history working at the height of their powers. They were Matsuo Bashô (1644-94), master of the haiku, the seventeen-syllable Japanese verse form; Ihara Saikaku (1642-93), popular novelist and chronicler of the lives of the merchant class of the day; and the great dramatist Chikamatsu Monzaemon (1653-1724), whose libretti for the Kabuki and for the puppet drama are still frequently performed today.

Two questions occur to one here. The first is, why should three such outstanding figures should have appeared together in the Genroku era? The other question is why they should have appeared not merely in the same age but also in the same area of the country – the Kansai region, centering on Kyoto and Osaka.

Saikaku, it seems, was an Osaka merchant, son of a relatively wealthy business family; but at an early age he handed over care of the business to the firm's head clerk and devoted himself to the study of the haikai. In all probability, his parents had died while he was in his infancy. He seems not merely to have put responsibility for practical matters in the chief clerk's hands, but to have made over the business to him entirely. This suggests difficulties in the family's affairs, and complex factors probably lay behind the fact that Saikaku used his mother's family name, Ihara, rather than his father's name, Hirayama.

Bashô too, having been born at Ueno in the province of Iga (present Mie Prefecture), can justly be called a Kansai man. It is known that he was in the service of Tôdô Yoshitada, head of a branch of the family that ruled

Ihara Saikaku; Collection of Kubo Katsutaka (Uwajima, Ehime Prefecture)

the clan, but much remains unclear as to his career following Yoshitada's death. It is certain that he pursued various scholastic and artistic studies in Kyoto, and it seems likely too that he underwent Buddhist training in Kyoto at one of the five great monasteries of the Rinzai school of Zen. Although a large part of his productive life was spent in Edo, his birth, upbringing, training, and other formative influences marked him indelibly as a Kansai man.

Concerning Chikamatsu's family background there are various theories, but the most plausible holds that he was born in Echizen (present Fukui Prefecture). While still a boy he went to Kyoto with his father and entered the service of a court noble, Ichijô Ekan, who was extremely close to the imperial family. He was only twenty-one, however, when Ekan died. He is said next to have entered the Gonshôji temple in Ômi (present Shiga Prefecture) as a Buddhist novice. Thus his career as a young man resembles that of Bashô, in that both entered Buddhist monasteries following the death of their masters.

The three great men, therefore, are alike not only in sharing the same period and district but also in experiencing major upheavals during their formative years. In the feudal age, to lose one's master was a great blow to the individual concerned. Tôdô Yoshitada had had a taste for haiku, and it is said that it was his influence that first interested the young Bashô in the form. It is also possible, however, that Bashô had already shown a literary bent in his late teens, and that this was what led to his being chosen to serve in the Tôdô family. The same may have been true in the case of Chikamatsu and his employer Ichijô Ekan. Either way, just as Yoshitada, though a member of the Tôdô family, was not head of the clan, so Ekan, despite his being an imperial prince, was only a ninth son of an emperor (in a shogun-dominated age). Neither were very important figures and since both Bashô and Chikamatsu were taken on in a more or less private capacity, the death of their masters necessarily meant the swift loss of their jobs.

When Chikamatsu Monzaemon was fifteen or sixteen, his father is said to have left the Echizen clan and become a *rônin* (masterless samurai), which would have meant a sudden decline in the family's fortunes. Bashô's family, too, was not unacquainted with financial distress; his elder brother is said to have borrowed money from him, and a letter survives in which Bashô presses a pupil for that purpose. In Saikaku's case, as we have seen, the fact that he handed over the family concern to an outsider suggests that though the family may once have been well-off it had since fallen on hard times. It seems safe to assume, in short, that all three men experienced upheavals in their personal circumstances, and consequent economic hardship, during their early maturity.

Their "hardship," of course, was doubtless insignificant compared with the lot of the povert-stricken peasants of the day, but what is important here is that, in their cases, penury came to them as offspring of relatively well-established families. The penury of the peasants, being with them from birth, was to that extent a less soul-searing experience: poverty always hits harder if one has known better times. It was, one suspects, this knowledge of hardship, underlying their other experiences of life, that gave all three artists such a clear-eyed view of the world. To exaggerate slightly, each of them had the toughness of one who, in his own way, has had a glimpse of hell.

Saikaku was born in 1642. Bashô was born two years later, in 1644. Chikamatsu was born nine years later, in 1653. The most important fact to bear in mind in appraising the nature of the age in which they lived is that the battle of Sekigahara had taken place in 1600. In that year, the Tokugawa family established a hegemony over the land that was to last until the Meiji Restoration of 1868. The long years of civil strife were over. The only major conflict that was to occur for almost three centuries was the Shimabara rebellion of 1637, directed at the Tokugawa Shogunate's suppression of Christianity.

A whole era had thus come to a well-defined end in 1600. During the long years of strife man as an individual had been utterly unimportant and dispensable, each fresh burst of conflict engulfing in a short time vast

Matsuo Bashô; Bashô-ô Kinenkan (Ueno, Mie Prefecture)

numbers of human beings, over whose corpses a new political system emerged. Human life was little more than a stepping-stone to power. The conviction, born of experience, that life was brief and of little value accorded well with the doom-laden tones of medieval Buddhism.

Such was the age on whicn the curtain had just descended. And just as the age of civil wars had had its own morality, so the new age of peace naturally developed a new morality to take its place. There were still, of course, plenty of cases of suffering and death, and life continued to be transient. Yet in a majority of cases, "death" now meant the death of an individual. Once peace was re-established, men were no longer crushed in droves, like so many ants, beneath huge and irresistible forces, but could to some extent influence their own lives and deaths by their own efforts. It was only natural that in such an age a new type of art should emerge, an art that sought to throw light on human life as such.

There are aspects of the Genroku era – the shift in values, the rediscovery of man – that remind one of the Renaissance in Europe. In the history of the Tokugawa period, it represents a peak of brilliance. Nowadays, the name "Genroku" is often used in a derogatory sense, as a synonym for frivolity and luxury; but this usage betrays an ignorance of the historical significance of those two qualities. In an age when, after the darkness of war, words gush out again like water from a long-disused tap, it is often frivolity that comes spurting forth first of all. One manifestation of frivolity is wordiness, another whimsicality.

Saikaku's haikai were dubbed *karukuchi kyôku* (comic verse that is glib, or easily produced in large quantities). Sometimes, they were described as "Dutch-style" – probably not so much in the sense of "exotic," as in the sense that to the average Japanese they were noisy chatter, as unintelligible as the language of the European traders of the day. In short, they were odd and they were turned out interminably. In Osaka at the time, the world of haikai was dominated by the old-fashioned, orthodox Teimon style (of the school of Matsunaga Teitoku), and in such circles Saikaku's type of verse must have met with disapproving frowns. He seems to have been aware of the criticism – and to have used it for his own purposes.

There was a fad at the time for what was known as *yakazu haikai.* At the Sanjûsangendô hall of the Myôhôin temple in Kyoto, regular archery competitions were held in which the participants would shoot arrows until they were too exhausted to go on any longer, the winner being the man who succeeded scoring the most hits. This type of contest, known as *yakazu* (number of arrows), was a far cry from the normal atmosphere of Japanese archery, in which the archer draws his bow in a calm, unhurried fashion and releases the arrow only after taking leisurely aim.

This idea was taken over into haikai, and contests known as *yakazu haikai* were held to see who could compose the greatest number of verses in one day. Attended sometimes by thousands of onlookers, they were held in the precincts of shrines or temples; the contestants would declaim their verses, which were set down on paper by the judges. The question was not the quality of the poems but the number.

Yakazu haikai is said to have originated when Saikaku composed one thousand verses in one day as a prayer for the soul of his deceased wife. Originally, no doubt, he intended it as a means of assuaging the sorrow of his loss; but when others came forward and tried to outdo his "record," he was not above taking on the challenge. In this way, the new vogue began.

On the fifth of the sixth month, 1684, when Saikaku was forty-three, he arranged an entertainment in the precincts of the Sumiyoshi shrine at which, in the space of one day and one night, he composed 23,500 verses. The figure – which implies the production of one verse every four seconds for twenty-four hours – seems well-nigh incredible, but the feat was performed before a large crowd of spectators and in the presence of Takarai Kikaku, an eminent haikai poet who had come all the way from Edo, so one can only accept it as fact.

Following this, Saikaku commemorated his feat by taking the pseudonym "Niman'ô" (Sage Twenty-thousand). The episode, nevertheless, shows how little weight he attached to haikai; to turn out twenty-thousand-

Chikamatsu Monzaemon;
Collection of Okada Rihei
(Itami, Hyôgo Prefecture)

odd verses in twenty-four hours is not so much literature as a feat of verbal acrobatics.

The first verse he produced on this occasion runs as follows:

A great number of arrows
To put an end
To the life of haikai.

The phrase "put an end to the life of" probably implies that the record he was about to set would never be broken. But a verse form that relied not on quality but on quantity was fated from the start to vanish rapidly – as art, at least. The whole absurd venture, indeed, may have been Saikaku's private farewell to haikai; at the time, he had already won great public acclaim with his first novel, *The Life of an Amorous Man* (*Kôshoku ichidai otoko*), and its sequel had been published in the fourth month of that same year.

In a literary form as brief as the haikai link, compression is of the essence. Saikaku's talent, however, tended not to the condensed but to the expansive. He himself realized this, yet was uneasy at the time as to whether he could make a successful living in any other way than as a teacher of haikai. The success of *Kôshoku ichidai otoko* resolved this uncertainty, and the performance at the Sumiyoshi shrine can be interpreted as announcing his change of course. Nevertheless, Saikaku's apprenticeship to the haikai had in no sense been a wasted effort. To it, in fact, is attributable the economy of the prose in his stories; the success of his style depends on the effect of haikai training in tightening up the prose of a writer who was by nature prolix.

Another reason for Saikaku's switch to the novel may well have been a desire for the admiration of a larger public. The meager audience of a dozen or so afforded by a poetry gathering was hardly likely to satisfy him for long. Even when the linked verse that was composed at such gatherings was published, readership was limited. As the *yakazu haikai* episode suggests, he seems to have enjoyed the applause of the masses, and the popular novelettes of the kind known as *ukiyo-zôshi* offered the prospect of a far wider following.

He was not alone in this desire to reach the man-in-the-street. It was shared both by Bashô, who was keenly interested in popularizing the composition of haiku and the organization of haiku societies, and by Chikamatsu, whose dramatic writing was always aimed at producing a popular "hit."

The public, in the Genroku era, could no longer be dismissed as the "ignorant masses." The memories of an earlier age of bloodshed, handed down from the preceding generation, had combined with the influences of more than half a century of peace to foster a new depth of outlook, one manifestation of which was a sharper critical judgment. It was obviously a desirable thing for an author to win the applause of such an audience – and the louder the applause the better; ingrained in the Kansai outlook was a sensible appreciation of the benefits of material gain; the "noble penury" of the samurai – so admired in Edo – tended to be dismissed contemptuously as spiritual window-dressing.

So far, I have emphasized the points that the three men had in common. Of their differences, one of the most striking is the absence in Bashô and Chikamatsu – at least on the surface – of the whimsicality that is so marked in Saikaku. Saikaku, again, is the only one of the three who, in examining the world from various angles, places emphasis on "cleverness" (the Japanese term *saikaku*, having the same pronunciation as the author's name, conveys a sense of "resourcefulness in achieving material gain"). It was an instance of his own "cleverness," perhaps, that he should have made such conscious use of his eccentricity in enhancing his own reputation. The crowd that gathered at the Sumiyoshi shrine to stare at Saikaku composing his verses doubtless went home and told its families and friends all about it. The story spread from mouth to mouth, and Saikaku found himself in steadily increasing demand as an author.

Though Saikaku might be prepared to make a spectacle of himself for such an end, Bashô and Chikamatsu were not; both of them may well have longed for popular fame in just the same way, but their only means of achieving it was through their works; personal showmanship was impossible.

One might explain this difference by noting that though all three were Kansai men, only Saikaku came from the merchant class. More relevant, though, would seem to be the fact that Saikaku alone had had no experience of monastic life during his youth. There seems little doubt – although there is no definite proof – that Bashô was for a time a novice in one of the five great Zen monasteries of Kyoto. Still more certain is the fact that Chikamatsu entered the Gonshôji temple. Granted that the effect of monastic life in character formation will vary vastly from individual to individual, it is impossible that it should leave no mark at all. Either way, it is significant that Saikaku, alone among the three, received no formal religious education. This difference in early training is surely more important in considering the nature of their literature than any difference in social status between samurai and merchant. In both Bashô and Chikamatsu, one senses the attitude that once things reach a certain pass they are in the hands of the Buddha. In Saikaku there is no such attitude. His pen forges steadily ahead, portraying only what the eye can see; there is no room in his works for shadows. It is ironic, perhaps, that although Saikaku might appear to be the most cheerful of the three, any portrait of him as a human being would reveal the darkest shadows hovering in the background.

Bashô's life had a stoic aspect that recalls a monk in training at a Buddhist monastery. Yet his school of haiku had more than two thousand members, and a picture was even painted showing him surrounded by his followers, rather in the manner of pictures of the dying Buddha surrounded by his devoted disciples. The haiku originated as the first three lines of a sequence of "linked verse"; such linked verses were customarily composed at gatherings of poetry lovers, and the haiku thus had from the outset an eminently "sociable" nature. In such a field, it was only natural that like minds should gather together. Even so, most of the members of Bashô's school were scattered about the country, and the kind of crowd that Saikaku drew to the Sumiyoshi shrine would have been impossible. Bashô himself, despite the large number of his followers, could still compose the following verse:

On the path I follow
No other passes;
This autumn twilight.

The very number of his followers was also a source of trouble to him, and the perpetual squabbles between them must have made him feel as if he were the head of a quarrelsome family. Yet it meant, at least, that wherever his travels about the country took him, there were always followers to welcome him and make him feel at home.

The most fortunate of the three men where human acquaintances were concerned was Chikamatsu. The success of his Kabuki libretti with the public was due in large measure to the cooperation of the celebrated actor Sakata Tôjûrô. The art of the two men was complementary, and their collaboration was further enhanced by the fact that Kabuki was in the process of moving out of its stylized shell towards a new realism. In the theater, the audience seems always to demand a certain relevance to "the times," and Chikamatsu was particularly sensitive to this demand.

In writing for the puppet drama, Chikamatsu was likewise fortunate in the collaboration of a brilliant reciter known as Takemoto Gidayû. Following Tôjûrô's death in 1709, Chikamatsu stopped writing for the Kabuki and concentrated on the puppet drama (another sign of how close had been the relationship between him and the actor). Gidayû in turn died in 1714, but Chikamatsu was to live on for another ten years and produce his last works for Gidayû II.

Chikamatsu was lucky not only in having able collaborators in his work but in being able, simply by going to the Takemotoza theater in Osaka, to experience directly the audiences' reactions to his drama. Saikaku had to content himself with hearing the public's reaction indirectly via his publisher, but Chikamatsu was in direct contact with them.

Mention of Chikamatsu automatically calls to mind the "double suicide" theme, so frequently does it occur in his works. His stories in fact were taken, with certain modifications, from incidents that had happened in real life. Thus the incident in question was already the talk of the town even before he wrote the libretto, and the play as it was performed must have had a particular relevance for the audience. The love-suicide theme, presenting as it does humanity in an extreme situation where the essentials of its nature are stripped of their veils and thrown into sharp relief, evoked an unfailing emotional response.

One further difference between the three men is that whereas Saikaku's novels and Chikamatsu's plays were directed at the average citizen, Bashô's poems were not. Moreover, although Saikaku's and Chikamatsu's work contains frequent references to Chinese and Japanese history and displays considerable classical learning, the context of the whole always makes them readily intelligible. In Bashô's short verse forms, however, the elements derived from the classics have a rather esoteric air.

In *The Narrow Road to the Deep North* (*Oku no hosomichi*), Bashô's poetic account of his travels in northern Honshu, there occurs the following haiku:

The passing spring:
A bird cries;
Tears in the eyes of the fish.

The expression "a bird cries" was suggested by the following passage in Tu Fu's "Spring Longing":

The flowers shed tears at the passing of the seasons,
The birds cry their distress at the sorrow of parting.

The reader, thus, is expected to be acquainted with Tu Fu. And what, precisely, is the significance of the "tears in the eyes of the fish? " The expression "eyes of the fish" is used in three different ways in the Chinese classics. First, (since fish have no eyelids) it signifies eternally wakeful eyes. Secondly, it signifies the spurious – something that, like a fish's eye, resembles a pearl yet is not. Thirdly, it signifies a highly prized breed of horse whose eyes were supposed to be moist and glistening like those of a fish. Obviously, Bashô does not use the phrase in its second sense. Possibly he is referring to tears of parting after a sleepless night, or possibly he is suggesting that there are tears even in the eyes of the horse that is to bear him away. Or perhaps the two images are intended to overlap. Either way, such intellectual games are not for the masses, but require quite a high level of education.

There exists a study showing the social position of Bashô's principal pupils. According to this study, the largest group (19) consisted of samurai in the service of various daimyo, followed by members of powerful local families (16). There were fifteen doctors, fourteen merchants, and thirteen priests. Bashô seems to have felt that the haiku needed to be still further refined before turning it over to the masses. In a sense, this was a reactionary attitude in an age when society was relatively open, yet it was an attitude supported by a clear idea of his own place in the trend of the times. At first, he had stressed that the haiku should have *karumi* (lightness of touch). Later, he came to place more emphasis on *sabi*, a quality of simple refinement that had at the same time a suggestion of sophisticated depth. But in his last years, he came to advocate a *karumi* that transcended even *sabi.* One may infer from this that he recognized the necessity for literature to make spiritual contact with the masses, but that he felt it necessary, before this, that the form should be allowed to soar to the heights for a time.

Another factor that distinguishes Bashô is the region in which he based his literary activities. While Saikaku and Chikamatsu worked in the Kansai district, Bashô's base was in Edo. It was only natural that a product of Edo, a city lying directly beneath the shogun's eye and reeking of authoritarianism, should differ from the products of the Kansai, where the relatively free merchant class predominated.

To return, finally, to a something that all three writers had in common: they all painted, in addition to their literary activities. There is a resemblance here to leading figures of the Renaissance, such as Leonardo da Vinci, who were men of many-faceted genius. In an age of liberation, the individual's talents are not content to follow a single track, but must radiate in many directions in search of expression. Of the three men, Saikaku was the most distinguished painter, and he sometimes did the illustrations for his own works. Chikamatsu's son was a painter, and he often wrote the literary inscriptions (*san*) for his son's works. The three men's skill in this field was hardly of the first rank, but the fact that they painted as well as wrote is significant when one is considering the Genroku era as a whole.

It was Saikaku, the most flamboyant of the three, who was to die the loneliest death. He lost his wife early on, and never remarried. Of his three daughters, two married and left home. The third, who was blind, stayed with him, but she too died one year before her father, so that there was no one to carry on the family after him. The next year Bashô also died while on his travels about the country:

Sick in a far place:
My dreams flit
About the desolate landscape.

Chikamatsu, the youngest of the three, died at the relatively advanced age of seventy-one. The following quotation is part of an inscription that he himself wrote on a portrait that he had requested his son to paint when he was already past seventy:

"Looking like a hermit, I am no hermit. Looking like a wise man, I have no wisdom. Looking like a man of much knowledge, I know nothing: the biggest sham there is. I talked my head off and scribbled my hand off as though there were nothing to the accumulated arts, skill, and humor of China and Japan, of which I knew nothing; I twittered emptily all my life like a bird. But now that death is at hand, and I want to write the most important thing of all, I find, to my distress, that I can think of nothing to say."

(Tr. by John Bester)

Scholars of the Tokugawa Period

Arai Hakuseki and Motoori Norinaga

by

THOMAS J. HARPER

Few periods in the history of any nation stand out from surrounding time as distinctly as the Tokugawa period (1603-1867) in Japan. So determined and successful was the Tokugawa Shogunate's attempt to isolate the nation from disruptive foreign influences that Japan developed virtually untouched by the intellectual, scientific, and technological advances that transformed Europe in the seventeenth, eighteenth, and nineteenth centuries. It is hardly surprising, then, that scholars of the twentieth century have looked back upon this period as one of reaction and stagnation. Foreign travellers to Japan in the sixteenth century describe it as an industrious and progressive nation, in no significant way inferior to European states. In the nineteenth century they found what seemed to them a quaint backwater of civilization.

As is often the case appearances were deceiving. Quaint dress and the lack of locomotives encouraged the notion that progress of every sort had been brought to a halt with the seclusion edict of 1639. In fact the peace and stability of isolation proved extremely congenial to certain sorts of cultural endeavor. This was particularly true in the field of scholarship. Far from stagnating, scholarship flourished as never before under the Tokugawa, and attracted many of the finest minds of the time. A new sixty-seven-volume edition of the classics of Japanese thought (*Nihon shisô taikei*) now in the process of publication will include about thirty-five volumes dating from the Tokugawa period alone. Nor is this to say that Tokugawa scholarship was notable mainly for its bulk. Many disciplines of modern scholarship trace their origins to this period, and some of the better works of Tokugawa scholars remain standard works in their field. Arai Hakuseki (1657-1725) and Motoori Norinaga (1730-1801) are but two of a very numerous and active group, and an examination of their lives and work can help to illuminate an important aspect of Tokugawa cultural history.

The great flourishing of scholarship in the Tokugawa period had its start in Tokugawa Ieyasu's (1542-1616) patronage of scholars of the Chu Hsi school of Neo-Confucianism and his encouragement of Confucian learning among the samurai class. Ieyasu appointed Hayashi Razan (1583-1657) as his official Confucian adviser, and in later years the ancient position of Director of the Academy (*daigaku no kami*) was revived. The academy itself was generously endowed, the directorship came to be held hereditarily by Razan's descendants, and its students often went on to hold influential positions in the Tokugawa feudal bureaucracy. In several daimyo domains local lords followed the example of the shogun, and even the smallest fief was likely to have its salaried Confucian scholar (*jusha*), while larger fiefs often maintained flourishing schools. Private teachers, too, found a ready market for their instruction in the larger cities. In short, learning became an essential part of the training of a samurai, and scholarship became a respected profession by which many made a respectable living and some rose to considerable eminence.

Arai Hakuseki is an outstanding example of a scholar in the orthodox tradition – a man whose learning lay in the officially sanctioned school of Neo-Confucianism, yet who never confused sanction with rectitude nor allowed it to dull his spirit of inquiry.

Hakuseki's career was no easy rise to prominence. He was the eldest son of a samurai of middling rank in the service of the daimyo Tsuchiya Toshinao, lord of a small domain in Kazusa. Hakuseki followed his father in the serivce of the Tsuchiya family, but in 1677 both lost their positions through their association with the losing faction in a succession dispute. For five years Hakuseki was left without employment or income. During this period, he tells us, he was twice offered the opportunity to marry the daughters of wealthy merchants, but in spite of the financial temptations, he turned down both offers as beneath the dignity of a samurai. He rejected too the opportunity to become a physician, as work of this sort, however respectable, would prevent him from devoting full time to his studies. In 1682 he obtained a position in the service of the Great Elder (*tairô*) Hotta Masatoshi. Only two years later Hotta was murdered. But unlike many of his less altruistic fellow retainers, Hakuseki followed the family to their new fief in Yamagata, and remained in their service until 1691, when the financial strain caused him to seek a new post. At this point he had only a paltry sum of cash and a small supply of rice to his

Arai Hakuseki; Collection of Arai Osamu (Nagoya, Aichi Prefecture)

name, and his first son had just been born. But telling his wife that "at least we won't have to begin begging right away," he set out for Edo where he managed to make a modest living as a private teacher of Confucian doctrine. In this period of adversity he again demonstrated the strength of his principles in rejecting an offer of employment from the Maeda family, holders of the richest fief in the nation, in favor of a friend who needed the position to support his aging mother. But in 1693 he at last found a position befitting his talents when his teacher Kinoshita Jun'an (1622-98) recommended him for the post of tutor to Tokugawa Tsunatoyo who was later to become the sixth Shogun Ienobu (1663-1712).

There was an obvious rapport between the young lord and his tutor. Ienobu was a diligent student, genuinely devoted to the study of the Classics, and Hakuseki's learning and strength of character seems to have made a strong impression upon him. It was only natural, therefore, that after Ienobu became Shogun, Hakuseki was frequently consulted on matters of state. The opinions he offered were often adopted as official policy, in many cases in preference to conflicting opinion submitted by Hayashi Hôkô (1644-1732), the incumbent Director of the Academy. Some scholars suggest that the hardship and poverty of the middle and early years of Hakuseki's career gave his interpretations of Confucian doctrine a common-sensical quality that the Shogun found more to the point than the airy and bookish submissions of Hayashi. This is no doubt true; but a close examination of his work reveals real depth of learning as well as good sense, and this must have carried its weight as well. In any case, the theoretical basis for official policy in this period was largely of Hakuseki's making, and though he never actually held a policy-making position, he wielded considerable political influence. It is interesting to note, though, that his influence never brought him great wealth. Even after his appointment as a direct vassal of the shogun (*hatamoto*) his maximum income was but a thousand *koku*.

Ienobu's rule was cut short by his premature death in 1712. Hakuseki continued to serve as an adviser to Ietsugu, who was only three years old at the time of his accession. But less than four years later, in 1716, Ietsugu fell ill and died. This brought an end to Hakuseki's career as a statesman. The new Shogun, Yoshimune (1684-1751), came from a different line of the Tokugawa family, the Kii branch, and the new regime rejected Hakuseki's ideals in favor of what was regarded a more practical policy. Hakuseki was relieved of his position and remained in retirement until his death. He speaks with some bitterness of this period. Yet it permitted him for the first time in his career to devote his full time to study and writing. Had he remained in public life he would probably never have found the time to undertake the work upon which his reputation as a scholar is based, for most of his major writings date from these last nine years of his life.

Hakuseki's bent for learning seems to have appeared early in his life and developed rapidly in spite of unfavorable conditions. Indeed, the record of Hakuseki's accomplishments sounds so much like the eulogistic biography of Chinese history that one might suspect its authenticity were he not telling the story himself. He wrote passable characters at age two, asked intelligent questions at lectures on the *Taiheiki* at three, learned to read and comment on Chinese poetry at six, and so on. Yet for all his talent he was deprived of the benefits of regular formal instruction. A local physician helped him with the Classics for a time, but for the most part he was self-taught: "I studied alone with only my dictionaries, and as I learned later, made many mistakes." He is probably too modest, for when a collection of his early poems was brought to the attention of the Korean Ambassador, this gentleman was sufficiently impressed to do Hakuseki the honor of writing a preface to the volume. But it was not until some time later, after he had followed the Hotta family to Yamagata, that his work came to the notice of Kinoshita Jun'an, tutor to the Shogun Tsunayoshi, who recommended him for the position of tutor to Ienobu in preferance to one of his own disciples of long standing. Hakuseki had had to wait until he was past thirty to become a properly enrolled student of an established teacher.

The first fruits of Hakuseki's scholarship date from 1701, during his service as tutor to Ienobu. This work, *Hankanpu*, is a collection of family histories of the lords of domains assessed at over ten-thousand *koku,* and was compiled at the request of Ienobu, probably in anticipation of his succession to the Shogunate. *Hankanpu* is not usually described as one of Hakuseki's more original works, but it certainly bears the marks that distinguish his later work – a rational and analytical approach to history, and a strong sense of its effects on human beings. He does at times tend to relate the rise or fall of a particular family to the degree of their loyalty to the Tokugawa house, but he also sees quite clearly that events can force a fate upon a person that his own actions or sentiments could never have controlled. And the anecdotes that constitute a goodly portion of the narrative show him to be a talented dramatist with a sharp eye for relevant detail.

Another work written in Hakuseki's years of service to the Shogun, but not published until the Meiji period, was *Seiyô kibun*, the report of his interrogation of the Italian Jesuit Giovanni Battista Sidotti. Sidotti arrived in Japan long after the prohibition of Christianity and the promulgation of the seclusion edict, and his arrival was thus the cause of some concern to the Shogunate. Hakuseki, having interrogated the man, concluded that he was an intelligent person, but that his religion was so ludicrous as to be no threat whatever. Accordingly he recommended that Sidotti be sent back to Rome to report that Japan was indeed determined to keep the country closed. Hakuseki's recommendation was not adopted, but Sidotti was spared the punishment of imprisonment. He was instead placed under house arrest in the charge of an old man and woman; whereupon he repaid the Shogunate for its lenity by proselytizing his custodians. Hakuseki thus felt called upon to explain the details of his interviews with Sidotti in defense of his recommendation. *Seiyô kibun* was the result.

If these works from Hakuseki's period of public service were his only writings, however, we probably would not know the full extent of his learning and his originality as a thinker. These qualities emerge fully only in his historical works, *Koshitsû* and *Tokushi yoron*, and his autobiography *Oritaku shiba no ki*, all of which date from his years of retirement.

Both of Hakuseki's major historical works were originally prepared as lectures at the request of Ienobu. *Koshitsû* is a survey of Japan's ancient history which attempts to reconstruct the actual course of events in this period from the often mythological accounts in the early chronicles. *Tokushi yoron* is an analysis of political change in Japan from early Heian until the point at which the Tokugawa came to power.

To appreciate the unique character of Hakuseki's historical writings they have to be viewed against the background of historical writing prior to his time. Speaking in the most general terms, two schools of historical interpretation, the Confucian and the Buddhist, dominated historical thought before Hakuseki's time. The Confucian view saw history as a succession of dynasties that rose and fell in accordance with the degree to which their leaders practiced or neglected the Confucian virtues. The task of the historian was to elucidate this pattern of events, giving proper credit to virtuous founders of dynasties and heaping opprobrium upon wicked rulers who brought on their downfall. The Buddhist view dealt in larger, in fact cosmic, units of time, but was generally compatible with the Confucian view. Virtue proliferated in times immediately following the appearance of a Buddha upon the earth, but evil gained ground as the years passed and the power of the Law waned. And since virtue and evil have their karmic consequences, history follows a course of inevitable decline until another Buddha appears.

Hakuseki, as an orthodox Neo-Confucian, would certainly have subscribed to the Confucian view of history. Yet his own writings are remarkably free of the determinism and the "encouragement of virtue and chastisement of vice" of the traditional historian. He examines events in and for themselves, rather than forcing them into a prescribed mould and looking for their causes solely in the ethical character of the participants. The "*kami*" or deities of the ancient chronicles were simply human beings who fought each other in order to gain wealth and power. The great houses of the middle ages rose and fell through skill in arms and strategy and management of resources. In early eighteenth-century Japan views of this sort constituted a revolution in historical writing. Tokugawa period thought is usually described as "rational" (*gôriteki*), and in comparison with that of the middle ages, which often dwelt upon the "strange" and "inexplicable," it is very rational indeed. To Tokugawa period scholars there were few mysteries that could not be explained. But in another sense, Tokugawa thought sometimes falls short of the objective analysis that modern scholars at least attempt to achieve. Many of the mysteries were too easily explained as the workings of a Neo-Confucian sort of cosmic principle, "*ri*." Hakuseki, though he might accept such explanations in principle, was so much the genuine rationalist in his own work as to set a new standard of historical inquiry.

If Hakuseki's historical writings show us the depth of his learning and the acuity of his analytical powers, his autobiography, *Oritaku shiba no ki,* shows us the high moral character and practical wisdom that characterized the application of his knowledge in both private and public life. It is a somewhat disorganized and rambling work, but a magnificent piece of writing, both for its crisp style and the vividness of the author's voice. Hakuseki here speaks not with the voice of some archetypal paragon, but of a man of many moods who is quite willing to let all of them be seen. He describes the precarious insecurity – often approaching poverty – of the first half of his life in the most matter-of-fact tones. Yet he can become quite heated when decrying the pedantry of Hayashi Hôkô, or the foolishness of the Shogun's councillors, or the corruption of lesser officials. In his defense of the policies of the Shogun's Chamberlain, Manabe Akifusa, he shows a strong sense of loyalty to a man he regarded as highly intelligent and of unquestionable integrity. In his descriptions of his recommendations on specific issues – the perpetual currency problem, dealing with the Korean embassy, petitions from unfairly treated farmers – he shows himself willing to offer opinions he knows will be unpopular but which he believes to be firmly grounded in the teachings of the sages. In short, we see in Hakuseki's autobiography the concrete realization in its finest form of the Confucian ideal of government by learning. Hakuseki speaks so directly to our own empirical sensibilities that it is easy to lose sight of the fact that he bases much of his opinion and action upon Confucian principle and Chinese precedent. Only when some obtrusively Confucian notion emerges – as for instance when he suggests that the failure of the Tokugawa line to produce an heir to the Shogunate was Heaven's retribution for their mistreatment of the emperor's offspring – do we realize the full extent of the learning and ideology that lies beneath Hakuseki's arguments. Other scholars may have rivaled him in the magnitude of their learning, but few attained such lasting relevance in the application of their knowledge as we see Hakuseki's work.

If Hakuseki is an exemplar of orthodox scholarship, Motoori Norinaga might be regarded as representing the best of the schools that arose in reaction to it. For the flourishing of Neo-Confucian scholarship was accompanied inevitably by the rise of schools that questioned the tenets of the orthodoxy. These schools were numerous and differed considerably in the degree to which they diverged. The school of National Studies (*kokugaku*) with which Norinaga came to be associated was perhaps the most extreme in its rejection of Neo-Confucianism, and after Norinaga's death was to provide much of the ideological basis for the movement that culminated in the Meiji Restoration. Norinaga's work is significant, therefore, not only for its intrinsic merits, but its influence on the thought and action of others as well.

Norinaga came from a very different background than Hakuseki. He was born in 1730 (five years after Hakuseki's death) to a family of cotton merchants in the town of Matsusaka near the Great Shrine of Ise. The Ozu family (he changed his name to Motoori much later) had once been wealthy, and had their prosperity continued Norinaga would no doubt have gone through life as a well-to-do merchant and left no mark in history. The severe economic recession of the mid-eighteenth century seems to have had much to do with his becoming a scholar instead. That at least is the impression the reader gets from his *Family History* (*Ie no mukashi monogatari*). Norinaga is tantalizingly vague about this period in his life. He tells of being sent to Edo in 1745 to learn the cotton business under the tutelage of his uncle; but only a year later he returned to Matsusaka under circumstances he neglects to explain. In 1748 he was taken into a family of paper merchants as the adopted husband of one of the daughters; but again he returned home, this time after two years. The only hint he offers of the reasons for the failure of his two attempts at a business career is that he was "only interested in reading books." One would like to know more; but his fondness for study obviously was a major force in his life and we are fortunate that ultimately it was to be the dominant one. Norinaga credits his mother, whom he describes as a paragon of maternal wisdom and self-sacrifice, with making this possible. In 1752 she arranged for him to go to Kyoto to study medicine, the profession by which he made his living for the rest of his life. This was the beginning, too, of his training and activity as a scholar.

In Kyoto he enrolled in a course of Confucian studies under a scholar named Hori Keizan, in preparation for more specialized studies in general medicine and pediatrics. Shortly thereafter he changed his name from Ozu to Motoori and adopted the dress and hair style of a physician – a transformation that brought his mother "great delight." For Norinaga himself, however, the change of name carried special significance. He was not merely choosing a suitably professional sounding name, but was reasserting a claim to samurai descent that had been lost when one of his ancestors, the widowed wife of a warrior, had taken the name of the plebeian family that had cared for her after her husband's death. Some modern scholars have made much of the spirit of the rising townsman class that they detect in Norinaga's scholarship, as opposed to the spirit of the samurai in the more orthodox forms of Confucian scholarship. Norinaga himself would probably have denied this vigorously, as intent as he was upon establishing a respectable samurai lineage for himself.

Norinaga spent about five years in Kyoto, perhaps the most important five years in his life. It would be impossible, and probably not very enlightening, to enumerate all of the "influences" on his thought. But at least two such shaping forces are worth noting. The first is that of the

Motoori Norinaga; Collection of Wada Sentarô (Fujisawa, Kanagawa Prefecture)

work of the Confucian scholar Ogyû Sorai (1666-1728), who rejected the Neo-Confucian interpretations of Chu Hsi and advocated a return to the original teachings of Confucius. Hori Keizan was a scholar of wide interests, and though he himself was an orthodox Neo-Confucian, he knew the works of Sorai well and found much to admire in them. Through his teacher Norinaga too became acquainted with Sorai's theories, and the influence was profound. At least one modern scholar has gone so far as to say that Norinaga had not a single idea he did not owe to Sorai. This judgment is surely extreme, but it cannot be denied that some of the most basic premises of Norinaga's scholarship – particularly his strict adherence to the language of ancient texts, his insistence on the importance of the emotional as opposed to the cerebral, and many of his attitudes to literature – bear a striking resemblance to Sorai's. The similarity seems to have been noted by Norinaga's contemporaries as well, for he is at great pains to insist that he owes no debt whatever to Sorai.

The other major shaping force – this being one that Norinaga acknowledges freely – is the work of the monk Keichû (1640-1701). Keichû's studies of classical Japanese literature, as Norinaga puts it, "opened his eyes to the true Way of Poetry." By this he refers mainly to Keichû's attempts to free the study of literature from the dogma of medieval tradition and focus attention on the works themselves – another constant theme in the work of Norinaga.

Norinaga had a long and productive career. But the ideas and methods at the core of most of his work took shape in his Kyoto years and are articulated in germinal form in his *Ashiwake obune* (1756), a work of poetic theory written toward the end of his professional studies. His rejection of any moral or didactic function of literature; his condemnation of medieval dogma and secret teachings; his assertion, reminiscent of Tsurayuki's Preface to the *Kokinshû* (905), of the basically lyrical nature of poetry; his insistence upon the importance of close philological study to the proper understanding of any work of literature – all the major themes of his later work are set forth quite clearly in this treatise written in his twenty-seventh year.

The following year, 1757, he returned home to Matsusaka and opened practice as a physician, specializing in the treatment of children. Shortly thereafter he inaugurated a series of lectures on the Japanese classics. From that time forward teaching came to be one of his principal activities, and he lectured several evenings a week in his home almost until the day he died. Ueda Akinari (1734-1809), the eminent scholar and fiction writer, once suggested that Norinaga's main interest in teaching was in collecting enrollment fees from his disciples. It is true that Norinaga did have a great many disciples – well over four hundred at the height of his career – but the detailed records of his finances which he kept show that neither teaching nor the sale of his writings ever constituted more than a fraction of his income. And considering the amount of time he devoted to his students, the return was almost negligible.

In 1763 he completed two more works of literary criticism, *Isonokami no sasamegoto*, a work of poetic theory, and *Shibun yôryô*, a treatise on *The Tale of Genji.* The former work is essentially a refinement of the ideas set forth in *Ashiwake obune*; but it is significant also because it contains one of the earliest uses of the term *mono no aware* – for which no single translation is adequate – that was later to become the central concept of his criticism of *The Tale of Genji.* This theory of fiction for which Norinaga is so justly famous is first articulated in *Shibun yôryô.* As Norinaga defines the term, "*aware*" was originally an expletive uttered in response to deeply felt emotion which later came to signify emotion in an abstract sense; "*mono no*" served to generalize the reference of the term. The emotion felt could be of any sort – joy, fear, love, sadness. And in early Japanese Court society, where great emphasis was placed on the refinement of the emotions, the person who responded with genuine emotion in situations where this was expected (*mono no aware o shiru hito*) was regarded with moral approval; while the unfeeling or insensitive person (*mono no aware o shiranu hito*) was the object of disapproval. To feign emotion where none was felt was the worst sort of deception. As

Norinaga points out, Japanese poetics had long held the expression of the subtleties of the emotions to be the chief function of Japanese poetry and the very source of its worth. In his treatise on the *Genji* he carries this argument an important step further. He argues that this is likewise the function of prose fiction – in particular the *Genji* – and for this reason novels deserve to be held in as high esteem as poetry and to be taken just as seriously. In support of this claim he cites Murasaki Shikibu's famous "defense of fiction" in the "Hotaru" chapter of the *Genji,* and documents his argument with a detailed explication of this passage. In the context of Japanese literary theory prior to the eighteenth century, this was an enormous step forward in the understanding of the novel. The *Genji,* almost from the time it was written, was recognized as a masterpiece. But its excellence always had to be explained in terms of some extrinsic worth – its didantic value, its poetic language, or the like. Norinaga was the first critic in seven centuries to recognize the importance of Murasaki's own views on fiction and to attribute the excellence of the novel to her skill in depicting the subtleties of human emotion. These ideas are best known from a later work, *Genji monogatari tama no ogushi* (1796), but they were first set forth in *Shibun yôryô* in 1763.

In that same year Norinaga had an experience which affected him profoundly and gave new purpose and direction to his work. By chance he heard that the great scholar Kamo no Mabuchi (1697-1769) was passing through Matsusaka on a pilgrimage to Ise, and he went to the inn where Mabuchi was staying and requested an interview with him. Mabuchi was impressed by the young man's interest in Japan's earliest chronicle, the *Kojiki*, and urged him to write a commentary on this work. Inspired by Mabuchi's encouragement, Norinaga began to work immediately on his *Kojiki-den.* It took him thirty years to complete the work, but it remains to this day the definitive decipherment of this difficult text and the basis of all *Kojiki* scholarship.

In the course of his study of the *Kojiki,* Norinaga's thought took on an ideological cast it had not had before, and the *"kami"* and their miraculous deeds in the Age of the Gods became the objects of belief as well as philological inquiry. As a corollary to this there appears a strong bias against the relentless rationalism of Confucianism and, by extention, against all things Chinese and foreign. It was this element of his work, which appears most prominently in his writings on the most ancient periods in Japanese history – *Naobi no mitama, Kuzubana* – that led ultra-nationalists in both the Meiji Restoration and World War II to look to Norinaga for ideological support. It should be remembered, though, that other by-products of his study of the *Kojiki* were of somewhat more constructive value. Norinaga's treatises on the language of ancient Japan, for instance, were pioneer contributions to the study of the grammar and vocabulary of classical Japanese.

As the years of work on the *Kojiki-den* drew to a close Norinaga found time to complete a number of other projects that had been postponed or lay unfinished. In 1793 he collected his essays and notes in a volume called *Tamakatsuma.* By 1794 he had completed a translation of the poems of the *Kokinshû* into the vernacular of his time; this work, *Kokinshû tôkagami,* was the first translation of any work of classical literature into modern Japanese. In 1796, through the patronage of the daimyo of a domain in Iwami, he published his famous treatise and commentary on *The Tale of Genji, Genji monogatari tama no ogushi.* In 1798 he wrote his *Family History* and an introductory essay on *kokugaku* studies called *Uiyamabumi.* These are only his best-known writings; the latest edition of his *Collected Works* will contain over twenty volumes when completed.

In his later years he enjoyed a degree of recognition for his scholarship. But the one opportunity he had to make his living as a scholar he turned down. When offered a position as director of National Studies by the daimyo of the Kaga domain, he chose not to accept the post because to do so would require him to leave his ancestral home in Matsusaka. He did, however, accept a modest stipend from the Kii branch of the Tokugawa family in 1792 as his services in this capacity could be performed without leaving Matsusaka permanently.

Throughout most of his career he supported himself through the practice of medicine, supplemented by fees from his disciples. He must have had an enormous capacity for work and extraordinary powers of concentration; for on most days the only time he had for study was late at night after the day's work and his evening lectures were over. And not until he was fifty-three did he even have a room of his own to study in. In 1782 he was at last able to build a small, second-story room for himself, the stairway to which was retractable, allowing him to retreat from the distractions of a large family without fear of interruption. He named the study *Suzunoya* after the string of antique bridle bells that hung on the wall, which he would jangle to revive himself when fatigue threatened to deprive of his study time.

When Norinaga died he left behind a large following of disciples to carry on the tradition of National Studies, but his successors were neither as versatile nor original as their master. Perhaps the best known were his son Haruniwa, his adopted son Ôhira, and Hirata Atsutane, who declared himself a disciple only after Norinaga's death. Haruniwa and Ôhira made notable contributions to the study of classical grammar, whereas Atsutane was plainly more interested in the political implications of Norinaga's thought. Norinaga himself held that political activity was not the province of the scholar. It was thus largely through Atsutane's interpretations of his work that he came to be the ideologue of the nationalists. The association was unfortunate not only because it distorted Norinaga's intentions, but because these distortions seriously damaged his reputation; in the years following World War II he was quite pointedly ignored by scholars. Happily the situation is changing now. A new and scrupulously edited edition of his works is nearing completion, and several excellent books on him have appeared in recent years. This new attitude is epitomized neatly in the opening pages of the latest of these books, Kobayashi Hideo's *Motoori Norinaga.* Kobayashi tells of the first time he called on the distinguished scholar and poet Origuchi Shinobu. In the course of their conversation Origuchi talked at length about Norinaga's *Kojiki-den*; this work had not agreed with Kobayashi's sensibilities and he had let his irritation show. Origuchi said nothing, but later when they parted at the railway station he said, "*Kobayashi-san, Norinaga-san wa ne, yahari Genji desu yo.*" The statement is difficult to translate concisely, but his point was that whatever else Norinaga had done, finally the real core of the man's work lay in his criticism of *The Tale of Genji.*

The contrasts between Hakuseki and Norinaga are obvious. Hakuseki, the orthodox Neo-Confucian, grounded his thought and work almost exclusively in Chinese principle and precendent. Norinaga rejected the orthodoxy – and all things Chinese – with a totality that at times approached bigotry. Hakuseki was born of samurai stock; Norinaga was raised to be a merchant. Hakuseki at the peak of his career was an influential statesman; Norinaga purposely avoided public life. Hakuseki the thorough-going rationalist; Norinaga the unquestioning believer in an Age of the Gods – and so on. The contrasts are worth noting, for they suggest something of the great variety and vitality of Tokugawa scholarship. Yet if the contrasts between the two men delineate the type, their similarities are more helpful in defining what sets them apart from their peers. For difficult though it is to define, the reader definitely senses a shared quality of excellence in the writings of Hakuseki and Norinaga that lies deeper than their surface differences. Both men were plainly of superior intellect and intensely devoted to their work; but there is more to it than this. There is a clarity of vision, a sureness of understanding, a directness of statement that has kept their work alive to this day and distinguishes them as superior minds in an age when scholarship attracted the best minds.

Forerunner of the Modern Statesman

Tanuma Okitsugu

by

JOHN W. HALL

Tanuma Okitsugu (1719-88), daimyo and official of the Tokugawa Shogunate, rose from minor office to great influence as the favorite of the tenth Shogun Tokugawa Ieharu. In an age when shogunal officialdom gave little opportunity for advancement and favored few changes in basic policy, Tanuma stood out both for the remarkable stretch of his rise to political power and for the unorthodox government policies which he presumably pushed. In the traditional historiography, Tanuma is harshly treated, being depicted as the very prototype of the "evil minister." Only in modern times, as scholars more removed in time and setting have been able to reevaluate Tokugawa history, has Tanuma been looked upon more generously as possibly a "forerunner of modern Japan."

The traditional historiography which reflected the official point of view, was mainly the work of Confucian-trained scholars. Confucian political theory, adopted as the official doctrine by the Tokugawa ruling class, laid great stress upon the maintenance of "proper order" in political, social, and economic matters. The political hierarchy of emperor-shogun-daimyo-samurai was kept in order through the loyalty of subordinate to superior. The class hierarchy of warrior-farmer-artisan-merchant was maintained when each class fulfilled its natural and proper function: the *bushi* to rule firmly but benevolently, the farmers to produce without indolence, and so forth. Merchants were placed at the bottom of the four-class system, because they were considered economically unproductive: they merely moved goods produced by others, and took a profit besides. The economic policy adopted by the Tokugawa government rested on the Confucian premise that agriculture was the "foundation of the state"; it gave no place to the possibility of profit through commerce

Tanuma Okitsugu;
Shôrinji Temple (Tokyo)

and trade. Since agriculture provided a relatively inelastic source of income, the samurai class was admonished to set an example for the other classes by living strictly within its means. Frugality was made a moral principle; luxury and ostentation were positive evils and were made the object of sumptuary laws.

From the Confucian point of view, the Tokugawa regime started off well but later ran into economic difficulties. The later half of the Tokugawa period is depicted as a series of routs and rallies, leading to inevitable demise in the confusion that followed the intrusion of Commodore Perry's "black ships" into Japanese waters in 1853-54. Routs were presumably brought on by "weak" leaders who allowed luxury and commercial economy to flourish, thus causing samurai government to overreach its income. Rallies were the work of "strong" shoguns or shogunal officials who rid the system of corruption and went back to first principles by tending the agrarian base. Of those "reform efforts" there were three: the Kyôhô (1716-45) led by the Shogun Yoshimune, the Kansei (1789-93) undertaken by the shogunal official Matsudaira Sadanobu, and the Tenpô (1841-43) advocated by the shogunal official Mizuno Tadakuni. Each of these efforts was preceded by a time of troubles; the one preceding the Kansei reform was credited to the misgovernment of Tanuma Okitsugu; hence his negative image. But much of the opposition to Tanuma came from the fact that he was a "new man" within the Tokugawa bureaucracy, raised above his betters through shogunal favoritism.

Tanuma Okitsugu's father Motoyuki had been an *ashigaru* (the lowest of samurai statuses) in the service of Tokugawa Yoshimune, daimyo of Wakayama and head of one of the three successor lines of the Tokugawa House. When in 1716 Yoshimune was selected to enter Edo Castle as the eighth Shogun, Motoyuki accompanied him, receiving the status of *hatamoto* (Bannerman). He served in a number of minor capacities and was at one time put in charge of the Shogun's private library.

Okitsugu succeeded to his father's estate in 1734 at the age of fifteen. His first appointment was that of Page (*koshô*) in service to Ieshige, the Shogun's heir. His initial annual stipend was 300 bales (*hyô*) of rice, roughly the income from a fief of 300 *koku*. (A *koku* was a measure equivalent to approximately five bushels. A fief of 300 *koku* assessment would normally harvest 300 *koku* or 1,500 bushels. Taxed at 40%, this would bring in 600 bushels in taxes. In bales of two bushels capacity, this would come to 300 *hyô*.) Ieshige became shogun in 1745, and in 1751 Tanuma Okitsugu was raised to the post of Chamberlain *(sobashû)* in the Shogun's service at a considerable increase in fief. In 1785 he acquired the status of daimyo as a result of having received lands assessed at 10,000 *koku*.

In 1761, Ieshige died and was succeeded by his son Ieharu. But Tanuma retained the new Shogun's favor. In 1767 he became Grand Chamberlain (*sobayônin*) the most important "inner" office in the Shogunate and one which placed him close to the Shogun with the authority to mediate between him and the Board of Senior Councilors. A concurrent raise in land holdings brought his total to 20,000 *koku*. All told Tanuma was to reach a total of 57,000 *koku* before his fall. His main holdings were based on the castle town of Sagara in the province of Tôtômi (now Shizuoka Prefecture).

In 1772 Okitsugu reached the pinacle of his career when he achieved the position of Senior Councilor (*rôjû*) in addition to the post of Grand Chamberlain. Meanwhile his son Okitomo (born in 1749) was advancing rapidly in shogunal service. By 1783 he had become Junior Councilor (*wakadoshiyori*). This created a most unusual condition in which a father and son together held high shogunal office and received shogunal favor. But this was not all, for Tanuma had carefully built up a faction of officials within the Shogunate, particularly in the Finance Office (*kanjô-sho*), consisting of partisans, his own appointees, and relatives by marriage.

Despite the high status and rank ultimately achieved by Tanuma Okitsugu, his political position remained precarious and rested heavily on the backing of the Shogun. Then when that support was lost, his fall was rapid. In 1784, the son Okitomo was assassinated, over a personal grudge, within the shogunal palace. Although the assassin, Sano Masakoto, was apprehended and punished, the incident tarnished Okitsugu's public image and weakened his factional base. That a considerable resentment had built up against Okitsugu both within Tokugawa officialdom and on the streets of Edo was made evident when Sano, after his death by ritual suicide (*seppuku*), was made a popular hero and his grave visited by hordes of worshippers.

Two years after Okitomo's assassination, the Shogun Ieharu died. The heir apparent, Ienari, was still a minor. This situation made it possible for the Tokugawa collateral heads, particularly those of the Three Successor Houses (*sanke*), to intrude into shogunal affairs. Tanuma was quickly stripped of his offices and reduced in rank and income. His principle policies were countermanded, and the members of his faction expelled from government. When Okitsugu died in 1788, his grandson succeeded to a minor domain of 10,000 *koku* in the northern province of Mutsu. Even before Okitsugu's death, Matsudaira Sadanobu, the author of the socalled Kansei Reform, had taken charge of shogunal policy with the avowed purpose of reversing the evils, as he presumed them to be, of the Tanuma influence on shogunal policy. Tanuma's official memory was vilified. To the public he became a scapegoat for the many difficulties the country was experiencing during the 1770s and 1780s.

The official case against Tanuma had a number of elements to it. First of all there was the matter of his modest origin and unusual career pattern. Tokugawa bureaucracy, especially at the top where offices were staffed by daimyo, was extremely conscious of inherited status and resentful of the appearance of "new men." The fact that Tanuma had risen through the "inner" offices – Page, Chamberlain, Grand Chamberlain – to become Senior Councilor, rather than by the usual course of assignment through the "outside" offices of Keeper of Osaka Castle or Junior Councilor before reaching Senior Councilor was held against him. The fact that shogunal favoritism was involved was also at issue, since it was presumed that the combination of a shogun working through his close, but inexperienced, inner officials produced less responsible government than when important decisions were left to the Board of Senior Councilors (*rôjû*). And here Confucian theory came into play; for it was piously assumed that Grand Chamberlains, like Tanuma, were motivated chiefly by personal ambition and that their influence, being private, was necessarily corrupt. Lurid tales were told about Ôoka Tadamitsu, Grand Chamberlain to Ieshige, the ninth Shogun. One of Ôoka's special holds over Ieshige, it was said, was that he alone was able to make sense out of the Shogun's defective speech. Others, including Tanuma, were whispered to have played upon the "unnatural" affection of the men they served. Certainly in the case of both Ôoka and Tanuma, personal friendships had grown up between page boy and heir apparent, and these were carried over into the years when Ieshige and Ieharu served as shogun. Along with the claim of unhealthy favoritism was the presumption that the combination of weak shogun and corrupt inner officials produced bad governmental policy, encouraged luxury and neglect of the moral foundations of samurai government. In Tanuma's case the accusation was that he was primarily responsible for bringing down upon the country a period of economic dislocation, social unrest, and even natural disasters.

The existence of two separate, and contradictory, paths to high shogunal influence is a matter of historical record. That the inner should be considered undesirable was not axiomatic, and the use of Confucian moralism to justify the accusation was very much a rationalization by the vested interests of the daimyo who staffed the high outside offices. From the very outset of the Tokugawa regime a battle had waged between the central interests of shogunal government and the interests of the Tokugawa house daimyo. It was to the interests of the 145 *fudai* daimyo that policy be debated and decisions made in the Board of Senior Councilors. By the middle of the Tokugawa period it had become apparent that there were broad areas of conflicting interest between the shogun's central needs and the desires of the daimyo for greater autonomy. And whether corruption or weak leadership on the shogun's part was involved or not, it is clear that the eras of "inside" influence (those periods in fact which Confucian historiography wrote down as routs) gave rise to forceful shogunate-centered policies. To turn the situation around, any shogun wishing to exercise positive political influence would have to bypass the Senior Councilors and find his own mechanism for carrying out measures of his own design. For Ieharu, Tanuma and the members of his faction provided such a mechanism. To this extent Tanuma was symptomatic of the effort to secure greater centralization of authority by the Shogunate, and as such his policies may be seen as presaging the policies adopted by the modern Japanese state. That these policies were vigorously opposed by the daimyo helps to account for the bitter attacks which Tanuma suffered while in office and the negative treatment afforded him in the official history.

The Tanuma age was indeed a time of troubles for Japan. There were numerous natural disasters, clearly "acts of God," but nonetheless blamed on Tanuma. The eruption of Mount Asama in 1783 spread ashes over three entire provinces, killing an estimated twenty thousand persons and making fields infertile for many years. Crop failures in 1782 and 1783 led to widespread famine throughout northeast Japan. The estimated death toll from such disasters between 1782 and 1786 was close to a million persons. Edo experienced one of its worst fires in 1772: destroyed were 178 temples and shrines, 127 daimyo residences, 878 daimyo establishments, 8,705 residences of bannermen, and 628 blocks of commercial residences and stores. Such calamities fed the flames of antagonism against Tanuma within official circles, while at large there were peasant uprisings in the countryside and mob violence (*uchikowashi*, literally "house smashings") in the cities. While neither the Shogunate at large nor Tanuma as a person, could be held directly responsible for these conditions, they were obvious scapegoats. Tanuma's sensitivity to public opinion is revealed in the "era name" (*nengô*) episode. In 1764 the era name Meiwa (Illustrious Peace) had been adopted. This was a prerogative of the imperial Court in Kyoto. The year 1772 (Meiwa 9) had seen the great Edo fire, calamitous tempests and crop failures. Meiwa 9 was pronounced "Meiwa-ku", which also could mean "annoyance" or "trouble." The populace made sport of this coincidence. Before the year was out the *nengô* had been changed at Tanuma's urging to An'ei (Eternal Tranquility). Yet, of course, the country's troubles continued.

But these troubles were not simply the result of natural disasters. Throughout Japan by the middle of the eighteenth century the relationship between government, the economy, and the people had become disjointed. Population and level of living had greatly increased for all classes in the century and a half since the Tokugawa takeover. Urban centers like Edo (with close to a million inhabitants), Osaka and Kyoto (with three to four hundred thousand apiece) had become great consuming centers. The agrarian economy was proving inadequate as the prime source of tax revenue, while commercial production received tremendous stimulus from the cities. A new economy in which rice was losing its absolute primacy to cash crops like cotton, tobacco, mulberry (for silk worm production), was already rampant throughout most of Japan. Confucian economic principles were no longer relevant to these conditions.

In meeting these new conditions the daimyo generally moved faster than the Shogunate. The primary method used by them was to establish domain-wide controlled economies in which local specialty products were exported for profit and paper currencies were circulated within the domains to prevent the outflow of specie. In essence the daimyo began to carry on a form of foreign trade in which the shogunal cities like Edo and Osaka served as foreign markets. This naturally created a potential conflict of interest between daimyo and Shogunate. The Shogunate was slow to adjust to the new economic conditions, in part because of the possibility of using techniques, such as currency debasement, which were unavailable to the daimyo. But also, since shogunal policy, when arrived at through "normal" channels, inevitably reflected the interests of the *fudai* daimyo, alternative policies were not forthcoming unless an outsider like Tanuma arrived on the scene.

The overwhelming problem which Tanuma and his associates confronted as they gained places of influence within the Shogunate was how to reverse the economic decline of the shogun's government. Not all of the measures adopted by Tanuma were unorthodox or even innovative, and in the main they were put forward as serious, even desparate, efforts to assist the Shogunate to meet its financial obligations. Efforts at increasing the efficiency of tax collection on the Shogun's lands (the *tenryô*) or the flow of precious metals from the shogun's mines, or efforts to extend the amount of land available for cultivation, were standard practices. One project for which Tanuma was soundly criticized was the Inbanuma reclamation plan. The objective was to contain the uncontrolled Tone River north of Edo and reclaim for paddy land cultivation large stretches of swamp along its course. The project was costly, but Tanuma pushed it to near completion before luck ran out. An unprecedentedly severe rain followed by flood washed out all construction, and the project had to be abandoned. Tanuma was not the first to attempt to reclaim Inbanuma, and others were to attempt to do so down to modern times. The project was in fact completed in 1969. But Tanuma bears the onus of having squandered government funds on an "illconceived and wasteful project."

It was in the commercial field that Tanuma's more controversial policies were to be found. Tanuma was, of course, not the sole instigator of such policies, and it is now quite evident that many of the ideas credited to Tanuma were products of an increasingly professionalized Shogunal Finance Office. Essentially what the "Tanuma policy" did was to attempt for the Shogunate what the daimyo were doing for themselves: create a favorable (that is expanding) monetary and fiscal structure, use government authority to control or license the production and sale of special products, regulate but also expand foreign trade.

Several actions of the Shogunal Finance Office during Tanuma's administration give evidence of a reasoned and flexible fiscal policy based on a fairly sophisticated understanding of market economy. In 1772 the Finance Office issued for the first time a minted silver piece (the *nanryô nishu* coin) which was to circulate as a fraction of the standard gold *koban.* Silver up to then had circulated by lump, meaning each transaction required the weighing and cutting of silver lumps. The main objective of the new issue, aside from convenience, was to increase the amount of currency in circulation. While the coins were in fact slightly overvalued, they were of good quality silver. The attempt was made therefore to accustom the people to the concept of fiat currency. And this to some extent succeeded. Another innovative plan tried under Tanuma's authorization was the effort in 1785 to create a Shogunate-managed loan fund for use by financially needy daimyo and bannermen. What with poor harvests, natural calamities, and diminished tax revenues, many daimyo were in extreme financial distress; many had borrowed disastrously from merchant financiers; the loan fund was to assist in such situations. The basic plan was to create a self replenishing pool of capital managed by the Shogunate for low interest loans. The initial contribution of capital was to come from affluent commercial houses chiefly of Osaka. But despite the fact that the Shogunate stood behind the loans, the merchants of Osaka declined to participate. A similar plan was successfully implemented a few years later under the reform administration of Matsudaira Sadanobu, but Tanuma went down in history as a corrupt schemer for having failed in this earlier attempt.

The aspects of Tanuma's economic policies which were most bitterly criticized were those in which the effort was made to use the political power of the Shogunate to profit from the country's growing commercial sector. The most obvious and direct way to do this was through the licensing of commercial agents and monopoly rights for certain goods and services where the Shogunate by virtue of its national prerogatives or because the location of the *tenryô* made monopolization possible. Some monopoly organizations were already in existence. Such were the *Ginza* (for the minting of silver) and the *Kinza* (for the minting of gold coins). A *Dôza* (copper monopoly) was also established for the control of the sale of copper. The Shogunate profited from control of the production and distribution of copper, since it monopolized the minting of copper cash and the export of copper to the Chinese and Dutch through Nagasaki. In addition to these traditional areas of central government monopoly, the Tanuma period saw the granting of monopoly patents in such commodities as iron, brass, sulphur, camphor, cinnabar, ginseng, lamp oil and a number of other products. This action put the Shogunate, or at least its commercial agents, in direct competition with the daimyo and their local monopoly organizations. Hence the outcry from many quarters but especially from the Tokugawa house daimyo.

One of the most interesting chapters in the Tanuma story concerned foreign trade. The Tokugawa seclusion (*sakoku*) policy adopted during the

1630s had left the country with a narrow and strictly regulated foreign trade concentrated at Nagasaki. For roughly a century the seclusion policy remained intact: trade was controlled by merchants licensed by the Shogunate, and information from foreign lands, especially writings about Christianity, was strictly censored. The eighth Shogun Yoshimune had relaxed these controls somewhat in 1720 by permitting Japanese to study Dutch and to import books on Western medicine and other sciences. But the Tokugawa government still held the West at arms length, while the Nagasaki trade was perceived more as an economic liability than an asset. The discovery that both the Dutch and Chinese traders were taking out of Japan large quantities of copper and silver had alarmed the Shogunate into putting ever more severe limitations on the Nagasaki trade.

During the Tanuma era there occurred a momentary relaxation in the negative official policy toward foreign contact and trade. Tanuma himself took an interest in articles imported from Europe, members of his administration had frequent contact with members of the Dutch factory on Dejima, from whom they sought information on the nature of the outside world and on the value of foreign trade. Two agents of the Dutch factory have left behind important records of the new atmosphere which prevailed under Tanuma. Karl Thunberg who stayed in Nagasaki from 1775 to 1776 wrote in his *Voyages de C.P. Thunberg au Japon* (4 vols. Paris, 1796) that many Japanese officials and scholars gave evidence of having studied the Dutch language and of a keen interest in Western science, especially medicine. Isaac Titsingh who was in Japan from 1779 to 1785 wrote even more explicitly of the interest of high level Japanese in learning about the West and possibly of expanding trade with the West. Titsingh in his *Illustrations of Japan* (London, 1822) listed the names of numerous Tokugawa officials, including Tanuma's son, who approached him with the prospect of "widening the road" of foreign intercourse. Thus for a brief moment Japan witnessed a "Western boom": European goods like clocks; scientific instruments including electric spark generators; Western books on geography, astronomy, medicine; Western paintings; articles of Western clothing were avidly sought after. Titsingh even goes to the point of suggesting that the Tanuma faction was on the verge of negotiating with the Dutch for the building of large ocean-going ships as the start of an aggressive foreign trade policy. He claims that the assassination of Tanuma's son "annihilated all our fine schemes."

However that might be, the fact remains that the Tanuma faction did try to expand the Nagasaki trade through the increase of Japanese exports. Copper export quotas were raised, but also substitute goods were vigorously sought. One of the most successful proved to be what were called *tawaramono* (bale goods). This was a generic name for dried sea products such as tangle (*konbu*), sea ears (*awabi*), sea slugs (*iriko*), and sharks' fins, all highly desired by Chinese traders. Bale goods came mostly from the far north, from the then little known island of Ezo (now Hokkaido). The Shogunate tried in various ways to derive income from the export of bale goods. It was under Tanuma's direction that in 1786 a shogunal monopoly was created and operated profitably.

Mention of the northern island of Ezo brings to attention another foreign problem, namely the appearance of Russian ships and explorers on Japan's northern frontier. Although the Shogunate had been alerted to the existence of Russian outposts in the Kuriles since the early eighteenth century, the first real "northern scare" came during Tanuma's time in office. This was the result of several incidents during the 1770s and 1780s when Russian ships entered harbors in Ezo in search of food and trade. In 1783 a physician attached to the daimyo of Sendai sent an analysis of the northern problem to Tanuma. Rather than reacting in alarm, Tanuma set in motion a series of activities – an exploratory expedition, and studies of mineral resources, colonization and trade possibilities in the northern area. But again, before any of these acts could lead to any relaxation of the seclusion policy in the north, the mood in Edo had changed with Tanuma's fall from power.

The Tanuma interlude in Tokugawa history presents the historian with an intriguing question. Since so many of Tanuma's policies and actions were in the direction of greater commercialization and more openness to foreign contact and trade, was there any prospect that the Shogunate might have abandoned its seclusion policy of its own accord? It is highly unlikely that any such drastic change in basic policy could have been instigated from inside the Edo government, but a moderation was not so unthinkable. Of this we can be sure, a continuation of the strong Shogunate-first tendency pursued by Tanuma could have built up a sufficiently confident central administration so that, by the time of Perry's arrival, the Shogunate itself might have been able to lead Japan in the process of rapid modernization which by abdication fell to the Meiji government.

In the final analysis Tanuma did in many ways anticipate policies which were adopted a hundred years later by Japan's modern government. It is important to point out as well that many of these policies, particularly in the financial area, were not "Tanuma's." These were policies devised pragmatically by the Shogunal Financial Office. And although they were discredited in Tanuma's name, most of them remained as part of a basic shift of shogunal fiscal policy in the direction of commercialization. As an historic symbol, Tanuma was representative both of the desire of the shogunal interest to strengthen its centralizing capacity and also of its inability to gain legitimacy for such a policy. Tanuma's personal weakness, his low-status origin and his vulnerability to accusations of corruption, were factors which complicated, but did not make inevitable, the bad repute of the policy with which he was associated.

[NOTE]

For further reading in English: John Whitney Hall, *Tanuma Okitsugu, 1719-1788: Forerunner of Modern Japan* (Cambridge: Harvard University Press, 1955). Conrad D. Totman, *Politics in the Tokugawa Bakufu 1600-1843* (Cambridge: Harvard University Press, 1967). Harold Bolitho, *Treasures Among Men, The Fudai Daimyo in Tokugawa Japan* (New Haven: Yale University Press, 1974). Herman Ooms, *Charismatic Bureaucrat, A Political Biography of Matsudaira Sadanobu 1758-1829* (Chicago: University of Chicago Press, 1975).

"Holy Foolishness"

Ryôkan

by

JOHN STEVENS

There is a certain irony in Ryôkan being included in a book on great historical figures of Japan. How is it that this beggar-monk whose only possessions were an old bowl and a tattered robe came to be placed beside emperors, feudal lords, statesmen, and patriarchs? What can be the historical significance of a Zen priest who spent the last thirty years of his life living in a mountain hermitage in one of the remotest parts of Japan and who in his lifetime was virtually unknown outside his local district? Other famous monks such as Eisai, Dôgen, Shinran, Nichiren, Ikkyû, Hakuin, etc. were founders or abbots of famous monasteries and had hundreds of disciples, but Ryôkan had neither a temple nor any disciples. In contrast to most of the other figures in this book, who were driven by some great ambition or desire, Ryôkan was totally without covetousness. If he needed anything he went to town to beg for it, and if there was anything extra he gave it away. Often he was so absorbed in playing with the village children or picking flowers he completely forgot his begging for that day and returned to his tiny hut empty-handed. However, it is exactly this kind of "holy foolishness" – Ryôkan's literary name was Daigu, "Great Fool" – that makes Ryôkan and his poetry so special to the Japanese. As D.T. Suzuki wrote, "When we know one Ryôkan we know hundreds of Ryôkans in Japanese hearts." The beauty of Ryôkan's life is what qualifies him as a great figure.

Ryôkan was born as Yamamoto Eizô in the year 1758 in the village of Izumozaki in Echigo Province (present-day Niigata Prefecture) on the west coast of Japan. This area is noted for its heavy snow, often two or three meters high, its earthquakes, and for the famous island of Sado which was visible from Ryôkan's home and whose beauty made a lasting impression on the young child. Ryôkan's father, the haiku poet Tachibana Inan, was the village headman and Ryôkan as the eldest son was expected to assume that position when he came of age. He was trained to that end and actually became headman for a time, but his quiet and sensitive nature made it difficult for him to deal with the many disputes, minor and major, that arose. In 1777 he renounced his inheritance, resigned his position, and entered the local Sôtô Zen monastery, Kôshôji. He was ordained a monk, taking the name Ryôkan (*ryô* means "good"; *kan* is "generosity" and "large-heartedness"). After practicing there for about four years he met a famous monk of that time called Kokusen, and Ryôkan became his disciple. They returned together to Kokusen's monastery in Bitchû Province (now known as Okayama).

Ryôkan stayed at the Entsûji temple for twelve years devoting himself to Zen practice. He became Kokusen's senior disciple and was given a certificate as Kokusen's Dharma-heir in 1790. During the period Ryôkan continued his studies of ancient poetry and other literary classics and also mastered calligraphy. Entsûji was flourishing in that period and Ryôkan had an opportunity to meet many other interesting religious and literary figures. One of them was his Dharma-brother Senkei (not to be confused with Sengai). Senkei seems to have been a real eccentric in the Zen manner. Ryôkan wrote this poem about him:

Priest Senkei, a true man of the Way!
He worked in silence – no extra words for him.
For thirty years he stayed in Kokusen's community –
He never practiced *zazen,* never read the sutras,
And never said a word about religion;
Just worked in the garden for the good of all.
I saw him, but didn't really see him;
I met him, but didn't actually meet him.
Ah – he is impossible to imitate,
Priest Senkei, a true man of the Way.

Kokusen died in 1791 and Ryôkan set off on a series of pilgrimages (this is a common Zen practice) to visit other famous masters and spent the next few years traveling throughout the country. His father had also left their native village after turning over his position to the second son, Yoshiyuki, and had settled in Kyoto after his own series of pilgrimages. Inan was an ardent supporter of the emperor and strongly opposed the repressive nature of the Tokugawa Shogunate. He felt so oppressed, in fact, that in 1795 he committed suicide by throwing himself in the Katsura River in Kyoto to protest the actions of the government.

Ryôkan, who never shared the political crusade of his father, was

Ryôkan; Board of Education, Itoigawa City (Niigata Prefecture)

greatly saddened to hear of his father's suicide and went to Kyoto to hold a memorial service. After spending some time in Kyoto Ryôkan decided to return to his native place which he had left twenty years before.

After searching several years for a suitable place to settle down he finally decided on an abandoned one-room hut halfway up Mount Kugami, about ten kilometers from his ancestral home. It was called "Gogô-an" – *"gogô"* is half a *shô,* the amount of rice necessary to sustain life for one day, and *"an"* means "hermitage". He wrote this poem about his new dwelling:

The wind blows through my tiny hermitage,
Not one thing is in the room.
Outside a thousand cedars.
On the wall, several poems are written.
Now the kettle is covered with dust,
And no smoke rises from the rice steamer.
Who is pounding at my moonlit gate?
Only an old man from East Village.

Although Gogô-an was deep in the mountains Ryôkan often visited the neighboring villages to play ball with the children, drink sake with the farmers, or dance in the local festivals. He was always smiling and greeted all with a cheerful face. He acquired his simple needs by mendicancy and kept nothing extra. Once a misdirected thief entered Gogô-an and finding nothing to steal took away Ryôkan's old and torn sleeping quilt and his *zazen* cushion. Ryôkan wrote this haiku:

The thief left it behind –
The moon
At the window.

Ryôkan loved children and was a great favorite with them. After the long winter finally ended Ryôkan would hurry to meet his small friends.

Hand in hand, the children and I
Pick spring vegetables –
What can be more wonderful?

*

Pants too short, top too long.
Smiling to myself I try to walk in a straight line.
As soon as the children see me
They clap their hands and cry,
"Please, please sing that song we use when we play ball."

Once Ryôkan was playing hide-and-seek with the children and he ran to hide in a nearby outhouse. The children knew where he was and decided to play a joke on him and ran away without telling him. The following morning a farmer's wife came into the shed and was startled to find Ryôkan crouching in the corner. "What are you doing here, Ryôkan? " she said. "Shh, be quiet please," he whispered, "or else the children will find me."

Another time some children were trying to fly a kite when they saw Ryôkan approach. "Ryôkan! Ryôkan!" they cried. "Please write something on this paper that will help make our kites fly." Ryôkan thought for a moment and then wrote the four characters *Ten jô dai fû,* "To heaven on the great wind." The subtle beauty of those four characters – among the simplest in the Japanese language and taught to every first-grader – written spontaneously for a group of children is indescribable, and that piece of calligraphy has become one of Japan's greatest treasures.

The long years of Zen training had not made Ryôkan remote or insensitive to others' suffering or hardships; on the contrary, it made him more open, gentle, and kind. The culmination of Zen practice is to "return to the market place with open hands." Ryôkan spent the last thirty years of his life among farmers, merchants, fishmongers, tavern owners, and children, making them all objects of religious salvation. Mingling with all types of people, he was living the unfettered life of Zen. There was no thought of condescension or even altruism. Indeed, the highest form of Zen is to be detached from one's detachment and to be free of all physical or spiritual materialism. It is life lived in the present, in harmony with nature, without pretense or clinging.

If you have no desires you will be happy with anything
But if you seek something, nothing will satisfy you.
Wild vegetables can fill your hunger
And you need only one robe to wrap around your body.
If you live alone tame deer will accompany you
And you can sing as loud as you like with the village children.
Wash the dirt and dust from your ears in the valley stream
And keep your heart among the mountain pines.

While other monks lectured for hours on the profundities of the sutras or officiated in gorgeous robes, Ryôkan wandered around the village in his tattered black cloak, always smiling and bowing to all – he was a living sermon, not unlike St. Francis of Assisi, God's Fool. (Ryôkan also shared St. Francis' love of birds. Often the sparrows would eat up the rice in Ryôkan's bowl while he played with them and once he let an expensive bird escape from a cage in a friend's home.) When Ryôkan appeared quarrels would immediately cease, and problems which seemed so important a few seconds before, would be completely forgotten.

Once the local daimyo wanted to construct a magnificent temple in a nearby town and install Ryôkan as head priest. He went to see Ryôkan at Gogô-an, but Ryôkan was out picking flowers and the lord and his party had to wait quite a while before he finally returned with his begging bowl full of flowers. The lord made his request, but Ryôkan remained silent. Then he wrote this haiku and handed it to the master.

The wind has brought
Enough fallen leaves
To make a fire.

The lord understood Ryôkan's feelings and quietly returned to his castle.

Ryôkan was very absent-minded, often forgetting his things or what to do, so he decided to make the following lists:

(a)

No. 1. Things to take along

cotton cap towel tissue paper fan coins ball marbles

No. 2. Necessities

bamboo hat leggings gloves belt staff short *kesa*

No. 3. For pilgrimages

clothes raincoat bowl bag

Be sure to read this before going out or else you will have some trouble!

(b)

Offer incense and flowers to Buddha.
Plant trees and flowers, clean the garden, water the
  plants, remove the stones.
Occasionally use moxibustion for the legs.
Do not eat oily fish.
Stay away from greasy things; always take light food.
Do not oversleep.
Do not overeat.
Do not make the afternoon nap too long.
Do not overexert yourself.
Do not be neglectful.
Do not talk when you have nothing to say.
Do not hide anything in your heart.
Always drink your sake warm.
Shave your head.
Trim your nails.
Rinse your mouth and use a toothpick.
Take a bath.
Make your voice clear.

Zen also means "when hungry, eat; when tired, sleep" and Ryôkan freely identified with all human emotions and shared all our feelings of joy and sadness, darkness and light.

Walking beside a clear running river, I come to a farm house.
The evening chill has given way to the warmth of the morning
  sun.
Sparrows gather in a bamboo grove, voices fluttering here
  and there.
I meet the old farmer returning to his home;
He greets me like a long lost friend.
At his cottage, the farmer's wife heats sake
While we eat freshly picked vegetables and chat.
Together, gloriously drunk, we no longer know
The meaning of unhappiness.

*

When I think about the sadness of the people
  in this world
Their sadness becomes mine.

*

I have returned to my native village after twenty years.

No sign of old friends or relatives – they have all died or gone away.
My dreams are shattered by the sound of the temple bell struck at sunrise.
An empty floor, no shadows, the light has long been extinguished.

*

First days of spring, blue sky, bright sun.
Everything is gradually becoming fresh and green.
Carrying my bowl I walk slowly to the village.
The children, surprised to see me,
Joyfully crowd about, bringing
My begging trip to an end at the temple gate.
I place my bowl on top of a white rock and
Hang my sack from the branch of a tree.
Here we play with the wild grasses and throw a ball.
For a time, I play catch while the children sing;
Then it is my turn.
Playing like this, here and there, I have forgotten the time.
Passers-by point and laugh at me asking,
"What is the reason for such foolishness? "
No answer I give, only a deep bow;
Even if I replied they would not understand.
Look around! There is nothing else besides this.

Ryôkan, too, knew love. Late in his life, after he had left Gogô-an and was living with Kimura Motoemon in Shimazaki village, he met the beautiful nun Teishin. Ryôkan was nearly seventy and Teishin just twenty-nine, but they fell in love immediately. They delighted in each other's company, composing poems, playing with the children, and singing songs as they walked through the countryside.

Singing *waka,* reciting poems, playing ball
Together in the fields.
Two people, one heart.

In the last four years of his life following his meeting with Teishin Ryôkan's poetry became even more lucid and pure. He died peacefully on the sixth day of the first month of 1831 with Teishin at his side. His death verse:

What will remain as my legacy?
Flowers in the spring,
The *hototogisu* in summer,
And the crimson leaves of autumn.

Teishin brought out a collection of Ryôkan's poems entitled *Dewdrops on a Lotus Leaf* in 1835. Ryôkan remained a rather obscure figure, however, until the beginning of the twentieth century when the scholar Sôma Gyofû and others began to introduce him to the general public. Since then his popularity has increased steadily and his name and poetry are known to every Japanese. His poems are especially popular among devotees of *shigin* (classical recitation of verse written in Chinese characters). The number of studies and editions of his poetry grows yearly and his hermitage and ancestral home in Niigata are visited by thousands of pilgrims each year.

Ryôkan's poetry was a reflection of his life – fresh, spontaneous, and without pretense. He wrote classical Chinese poems, *waka,* haiku, folk songs, and *Man'yô*-style poems. The majority are free-style *waka* (he frequently ignored the traditional 5-7-5-7-7 syllable pattern) but his Chinese style poems (*kanshi*) are perhaps more popular. Ryôkan is often compared to Kanzan (Han-shan), the eighth century Chinese hermit-monk. Prior to Ryôkan, Kanzan was considered to be the epitome of the "Zen fool" and was a favorite subject of Zen painter-monks. He is represented as a shabbily dressed recluse with a lunatic grin and often shown with his equally mad side-kick Jittoku (Shih-te). However, Kanzan's poems seem to be somewhat more cutting or disparaging than Ryôkan's; although Kanzan praises the freedom of his hermit's life and heaps scorn on those caught in the world of desire, there is a certain bitterness at being ignored by his contemporaries. (This tendency is present in much Chinese poetry, a great deal of which was composed during the poets' periods of exile.) Such a feeling is rarely present in Ryôkan. He did write a few admonitory Buddhist poems, but his feeling toward others is best shown in these two *waka*:

Thinking about the people in this floating world
Far into the night –
My sleeve is wet with tears.

*

O that my priest's robe was wide enough
To gather up all the suffering people
In this floating world.

In some ways Ryôkan had more in common with his two contemporaries, the painter-monk Sengai (1750-1837) and the haiku poet Issa (1763-1827). In 1788, Sengai was appointed abbot of Shôfukuji in Hakata, Kyushu. His Zen paintings, the most famous ever done, are full of humor and insight. Sengai too avoided philosophizing and pomp, and was happiest living close to nature and the common people. Issa also left his home when young and traveled around the country for many years and finally returned to his native village at the age of fifty, married, and led a poor and rather sorrowful life – his wife and four children all died within a ten year period. Yet Issa, like Ryôkan, retained a gentleness, a feeling for all types of people and things (both Ryôkan and Issa had a particular affection for lice). All three of them were unconventional, free spirits and in a time of vulgarity and decline they preserved the detachment and closeness to nature of earlier poets.

Ryôkan lived in a period of transition from old feudal Japan to the first stirrings of the establishment of a modern state. Ryôkan himself was relatively untouched by the historical currents of his time and was therefore able to maintain the simple elegance of traditional Japan. In fact, Ryôkan seems to be the last of those poets who actually led a poetic life. Ryôkan's life is a symbol of the purity and open-heartedness that once existed. Since the Meiji Restoration, Japan has lost much of its natural beauty and a great deal of its attractiveness. There has been a gradual weakening of the Japanese spirit. Life is too complex, people have spent too much time in school, society is being choked by mass media, everyone is too busy doing nothing. Ryôkan's life and poetry is an antidote for this modern world-wide sickness; it is a valuable treasure that must not be lost.

The number of days since I left the world and
Entrusted myself to Heaven are long forgotten.
Yesterday, sitting peacefully in the green mountains;
This morning, playing with the village children.
My robe is full of patches and
I cannot remember how long I have had the same bowl
    for begging.
On clear nights I walk with my staff and chant poems;
During the day I spread out a straw mat and nap.
Who says many cannot lead such a life?
Just follow my example.

Historian and Master of Chinese Verse

Rai San'yô

by

BURTON WATSON

A major Japanese writer who wrote almost nothing in Japanese: not really the paradox it appears to be, but a description of the Osaka-born poet, historian and essayist Rai San'yô (1781-1832). He lived at a time when the majority of his educated compatriots could read classical Chinese in addition to their own language, and he chose the former as his literary medium. So skillfully did he employ it that his poetry gained an enthusiastic following and the *Nihon gaishi* (*Unofficial History of Japan*), a history of medieval Japan that he wrote in Chinese, became one of the most widely read and influential works of the period.

Before turning to the story of his life, it may be well to explain in brief why it was possible for Rai San'yô to gain such renown among his countrymen by writing in a language not his own.

The Japanese in ancient times had no system of writing. The first writing system they encountered, and almost the only one they had any great familiarity with in early times, was that devised by the Chinese. For all practical purposes, writing for the early Japanese meant writing in Chinese. During the period from the sixth to the tenth century, Japan borrowed heavily from Chinese culture, and classical Chinese was the medium through which much of this borrowing took place. Japanese not only studied the classics of Chinese literature and philosophy, and the texts of Buddhism in Chinese translation, but wrote original works of history and literature in Chinese, as well as employing the language for government papers and records. Though snobbism played a part in this fashion for writing in Chinese, it was inspired largely by a sincere desire to participate in the experience of Chinese culture, particularly during the centuries when China's power and prestige were at their height. At the

Rai San'yô; Rai San'yô Kyûseki Hozonkai (Kyoto)

same time, classical Chinese provided a means of communication not only with China but with the Korean and other mainland peoples who used it as a lingua franca.

For recording their own language, the Japanese at first employed a cumbersome system in which Chinese characters were used sometimes for their meaning and sometimes for their sound. In time a syllabary was devised which greatly simplified the writing of Japanese, and the literature in the native language benefited accordingly. Soon all real creativity was being channeled into Japanese literary forms, and interest in composition in Chinese waned. This development, not surprisingly, corresponded with a period when China's glory was temporarily eclipsed by internal strife and when Japan had relatively little direct contact with the continent.

The introduction of Zen Buddhism to Japan in the thirteenth century awakened a new interest in the Chinese language. Many Japanese monks journeyed to China to study Zen, often spending many years there and becoming highly proficient in the language. Zen laid great emphasis on the doctrinal significance of Chinese verse, and in time the great Zen monasteries of Japan became centers of learning and literature where much attention was given to composition in Chinese. The resulting voluminous body of poetry and prose in Chinese is known as *Gozan bungaku* or the "Literature of the Five Mountains," in reference to the major Zen temples of Kamakura and Kyoto.

A third great period of enthusiasm for Chinese studies and composition in Chinese was ushered in by the founding of the Tokugawa Shogunate in 1603. The Shogunate in time enforced a seclusion policy that prevented Japanese from traveling to China or having much direct contact with the Chinese. But it adopted the Neo-Confucian school of philosophy as the official doctrine of the state and actively encouraged Confucian studies, founding a college devoted to such studies in Edo, the seat of the Shogunate. Similar schools were established under official auspices in a number of important feudal domains, while many scholars in the large cities opened private schools to teach Confucianism and Chinese literature. Thus the samurai of the period, and those townsmen and farmers who could afford an education, spent their childhood poring over Chinese texts and learning to imitate the classics of T'ang and Sung poetry and prose, much as their counterparts in England pored over Latin and Greek and imitated the Roman poets.

Rai San'yo's family was deeply involved in this Tokugawa period tradition of Confucianism and Chinese studies. And without it, San'yo's career would have been wholly different, for he would have had no readership to write for. At the same time, he shaped the tradition and helped to bring it to a height of proficiency and popularity it had in many ways not known before. And, though few could have predicted it at the time, he was one of the last great figures in the tradition, since it began to decline in importance not long after his death, as the Japanese increasingly turned their attention to the study of Western languages.

Rai San'yo was the eldest and only surviving son of a Confucian scholar named Rai Shunsui of the domain of Aki in present-day Hiroshima Prefecture.[1] Rai Shunsui, the son of a well-to-do farm family of Takehara, went to Osaka in his youth, where he studied Chinese and became an enthusiastic supporter of the Chu Hsi school of Neo-Confucianism. He also became a member of the *Kontonsha* or Chaos Society, a group of scholars and literary-minded townsmen who gathered once a month to compose poems in Chinese and criticize each other's works, consuming considerable amounts of sake in the process, we are told. He opened a small private school in Osaka to teach Chinese and Confucianism, and married a well-educated young woman who went by the literary name Baishi, the daughter of a Confucian scholar and physician. San'yô, their first child, was born on the twenty-seventh day of the twelfth lunar month of An'ei 9, a date that by the Western calendar would fall early in 1781.

Shortly after, Shunsui was invited to become an official Confucian scholar of his native domain of Aki. He returned with his family to Takehara, and eventually took up residence in Hiroshima, where the castle of the domain was situated. San'yô began his studies under his uncle Rai Kyôhei, a distinguished scholar and writer of poetry in Chinese and, like San'yô's father, an official Confucian scholar of the domain. San'yô was extremely bright, diligent in his work and especially fond of history, but physically rather weak and so moody and temperamental his parents could barely manage him. A poem in Chinese written when he was thirteen (fourteen by traditional Japanese reckoning) reveals the high goals he set for himself, and his impatience to reach them. (I quote the original version of the poem, which was later somewhat reworked.)

> Thirteen springs and autumns,
> springs and autumns that went by like water;
> when will I realize my ambition:
> for countless years, a place in history?

At the age of seventeen San'yô went to Edo with his uncle Kyôhei, who had been assigned to temporary duty there. San'yô became a student in the Shôheikô, the school for Confucian studies operated by the Shogunate. But for reasons no biographer has so far been able to determine for certain, he left the school after a year and returned home. Quite likely, like many precocious students, he was bored with his courses, which in this case would have consisted merely of more of the Chu Hsi Confucianism he had already been so fully exposed to at home. Other explanations have been offered, among them a rumor that he got into trouble by making advances to the maid at the home of the scholar and in-law with whom he was lodging.

Back home in Hiroshima, San'yô continued more moody and restless than ever. His parents, hoping that marriage would settle him down, arranged for him to take as a bride the fourteen-year-old daughter of a local physician. But, as repeated rueful entries in his mother's diary attest, the marriage failed to have the desired effect, and San'yô seized every excuse to leave the house, often drinking heavily and not returning until after midnight. The bride, reduced to a state of hysteria, was eventually sent back to her own home and the marriage dissolved. She was already pregnant and bore a son, named Mototada, who was adopted and raised by San'yô's father.

In 1800, the year previous to this, San'yô's father was summoned to Edo to lecture for half a year at the Shôheikô, an honor he no doubt welcomed with delight. But while Shunsui was covering himself with academic glory in Edo, San'yô struck off in a quite different direction. Freed from his father's surveillance and sent by his mother to convey condolences to a bereaved relative in Takehara, he took the opportunity to run away from Aki, a grave offense, since official permission was required for all journeys outside one's own domain. He was eventually located in Kyoto and brought home where, as a result of his parents' pleas, he was pardoned from more severe punishment on grounds of insanity and placed under house arrest. He was disinherited by an understandably irate Shunsui and a cousin was adopted as heir in his place.

San'yô's erratic gesture of rebellion, while it sullied the family name, ended by having a highly salutary effect on his growth as a scholar and writer. Though the conditions of his confinement were severe at first, he was soon allowed to have what books and writing materials he desired. He spent his three-year term of confinement studying and writing, beginning the work that in time was to make him famous, the *Nihon gaishi,* of which I shall say more later.

In 1809, his period of opprobrium ended, San'yô was sent to study under and assist Kan Sazan (or Chazan, as the name is sometimes read), a scholar who ran a small school in Kannabe in the neighboring province of Bingo. Kan Sazan is a figure of major importance in the history of *kanshi* or Chinese poetry written by Japanese. Most Japanese *kanshi* writers in the eighteenth century had modeled their works on those of T'ang dynasty China, endeavoring to reproduce the lofty and often mythic tone of T'ang poetry. The results, though polished and elegant, tended to lack individuality, seldom achieving anything more than a stilted imitation of a far-off country and age. Toward the close of the eighteenth century Japanese writers, following an earlier shift in taste in China itself, began to take greater interest in the poetry of the Sung period and to attempt to capture its spirit in their own works. Sung poetry, particularly in comparison to that of the T'ang, is more homey and discursive, dealing realistically with the scenes and activities of everyday life, often in a light and humorous manner.

Kan Sazan, who lived from 1748 to 1827, was one of the first important poets to write in the Sung manner, and his works, simple and unpretentious in tone, did much to popularize the style. Both San'yô's father and his uncle Kyôhei were distinguished poets, employing the same simple style as Kan Sazan, and as we have seen, San'yô himself had begun writing verse in Chinese at an early age. Yet the fact that he had an opportunity to study and live with so distinguished a poet as Kan Sazan no doubt spurred his interest in poetry and helped him to refine the skills that were later to win him wide acclaim as a *kanshi* writer.

But San'yô was scarcely the kind to be contented with the lot of a teaching assistant in a country school. As he made clear in a letter written at the time, he was firmly convinced that one must be in the big city if one hoped to be a success in literature and learning. In 1811, therefore, after a year with Kan Sazan, he made arrangements to go to Kyoto, where he opened a small school of his own. The move was probably a disappointment to Kan Sazan, who apparently had contemplated adopting San'yô as his heir, though the two remained good friends.

Since San'yô had been disinherited and had no kind of official position or stipend, he was dependent entirely upon what money he could make from his teaching and writing. Though in time he gained sufficient fame to be able to make a relatively comfortable living in this manner – indeed, he is noteworthy as the first Japanese man of letters to do so – life in Kyoto must at first have been rather lonely and precarious. He made occasional trips to nearby provinces, on one of which in 1813 he stopped at the home of a scholar and physician named Ema Ransai in Mino. There he met Saikô, Ransai's eldest daughter. The two appear to have been immediately attracted to one another, and San'yô in time requested permission to marry her. Ransai turned down the request on the grounds of San'yô's unpromising financial situation. Saikô nevertheless became San'yô's disciple, studying *kanshi* writing under him and visiting him often in Kyoto. It is difficult to say just how intimate their relationship was. A poem written by San'yô in 1830 suggests that, seventeen years after their meeting, he was still very fond of her:

"Farewell Talk with Saikô by a Rainy Window"

A parting meal, low lamp – stay and enjoy it a bit longer;
new mud on the road home – better wait till it dries.
On peaks across the river, clouds only now dispersing;
strings and songs in the house next door just beginning to fade in the night.
Intercalary month this spring – my guest lingers on,
though last night's rain heartlessly scattered the cherry flowers.
From here you go to Mino – not a long way away,
though growing old, I know how hard it is to meet now and then.

Saikô, who remained unmarried, has left the following testimony indicating how deeply she regretted that she had not become San'yô's wife, though she suggests that she herself was to blame:

"To Inscribe on My Portrait"

Lonely room, fiddling with a brush as the years go by;

one mistake in a lifetime, not the kind to be mended.
This chaste purity to rejoice in – what do I resemble?
A hidden orchid, a rare bamboo – sketch me
in some such cold form.

San'yô, resigned to failure in the case of Saikô, in 1815 married Hikita Rie, the daughter of a farm family of Ômi Province. She was anything but a literary type like Saikô, though apparently she made San'yô a very devoted wife. San'yô in his writings speaks of her with affection, and in fact became known in current parlance as a *rakuda* or "camel," a man who, contrary to custom, takes his wife along with him on outings and social visits. She bore him three sons, Tatsuzô (died in childhood), Matajirô, and Mikisaburô, and a daughter.

San'yô's most extended journey was that made in 1818 to Kyushu, which occupied over a year and inspired numerous poems on historical and scenic spots. One poem begins with the following vivid description of a Dutch ship entering the harbor of Nagasaki, where the Dutch and Chinese were permitted to carry on limited trade. The poem illustrates San'yô's remarkable skill in handling themes that had little or no precedent in traditional Chinese poetry:

In Nagasaki, southwest where sky and water meet,
suddenly at heaven's edge a tiny dot appears.
The cannon of the lookout tower gives one roar
and in twenty-five watch stations bows are bared.
Through the streets on four sides the cry breaks forth:
"The redhaired Westerners are coming! "
Launches set out to meet them, we hear the drum echo,
in the distance signal flags are raised to stay alarm.
The ship enters the harbor like a ponderous turtle,
so huge that in the shallows it seems certain to ground.
Our little launches, so many strings of pearls,
tow it forward amid a clamorous din.
The barbarian hull rises a hundred feet from the surface,
sea winds sighing, flapping its pennants of felt.
Three sails stretched among ten thousand lines,
fixed to engines moving up and down like wellsweeps.
Blackskinned slaves nimble as monkeys
scale the masts, haul the lines, keeping them from tangling.[2]

In Kyushu, San'yô called on Hirose Tansô, a distinguished *kanshi* poet who was San'yô's age. Tansô, who left a record of his impressions, found San'yô ambitious, highly confident of his ability, and lacking in manners, and adds that he was widely disliked in Kyushu and reportedly was the target of much criticism in Kyoto as well. He concedes, however, that San'yô was extremely talented and expressed regret that he was not better treated by society.[3]

This is no more than one man's opinion, but there are other intimations that San'yô often impressed people unfavorably. All his life he appears to have been impatient for recognition, and this, along with the temperamental nature that had characterized him from childhood, led him at times to assume an offensively brash and boastful manner. It should also be noted that, although San'yô's poetry, calligraphy, and literati-style painting were fairly well known during his lifetime, his most important works, particularly the *Unofficial History of Japan,* did not circulate widely until after his death. His contemporaries, therefore, did not have the means to judge the full extent of his ability.

San'yô returned to Kyoto in 1819 and the following year his first child by Rie, a son named Tatsuzô, was born. The following are three of six poems he wrote on the occasion:

No fields, no house, one poor scholar,
but I have a child, and to my delight it's a boy!
A few paintings, a pair of old inkstones:
your father offers them to you – but will you accept them?

So stupid of me to hope you'll take to books;
a scholar all my life, I want to raise you the same way.
Baby squalls that to other ears are nothing but noise –
sooner or later they'll give way to the student's drone.

Fist like the mountain fern half unfurled,
skin like the pomegranate when the blossom has just dropped;
all you do is howl, searching for your mother's breast;
beautiful baby eyes that have not learned to tell their father.

In 1822 San'yô was well enough off to move to a new house on the west bank of the Kamo River just north of Marutamachi, where he lived for the remainder of his life. The Rai family continues to occupy the house, and San'yô's small thatched-roof study in the garden, added in 1828, is kept as it was in his time. He describes the house in the following poem written on New Year's day, which, according to traditional reckoning, marked the beginning of spring:

In a new house greeting the first of the year,
opening doors on bright clear weather:
below the stairs, shallow water flows,
rippling already with the sound of spring.

Bending by the current, I wash my inkstone,
purple of the stone reflecting green of hills.
In such an out-of-the-way spot, few visitors –
I'm pleased to be spared all that greeting and goodbying.
A place to live this peaceful –
it fits exactly with what I've always wanted;
only I regret that business of my mother,
not arranging to have her come live with me.
How can I share this wine with her,
see her gentle face smiling as she lifts the cup?
I grind some ink, write a letter home
in a drunken hand that keeps straying out of line.

San'yô's mother, mentioned in the closing lines, is a familiar figure in his poems. His father died in 1816, and it was only shortly before his death that father and son were fully reconciled. But San'yô's mother remained well and active throughout his lifetime, and outlived him by eleven years. Partly perhaps out of guilt over the grief he had caused his parents in his youth, San'yô treated his mother with unusual respect and attentiveness. She continued to live in Hiroshima – whether out of choice or because San'yô never got around to making other arrangements, we do not know – but she visited Kyoto frequently and took trips here and there with her son. The following poem was written in the fall of 1829. In the spring, San'yô's mother had come to Kyoto for a visit, and in the fall San'yô escorted her part of the way home.

"Escorting My Mother Home: a Short Song for the Road"

East winds to greet my mother when she came;
north winds see her on her way back home.
She arrived when roads were fragrant with blossoms,
now suddenly this cold of frost and snow!
At cock crow already I'm tying my footgear,
waiting by her palanquin, legs a bit unsteady.
Never mind if the son's legs are tired,
just worry whether her palanquin's fit for riding.
I pour her a cup of wine, a drink for myself too,
first sunlight flooding the inn, frost already dried.
Fifty-year-old son, seventy-year-old mother –
not often you find a pair lucky as we!
Off to the south, in from the north, streams of people –
who among them happy as this mother and son?

Though San'yô's little boy Tatsuzô died of smallpox in 1825, a second son was born in 1823 and a third in 1825. He was nearing completion of the *Nihon gaishi,* and if he sometimes had trouble making ends meet, life on the whole seems to have been relatively tranquil. In the following poems, two of a set of eight written in 1828 and entitled "Reading Books," the grumbling is largely feigned; the overall mood is one of contentment.

This morning, splendid breeze and sunlight,
north window where the new rain passed;
visitors sent off, I open my book;
then my wife comes with her story:
"No money coming in – all these relatives –
eight mouths – how can we get along alone?
No one important ever comes to call –
poverty and cold – that's all we'll ever know!
If only you'd be a little less sharp –
try being pleasant to others for a change – "
My illness, who can cure it?
The bones I have are the ones Heaven gave me.
If I'd stayed in my father's domain
I'd never have forgone official service.
But if I went back to that petty routine,
wouldn't I be false to my father's hopes?
Go away – don't bother me!
I'm trying to converse with the men of old.

Eastern hills – dense and lush,
turning purple in the evening sun.
Kamo River ripples have all subsided,
only here and there the glint of a white gem.
Our family ducks know the day is ended;
they quack to each other, time to go home!
I too put away my books,
call to my wife to get out the cask of wine.
Fresh fish from the river, just right for grilling;
bamboo shoots – we dig them ourselves.
I'm going to sit by the eastern eaves,
share a drink with the hills over there.

After completing the *Nihon gaishi* in 1827, San'yô began work on a second historical study, the seldom-read *Nihon seiki* (*Political Record of Japan*). Though taking off time for trips with his mother, he remained hard at work at it and other writings until the summer of 1832, when he suddenly spat up blood. Examination revealed that his lungs were in serious condition. Entertaining no illusions about his chances for recovery, he utilized what time and strength remained to put his writings in order. On the seventeenth day of the ninth month, Yanagawa Seigan, a poet, scholar, and old friend, called on San'yô to inquire of his condition before setting off for Shinshû and Edo. San'yô, who knew it was the last time he would see his friend, wrote the following poem and died six days later.

Lamp by the yellow chrysanthemums, close onto midnight;
tomorrow morning you set off to tread the Shinshû clouds.
Our one pot of wine gone, but stay a little longer –
In this sickness near to death, must I say goodbye to you?

I have already quoted enough of San'yô's *kanshi* to indicate some of the qualities that make them outstanding: their descriptive power and simple, unaffected treatment of actual events in the poet's life. Though Japanese *kanshi* poets, particularly in the Tokugawa period, had ready mastery of the technical requirements of Chinese verse and could turn out pieces that met conventional standards, few were able to be truly creative in the medium. Sugawara no Michizane, the famous ninth century scholar and statesman, who was one of San'yô's idols, was a rare exception in the early period, leaving a collection of poems in Chinese that include not only ornate state pieces but highly personal and moving accounts of his private life, particularly of the bitter years of exile in Kyushu.

San'yô, like Michizane, had sufficient command of his medium that he could shape it to any theme or emotion he desired, though his low-keyed pieces on daily life perhaps hold the greatest appeal for us today. San'yô has been particularly admired in the past as a writer of poems on historical themes, a genre he did much to popularize. Especially famous are his *Nihon gafu* (*Ballads of Japan*), a series of sixty-six poems on famous events in Japanese history cast in *yüeh-fu* or ballad form, which uses lines of varying length. The series, completed in 1828, is modeled on similar works by the Ming poet Li Tung-yang. The poems are difficult to appreciate without a thorough knowledge of the events they treat, and are rather bombastic in tone. But their ardent patriotism and expressions of support for the imperial institution insured them wide popularity in the period following San'yô's death.

San'yô's shorter prose writings in Chinese include travel pieces and biographical sketches of unusual personalities of the Tokugawa period. Among the latter are the wry and humorous account of O-Yuki, the lady swashbuckler of Osaka, and the warmly sympathetic account of Yuri, a Kyoto teahouse attendant and poet.[4]

But although San'yô's poems and miscellaneous prose writings in Chinese charmed his contemporaries, it was the *Nihon gaishi* that made him a figure of towering importance in the literary world in the century following his death. As we have seen, he began work on the history when a young man under house arrest. He completed it in 1827, some twenty-five years later, and presented a copy to the eminent statesman and friend of the family Matsudaira Sadanobu, who was by this time living in retirement and had asked to see the work. Matsudaira praised it highly, and from this time it began to circulate in manuscript. Some ten years after San'yô's death it was printed, and ran through countless editions.

The work, in twenty-two chapters, deals with the various military families who wielded power in Japan from the close of the Heian period in the late twelfth century to the founding of the Tokugawa Shogunate in 1603. San'yô takes up each family individually and traces its background, rise to power, and eventual downfall (his account of "our Tokugawa," needless to say, being an exception in this last respect). Here and there, in carefully marked appraisal sections, he comments on the causes behind the flow of events and passes judgment on the participants. In tracing the history of individual families and confining his personal observations to specially marked sections, he was following the example of the Chinese historian Ssu-ma Ch'ien (145? -90? B.C.), whose *Shih chi* (*Records of the Historian*) he admired intensely and took as his model for prose style.

The entire work, as San'yô makes clear in the opening pages, is motivated by his boundless regret that the imperial house in the centuries following the late Heian was forced to relinquish the actual power of government to a succession of warrior families. His sympathies throughout are manifestly on the side of the largely impotent emperors and their supporters, and against the shoguns and military dictators who exercised de facto rule. In a long digression on the history of the Fujiwara family, he apportions them a share of the blame in bringing about the eclipse of imperial power, and does not hesitate to chastise the emperors themselves for calling upon the warrior class for protection in the first place instead of wielding military power in person. His work thus is dominated by a unified theme and point of view, one that was becoming increasingly prevalent as reverence for the imperial institution grew and the weakness of the Shogunate became ever more apparent.

But the fact that its outlook so aptly tallied with the trend of the times does not fully account for the enormous popularity that the *Nihon gaishi* enjoyed. San'yô appears to have made little effort to ferret out new source materials or to subject the traditional accounts to any original or penetrating analysis. His work thus bears no comparison with that of more critical and creative historians such as Arai Hakuseki. His interest lay rather in the literary aspects of his material, in history as a series of stirring and heroic tales. He was content to follow traditional accounts even when, as in works such as the *Taiheiki* (*Chronicle of the Great Pacification*), they are idealized almost to the point of fiction. His unique contribution lay in organizing the material into a comprehensive account of the period, in recasting Japanese sources into clear and lively Chinese prose, and in adding passages of reflection that, if seldom outstandingly acute, are often moving as poetic evocations of the past.

To report that the *Nihon gaishi* is written in classical Chinese immediately suggests that it must be rather forbidding and pedantic in nature – a Macaulay in Latin instead of English. But several points must be noted if one is not to misconstrue the situation. First is the fact that educated Japanese of the period began the study of classical Chinese at a very early age, receiving extensive exposure to historical texts such as the *Shih chi* that constituted San'yô's models. Thus they were able to read San'yô's text rapidly and with ease. It should also be kept in mind that they were already thoroughly familiar with the main personages and events of San'yô's narrative from their reading of earlier works in Japanese. What interested them in the *Nihon gaishi* was to observe how San'yô wove together all the scattered accounts of the past, what comments he had to make on them, and how he rendered into Chinese the famous episodes and utterances of Japanese history. San'yô did not disappoint them, taking care to present in vivid, powerful language the battles, death scenes, and other dramatic highlights of his Japanese sources. Moreover, because classical Chinese is intrinsically far more compact and economical in expression than classical Japanese, San'yô's narrative, while preserving all the essential details of its prototypes, moves along with a briskness that is positively exhilarating.

Far from striking his compatriots as tedious, the *Nihon gaishi* was welcomed with great enthusiasm, particularly by youthful readers of late Tokugawa times. One more fact may be adduced to explain such popularity. Although the work deplores the appearance in history of the great military families, it deals entirely with their exploits, in chapter after chapter detailing the bold schemes and deeds of valor by which they rose to power. But the Tokugawa was a period of profound peace and social stability, when samurai grew old and died without ever having tasted actual combat; only in dreams could one battle one's way to glory. For the youth of late Tokugawa times, grown restive with this long peace, the *Nihon gaishi* provided such a dream, a stirring reminder of how different the situation had been in the past. And, with its sentiments of strong support for the imperial house and implied condemnation of the Shogunate, it must have suggested to them that a new period of social upheaval was not far off, when deeds of valor and meteoric rise to power would once more be within the realm of possibility.

San'yô himself took care to see that his works, though pro-imperial in tone, should contain nothing that would offend the Shogunate. His youngest son Mikisaburô or Ôgai was less cautious. Only seven at the time of San'yô's death, he carried on the family tradition of learning and like his father attended the Shôheikô in Edo, though his undisguised contempt for the Shogunate soon led to his expulsion. Back in Kyoto, he joined the group associated with San'yô's old friend Yanagawa Seigan, mentioned above. Seigan in his late years became increasingly active in supporting the *Sonnô jôi* movement, which called for restoration of power to the emperor and expulsion of the foreign traders. He and his group were marked for surveillance by the Shogunate, and in 1858, in the so-called Great Persecution of the Ansei Era, measures were taken to silence them. Seigan died of cholera just before the authorities moved into action, but Mikisaburô was arrested and imprisoned in Edo, where he was beheaded in 1859. While in prison he wrote the following poem:

I wanted to drive back the clouds,
with these hands sweep clear the evil stars,
but the ground gave way beneath my feet,
I plunged to Edo Prison.
Idiot frogs fret at the bottom of their well;
the brilliance of the great moon falters on the horizon.[5]
I wait the death sentence, no news from home;
in dreams, the ring of swords: I slash at sea monsters.
When the wind and rain of many years have cloaked my stone in moss,
who will remember this mad man of Japan?

Thus the cause so eloquently pleaded by San'yô in the end claimed the life of his son, as it did those of so many of the promising young men of the period. Today Mikisaburô rests beside his father and other family members in the graveyard of Chôrakuji in Kyoto, under a stone by no means forgotten or unduly moss-grown.

The eminent Meiji period critic Okakura Tenshin, in a work written in English, described the *Nihon gaishi* as "that epic narrative of the country from whose poetic pages the youth of Japan still learn the intensity of the raging fever that moved their grandfathers to revolution."[6] It is unlikely that any present-day reader, Japanese or otherwise, could wax so enthusiastic. The *Nihon gaishi*'s value as history was dubious to begin with, its political views have severely dated, and few readers today command sufficient fluency in classical Chinese to appreciate its felicities of style. It was a work of indubitable and far-reaching importance in its day, but that day seems definitely to have passed.

Time has been kinder to San'yô's poems and informal prose works. These, as I hope I have suggested, reveal a man of warmth, intellect, and engaging sense of humor. Though San'yô can never again be the literary idol and kindler of youthful ardor he was for past generations, he remains an author eminently worth knowing. If he was inordinately admired in the past, he is at present neglected to an unjust degree. One hopes the time has come for the pendulum to take another swing.

[NOTES]

1. I refer to Rai San'yô and other literary figures by their *gô* or literary names, by which they are best known; San'yô's personal name was Noboru.
2. Javanese servants of the Dutch.
3. Tansô's remarks are translated in Donald Keene, *World Within Walls: Japanese Literature of the Pre-Modern Era 1600-1867* (New York: Rinehart & Winston, 1976), p.552.
4. Both are translated in Burton Watson, *Japanese Literature in Chinese*, Vol.2 (New York: Columbia University Press, 1976), pp.162-170; it also contains a selection of San'yô's poetry from which the examples above are quoted.
5. The frogs are the shortsighted statesmen of the Shogunate, the moon is the powerless emperor in Kyoto.
6. Okakura Kakuzô, *The Ideals of the East* (New York: E.P. Dutton & Co., 1904; reprinted by Charles E. Tuttle: Rutland, Vermont and Tokyo, Japan, 1970), p.210.

Leader of Peasant Rebellions

Miura Meisuke

by

HERBERT P. BIX

> I don't think you realize how hard it is for the oppressed to become united. Their misery unites them – once they recognize who has caused it. "Our sufferance is a gain to them." But otherwise their misery is liable to cut them off from one another, for they are forced to snatch the wretched crumbs from each other's mouths. Think how reluctantly men decide to revolt! It's an adventure for them: new paths have to be marked out and followed; moreover the rule of rulers is always accompanied by that of their ideas. To the masses revolt is the unnatural rather than the natural thing....
> (B. Brecht, "Study of the first scene of Shakespeare's *Coriolanus*")

The Setting

Nanbu lay against the Pacific coast in the rugged mountainous region of northeast Honshu, a large *tozama* fief valued originally at 100,000 *koku*.[1] To its south lay Sendai, to its west and northwest the fiefs of Akita and Tsugaru. Bordering it along the northern coast was the small, independent branch fief of Hachinohe, where the great Andô Shôeki lived out his life in the first half of the eighteenth century. Called in modern times the "Tibet of Japan," this was the region whose people would later be known for their tenacity and stubbornness (like the *Nanbu hanamagari* – local salmon ascending a river), where peasant families during the great depression of the 1930s were reduced to selling their daughters into prostitution, where children grew up before the war not having known the taste of sugar.

Since the Kamakura period the old and powerful Nanbu family had ruled over the region from their headquarters in the castle town of Morioka. During the first century of Tokugawa rule, which began in 1603,

Nanbu's economy grew on the basis of mining and the development of commerce, in a manner similar to the other semi-autonomous fiefs into which feudal Japan was divided. But soon enough the country's rice economy evolved into a money economy, without any accompanying political legitimation. The feudal lords of Nanbu then grew more oppressive, as they themselves were oppressed by the Shogunate in Edo. As the eighteenth century drew to a close, a marked decline could be seen in the fortunes of three of the four official classes caught up in the self-destructive *bakuhan* system. Only the lowly merchants continued to prosper.

In the northeast the crisis of feudal disintegration worked itself out with particular severity, aggravated by a succession of devastating famines and droughts. Nanbu lost 49,600 people through starvation in the great Hôreki famine of 1755, more than ten percent of the fief's entire population of 358,000. The scars of that disaster had hardly healed when the famines of the Tenmei era (1781-88) struck, taking another 65,000 lives and causing over 10,500 dwellings to be abandoned.[2] With rice productivity low even in the best of times, the peasants were compelled for their very survival to seek other sources of food and income. Whereupon the daimyo of Morioka levied new taxes, obstructing rather than encouraging the development of new lines of industry and commerce. Not content to take tribute from the peasants in accordance with the standard ratio of "six to the prince and four to the people," they devised taxes on every form of profitable activity. Finally, because the fief's treasury and cash reserves were chronically depleted, and pressed by the unending burdens of the *sankin kôtai* system, they moved toward a strategy of reinforcing samurai control over the countryside and squeezing the peasants even harder. The peasants of Nanbu, although unarmed by law and at the mercy of the fief's officials, answered back, drawing on a long tradition of peasant rebellions.

During the Tokugawa period there were at least 2,967 peasant uprisings (*ikki*), and if urban and rural disturbances are included the figure comes to over 4,000.[3] The authors of *Nihon zankoku monogatari* (*Tales of Cruelty in Japan*) give a figure of 1,240 major peasant uprisings during the early modern period and claim that as many as 361, or 29 percent, occurred in the northeast. And more occurred in Nanbu than in any other fief in Japan – 96 by one count and 120 according to another.[4]

As the nineteenth century unfolded and Western military pressure on Japan grew, the rebellions in Nanbu intensified: in tempo, size, planning, degree of organization, and militancy. Finally, in the year of Commodore Perry's arrival at Uraga, they culminated in one of the greatest and most

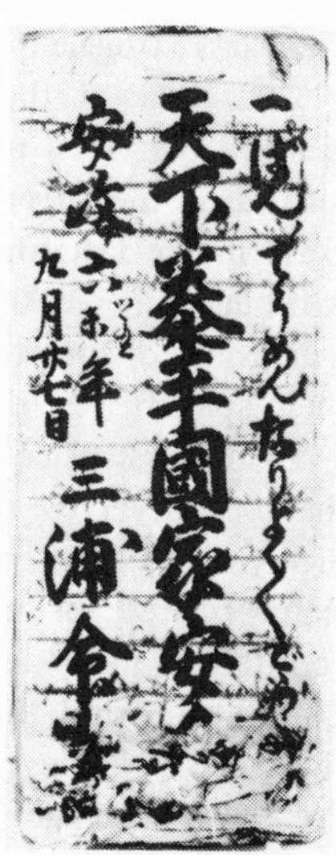

Miura Meisuke's *Gokuchûki* Notebook No. 1;
Miura Karoku (Kamaishi, Iwate Prefecture)

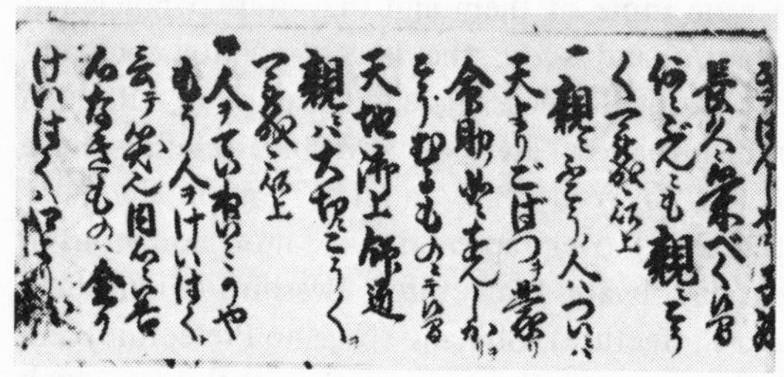

anti-feudal peasant uprisings in all of Tokugawa history. This was the uprising that began in May 1853 and twice swept Kunohe, Shimohei, and Kamihei – Nanbu's Three Hei Districts (Sanheidôri) – toppling the corrupt regime in Morioka castle and forcing its successor to accept and implement most of the demands of the people. Directed against the authority of Nanbu itself, it brought 16-17,000 people onto the road in a meticulously planned and executed mass exodus from the fief; and it represented, in the last analysis, the striving from below for a wider market free from feudal restrictions.

This short essay has two objectives. The first is to present a few of the more important economic and political factors behind the famous 1853 rebellion against Nanbu fief that have a bearing on the thought of Miura Meisuke (1820-64). Meisuke, at age thirty-three, joined the command group of the rebellion at a critical stage and was probably the main drafter of the forty-nine peasant demands. Later, while in prison, he went on to produce a unique document, the "Prison Memorandums and Letters," which historian Mori Kahei, the scholar who discovered it, has named the *Gokuchûki.* Secondly, by describing the contradictions in Meisuke's class position it is possible to point out some salient features of his thought as revealed in the *Gokuchûki,* and to show the contribution that the peasants, particularly those of the dissolving *nanushi* stratum from which Meisuke sprang, made to overthrowing Tokugawa feudalism from within and preparing for the Meiji Restoration.

The Class Struggle in Nanbu Fief

The story of the Nanbu uprisings and of Miura Meisuke, whose life spanned the worst period of misgovernment in the fief's history, must be set first in the larger framework of peasant rebellions (*hyakushô ikki*) that arose in the last forty years of the *bakuhan* system and feudal society. Although nineteenth century rebellions displayed an essential continuity with those of the preceding centuries, they also had characteristics that set them apart from earlier Tokugawa rebellions.

In the first place there were more of them and they were paralleled at the local level by *uchikowashi* and *sôdô,* the largely spontaneous and highly destructive collective actions of peasants and urban poor. Although exact figures for minor disturbances are not available, scholars have counted as many as 479 *ikki* between 1830 and 1867. As in the early Tokugawa period, they occurred all over Japan but were most numerous in five areas: Nanbu (present-day Iwate Prefecture), Iwashiro (Fukushima Prefecture), Echigo (Niigata Prefecture), Shinano (Nagano Prefecture) and Iyo (Ehime Prefecture).[5] By contrast, the fiefs of the southwest which were to launch the Meiji Restoration – Satsuma, Chôshû and Tosa – and which have been studied the most intensively by Western scholars, experienced comparatively few.[6]

Secondly, where nearly all the rebellions of the Tokugawa period can be regarded as expressing the structural contradictions of the closed *bakuhan* system and the peasants' desire for liberation from feudal oppression, those at the end of the period expressed both in a more self-conscious, if not class-conscious, way. They also expressed the peasant belief in the *ikki* as an actual right, to be exercised when all other peaceful tactics had failed and their very existence was threatened by intolerable feudal tax levies and corvées.[7] Peasants who rose up in late feudal society, when the possibility for material progress – even in backward Nanbu – was becoming self-evident, gave freer reign than ever before to their underlying moralism, to their pride at being society's producers, and to their belief in their own indispensability to the fief.[8]

Thirdly, the form of protest at the fief level underwent a subtle change. In earlier uprisings, either individuals or councils representing entire villages, would draw up a petition of grievances and take it personally to some higher feudal authority, often the domanial lord himself, or even the shogun, thereby violating the feudal chain of command. This was the *daihyô osso,* a traditional form of protest that ran the penalty of death, but which expressed in a veiled way the groping from below for a new system of rule.

By the 1840s and '50s, however, the mass *osso* began to acquire a dual

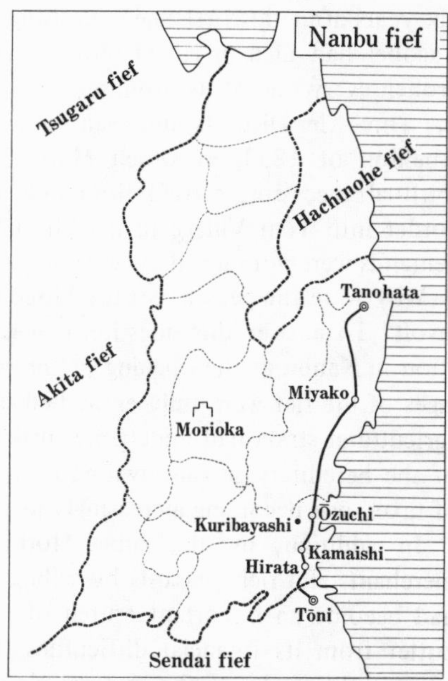

significance as the feudal system itself entered the final stage of disintegration. Not only did the *osso* break the feudal chain of command and reveal a *scale* of class consciousness that was more national than fief-bound, but the peasants in the process were starting to proclaim the illegitimacy of the fief itself – first by threatening, and then by actually implementing the threat to seek redress in other fiefs. This was a progression in anti-feudal consciousness and nowhere was it more clearly expressed than in Nanbu. Thus, when the first rebellion of the Three Hei Districts erupted, on December 2, 1847, over 12,000 peasants followed the seventy-year-old Yagobei, their leader, but only as far as Tôno, a dependent fiefdom within Nanbu domain. It was to Tôno's *karô*, Nitta Kojûrô, also a direct retainer of the Nanbu family, that the rebel petition and demands were submitted.[9] The implied threat to go outside the fief, as well as the tone of despair, are unmistakable.

> We are coming out to the door of the Shogunate because the Nanbu family is so crude. Peasants are people of the country [i.e., not of a particular fief] and therefore we want benevolent intervention by the Shogunate.... We can hardly live in this fief. So that even if we seize all the boats on the coast and row out with the winds as far as the coasts of such foreign lands as China or India, we will find a better place to live than this.[10]

Six years after this first major uprising of the Three Hei Districts – after Yagobei had died in jail at Morioka and after the fief government had broken every one of its promises to the peasants – they rose up again in the Three Hei Districts, not even bothering to appeal to the fief at all. The rebellion of 1853, in which Miura Meisuke participated as Yagobei's spiritual successor, carried thousands of peasants southward across the border into Tôni Village in neighboring Sendai fief. From there, if their demands were not met, they were prepared to go on to Edo.

Why were the peasants of the Three Hei Districts driven repeatedly into revolt? To answer this question it is necessary to review briefly the situation in Nanbu at the opening of the nineteenth century. By then the villages of the fief were fully enmeshed in the money economy; the various agricultural strata had undergone further differentiation; and the position of the hereditary servant-owning *nanushi* stratum, which bore the brunt of taxes, was becoming increasingly unstable.[11]

In addition, by this time, Morioka's policy of raising cash from merchants and rich peasants by selling them samurai ranks at fixed prices had become an important crutch of the regime. Desperately seeking an outlet from its financial difficulties, the fief government continued to expand the ranks of the samurai class.[12] It did this by reviving in the countryside the medieval "retainer" system, implied by the term *jikata kyûnin.* In its new (pseudo) incarnation, *jikata kyûnin* meant "local resident official." Originating from the *nanushi* stratum, the *kyûnin* had acquired considerable wealth through land reclamation, iron mining, fishing and money lending. Significantly, after purchasing samurai status and becoming enfeoffed, they continued living right in the villages, supervising the activities of the peasants and directly participating in the suppression of their rebellions. This despised stratum of pseudo "retainers," the "local resident officials," totaled only 361 in 1738. By 1827 their number had swelled to 559. But thereafter they grew by leaps and bounds, going from 760 in 1831 to 1164 in 1858 and 1151 in 1861.[13] The greatest proliferation of *kyûnin* occurred in the heartland of the Three Hei Districts – Ôzuchi, Miyako, and Noda – and that was a major factor in the rebellions of those years.

Besides spawning *kyûnin,* who lived in the villages like the *gôshi* ("rustic samurai") of Satsuma, Morioka also established a stratum of *kaneage-zamurai* (literally, "money contributing samurai"), who were really privileged merchant capitalists. Unlike the *kyûnin,* the latter went to live in Morioka castle in direct service to the lord, under whom some of them set fief policy. Ishihara Migiwa, who figured prominently as an object of peasant hatred during the 1853 rebellion, was an oil merchant who rose to the position of *karô* (fief elder) after his daughter became Lord Toshitada's concubine. A document quoted in the *Nihon zankoku monogatari* captures the image of this *kaneage-zamurai* in the eyes of a samurai chronicler.

> The high official Ishihara Yasubei [Migiwa] of Nanbu, who came from the *chônin* class and by mysterious fortune became a fief retainer, was gradually promoted. Sitting beside the lord, he flattered and seduced him with his sycophantic words just as Chao Kao of the Ch'in dynasty did. Flatterers and sycophants who became familiar with Migiwa, at both upper and lower ranks, indulged themselves in selfish desires. Meanwhile Migiwa, who was in command of those people, sought to cover his own corrupt practices through them. He developed his evil schemes day after day, with the result that tributes were doubled every year, causing great suffering among the people.[14]

If the emergence of *kyûnin* most vividly signalled the blurring of the line between samurai (*shi*) and peasants (*nô*), then the *kaneage-zamurai* symbolized the fief's policy of sheer tax pillaging, as another document cited in the above source confirms.

> First they [fief authorities] would contrive excuses and demand tax payments on unjustifiable grounds. But later, because the peasants were reluctant to comply, they resorted to illegal means, treated people harshly and even arrested them. And if the peasants failed to pay assigned taxes on the day due they would press them unmercifully. And, in addition to taxes, those rascals in lower offices and the ruthless prison guards would seize household effects as reminder fees. One can hardly bear to see their insatiable greed.[15]

The tax abuses, peasant protests and turmoil which accompanied the rise of the *kyûnin* and the *kaneage-zamurai* means that the very groups Morioka was relying on to keep the peasants under control and augment its wealth were actually undermining the framework of the fief itself. Yet the threat of fiscal insolvency, which grew as the Shogunate added to Nanbu's coastal defense obligations, compelled Morioka to continue its rule over the peasants with the aid of big merchant capital. The years 1820-40 saw the establishment of new monopolies on silkworm egg-cards and cotton thread (1822), on salt (1823), and on marine products (1832 and 1837),[16] together with new taxes of all sorts – all at a time when famine raged in the countryside. It was in this period that the thirty-eighth daimyo of Nanbu, Toshitada, by his indiscretions managed to crystallize the discord at his court into two factions: one that supported him together with the *kaneage-zamurai,* and another that supported his eldest son,

Toshitomo. As friction between the pro- and anti-Toshitada cliques deepened, the peasants stirred themselves. Rebellions occurred in 1836-37 and in 1847 the peasants of the Three Hei Districts rose up, organized and led by the intrepid Yagobei. The 1847 uprising, seventeen years in the planning, succeeded in forcing the Shogunate's intervention and Toshitada's retirement for the headship of the Nanbu family; but little else. He continued to rule the fief with an iron hand, hastening its ruination, while his weak-kneed son, Toshihisa, ruled as nominal daimyo. Moreover he immediately returned to the only financial policy he knew – forced loans and donations and crushing taxes, thereby breaking his promise of a moratorium on taxes to the Sanheidôri peasants. The ingredients for a new social explosion piled up until finally, in 1853, a year in which the lord was scheduled to make the costly journey to Edo, the peasants of the Sanhei seized their chance.

The Nanbu Uprising of 1853

The uprising staged on May 20, 1853, by the peasants from Tanohata Village in the Noda District of Nanbu, quickly developed into a great rebellion. Young and old, men, women, and children, whole villages participated, carrying with them in straw backpacks food and provisions for a long exodus from the fief. The object was to flee into Sendai, smashing any resistance encountered on the way. The march was led by a command group, numbering 300, which raised a great banner inscribed with the words, "In Distress" (made by combining the character *ko* [small] with a circle [*maru*] to be read as *komaru*). Each participating village constituted a military unit with its own banner of identification: a number. As new villages joined the march, armed marshals from the command group, calling themselves "petty magistrates" (*kobugyô*), some wearing white *hanten* with red sashes and others wearing yellow *hanten* with white sashes, were deployed to meet them. During the course of the march they attacked the Daikan's office in Nodadôri, smashed a samurai detachment sent out to stop them and destroyed the sake shop of Satô Gisuke, a large mine operator and *kaneage-zamurai.*

In June 1853, the organized peasants of the Sanhei, reduced by half to approximately 8,500, crossed the border into Sendai fief. Up to that point their leadership seems to have been a large council. But sometime after the marchers reached Tôni Village in Sendai the command seems to have fallen to three men, the main one of whom was Miura Meisuke, a stoutly built, eloquent, minor official from Kuribayashi Village who had not been part of the core group at the start of the uprising. However, as one source speculates, Meisuke may already have been involved at the planning stage of the rebellion under several pseudonyms, one of which was Yakichi.[17]

Of the actions of the peasant leaders after entering Sendai only two need concern us. One was the presentation of their petition to the daimyo of Sendai, the Date family, who had long had territorial ambitions on the adjacent districts of Nanbu; the other was their submission of a list of grievances and demands. These documents summarize the history of peasant oppression in Nanbu and constitute as well a damning indictment from below of late Tokugawa feudalism in general.

To The Lord of Sendai from the Peasants of the Sanhei
–We Respectfully Make This Petition–

1. We sincerely aspire to see that Lord Kai no Kami [Toshitomo] now retired in Edo, comes back to the fief.
2. We sincerely aspire to see you keep benevolently in your fief all the peasants coming from Sanheidôri and save their lives.
3. We aspire that you designate Sanheidôri to be a part of the *Shogunate's* domains and if this is not possible, designate it to be part of Sendai domain.[18]

After presenting this petition to Sendai officials in Tôni, the peasant leaders were questioned as to what had caused them to rebel. Miura Meisuke is then believed to have drawn up this list of forty-nine specific complaints against Nanbu fief, only some of which are quoted below. The grievances show that despite the economic advances made in Japan since the seventeenth century, the mechanisms for extracting the surplus from the peasants devised at that time, as well as the political control structure at both upper and lower levels, remained essentially intact right down to the early nineteenth century; thereafter, starting in the 1820s, new controls and exorbitant taxes were piled on top of the old in an endless succession.

The peasants are suffering from these things:

1. Advance payment of fixed corvées.
2. In addition to taxes in lieu of fixed corvées, excessive taxes have been levied on the peasants several times a year for the past twenty years, and ten times last year; and twice this year large sums have been ordered to be paid.
3. Exorbitantly high prices have been fixed for the annual rice tribute, though formerly peasants paid in cash at the rate quoted at the Miyako [Kyoto] exchange.
4. We are suffering because ever since the Bunsei era [1818-29] all

sorts of public works [*ukeoigoto*] have been imposed.

5. We are suffering from the fief's hoarding [*okaimono*] of soybeans, floss silk, and other things.

6. In recent years we have had four Daikan; previously we had only two.

7. In recent years we have had six Forest Magistrates, though in the Bunsei era Daikan usually held the two posts concurrently.

8. In recent years we have had four officials under the Daikan sent from the castle town, while formerly we had two local resident officials [*kyûnin*].

9. In recent years we have had four clerks [i.e. lowly samurai, equivalent to *ashigaru*]; formerly we had one clerk. (Since food is paid for by the peasants, as the number of officials increases, the peasants suffer accordingly.)

10. In recent years we have had four officials in charge of cattle and horses whereas previously we had only one.

12. The villages are suffering from the burden of having to care for [fief] horses and cattle until they foal and calf.

33. We are suffering from the losses involved in the manufacture of gunpowder, i.e. having to furnish firewood for the making of gunpowder and supplying our own houses as sites for this manufacture.

39. We are suffering from matters relating to fief copper mines.

46. We are suffering from the increased transport, communication, and travel corvées that have accompanied the increase in the number of officials [we must support] since the Bunsei era.

47. Speaking of contributions to the lord, we would like to have the *kimoiri* bring the tribute directly to the lord while he is in the fief as was the practice in the past.

48. We are suffering because the various ranks of samurai who were promoted to that status fifty years ago were formerly peasants.

49. Chûtarô and Shunji of Atsuka Village, two leaders of those who assembled in Tôno seven years ago were banished to Ushitaki.[19]

In October 1853, months after the Nanbu peasant leaders had secured Morioka's immediate acquiescense to all but eleven of the above demands,[20] they made the return of the remaining forty-five to Nanbu fief conditional on the acceptance of four additional demands, and exchanged papers with officials of Sendai fief as follows:

1. that various types of taxes be paid directly as in the previous year;

2. that debts of all peasants of the Sanhei be paid in installments for thirty years;
3. that upon their return to the fief the people assembled not be arrested;
4. that Ogawa Kiyoshi, Ogawa Ichizaemon, and Ogawa Naoemon [*kaneage-zamurai*] not be appointed officials.[21]

Miura Meisuke

Let us now see who was the man who had carried the second Sanheidôri uprising to its successful conclusion.

Meisuke was an educated peasant whose position in the market and administrative structure of his home village was hereditarily privileged, giving him a status above the majority of the villagers. A minor village official, he also operated as a small rural merchant who, when the need arose, lent money to other peasants. Breaking down the various determinants of his class position:

First, he was a small-scale, independent landowner and agricultural producer whose family worked the land with the help of four hereditary servants or bondsmen, remnants of the historically superceded serf system. After his participation in the Sanheidôri uprisings, this agricultural-producer aspect of Meisuke seems to have waned, a fact that also reflected the difficulty of farming under the onerous system of tax levies imposed by the fief government.

Secondly, he was a petty merchant who "purchased rice from Tsuchizawa and Hanamaki and marketed it in the Three Hei Districts."[22] Another source describes him selling "agricultural produce from the interior of Nanbu in exchange for marine products from Ôzuchi and Kamaishi."[23] This second aspect of Meisuke, his merchant concern, apparently grew throughout his life. By the time of his arrest, he appears to have resolved to enjoy the freedom of the middleman, earning as lucrative a living as possible through merchant trade.

Thirdly, as the son of a *kimoiri* (literally, village "caretaker") Meisuke was a hereditary member of Kuribayashi village's official elite. *Kimoiri* families belonged to the dissolving *nanushi* stratum mentioned earlier. They traced their origins back to the *Sengoku* period of the fifteenth and sixteenth centuries, when their ancestors fought side by side with local samurai, which is why Meisuke retained his surname. It is worth noting that Meisuke showed no particular distaste at being a privileged member of the old village elite. In fact, holding such a position was perfectly congruent with his ideal of material affluence and living life to the fullest.

Carrying this discussion of Meisuke's class position a step further, it is possible to extrapolate two principal features. Meisuke may be seen as reflecting the interests of petty merchant capital in a period of feudal disintegration, when strong possibilities existed for the rapid rise or rapid fall of different social strata. His own family stood in an intermediate position above ordinary (lower- and middle-echelon) peasants and below the new *kyûnin* or pseudo-retainer class of local resident officials that Morioka re-created for the dual purpose of keeping the peasantry under control and meeting its own dire need for money. Had Meisuke himself been more venal, had he not hated the growing absolutism of the fief government, had he not chaffed at the poverty, isolation, and countless restrictions on life and trade in Nanbu, then it is possible that he might have sided with the *kyûnin* who also sprang from the *nanushi* stratum. Instead, to his credit, he chose to share the indignation of the majority of poor peasants of the region and participate with others in leading the rebellion against the fief.

Secondly, by virtue of his position as a Village Elder (*otonayaku*) Meisuke stood in an objectively antagonistic relationship to the poor, the majority of the village, his own personal integrity and uprightness notwithstanding. In March 1853, two months before the rebellion, he had advanced a loan of 76 *kan* 300 *mon* to someone, accepting as security the labor of a forty-eight-year-old man.[24] His family account book of 1856 reveals also that he had earlier lent over 93 *ryô* to peasants living within Kuribayashi Village and to others in Ôzuchimachi, Senbokumachi, Tôno, and Kamaishi.[25] Meisuke however seems not to have confronted the pitfalls in his own position. Yet once the lord of Morioka submitted to the peasants' demands, the unity of the villages would dissolve and the smaller contradictions inherent in his situation would inevitably reassert themselves. The optimistic Meisuke's failure to anticipate that natural reversion may have contributed to his own undoing.

Morioka had publicly pledged itself not to arrest or punish any of the forty-five peasant representatives who had remained in Sendai to negotiate. But its officials, believing that the house of Nanbu had lost face, seethed with resentment and were looking to revenge the humiliation inflicted by the peasants. They had somehow to find a scapegoat through which to exorcise the spirit of the successful *osso*. When Meisuke returned home from Sendai fief after the uprising, he immediately resumed his duties as a Village Elder in Kuribayashi. The fief officials thereupon moved to exploit the vulnerability of the man they remembered as the tough peasant negotiator and drafter of the rebel demands. That they could do so presupposes the latent resentment of the majority of the poor against the village officials who doubled as merchants and exploiters of the lower- and middle-echelon peasants. For what occurred next was, according to one authority, nothing less than a dispute in which the entire village, represented by six peasants, appealed to the Daikan's office for the removal of the *kimoiri,* Heiemon, and the appointment of Zen'emon to *otonayaku,* whereupon all the *otonayaku,* including Meisuke, offered to resign.[26] Another writer, emphasizing the machinations of the fief, describes Meisuke's downfall as follows:

> An *ikki* of thirty people under Rokuzaemon arose in Kuribayashi Village on July 5, 1854. Meisuke tried to stop it but it broke out again on July 21. The Daikan [of Ôzuchi],without investigating the case, railed at Meisuke who had tried to get the peasants to listen to reason, and rebuked him for his role at the time of the uprising of the Three Hei Districts.... This has the very strong smell of an *ikki* instigated by the fief. Meisuke, unable to bear the pressures, fled the fief on July 23 and was charged with the crimes of seizing public money and illegally leaving the fief. Later Meisuke repeatedly said that leaving the fief was a mistake.
>
> He was doubly stigmatized because of this and his pride as an *ikki* leader was wounded. Here is why, despite all the dangers, he had to return to the fief, issue various public confessions, and make personal explanations. They demonstrated his sincerity but at the same time they provided grist for the mill of those who were out to get him.[27]

Meisuke fled Kuribayashi Village and the jurisdiction of the Ôzuchi Daikan on July 23, 1854, leaving behind his pregnant wife and five children.[28] From then until his arrest and imprisonment in Morioka in 1857, his actions and motivations are not entirely clear. By his own account, as reconstructed by Mori Kahei, he stayed nearly three months in Nanbu before crossing into Sendai in early October 1855. While in Sendai he became affiliated with two Tendai sect temples that seem to have been connected with the Nijô family in Kyoto. These were Sekiunji, where his brother served as a resident priest, and Nishinobô, where he stayed for a year, becoming a priest himself and practicing a type of ascetic mountain worship. In late October 1856 he returned secretly to Nanbu staying at different places and managing somehow to communicate with his family. His diary entry for November 21, 1856, states, "Finally I am ready to go." On December 23, 1856, he arrived in Kyoto, where he later said he became a retainer to the noble family of the Nijô. After staying only four days in Kyoto he departed for what was to be his last return journey to Nanbu. Meisuke was arrested on July 4, 1857. It was recorded that at the time "he was calling himself Miura Meisuke, a retainer of the Nijô, bearing a signboard saying 'In the Service of Lord Nijô,' wearing two swords, accompanied by servants and walking swaggeringly past the guard house at Hirata Village."[29]

In 1864, in the sixth year of his imprisonment, Meisuke died, too soon by three years to witness the dismantling of the feudal political order, an historical event he had helped further by his own actions. The invaluable record of his thoughts which he left behind, the *Gokuchûki,* is essentially a collection of four notebooks of letters and diaries to his family written between June 1859 and February 1861. (The first three were completed between September 26, 1859 and sometime in 1860, and the last in February 1861.)[30] Notebooks one and two open with an invocation to three popular peasant deities, under whose banner peasant uprisings often occurred:

Hachiman Daibosatsu: May Peace Prevail Under Heaven
Tenshô Kôtaijingû: A Prayer
Kasuga Daimyôjin: Safety for the Country[31]

Hachiman was a quasi-Buddhist deity and the ancestral god of the Minamoto. Kasuga Daimyôjin, the god honored in the Kasuga shrine in Nara, was the ancestral god of the Fujiwara family and a figure associated with syncretic Shintoism. Tenshô Kôtaijingû, the sun goddess in Japanese mythology associated with the creation of Japan, was another object of peasant folk belief, though her connection at this time with the emperor living in seclusion at Kyoto is a matter of dispute among scholars. A prayer offered to Tenshô Kôtaijingû did not, one suspects, necessarily connote a peasant belief in loyalty to the emperor.

But having stressed the very mundane and non-nationalist content of the opening invocation, it is still possible to interpret it, as Yasumaru Yoshio has, as expressing the intimate connection Meisuke made between certain "universal tasks on a national scale – peace and safety for the country" – and the way he devised to achieve "wealth and prosperity and the perpetuation of the family line for all the descendants."[32]

In fact, Meisuke's prescriptions for his family for achieving that goal constitutes the main theme of the *Gokuchûki.* And in describing "the way of wealth and prosperity" (*gokuraku no hô*) – the title of a letter addressed to his family on June 16, 1859 – Meisuke implies that even in backward Nanbu fief a market for handicrafts exists and that, when all land is lost, it is still possible not only to survive but to live comfortably, provided one works hard and diligently.

Man should go to bed late in the evening to do work worth 30 *mon.* By day earn 35 *mon,* thus totaling 65 *mon.* With this much he may support himself for a day.... First let me write down the day's expenses: for each person, 30 *mon* for rice, five *mon* for miso, 5 *mon* for fish, 5 *mon* for radish, 10 *mon* for kimono and another 10 *mon* for services. Thus totaling 65 *mon* to be needed everyday. Therefore, each should work for 65 *mon* for one day and one evening in order to live a comfortable life. This method of living is devised to meet requirements when our fields [lit. paddies and uplands] are lost to us. Keeping this in mind, each of you should earn 65 *mon* by doing some suitable handicraft in an emergency, so that you may not disclose your weaknesses to your enemies. To show your back means flight [i.e. stay in the village by doing handicrafts].

Man should seek to earn money. I mentioned this method for the time when one has insufficient land to support oneself.[33]

An essential part of Meisuke's outlook, boldly stated at the beginning of the *Gokuchûki,* was a belief in man rather than land as the source of all value. After telling his family, who had fallen into distress because of his escape and imprisonment, not to be afraid of debts or loss of land, he goes on to declare,

If one compares men and the rice fields, man is the Udonge flower [i.e. the magical flower that makes fortune] that blooms only once in three thousand years.[34]

And a little later he adds

On holidays go to bed early. You should revere your spirit from the bottom of your heart. If I may say, the figure of a man is quite like the moon and sun. Just as you worship them, every morning you should pray to your own soul.[35]

Where feudal theory saw all value as emanating from land and its possession, Meisuke locates its source in man and his labor. A small merchant and agricultural producer, Meisuke played his role on the stage of history just at the moment when a break had occurred in the disintegration of Japan's feudal mode of production – a break symbolized by the linking of the country to the expanding world capitalist market system and by the virtual revolution against Nanbu fief, both in the year 1853. At this juncture, a merchant with Meisuke's experience could perceive the possibilities of the situation and the power of the individual ruled by peasant values of diligence, thrift, hard work and honesty, to realize those possibilities. The foundation for his self-confidence and his modern insight that man was the very "Udonge flower" – the source of all value – lay precisely in his immersion in the developing capitalist market sector.

But that immersion in the market also accounts for his despair with the fief, which retarded the economy and the peasants' desperate efforts to eke out a living by developing trade and handicrafts. Meisuke's mood changes as his years in prison go on. A letter to his family dated September 27 [probably 1860] states,

> Whenever you have to leave the fief, you should make the rumor that you are moving to Morioka. Wherever you may move to you should make that rumor. You should arrange things very carefully. However, if I am not killed you should not go anywhere. If I am killed, I sincerely hope you will move to one of these five places: Edo, Matsumae, Tsugaru, Shiogama [a port near Sendai], or Ishinomaki [a port within the fief of Sendai].[36]

Finally, in one of the rare political statements in the *Gokuchûki* and one often dwelt on by writers,[37] he observes, "Heaven is benevolent but because the lord of the domain lacks benevolence everything is difficult."[38]

Conclusion

Rebel leaders like Miura Meisuke expressed a vague longing for a larger public authority, which *to them* meant greater freedom – and, in a sense, greater freedom could be expected under the direct rule of the Shogunate than under Nanbu fief. But their criticism of local fief authority did not entail a grasp of the limitations of the *bakuhan* system itself. Lacking opportunities for communication across feudal boundaries, lacking the intellectual catalyst of a community of revolutionary intellectuals, they found it difficult to build on their own historical experiences and to develop their own analytical capabilities for grasping political realities. In other words, a continuous tradition of peasant rebellions such as existed in Nanbu, where the memory of Yagobei was still fresh in 1853, was not the same thing as an intellectual heritage of revolutionary thought. The tragedy of Miura Meisuke and others like him was that, lacking such a heritage, they could find no way to raise their desire for human freedom to a self-conscious and anti-feudal ideology.[39]

Yet in two basic ways Meisuke at least did effect a transcendence and transvaluation of feudal ideology. Through involvement in the market economy of the fief he came to perceive that man and his labor, rather than land, was the source of all value, and that it was better for man to serve an impersonal master – the Shogunate or even the emperor – rather than remain the private possession of a feudal lord. Ultimately, Meisuke's outlook had acquired, by the time of his arrest if not earlier, a specifically non-feudal, indeed bourgeois content. Then, toward the end of his life, deprived of physical freedom and the hope of ever again being able to satisfy his nature through labor, he even displayed the characteristic dualism of the petty bourgeoisie. The optimism of the early letters of the *Gokuchûki* changed swiftly to despair, and the *gokuraku no hô,* that prescription for the good life, revealed its essential ambiguity: the temporal way of wealth and prosperity reverted to the religious way of paradise. The last entry in the *Gokuchûki* reads:

> Discard the sense of rivalry;
> Be free from stinginess;
> Do not mind being laughed at by people;
> Do not care where you end your life....
> On this day of February 24, 1861
> I abandoned desires.[40]

* I wish to thank Ôkubo Genji for many pleasant occasions on which we discussed Nanbu *ikki* and Kano Tsutomu for reading and commenting on the text.

[NOTES]

1. See Kodama Kôta et al. (eds.), *Kinseishi handobukku* (*Handbook of Early Modern History*; Tokyo: Kondô Shuppansha, 1972), p. 58. Nanbu, also called Morioka fief, had its seignorial value in rice, that is to say its ranking in the feudal order, increased to 200,000 *koku* in 1808. A useful annotated bibliography on Nanbu is found on pages 58-60.
2. Miyamoto Tsuneichi, Yamamoto Shûgorô, et al. (eds.), *Nihon zankoku monogatari, daisanbu – sakoku no higeki* (*Tales of Cruelty in Japan,* Part 3, "The Tragedy of Seclusion"; Tokyo: Heibonsha, 1960), p. 304.
3. Shôji Kichinosuke, Hayashi Motoi, and Yasumaru Yoshio (eds.), *Nihon shisô taikei 58 – Minshû undô no shisô* (*Compendium of Japanese Thought,* Vol. 58, *The Thought of the People's Movements*; Tokyo: Iwanami Shoten, 1970), p. 391.
4. *Nihon zankoku,* p. 307, and Sasaki Junnosuke (ed.), *Nihon minshû no rekishi 5, Yonaoshi* (*History of the Japanese People,* Vol. 5, *Millenarian Movements*; Tokyo: Sanseidô, 1974), p. 209.
5. Murakami Hyôe, *Seinen no sanmyaku – ishin no naka no sei to shi* (*Youth Who Made History – Life and Death in the Meiji Restoration*; Tokyo: Tokuma Shoten, 1966), p. 58.
6. Perhaps one reason for the one-sided, rose-colored interpretation of the Tokugawa period in most postwar Western accounts is the neglect of peasant rebellions and, indeed, the history of the plight and aspirations of peasants.
7. *Minshû undô,* p. 397.
8. See Kano Tsutomu, "Peasant Uprisings and Citizens' Revolts," in *The Japan Interpreter,* Vol. 8, No. 3 (Autumn 1973), pp. 279-83.
9. *Nihon zankoku,* p. 313.
10. Quoted in Sasaki, *Nihon minshû,* p. 210.
11. See Moriya Yoshimi, "Bakumatsu kôshinhan no keizaiteki jôkyô – Morioka han bakumatsu hyakushô ikki no yobiteki kôsatsu no tame ni," in *Nihonshi kenkyû* Nos. 150-51 (March 1975), pp. 184-86.
12. According to Moriya (*Ibid.,* p. 187) the full-scale sale of samurai ranks began in 1773 though the policy itself antedated the 1770s.
13. I am indebted to Kikuchi Hayao for kindly giving me data on the growth in numbers of *kyûnin* from his own research on Nanbu fief. Kikuchi's most recent essay is "Miura Meisuke 'Matsumae' ijûron no shiteki igi," in *Rekishi hyôron,* No. 331 (November 1977), pp. 68-79.
14. *Nihon zankoku,* p. 320.

15. *Nihon zankoku*, pp. 320-21.
16. Moriya, "Bakumatsu kôshinhan," p. 192.
17. *Nihon zankoku*, p. 321.
18. Mori Kahei, *Nanbuhan hyakushô ikki nò shidôsha, Miura Meisuke den* (*A Biography of Miura Meisuke*: *A Leader of the Nanbu Peasant Uprisings*; Tokyo: Heibonsha, 1962), p. 41.
19. *Ibid.*, pp. 41-45.
20. Morioka rejected four of the demands outright (33, 39, 47, 48), promised to investigate three (20, 25, 40) and claimed that five others (23, 26, 31, 32, 37) were not clear.
21. *Miura Meisuke den*, p. 73.
22. *Nihon zankoku*, p. 332.
23. *Minshû undô*, p. 421.
24. Fukaya Katsumi, "Kôseitaiteki kiki no dankai ni okeru jinmin – 'Miura Meisuke *Gokuchûki*' no kentô o tsûjite," in *Minshûshi kenkyû*, No. 75 (April-May 1969), p. 61.
25. *Ibid.*, p. 61.
26. Fukaya, p. 62.
27. *Minshû undô*, p. 443.
28. This paragraph summarizes Mori Kahei's account in *Minshû undô*, p. 443.
29. Cited by Mori in *Minshû undô*, p. 444.
30. *Ibid.*, 445.
31. *Miura Meisuke den*, pp. 219, 228.
32. *Minshû undô*, p. 428.
33. *Miura Meisuke den*, pp. 234-35.
34. *Ibid.*, p. 220.
35. *Ibid.*, p. 221.
36. *Ibid.*, p. 245.
37. See Sasaki, p. 212; and Yasumaru Yoshio in *Minshû undô*, p. 448.
38. *Miura Meisuke den*, p. 253.
39. *Minshû undô*, p. 421.
40. *Miura Meisuke den*, p. 254.

Young Activist of the Meiji Restoration

Sakamoto Ryôma

by

MARIUS B. JANSEN

After a long period of quiet, Japanese politics were suddenly transformed by the intrusion of Commodore Perry in 1853. Long before his coming many scholars and bureaucrats had been aware that the military and industrial advances of the nineteenth-century West could contain future problems for Japan. There was knowledge that economic crisis would hamper rearmament. And although the Perry challenge was new, it had been preceded by awareness of China's defeat at the hands of Great Britain. Perry's demand for treaty relations thus served to confirm earlier misgivings at the same time that it revealed new weakness. At the least it required political decisions, and the search for agreement on these produced a new age of politics. For almost two decades Japan was torn by disagreement that strained every type of loyalty and belief. Action, commitment, and even extremism replaced conformity. The age was one favorable to the emergence of strong and colorful individuals. Sakamoto Ryôma was one of the most striking of these.

Sakamoto was born in 1835 in Tosa in Kôchi, the castle town of the Yamanouchi domain in the island of Shikoku. Sakamoto and his province fit the conventional categories devised for description of Tokugawa Japan only imperfectly. The Yamanouchi daimyo was an "outside lord" (*tozama*), but only in the sense that he had not followed Tokugawa Ieyasu from the first. Unlike his counterparts in great southwest domains like Satsuma and Chôshû, he had not fought on the wrong side in the great battle of Sekigahara that established the Tokugawa hegemony in 1600, and he had been granted his imposing realm as a reward for benevolent neutrality. In all but a technical sense he was thus closer to liege vassal (*fudai*) status than his designation would suggest. Sakamoto himself, while technically a member of the ruling samurai class, in actuality had only a second-class membership. His forebears had been farmers, merchants, and brewers before requesting status as *gôshi* in 1771 under regulations that made it possible to seek such advancement as reward for the reclamation of land. Not only was Sakamoto's family status that of a merchant-turned-"rustic samurai," but he himself was a younger – in fact youngest – son, unlikely to achieve importance. His education also was spotty. On the other hand the times favored the unconventional and the adventurous. Sakamoto's participation in national politics was the more joyous for the contrast such excitement had for the dull career that would have awaited him in normal times, and his earthy, pithy letters to his favorite elder sister convey this excitement so directly that modern Japanese still relate to this colorful *gôshi* son.

Sakamoto had a brief and largely unprofitable exposure to book learning in a private academy near the Kôchi castle, and the chief element in his early education came in the fencing academies to which his family sent him. There he acquired a fascination with martial arts, a concern with national defense, and from his peers, an identification with country and the Kyoto monarch. Fencing academy activities included regional tournaments that made possible contact with vigorous young swordsmen from other areas, especially when in 1853, Sakamoto's family sent him on to the shogunal capital at Edo for further study. Sakamoto was in Edo when Perry's flotilla entered Edo Bay. He was enrolled in special levies that were hastily organized to withstand the Americans, and sufficiently excited to send home a promise that he would take a foreign head in the war that seemed inevitable. Tokugawa agreement to the new treaty with the United States warded off that war. Sakamoto returned to Kôchi, but before long resumed his studies in Edo again.

He now came under the influence of the leading Tosa loyalist, Takechi Zuizan. Takechi, a dynamic and charismatic figure, was entrusted with responsibilities for education in swordsmanship by the domain administration, and Sakamoto was among the young swordsmen included in the Loyalist Party which Takechi formed in 1861. The impetus for this organization came from the turbulent state of national politics. The Harris commercial treaty (negotiated in 1858) had been signed in disregard of the imperial will, and immediately thereafter shogunal traditionalists had expressed their disapproval of those who had organized opposition to it by ordering a purge of daimyo dissidents and their advisers. The Tosa daimyo had been among those forced into retirement by this purge. Within months the chief author of that repression, Ii Naosuke, the Shogunate's first minister, was assassinated by samurai activists from Mito who sought

Sakamoto Ryôma

revenge for their lord's punishment. With this deed, which came in the spring of 1860, the era of loyalist violence was at hand. Takechi's party was a Tosa version of this indignation. His followers subscribed to a document stressing the emperor's grief that the "divine country has been humiliated by the barbarians"; their former lord too had been punished for his opposition to this. They, in turn, swore to bring about the "rebirth of the nation," to "ease the Emperor's mind," and "carry out the will of our former lord, and purge this evil from our people." Their document assumed an identity of purpose between "former lord" and *tennô*, but its wording left little doubt of the special priority they accorded the latter.

While these events were in progress an administration of reforming officials in Tosa did its best to keep a low posture in national politics for fear of bringing further punishment on the now-retired daimyo. This seemed cowardly to the young loyalist extremists, and in the spring of 1862 Yoshida Tôyô, the chief figure in that administration, was murdered by them. By then Sakamoto had already fled Tosa to immerse himself in loyalist politics on the national level.

The murder of Ii Naosuke in 1860 ushered in an era of violence in which many low-ranking swordsmen found it possible to attach themselves to the establishments of Kyoto nobles and anti-foreign daimyo as secret agents and messengers. Still others added to the insecurity of life and politics by individual violence directed against officials and individuals who were thought to be treasonous by virtue of contact with foreigners or advocacy of "pro-foreign" policies. Conventional standards of discipline and conduct were temporarily in abeyance, subordinated to professions of obligation to a "higher duty" to country and monarch. National politics, meanwhile, were dominated by a steady tug of war for influence between court nobles, Satsuma, Chôshû, and the Tokugawa Shogunate.

The Shogunate needed the cooperation and at least tacit approval of the great domains to legitimize its enforced departure from the institutions of seclusion so long associated with its rule. Domains that chose to participate in politics needed the imperial Court as justification for their own increasing interference in national affairs, and in turn the Court could gain influence only as others found it possible to take up its cause. The great Tokugawa domain of Mito, whose dissidents had murdered Ii Naosuke, was ineffective in the power struggle because of internal disputes. The ground was thus prepared for the advance of non-Tokugawa, "outside" (*tozama*) lords to propose alterations in the balance of power that would strengthen, as they saw it, the national response to the foreign danger. In 1861 Chôshû put forth the first proposal for a better cooperation between Court and Shogunate (*kôbu gattai*); and the next year Satsuma advanced proposals somewhat more favorable to the Court. By the end of that year the young Tosa daimyo was also drawn into these moves by new advisers who had taken over from the murdered Yoshida Tôyô. Sakamoto's loyalist friends in Tosa seemed to be gaining in influence. He himself, however, was developing a new understanding of national problems.

Late in 1862 Sakamoto, now twenty-seven, resolved to murder Katsu Kaishû, a Tokugawa bureaucrat. Katsu got him to hear him out first, however, and persuaded him of the necessity for Japan to strengthen itself by Western-style reforms before trying to drive out the Westerners. Sakamoto was so fully persuaded that he became Katsu's follower, and Katsu in turn was so convinced of the quality of his would-be assailant that he secured a Tosa pardon of Sakamoto's flight from domain jurisdiction. Sakamoto now found himself at the center of Tokugawa reform politics, for his patron was to become a leading figure in preparedness at a time when military policy was the central issue for the government. Sakamoto helped Katsu to recruit and train young samurai from many parts of the country for a naval training institute that was established at Hyôgo, near present-day Kobe. He was thus productively occupied, and learning a great deal about Japan's problems, during the peak years of anti-foreignism and terrorism.

The loyalist tide ebbed for a time; and when Chôshû extremists tried to seize control of the Kyoto palace in 1864 and failed it seemed to have spent its force. Tokugawa conservatives now thought they saw an opportunity to resume a harder line with their opponents and to discontinue some of the reforms that had been set in motion. Katsu, Sakamoto's patron, was dismissed from his post, and shortly afterward shogunal forces launched a military expedition to punish Chôshû for its action in Kyoto. Under pressure of defeat Chôshû conservatives replaced the administration that had incurred Tokugawa displeasure. In Tosa, also, the retired daimyo, restored to influence again, had reasserted his control of domain policy, ordered the apprehension and punishment of the loyalist leaders who had allied Tosa policy with that of Chôshû and Satsuma, and forced the suicide of Takechi and other loyalist leaders. Sakamoto had lost his Tokugawa patron, and he could expect little support in Tosa.

Sakamoto now found refuge in Satsuma, a domain whose leaders had supported shogunal reform cautiously but had no desire to see Chôshû crushed decisively. Sakamoto retained his ties with Tokugawa reformers in the Katsu camp, men who would return to power and influence in 1867 after the failure of a second effort to crush Chôshû. He also knew the radicals who seized control of Chôshû policy again shortly after the Tokugawa armies were pulled back. As the balance slowly shifted Sakamoto also became important to the administrators of his own domain of Tosa, who saw the advantage of reclaiming this once-obscure *rônin* who could claim membership in what was becoming a circle of possible national leaders.

From 1865 to 1867, the year of Sakamoto's murder, Satsuma played an increasingly important part in national politics. With Satsuma help he formed a small commercial company, the *Kaientai,* whose ships, often armed, ran between Nagasaki, Satsuma (Kagoshima), and Chôshû (Shimonoseki) to ferry Western small arms to those two domains. In 1866 Sakamoto mediated between Satsuma and Chôshû to bring about the political alliance between those two great domains that foreshadowed the fall of the Tokugawa and the make-up of the later Meiji leadership group.

In 1867 Sakamoto, sensing the speed with which his friends in Satsuma and Chôshû were preparing for a frontal attack on the Tokugawa, moved closer to his former superiors in Tosa. Aware that a military solution might rule out Tosa influence in the future, and conscious of a lingering obligation to the Tokugawa house, the former Tosa lord was receptive to proposals that he petition the Shogun to resign his powers voluntarily against the assurance that a new, conciliar form of power would be worked out. In such an arrangement the Shogun would have remained the largest single lord. The actual details were worked out by Sakamoto, in an eight-point program that projected the appointment of the "most able men" as councillors, "able daimyo" as Court officials, formal relations with foreign countries, more uniform codes of administration and laws, upper and lower deliberative assemblies, army and navy ministries, an imperial guard, and revaluation of Japan's precious metals in line with international usage. Sakamoto's plans retained the terminology of feudal times, but they also contained essential steps toward the establishment of a centralized state with a single center of political decisions.

Late in 1867 the Shogun accepted the proposals submitted to him by the Tosa daimyo and petitioned the Court to accept the return of his political powers. Satsuma and Chôshû leaders nevertheless outmaneuvered him by demanding he surrender his lands as well, and forced him into the position of rebel. In 1868 "imperial" (Satsuma, Chôshû, Tosa) forces marched through Tokugawa territories to complete the "Meiji Restoration" that had been proclaimed in January. Sakamoto, however, had been killed just before this announcement, presumably by pro-Tokugawa vigilante units.

Throughout these tumultuous years Sakamoto's correspondence and activities show the rapidity with which this low-ranking, poorly educated, and impulsive young swordsman learned the realities of Japan's place in the modern world and adapted his personal and political thinking accordingly. He began by protesting the decision to open Japan to Western intercourse, assuming that his feudal lord was of the same mind and that there was no conflict of loyalties. On finding this was not so, he chose the national and imperial cause and prepared to work toward a resolution by assassination and terror, only to be persuaded of the inadequacy of such a piece-meal response to larger problems. After a time as assistant to a modernizing Tokugawa administrator, he was forced to abandon that course also, and now chose his companions in the great anti-Tokugawa domains to the southwest. When he saw them nearing power he altered course once more to work for a compromise settlement in which no regional force would be all-powerful. Sakamoto died at the moment of success, before the discovery that the Tokugawa influence was to be extinguished completely. Most remarkably, his letters, plans, and a pamphlet posthumously ascribed to him show him increasingly aware of the inadequacy of feudal institutions and leadership in the Japan of his day, and prepared to work for institutions of central government that could provide a surer basis for national unity and strength. Throughout he maintained a buoyant optimism and zest in everything he did. It is small wonder that contemporary novelists and television dramatists have found Sakamoto congenial to their purposes of dramatizing the excitement and adventure of the Restoration experience.

Architect of the Modern State

Ôkubo Toshimichi

by

MASAKAZU IWATA

One of the many great figures in Meiji history was Ôkubo Toshimichi. But unlike the legendary Saigô Takamori, the talented Kido Kôin, and the courtly Iwakura Tomomi,Ôkubo never won the hearts of his countrymen. While the charismatic figure of Saigô stands as a monument in bronze in Ueno Park, no such monument was erected in honor of Ôkubo prior to World War II. Since the defeat of Japan in the Pacific War and the influx of democratic principles into Japanese thinking, all vestiges of political authoritarianism have been repelled by the people. Authoritarians led the country into war, and hence historical personalities of this bent were denigrated.

In proper historical perspective, however, this correlation of authority with evil in a nation's development is not an objective approach to the analysis of the past. If Katsuda Magoya's prewar assessment of Ôkubo Toshimichi's role in Japanese history is unduly eulogistic, younger postwar historians such as Ikeda Kiyoshi have added balance to the significance of the Meiji leader. He stresses the seemingly valid theme that Ôkubo was the man of the hour for a Japan emerging from the chrysalis of feudalism and confronting the encroachment of Western power in East Asia. Like Moses in Judaic history who was destined to lead the Israelites out of bondage and into freedom, Ôkubo, with his coldly analytical approach to political problems; his loyalty to the symbol of the people, the emperor; his dedication, that verged on a sense of mission, to building a strong, united nation retaining its autonomy and uniqueness; served much the same role for Meiji Japan. Without leaders of this caliber in the mid-nineteenth century, Japan would not have become a world power prior to 1941, nor would she be what she is today, once more an economic and political power whose basic philosophy of progress and development in all areas of national life was established in the Meiji period.

For better or for worse, Ôkubo Toshimichi was not only a politician but also a statesman, a leader with intellectual superiority, fortitude, a sense of mission, Machiavellian realism, and a pragmatic inclination, in short a strong-willed, coldly courageous authoritarian state-builder.

Born in Kagoshima in 1830 when the Western powers were already preparing to make inroads into China, Ôkubo was one of several Satsuma men who assumed national prominence, such as Saigô Takamori, and later General Ôyama Iwao and Admiral Tôgô Heihachirô. Ôkubo spent his formative years in a provincial environment as the only son in a family of seven. His father, Jûemon, was a retainer in the service of the Satsuma daimyo, the Shimazu, and was a man of strong convictions and determination, a "revolutionary" in more modern parlance, inasmuch as he was involved in a movement to oust reactionary advisors surrounding Shimazu Narioki.

Another influence on the life of the young Toshimichi besides his father was his grandfather Minayoshi Hôtoku, a physician who had acquired Western learning at Nagasaki and Edo, and hence instilled in his grandson the character of Western civilization.

Ôkubo acquired the normal education of a samurai, which included the martial arts as well as literary pursuits, the latter of which he favored because of his physical limitations. Confucianism and Zen Buddhism were significant aspects of the curriculum. Saigô, who was a classmate, marvelled at his friend's mental acuity. At the age of sixteen Toshimichi was given a position as assistant in the archives of his domain.

In 1849, upon the exile of his father for political activities, Toshimichi was not only relieved of his position but also placed under a six-month house arrest. With no source of income and the responsibility of his family on his shoulders, the young samurai began a period of dire poverty during which he was forced to borrow money to keep the family in necessities. He wrote to his brother-in-law in a letter requesting a loan: "No amount seems sufficient for our present needs... [and] if it is impossible to spare eight *ryô,* then even five *ryô* would help." The difficult years of 1849 to 1853 should have rounded out Ôkubo's character. Adversity, however, had a negative effect upon him because he emerged from his experiences as a cold and reserved individual, somewhat of a rebel obsessed with a desire to forge ahead in life regardless of adversities.

His coldness did not hide his talents; the new daimyo, Shimazu Nariakira, in 1853 reassigned Toshimichi to his former post as archivist, and in 1858 he was advanced to a position handling tribute rice. By this

Ôkubo Toshimichi

time, traits of activism in the youthful samurai were already noticeable; he had been involved in two reform movements within the domain. He was no less averse to traditionalism within the Satsuma domain than on the national level, where two factions were developing, those who would open Japan to Western contact and their opponents who were for achieving reform and national unity before doing so. Ôkubo considered national reform of politics and society as well as changes at the domain level as *sine qua non* for a strong state. Satsuma was to feel the impact of Ôkubo's reforming zeal, just as Japan itself would subsequently. From the fires of political strife (between the progressives and the conservatives) on the domain level were to emerge the new authoritarian leaders of the later Meiji government.

The death of Shimazu Nariakira in 1858 left unfinished the Satsuma plan to force the Tokugawa Shogunate in Edo to carry out reforms to cope with internal and external problems. Since the conservative chief minister of the Shogunate, Ii Naosuke, displayed arbitrary opposition to reform, Ôkubo and his like-minded peers resolved to take matters into their own hands by severing relations with their domain, becoming masterless samurai, and to implement a plan to force reformation by attacking the Kyoto headquarters of the shogun as well as Ii in Edo. Toshimichi's friend Saigô advised that vacillation at this time would indicate the lack of a sense of loyalty and assured his support. Saigô, who commanded the confidence of both Nariakira, whom he served as secretary, and the reform element of the domain, had risen to national political prominence even before Ôkubo. During the oppressive rule of Ii Naosuke, Saigô, realizing that he was helpless in protecting the life of the loyalist priest Gesshô, who had turned to Satsuma for asylum, decided one night after a farewell repast with his fellow thinker to commit double suicide with Gesshô by drowning at sea. The decision was carried out and resulted in Gesshô's death, while Saigô, resuscitated, lived to see another day. As his punishment he was exiled to an island. And from Saigô's manifestation of a high sense of responsibility Ôkubo learned a lesson.

The radical party of about fifty samurai loyalists, soon formed at Ôkubo's insistence, installed as its leader Iwashita Hôhei, a samurai of relatively high status, and received the financial backing of a Kagoshima merchant. But he did not attempt to utilize the group immediately for destructive purposes. Rather he intended to direct its energy toward political reform within the domain. Realizing that without the support of the domain their objective could not be attained, Ôkubo strongly warned his *Seichû-gumi* comrades against taking positive action. He then planned to draw closer to the new Satsuma daimyo, Tadayoshi, and his influential father, Hisamitsu, in order to gain their support for his cause. Under the feudal system it was almost impossible for a lower-ranking samurai to meet with and express his opinions to a daimyo or his father. When Ôkubo learned that Hisamitsu, who was enamoured with the game of *go,* regularly used as his partner a certain priest, he sought to have the latter give him lessons. And when he learned that Hisamitsu, a voracious reader, borrowed certain classics from the priest, Ôkubo inserted between the pages of such a book a slip of paper on which he had written out his views. Hisamitsu who had been endeavoring to establish a stronger position within the domain, himself extended his hand to Ôkubo. It came in the form of an urgent message which expressed his faith in the group, a fact which tended to pacify its members as they acknowledged Hisamitsu's sympathy for their feelings. As for Hisamitsu, this in fact served to elevate his standing within the domain – precisely the outcome that Ôkubo had anticipated.

Before long Ôkubo was given an audience with Hisamitsu and thereafter rose within the domain hierarchy, becoming in a short time a member of its council. In an advisory capacity he was soon in a position to influence the policy of Satsuma within the framework of the tradition-encrusted feudal system. Such rapid advancement was unprecedented. Although phenomenal, it was, however, not limited to Ôkubo or to Satsuma; there were others, not necessarily men of influence and power, who were given

Saigô Takamori; Collection of Saigô Kichinosuke (Tokyo)

similar preferment based upon ability alone. The new pattern was dictated by the social forces of the age. Similar changes were taking place within the influential domains which subsequently were to make an impact upon the politics of the Meiji Restoration.

In 1860, the year Ôkubo met with Hisamitsu, Ii Naosuke was assassinated by dissident *rônin* from Mito and Satsuma (the element within Ôkubo's *Seichû-gumi* that did not heed his admonition). The primary grievance of the assassins was Ii Naosuke's insistence upon opening ports to foreigners in direct opposition to the imperial will. Although itself opposed to the opening of ports, the Shogunate was forced to bow to external pressures. Whereas in the past the Shogunate was relied upon to conduct political affairs, the fact that it was now forced to consult the opinion of the Court indicated its loss of authority. Moreover, the assassination of the one in whose hand rested the reins of government spurred the decline of the Edo government. The influential daimyo who had heretofore been deprived of the right of self-expression within the Shogunate system now hurried to fill the power vacuum, chief among them being those of Chôshû and Satsuma.

In 1862, Hisamitsu at the head of his troops proceeded to Kyoto and tried to induce the Court to issue an imperial order for a fundamental reformation of the Shogunate. This was a daring move challenging the very structure of the Shogunate. The person most responsible for this plan was none other than Ôkubo. It was at this juncture that he stepped from the stage of Satsuma to that of national politics. It was at this time also that he was to meet the one with whom he was destined to work together in the formulation of the Meiji government, the courtier Iwakura Tomomi.

Meanwhile in Kyoto there were a number of high-spirited *rônin* who interpreted Hisamitsu's march on the imperial capital as part of a movement to overthrow the Shogunate. At the same time there were the extremists who would not be satisfied merely with the reform of the Shogunate. Ôkubo had his hands full in attempting to placate them. It was at this point that Saigô, whose appeal to the samurai element was well known, was summoned. Saigô, who had been absent from politics for some time, now reappeared on the scene. But instead of obeying the orders of Hisamitsu he displayed sympathy for the radical faction which resulted in his banishment from Satsuma. And to deal with the group extreme measures were taken; agents were dispatched and the ring leaders murdered. Ôkubo's attitude toward the incident is a matter of conjecture, but the likelihood is that he supported Hisamitsu's action. For Ôkubo, in politics the end justified the means. As the result of negotiations in Kyoto, Satsuma was given the imperial order for the reformation of the Shogunate, and Hisamitsu was to deliver this to Edo. The order stipulated that members of the reform element be appointed as officials in the Shogunate and that the shogun and various daimyo visit Kyoto for consultation with the imperial Court. While in Edo, Ôkubo was among the chief negotiators with the Shogunate, and the success of the negotiations was facilitated by his aggressive attitude and approach; he was prepared to put to the sword the Shogunate negotiators should they fail to accept the imperial order.

The negotiations, to be sure, served as a valuable experience in politics for Ôkubo, but the actual implementation of the agreement was soon to meet obstacles. Although the Shogunate appointed reform-minded daimyo officials, there soon arose differences of opinion among the appointees. It took some time before Ôkubo was to realize that the Shogunate's structure had become so outmoded that it no longer was compatible with the times.

It was on the return trip from Edo after the conclusion of this mission that the Namamugi incident occurred in the eighth month of 1862. Having cut athwart the daimyo procession conveying Hisamitsu back to Satsuma, the Englishman, C. L. Richardson, was cut down by the sword of a Satsuma retainer who took offense at the breach of propriety. As a realist, Ôkubo advised those who wished to attack the English party that the matter should be dealt with through negotiation. The incident, however, took on unexpected seriousness. England demanded of the Shogunate an apology as well as a huge indemnity. Having obtained this, it moreover made strong demands upon Satsuma. In the sixth month of 1863, an English fleet sailed into Kagoshima Bay. Negotiations halted and firing erupted from both sides. Ôkubo, who in the meantime climbed to the roof of a building to observe the exchange between the two forces, slipped and fell to the ground. Those who envied his rise to success declared that he was in actuality a coward despite the image of courage he normally tried to project. There was no clear-cut victor in this particular engagement, but to Satsuma and Ôkubo and those in favor of expelling the foreigners, the superiority of Western naval power was obvious. The British incident opened the way for the entry of foreign influences into Japan. Even while the Shogunate's ban on foreign travel was in effect, Satsuma was to send students to England, a move that Ôkubo strongly supported.

Ôkubo also firmly insisted that the Shogunate loan Satsuma the $100,000 indemnification demanded by England. He was aware of the consequences to the Shogunate if it were to refuse and the negotiations fail. Hence, he threatened the Shogunate that if it refused his request, he would have the British minister cut down to add further to the woes of the Edo government. The Shogunate complied with Ôkubo's demand. There is, however, no indication that this "loan" was ever repaid, according to the contemporary English diplomat, Sir Ernest Satow.

In the meantime, the political situation in Japan shifted drastically. At the time Hisamitsu returned from Edo to Kyoto, there was accelerated and uncontrollable activity by the *sonnô-jôi* literally "revere the emperor and expell the barbarians" faction. After dealing with the Namamugi affair, Satsuma joined with the Aizu domain, which was responsible for the preservation of order in Kyoto, and by means of a *coup d'état* expelled the *jôi* elements comprised essentially of Chôshû warriors from the imperial capital. Ôkubo's *kôbu gattai* "amalgamation of Shogunate and Court" policy was now realized, but internal friction caused the alignment to be short-lived. Ôkubo, deciding to observe events within the land, made no further commitments. Within Satsuma, his efforts were directed to strengthening its military and economic position, a policy which after the Meiji Restoration in 1868 reappeared in the guise of the *fukoku kyôhei* "rich nation, strong military" policy.

Shortly thereafter in Kyoto a conflict erupted. The anti-Shogunate Chôshû forces confronted the troops of Satsuma and Aizu and went down to defeat. As a punitive measure the Shogunate dispatched a force to Chôshû, and in order to reestablish its credibility, stipulated severe terms. Satsuma, however, opposed this. Saigô was sent as commander of a punitive force and managed to reach a settlement based on generous terms. Highly dissatisfied, the Shogunate once more planned to send an expedition against Chôshû which at this point clearly brought the policy of the Shogunate and Satsuma into sharp conflict. Ôkubo realized that the Shogunate's most recent move against Chôshû would mean its collapse. He in the meantime increasingly emphasized the policy of "rich nation, strong military," and rejecting Aizu's advances and establishing instead a military alliance with Chôshû, he awaited future developments. The year after the bombardment of Kagoshima by the British fleet, Chôshû batteries were shelled by the naval forces of England, France, America, and Holland, an experience that impressed upon the domain the folly of an anti-foreign policy. Hence, Chôshû opinion was to swing toward that which underlay Satsuma's policy, namely *fukoku kyôhei.* The Shogunate's troops in their second expedition against Chôshû were defeated on all fronts by an army that was becoming increasingly modernized. It was at this juncture that the Shogun died and the punitive action against Chôshû was terminated with Tokugawa Yoshinobu's succession as the fifteenth Shogun.

There was hope now of a peaceful revolution based upon Court-Shogunate unity. However, the views of the new Shogun and those of the major domains clashed in a conflict involving Yoshinobu who shrewdly wished to dissolve the domain system and establish a strong centralized government with the Shogunate as a core; while such domains as Satsuma envisioned an administrative structure emphasizing participation by the major domains. Ôkubo and Saigô decided upon the ultimate forceful overthrow of the Shogunate and therefore in cooperation with Iwakura secretly secured from the imperial Court an order to overthrow the Shogunate. Yoshinobu's response to this strategy was to relinquish his commission as Shogun. Late in 1867, the Yoshinobu and Ôkubo factions met at Court and deliberated under considerable tension. Thus on the ninth day of the last month, with troops under Saigô guarding the imperial palace, the Restoration edict formulated by Iwakura and Ôkubo was issued. Yoshinobu was accordingly stripped of his powers. His supporters, however, reacted violently, and as a result even the stout-hearted Ôkubo could not but be pessimistic about the new developments. Yoshinobu, however, made a fatal decision. After withdrawing to the Osaka castle he ordered his troops to march on to Kyoto where they met and suffered defeat at the hands of the Sat-Chô forces. The birth of the new Meiji government was obviously integrally related to the final outcome of this military engagement.

One of the chief protagonists on the Restoration stage was without a doubt Ôkubo Toshimichi who worked closely with Iwakura Tomomi and the Chôshû loyalist, Kido Kôin. Selected by Hisamitsu for domain administrative duties, Ôkubo represented Satsuma ably and with courage in complicated negotiations and thereby helped to consummate the Restoration. This was the first phase of his political career. In the next phase he was to emerge as a great state-builder.

Despite the political instability of the period, Ôkubo's focus was constantly on the future of the government as he groped for answers, made plans, and implemented them. He can thus be termed the "prime architect of modern Japan."

Ôkubo became an integral part of the early Meiji government, serving within the important Department of Home Affairs. In order to display the force of the new government, Ôkubo received imperial permission to put in review the troops of the domains which comprised the core of the coalition government, namely, Satsuma, Chôshû, Tosa, and Aki. Seventy-five hundred troops served notice to the other domains that vacillation and disloyalty would find its nemesis.

As an officer in the Department of Home Affairs Ôkubo helped institute progressive reforms designed to create a forward-looking and strong state. He proposed to "humanize" the Emperor Meiji by bringing him out of his traditional seclusion, and to move the imperial capital from tradition-bound Kyoto to the seat of the former Tokugawa Shogunate in Edo. This move to the newly renamed city of Tokyo would remove the Court from regressive influences. In 1869 the Emperor made Tokyo his permanent abode.

Especially critical in the early Meiji years were Japan's foreign relations, as anti-foreign elements continued to attack aliens in Japan. Ôkubo was usually involved in dealing with foreign states with grievances that required settlement over deaths of their nationals. For instance, he met for two days with the French representative M. Leon Roches aboard the *Dupleix* in order to arrange a settlement of a murder case which had occured on the fifteenth day of the second month of 1868, in which a samurai killed eleven French seamen at Sakai. Usually, the Meiji government showed a willingness to conciliate rather than the rigidity that had been their normal reaction prior to 1868. It was essential for Japan to avoid becoming entangled with foreign powers during its formative years as a modern state.

Soon after the issuance of the Charter Oath in the third month of 1868, a statement of policy, liberal in its connotation, whose basic aim was to invite all factions to support the new government, Ôkubo had the exhilarating experience of becoming the first among the retainer class to be given an audience with the Emperor. He noted that the experience "moved him to tears."

If such experiences gave him momentary joy, the realities of bringing a newly established government to the take-off point weighed upon him. In financial matters, although Ôkubo sanctioned the issuance in 1869 of government notes amounting to 48 million *ryô* and the borrowing of money from influential merchant families such as the Mitsui to finance government operations, he was reluctant to pursue an inflationary policy that might lessen the fiscal integrity of the state.

Other problems plagued the new leaders. The court nobles were uncertain as to the import of the call of *sonnô* ("revere the emperor") which inspired the Restoration movement, when now in actuality the samurai class was in charge of administration. The domain leaders not involved in the Meiji government displayed antagonism toward the Satsuma-Chôshû coalition. Returned soldiers who had participated in the civil war following the Restoration proclamation also caused dissension within the nation. Hence as early as 1869, Saigô and Kido considered a Korean expedition as an expedient means to calm troubled domestic waters. Ôkubo, however, opposed such a foreign venture; he considered first of all the stability of the state which such a move would weaken. Better, he said, to recruit the dissatisfied elements into an imperial army comprised of troops of various domains. To deter further opposition against the Sat-Chô government, the Meiji leaders conceived the idea of returning their fiefs to the throne as a display of devotion to the emperor. Ôkubo at first showed little enthusiasm for this plan because of possible domain reactions against the government. Instead Ôkubo continued to stress the strengthening of the central government through a series of moves to rationalize the government that culminated as early as August, 1869 in the establishment of a structure representing a return to traditional authoritarianism in which the Department of Shinto (*Jingikan*) became superior to the Executive Department (*Dajôkan*).

Ôkubo saw that the earlier attempts at liberalization in line with the dictates of the Charter Oath proved to be divisive and weakening. Hence he discouraged public debate by abolishing bodies established as public forums such as the *Kôgisho.* As a Councilor of State (*sangi*), he furthermore urged a rigid stand by government officials against outside pressures and called for withholding government secrets from the public. The powerful oligarchy of the Meiji period was coming into being as the top officials pledged to implement policy as a united group. Later, for obvious reasons, he established strong government control over the Departments of Finance and Civil Affairs.

In the meantime, Ôkubo, true to the tradition of Japan, saw the need for learning from civilizations technically superior to his own. If Japan in the eighth century launched the world's first studies-abroad program by sending students to China, Ôkubo was responsible for reinstituting the concept in the nineteenth century by sending young men to France, England, and the United States who would become capable of "blending together the civilizations of Japan, China, and the West."

For the Japanese of the time, Western culture as manifested in Japan was at times eye-opening. In receiving the Duke of Edinburgh, the first foreign prince to be a guest of the Emperor, the Japanese government feted the royal visitor in 1869. At a return dinner at the British legation in Yokohama, Ôkubo and his colleagues "witnessed, wide-eyed, members of the opposite sexes dancing together."

In personnel policy, Ôkubo was perceptive and utilized men who were capable of strengthening the government. Hence in the sixth month of 1871, he stepped down as Councilor of State of the position of finance minister in order to allow Kido Kôin and Saigô Takamori to assume the position of Councilor of State. By now Ôkubo felt the time ripe for the abolition of the domains, and to implement this policy a united government stance was essential. The "self-relegation" of power to Kido and Saigô did not mean, however, that Ôkubo relinquished any real power; he was head of the Ministry of Finance (*Ôkurashô*) which controlled not only finance but also supervised local administration, a role ordinarily assigned to the Home Ministry (*Minbushô*). (The unique situation at this time resulted from the temporary incorporation of the *Minbushô* into the *Ôkurashô.*)

With the stage ready for the abolition of the domains and the establishment of the prefectures and all that this implied in terms of political centralization, Ôkubo proceeded with the help of Kido and Saigô (who had sold the idea to his childhood friend) to win support for the move. Ôkubo, therefore, in 1871, utilizing the influence of a united oligarchy implemented the dreams of Kido and Saigô, destroying the Japanese feudal structure and establishing a unified Japan under central government control, a *sine qua non* for the establishment of the later constitutional government.

Among the social reforms instituted in 1871 were included relaxed marriage and travel regulations as well as the abolition of the *eta* or pariah class.

With the abolition of the feudal domains domestic equilibrium was attained, at least temporarily, and the leaders turned their attention to foreign relations. The Iwakura mission (1871-73) went to the United States and the European countries to renegotiate the unequal treaties of 1858 as well as to give its members an opportunity to observe and absorb the culture of the West. Despite opposition from some of his colleagues and after a consultation with Saigô, Ôkubo decided to accompany the mission; he wished to see the West as well as to enroll his two sons in Western schools. Another motive was to cool the developing antagonism within the government between the Saigô-led war party and the Ôkubo industrial expansion advocates in the Ministry of Finance. By stepping out of the picture temporarily and allowing the Saigô faction to assume nominal leadership, he felt the situation would be ameliorated. Before leaving, however, Ôkubo made certain through a pledge signed by members of the Council of State that no drastic changes in personnel or domestic policy would be made prior to the mission's return to Japan. It is not clear why Saigô signed such a limiting pledge.

Ôkubo and the mission travelled through the United States after landing in San Francisco in the twelfth month of 1871, where they were received with great interest and warmth. The *Daily Evening Bulletin,* commenting on the Japanese, editorialized that "they are, as a race, impulsive, highly intelligent, brave to rashness, have a high sense of personal honor, and are universally polite, from the highest dignitary to the lowest in the land, and withal are kindly disposed toward foreigners, especially Americans." En route to Salt Lake City, Ôkubo noted the dimensions of the Lake and observed the interesting aspects of Mormon culture such as their practice of polygamy. After a meeting with President U.S. Grant in Washington, D.C., the party went on to Europe. In England, Ôkubo was interested in British industrial progress as he visited mills, shipyards, and iron founderies. In France he revealed his plans for government establishment and/or subsidization of industrial enterprises, to which Kido assented. In Germany the Iron Chancellor Bismarck impressed the Japanese; here was a strong leader and state-builder that could be emulated as by those absorbed with the *fukoku kyôhei* policy.

Meanwhile, at home the government was being pressed by internal as well as external problems relating to Korea, Formosa, and Karafuto. Hence, Kido and Ôkubo were urged to return to help settle differences arising over decisions to be made. The most delicate problem involved the conflict between Saigô's plan to chastise Korea for non-recognition of Japan following the Meiji Restoration and Ôkubo's belief that Japan's politico-economic position must be strengthened prior to pursuing an expansionist policy. Saigô was motivated by the desire to utilize the restive former samurai in a foreign war, the desire to enhance Japan's prestige, the fear of Korea coming under foreign domination, and the growing resentment and frustration caused by the opposition clique in government.

It was over the issue of Korea that the leaders of the two opposition factions were brought into heated confrontation in 1873. On October 24, Saigô along with others of his clique resigned, and the civilian faction under Ôkubo carried the day. A week after Saigô's return to Kagoshima there were rumblings of a possible military uprising against the government.

With opposition within the government minimized, Ôkubo could begin consolidating his position. By the end of 1873, he had formed the "Ôkubo government" filled with men of Satsuma, Chôshû, and Hizen. He himself served concurrently as Councilor of State and Minister of Home Affairs. He was henceforth to exercise virtually the power of a prime minister until he was struck down by an assassin's sword in 1878.

In political philosophy, Ôkubo cannot be described as a proponent of an absolute state as Tôyama Shigeki has argued. He favored the gradual evolution of representative government, stopping short of that epitomized by Western democracies, at approximately the point represented in the Japanese Constitution of 1889. This in itself is significant inasmuch as it raises the question as to what extent Ôkubo's views influenced Itô Hirobumi, the father of the Constitution of 1889. If Ôkubo's actions bespoke those of an autocrat, it was not because of his philosophy but rather the dictates of circumstance. Realism induced him to utilize those means that would assure the achievement of his basic objective of establishing a strong, independent Japan.

Circumstances that seemed to warrant strong exercise of authority included the Iwakura incident of January 14, 1874, involving samurai dissidents who made an attempt on the life of Prince Iwakura, and the Saga rebellion led by Etô Shinpei, a Saigô protege and a former member of the Tokyo government. Given dictatorial powers, Ôkubo suppressed the rebellion, and by April Etô had been tried and executed, thus assuring for the time the stability of the young government.

But other problems arose to plague the government as the Formosan question ripened into a major issue, taxing the ingenuity of the Meiji oligarchy. The question had its roots in the 1871 murder by Formosan tribesmen of fifty-five shipwrecked seamen from the Ryukyu islands. The Ryukyus were considered dependencies of the Japanese government and their people deserving of protection and redress for wrongs suffered. Since China failed to assume responsibility for the murders, the Japanese decided to take action, partially upon the advice of Charles E. De Long, the American minister to Tokyo (1869-73), and General Charles W. Le Gendre. The Japanese felt that positive military action was necessary to seize Formosa, a part of China, in order to establish a base which would strengthen Japan's defenses thus precluding English and French encroachment into Japanese affairs. By early 1874 Saigô Tsugumichi was ordered to investigate the question and recommended the organization of a military force for a punitive expedition to Formosa. By this time Saigô brothers and Ôkubo were in accord as to the Formosan policy. On April 27 Ôkubo received powers to make decisions regarding the expedition which had in the meantime been organized under Saigô Tsugumichi's command. But before Ôkubo arrived, Saigô ordered four ships of the fleet to sea and awaited Ôkubo's arrival. Ôkubo was hence confronted with a *fait accompli*, an early example of the Japanese military acting independently of the government. The reaction from China was positive as the Japanese took Ôkubo's advice not to withdraw Japanese troops.

Ôkubo was made envoy plenipotentiary to China in order to achieve a peaceful settlement of the Formosan crisis. Having made full plans for a possible war with China if the negotiations failed, he left for China on August 6, going directly to Peking, contrary to the diplomatic practice demanded by China. Throughout September and most of October he prepared for and then conducted vigorous negotiations, manifesting shrewd boldness and force. Finally, on October 31 a settlement was reached, and war between China and Japan was averted. Hence, the Formosan enterprise and its settlement were responsible for the early recognition by foreigners that Japan was indeed capable of preserving law and order within its realm. Significantly both the French and the English soon thereafter withdrew their forces from Yokohama.

Ôkubo played his role as a diplomat superbly, and upon returning to Tokyo in November expressed a desire to return to China the greater portion of the 500,000 *tael* indemnity promised to Japan. In this way, he hoped to win China's respect, since it was obvious that future cooperation would be imperative if the two countries in East Asia were to prosper. For his achievement, Ôkubo received the gratitude of the Emperor Meiji in the form of a ten thousand yen grant which he returned with the request that it is used for philanthropic purposes. The Emperor would not accept the refusal, and Ôkubo's critics have pointed out that with this money he built a large Western-style home in 1876.

After the settlement of the Formosan crisis Ôkubo had become the most important member of the government, but this was no consolation inasmuch as he had lost key leaders. Kido had left the government in protest over the Formosan adventure while Saigô Takamori was in his home province quietly rallying samurai malcontents. Under the circumstances he could do no better than to establish a reconciliation with Kido, the Chôshû leader.

The reconciliation was effected through the Osaka conference in 1875 which brought into being a Satsuma-Chôshû-Tosa coalition government after Kido and Itagaki Taisuke agreed to join Ôkubo on the latter's promise to work toward a more representative national structure. The conference agreed to the establishment of a senate to serve as a basis for a future national assembly, a supreme court, a conference of prefectural governors, and the limitation of the power of the Council of State. The program was obviously designed to curb the power of the Satsuma bureaucrat. That this was apparent to Ôkubo is clear, and the inference must be that he felt the need to begin laying the groundwork for a more liberal form of government, a structure that was established in 1875 as a check against increasing authoritarianism.

Ironically the Osaka conference with its democratic emphasis led to suppression of the press, a result of the journalists' lack of restraint in criticizing the despotic nature of the government. The laws authored by Ôkubo were intended to preserve the integrity of the government and were hence from his standpoint legitimate.

In economic policy, Ôkubo adhered to a mercantilist philosophy that had its roots in seventeenth and eighteenth century Europe, and was perhaps best represented by the French monarch, Louis XIV. He therefore sanctioned government encouragement of industry with the aim of establishing a sound fiscal basis for the country's political and military position. He stressed the development of a favorable trade balance for Japan. The traditionally close association of government and business in Japan can be traced to this period. The Mitsui, Mitsubishi, Shimada, and Ono merchant families owe their rapid rise to the Meiji government and its economic practices that favored entrepreneurship. Ôkubo encouraged agriculture by establishing in 1874 an agricultural school, an agricultural experimental station at Mita, and a stock-breeding center at Shinjuku. He established a silk filature in Gunma Prefecture, assuring its manager that it would be sold in time to private enterprise. Ôkubo offered government subsidies to shipping companies and established a navigation school to train seamen for the merchant fleet.

Ôkubo rightly believed that industrialization could work economic miracles that would in time alleviate samurai dissatisfaction of an economic sort; many could be absorbed by industries. For those who favored agricultural careers, Ôkubo initiated a program to settle samurai on land in Fukushima Prefecture.

But for many samurai this was not enough to still discontent. When in March, 1876 the government prohibited the samurai from bearing two swords, the badge of the warrior class, a roar of indignation could be heard from their ranks. Later the commutation of all feudal stipends added to the unrest.

The plight of the peasant class also caused ferment that affected national unity. To mitigate their plight the land tax of 1873, which had been a definite improvement over that of 1872, was further reduced from 3 to 2.5 per cent by the new tax law of 1877.

Samurai unrest was to culminate in the Satsuma rebellion of 1877, the last serious attempt of the military class to gain control of the government. The leader around whom the dissidents had rallied since the defeat of the war party in 1873 was Saigô himself who is said to have been indirectly involved in the Saga rebellion in 1874. In Kagoshima he established a school to nurture the traditional Satsuma samurai spirit and instilled *jôi* sentiment in his students. There are those who would contend that among his motives was the overthrow of the government in order to reassert his own control over it. If this was actually his innermost thought, it was induced by his disappointment with the direction in which the Meiji government was moving, which was counter to what he thought proper. His feeling of utter helplessness in influencing policy that would elevate the general welfare could conceivably have motivated his activities in Kagoshima. It could also be argued that as a Japanese samurai imbued with the spirit of *bushidô* he undertook the leadership of a rebellion that he realized had no possibility of success, a movement that would fulfill his "death wish." Death for what to him was a righteous cause was most honorable. Whatever the exact motivation, by 1875 there were seven thousand followers in Kagoshima alone and an additional thousand in branch schools. By 1876 Kagoshima fell under the influence of Saigô adherents. Ôkubo therefore observed closely the activities of Saigô's followers. In 1877 arms and munitions from the Kagoshima arsenal were ordered removed. Upon learning of the government move, the Kagoshima samurai on January 29 and 30 broke into the arsenal and the naval shipyard and carried off large quantities of weapons and war materials. By early February, Saigô and a force of fifteen thousand men began a march northward, and on the nineteenth the government proclaimed a civil war against the Saigô rebels. The imperial forces in the battle of Shiroyama on September 24 wounded the rebel leader who, noting the impossibility of the situation, ordered a lieutenant to sever his head to spare him from falling into enemy hands alive. Hence, a victorious termination of the war was realized after Kagoshima itself and the greater part of Kumamoto were reduced to ashes and over thirty-three thousand were killed or wounded. The modern conscript army had carried the day.

Historians have argued over whether Ôkubo had considered having

Saigô assassinated in order to prevent a civil war. This remains a controversial issue. There are scholars who say Ôkubo in fact attempted to meet with Saigô in order to prevent the carnage.

The civil war was inevitable considering the circumstances of the period. Ôkubo and Saigô represented two divergent political philosophies one emphasizing civil leadership of government while the other believed that the traditional spirit of the samurai in its pristine form was a *sine qua non* for the building of a strong and respected Japanese state. Ironically the rebellion pitted two Satsuma friends against each other – the one staunchly loyal to the new imperial government and the other to Satsuma which represented the samurai cause. Hated by his own domain, Ôkubo nevertheless maintained his tough-minded stance and never allowed sentiment to cloud his vision. Had the Meiji government been overwhelmed by forces of Saigô conservatism, Japan might well have reverted to a feudal state, a position from which her rise to modernism would have been vastly difficult.

On May 14, 1878, Ôkubo was assassinated by six samurai conspirators while riding in a carriage from his residence in Kasumigaseki to attend a meeting at the imperial palace. Saigô Tsugumichi had the sorrowful task of taking the body back to the Ôkubo home.

Ôkubo was murdered because of his seeming arbitrary exercise of authority, and his death was in a sense the direct consequence of the Satsuma rebellion. His assassination perhaps led to discussion of a more liberal government and hence hastened the arrival of constitutional government; in July the government announced that prefectural assemblies would be established with members elected by a restricted male electorate.

Although Ôkubo's life ended at the height of his power, by 1878 he had through his coldly calculating approach helped bring about the Meiji Restoration and placed on a firm basis the new Meiji government. His dedication to the cause of state-building never wavered. He was in essence the architect of modern Japan – a statesman of fortitude who appeared at a propitious moment in Japan's development toward modernism. Although an authoritarian, he deserves new consideration from the perspective of this moment in history.

From Xenophobe to Business Leader

Shibusawa Eiichi

by

WILLIAM D. HOOVER

Shibusawa Eiichi easily qualifies for the appellation "great historical figure." As a minor participant in the turbulent events at the end of the Tokugawa period, as a government official with brief service but significant accomplishments, as the premier businessman of the Meiji period, as an advocate of internationalism, and as a champion of philanthropic causes, Shibusawa definitely earns his many adulations. Indeed, he not only deserves these honors, but in many ways his career epitomizes the dynamic changes which swept Japan during this crucial era.

Born in a farming village north of Tokyo in 1840, Shibusawa had an advantageous, but hardly exceptional, childhood. His father was a farmer who profitably engaged in the production and commercial handling of indigo. As a child, Shibusawa received more schooling than the average youth of his day. An older cousin tutored him in the Confucian classics for seven years, instilling a lifelong love of the *Analects*. Shibusawa's threadbare copy attests to its shaping moral influence. In childhood Shibusawa became a voracious reader, a trait which he retained throughout life. Apocryphal though the story may be, he reportedly fell into an irrigation ditch while reading as he walked along a narrow road. The fact that he ruined his New Year's clothes irritated his parents but did not cause them to stifle his interest in reading. Instruction in swordsmanship and calligraphy helped mold and discipline his personality and manner. Along with his formal education, Shibusawa received practical experience in farming, manufacturing, and commerce through participation in his family's business. He also learned at first hand of social and political frustrations.

One particular episode illustrates the dilemma faced by the young

Shibusawa Eiichi

Shibusawa. When the local magistrate summoned Shibusawa's father to a meeting, the ill father appointed his sixteen-year-old son as his representative. The tax system at that time was quite arbitrary since, in addition to the regular general tax, the feudal lord could force special additional payments from wealthy villagers. The magistrate intended to levy such a special assessment on the Shibusawa family. When he demanded such a payment, Shibusawa, however, replied that he could not decide such a matter without consulting his father. The magistrate angrily rebuked him for lacking the authority to make such a decision in spite of his mature sixteen years. However, Shibusawa adamantly refused to change his attitude and said he could consent to such a payment only after consulting his father. Reminiscing about the incident in later years, he indignantly claimed, "If it weren't for my father, I'd have boxed the magistrate's ears and run away for good." Shibusawa came to realize that people without great rank could not challenge the political officials who oppressed them. He grew to detest the class system under the degenerate Shogunate.

In 1863, the contradictions which plagued his world became intolerable. Thus, the twenty-three-year-old Shibusawa brazenly approached his father and conveyed his desire to abandon his responsibility as successor to the family headship. He took this drastic step in order to journey to Edo to work for the reform of the nation. His father vigorously contended that he could adequately serve the nation as a farmer. A heated argument continued throughout the night. As dawn broke, Shibusawa's father finally consented to his son's request, magnanimously saying,

> "I understand. Even though you are not here, I will grow young again and protect the family. While the Shogunate exercises its tyrannical government and officials commit unfair acts, I will remain obedient. Since you say you can not do that, you may do as you please. Father and son must always follow the respective paths in which each believe."

Thus, Shibusawa left the family home to involve himself in national politics.

Provoked by foreign intrusions, Shibusawa vented his youthful exuberance by joining a movement to rid Japan of her foreign invaders. Together with other young exponents of anti-foreignism, he plotted an attack on the foreign settlement at Yokohama. Disgusted that the incompetent Shogunate would not rid Japan of the foreign menace, these exacerbated individuals conspired to cut down the foreigners and raze their settlement. Shibusawa presumed this attack would create a general uprising which would ultimately topple the totally ineffective Tokugawa regime.

The plotters secretly gathered weapons and planned the raid. However, the night before the attack, one of the leaders raised serious doubts as to the probable outcome of the mission. A heated argument ensued during which time it was decided to postpone the attack. Actually, this early anti-Shogunate insurrection was no more than a small, local uprising destined to end in pitiful failure. Shibusawa, fearing the strong arm of the law, fled to Kyoto. There he visited Hiraoka Enshirô, a talented retainer of Tokugawa Yoshinobu. Although Yoshinobu had not yet assumed any major public office, he was regarded by many as the future hope of the Tokugawa family. Hiraoka, who had previously met Shibusawa in Edo, saw his great potential and persuaded him to become a retainer of Yoshinobu. The Shogunate's search for the plotters had already begun, and without the status of a retainer Shibusawa would easily have been arrested and thrown in jail. Therefore, he accepted Hiraoka's offer. The abrupt change from participant in the anti-Shogunate movement to agent for the Tokugawa family caused Shibusawa serious pangs of conscience. He wanted to meet Prince Yoshinobu directly and convey his ideas concerning the reform of the Shogunate system. He made this a condition of his acceptance of the position as retainer. Hiraoka said that there was no precedent for such a thing, but Shibusawa quickly countered with the argument that neither was there a precedent for an individual farmer to be appointed a retainer. When Hiraoka finally accepted Shibusawa's condition, the young anti-foreign advocate agreed to radically shift his attitude.

Shibusawa, as Yoshinobu's retainer, demonstrated considerable ability by successfully applying his practical business knowledge to improve the administrative and financial affairs of the Tokugawa domain. Within a short while, Yoshinobu became the fifteenth Tokugawa Shogun. Shibusawa, who believed that the Shogunate should be dismantled, was not pleased with this development. While thinking he ought to resign, Shibusawa was suddenly ordered to accompany Yoshinobu's younger brother to Europe. Shibusawa abandoned the idea of resigning and willingly accepted this opportunity.

Extensive foreign travel can be an eye-opening experience for anyone. For a young Japanese of the mid-nineteenth century, living in Europe for one and a half years was a particularly exciting adventure. Shibusawa traveled to Europe in early 1867 as a retainer of Prince Minbu, the younger brother of the Shogun. The group went to represent the Tokugawa government at the International Exposition in Paris and to study the conditions of the West. Although he began the European trip as a committed anti-foreign devotee, Shibusawa had an open mind.

> "I am decidedly anti-foreign, but without knowledge of foreign matters. I am now of the opinion that one should know matters at first hand before he opposes or criticizes them. Moreover, I believe that there are many things which we should learn from foreign countries. From this point of view, I am pleased to accept the appointment."

His observations in Europe quickly convinced him of the futility of trying to drive the "barbarian" from Japan's shores.

Arriving in Europe, the inquisitive Shibusawa took great interest in everything around him. Western foods and eating habits, especially the consumption of large quantities of milk and coffee, amazed him. Gas street lamps, telegraph wires, train rides, and the municipal amenities fascinated him. His diary reveals the enthrallment with which he witnessed French military reviews, inspected schools, reverberatory furnaces, and various machine shops, and visited silk spinning factories. He stood in awe of the majesty of Emperor Napoleon III and his court. Theater performances, parties, and costume balls introduced a new social life. In

Switzerland, Belgium, and the Netherlands, he saw what industry and commerce could accomplish for a nation. Italy's dockyards, factories, and iron foundries revealed their potential. Witnessing a military ceremony, touring the textile mills, and having an audience with Queen Victoria all elevated the status of Great Britain in Shibusawa's eyes.

European travel opened new vistas for Shibusawa in the business world. The flourishing economic activity shocked and spurred him to action. Extensive observations of the European industrial world convinced him that the source of wealth and power of any country rests with its commerce and industry. He recognized that Japan's future was contingent on economic and technological development. During this crucial formative experience he committed his life to the economic modernization of Japan.

Four specific European observations greatly influenced Shibusawa's entrepreneurial career and public life. First, the favorable social status and respect which the European businessmen enjoyed deeply impressed Shibusawa. In direct contrast to the negative image attached to merchant activity in traditional Japan, Shibusawa saw the Ruropean businessman moving in the highest social circles, working as equals of government officials, and having a place of respect in his society. Secondly, by observing that the European businessman owned and operated his business enterprise in cooperation with others, Shibusawa discovered the advantages of the joint-stock corporate form of business. He concluded that the corporate form of organization must have something to do with the European industrial and commercial success. Thirdly, he observed the stock exchanges and banks in Europe and found them so impressive that he felt Japan must also develop the same. Finally, the way French businessmen contributed to various philanthropic causes aroused Shibusawa's admiration. Shibusawa resolved to implement these European features upon his return to Japan.

Although forced to return home in October 1868 due to the fall of the Shogunate, Shibusawa had seen enough to be dazzled and intoxicated by the magic of Western material civilization. Everything from Western machinery to the large sturdy houses, even the beauty of Western women stirred the lively Shibusawa.

> "I was surprised by everything I saw in France. The degree to which the West has progressed is much greater than I had imagined. I wish you could see it at first hand. I am happy to hear that the Shogunate decided to open two ports, Osaka and Kobe, for European traders... It is my sincere view that Japan should establish contacts with other nations, deeply and widely, and learn as much as we can from them; and that we should utilize the knowledge we learn from them.... It

> seems that a secluded Japan is out of the question now. Prices here are very high, as much as five times those in Japan. Currencies circulate very smoothly, and paper monies are being circulated like specie. Since Japan now has commercial relations with others we should have a monetary system corresponding to those of the Western nations."

Shibusawa soon had a chance to implement some of these ideas through official channels. In November 1869, he reluctantly postponed his business career and yielded to Ôkuma Shigenobu's request to join the Finance Ministry. There he headed the Bureau of Reorganization which led in such efforts as tax reform, standardization of weights and measures, abolishment of domain debts, and strategic surveys of natural resources. Energetic and creative, his progressive approach plus his opposition to excessive military expenditures earned him the hostility of some of the less enlightened bureaucrats.

Banking provides the most obvious link between Shibusawa's brief government career and his more enduring role as a businessman. Shibusawa was one of several individuals to bring various financial interests together to form the First National Bank of Japan. He served as the bank's general superintendent and soon became its president, a position he held for more than forty years. While both a government official and a private banker, he contributed his time and energy to educate and train bankers, to work out banking practices to serve the needs or industrialization, to assist banks over severe crises, and to carry out national banking reform measures. As an indication of Shibusawa's contribution to banking, rival banks unabashedly sent their employees to him for training. He was particularly active in developing such banking techniques as the issuance of bank notes, interest calculation procedures, bookkeeping, and financial reporting. He even prepared two useful booklets which explained banking procedures. For Shibusawa, the importance of banking could not be overemphasized. Banking was the life blood of a country's economic development. As he put it, "the circulation of money in the economic world may be compared to the circulation of blood in the human body. Both are equally important to healthy activity."

While observing the role of the businessman in Europe, Shibusawa decided that any political activity he might engage in must be secondary to his goal of developing commerce and industry. Publicly he deplored the superabundance of government officials in contrast to the paucity of capable, progressive businessmen. He explained his resignation from government as a necessary step to enable him to devote full time to the advancement of business. Though his personal life he sought to enhance the image of the businessman in the public eye. He was fully aware that, unless the public image of the modern businessman reached a new level of respectability, it would be difficult to attract ambitious, talented men to entrepreneurial careers. Since the private business sector was very weak in early Meiji Japan, Shibusawa sought to elevate it by providing leadership, ideas, organization, and performance. He deliberately left a promising government career in 1874 to engage systematically in entrepreneurial activity.

It is no easy task to grasp the significance of Shibusawa's contributions to the commercial and industrial development of Japan. To start with, he helped organize and direct as many as two hundred and fifty industrial and commercial enterprises. He engaged in the manufacture of paper, textiles, and cement, the processing of gas, fertilizer, electricity, iron, coal, and other natural resources, and the operation of breweries, shipping companies, and railway lines, warehousing, and insurance companies. Obviously, not all these enterprises flourished nor could Shibusawa devote much time to any one of them. In most cases he was not directly involved in the everyday managerial details but lent his name in support, built capital resources, provided technology, encouraged entrepreneurial talent, and worked to solve troublesome problems. Shibusawa, while having little interest in the routine details of management, prided himself on being "a problem solver for industrial bottlenecks" and "a strategist of modern industrialization." If the scope of his involvement is expanded to include the roles of director, adviser, and major shareholder, Shibusawa may be said to have had nominal connections with as many as five hundred diverse enterprises.

Second, a measure of his contribution to the business world can be gained from the fact that he actually coined a new term, *jitsugyôka,* for businessman. *Jitsugyôka,* "a man who undertakes a real task," seemed more appropriate to describe a businessman than the old term *shônin,* "trade person," with all its negative images. Shibusawa defined a *jitsugyôka* as a person who worked with diligence and honesty for the establishment of modern industrial development. The application of this new term helped elevate the status of the Japanese businessman and provided him with a better image.

Third, Shibusawa sought to be a leader and shaper of the business world. As he viewed the situation, Japan's chief economic problems stemmed from a scarcity of capital, poor organization in the business world, and a lack of capable entrepreneurs. He devoted a great deal of effort to solving these problems. To meet the problem of a scarcity of capital, he championed the joint-stock company form of business enterprise. He organized his own enterprises on this basis thus providing broader popular participation in capital formation and corporate leadership. For Shibusawa, large scale enterprises were essential to Japan's development. Joint-stock companies not only made this possible but gave men of ability an opportunity for honor, responsibility, and self interest while promoting the wealth and power of the nation.

In order to counter the poor quality of organization in the Meiji business world, Shibusawa took the lead in forming several business oriented groups. His first major undertaking was the formation of an association of the nation's bankers. This organization provided educational experiences for bankers and offered an opportunity to discuss banking procedures. It eventually became the powerful Bankers' Association of Japan. Again remembering his European experience, he helped found the Tokyo Chamber of Commerce and served as its president for many years. The Chamber of Commerce unified and gave direction to the Tokyo business community. To advance the business world, Shibusawa even published and wrote for a journal devoted to entrepreneurial development and business morality.

Believing that capable entrepreneurs would emerge only after people received the proper education and training, Shibusawa developed his own business school. Once, to illustrate his point, he refused a loan to a sugar refining developer because he felt the man inadequately educated for the task. Shibusawa contributed significantly to the success of Japan's first commercial high school by collecting funds for it, acting as its patron, and advising it. Later, this school became Hitotsubashi University, a noted institution of economic learning.

Shibusawa stressed the need to create a new attitude toward economic activity and instill a new social conscience in Japan's businessman. To raise his status, the businessman had to assume new social responsibilities, devote himself to the national welfare, and promote morality in business. He explained the subordination of his personal interests to national advancement in a speech in 1915.

> "The cause which led me into business life was neither a desire to increase my own wealth nor to attain pomp or glory. I wanted to awaken the business spirit in Japan so that the country could survive and prosper. Although I profited from salaries and the increase in value of my stocks, that was not my real purpose. I sought to straighten out the chaotic Japanese business system, develop it, and bring respectability to the businessman. Never for a moment did I aim at my own profit."

While these words ring of self-effacement, they do contain a measure of accuracy. For all his business acumen and extensive involvement, Shibusawa never accumulated wealth on a really great scale. Unlike the Iwasaki, Mitsui, or Yasuda families, Shibusawa did not leave a gigantic financial legacy. In addition to his attitude of self-denial, many other reasons explain his lack of financial accumulation. Most of his enterprises were backed by the joint-stock form of capital accumulation which gave financial strength to the corporation but did not provide great windfalls in exchange for his modest personal investments. As president, and not owner, of the First National Bank, he had significant influence but did not reap great personal profits from his labors. Rather than consolidate his efforts on only the most profitable enterprises, he frequently invested in ventures he thought to be important to the nation's development, even at his own personal financial disadvantage. Stressing the need for national economic growth, he was not a single-minded, profit-maximizing businessman.

Statements concerning the businessman's individual subordination to the national good were more than mere platitudes for Shibusawa. The accumulation of personal wealth was fine as long as the process served the national good and did not deny others the opportunity for profit. As he explained:

> "Civilization must depend upon the advancement of economic power. Economic progress cannot be achieved by simply aiming for personal gain and the prosperity of commerce and industry *per se,* unless it is based on the strong foundation of morality. There is no other way but to fall back on the practice of the principle of the union of economics and morality, if we desire human progress."

One should easily detect the tones of a moralist in Shibusawa's statements and actions. Schooled in Confucianism, he regularly quoted the *Analects* and tried to apply them in his daily economic life. He reinterpreted Confucianism in such a way as to make profit and morality thoroughly compatible. He tried to build modern enterprise using the abacus and the *Analects.* His unwavering adherence to his moral convictions demanded that on occasion he even sacrifice personal profit in business when the methods required did not coincide with his sense of morality. Once he complied with a ship building contract at a personal loss when a less honorable method of escape was possible. On another occasion he objected to selling a gas company to individuals for personal gain, even his own, when he thought the profit should go to the people of the nation. His "business ethics" of honesty, independence, cooperative spirit, and social responsibility were a blend of samurai ethics and modern business procedures.

By 1916, Shibusawa, then in his mid-seventies, had withdrawn from all positions of active leadership in his many businesses. In his remaining fifteen years, he intensified his participation in public service projects and in the improvement of international relations. Inherent in such a shift was Shibusawa's desire to utilize his wealth and status for the public good, to demonstrate that a life of morality was thoroughly compatible with success in business, and to convey the possible range of public service open to Japanese businessmen. By reliable estimates, he participated in as many as six hundred different organizations dedicated to public service, philanthropic endeavors, and international exchange. Obviously, in many cases, his participation could not have amounted to much more than lending his name or contributing some money to a specific cause. In other cases he gave more fully of himself. A few examples will illustrate the depth and breadth of his concern. For a businessman whose life was devoted to economic gain, the problem of poverty in his society was particularly perplexing. For sixty years Shibusawa contributed his time, efforts, and money to the founding and operation of the Tokyo City Poor House. Always oriented toward the self-improvement approach, Shibusawa stressed rehabilitation, education, and health care measures as key means of overcoming poverty.

Exposed in childhood to the tragic conditions facing Japan's lepers, Shibusawa carried a deep compassion for them throughout his life. "The community must," he said, "wake up and look after these unfortunate people." He took the lead in founding an institution to care for lepers and to work for the prevention of leprosy. He visited lepers' asylums in Hawaii and learned of efforts to eliminate the disease. He vigorously called attention to the lepers' plight and helped found other institutions to work for their welfare. In 1930, he capped his efforts on behalf of lepers with the organization of an association of major Tokyo businessmen to work on behalf of lepers.

Contributions to public education represent another example of Shibusawa's public involvement. Linking his concern for commercial education with public service, Shibusawa helped develop the previously mentioned Hitotsubashi University to train young men in entrepreneurial careers. He did not overlook women's education either. He contributed to the Meiji Girls School, served as a committee member of the Society for the Encouragement of Girls Education, and helped with the founding and financial support of Japan Women's University.

The elderly Shibusawa daily received visitors in his home during the early morning hours. Every day he saw anyone who wanted an audience regardless of whether or not the person had a formal introduction. The financial condition and status of the interviewer made no difference. People who came to see him were received in his parlor in the order in which they arrived. Listening to both great social problems as well as trifling personal matters, Shibusawa thoroughly considered the issues, judged them, and responded thoughtfully. If the issue concerned the establishment of a company, Shibusawa diligently applied a yardstick of evaluation seeking to determine if it was something which was reasonable, if the time was favorable, if it would benefit the peace of mankind, and if the planners had sufficient capability to succeed. Further, in the case where an individual's conversation was trivial, Shibusawa would recount a favorite proverb from the *Analects* or relate his own personal experience, thus kindly advising the visitor. He regularly made himself available for interviews until ten o'clock. Frequently, however, since these interviews did not end promptly at ten, there were telephone calls inquiring as to his expected arrival at some important meeting. Many times when financial magnates at the Banker's Club irritatingly asked, "Hasn't Shibusawa come yet?" he was in his parlor patiently explaining an important point to an impoverished student.

The promotion of international peace and good will was another important activity for Shibusawa. His views on the desirability of foreign relations shifted dramatically from his youthful xenophobic utterances and plans. In broadminded fashion, he developed an intense interest in the promotion of international good will and world peace. Several of the organizations which he either helped found, support, or serve endeavored to promote friendship between nations and find peaceful solutions to international problems. Organizations such as the Japan Peace Society, the Japanese-American Relations Committee, the America-Japan Society, the League of Nations Association of Japan, and the Japan branch of the Institute of Pacific Relations increased international contacts and thereby provided the opportunity for an exchange of information and sentiments.

Shibusawa zealously crusaded to improve relations with the United States. America, for which Shibusawa came to hold considerable admiration and affection, represented progress, power, and world popularity, all features which he hoped to see developed in Japan. In 1909, he traveled to the United States with a group of businessmen to promote better understanding and closer relations between the peoples of the two countries. There he made personal contacts, gave speeches, inspected facilities, and talked with leading citizens including President Taft. He made three other trips to the United States, all after his seventieth birthday. In 1913 during the height of anti-Japanese activities in California, he helped organize and served as the president of a joint

Japanese-American committee to seek an honorable settlement to this problem. In 1915 he again journeyed to the United States to cultivate positive ties of international friendship. In 1921 he ventured to America as an unofficial delegate to promote the Washington Conference. Spokesmen for internationalism throughout the world regarded Shibusawa as an outstanding practitioner of "people's diplomacy," the art of non-official, individual effort at improving international relations.

Ability, hard work, fortunate circumstances, and a strong desire for success all helped Shibusawa gain distinction as Japan's outstanding business leader. To no one's surprise, he received such honors as selection to membership in the House of Peers on its inauguration in 1890, and the title of Viscount in 1902. As Japan's original "organization man," the name Shibusawa Eiichi was repeatedly invoked as the model for Japanese businessmen. His efforts at creating new forms of business organization, advancing the level of business knowledge and responsibility, raising the moral standards, and advancing the national purpose rightly earned him this distinction. His service as a businessman, stateman, philanthropist, and internationalist brought him the imperial designation "a princely civilian."

Throughout his career, Shibusawa demonstrated a strong proclivity to seek order and stability in his world. Whether it was organizing and managing a business empire, solving problems of business organization, bringing respect to the role of the businessman, contributing to philanthropic causes, or working for a better international order, Shibusawa spoke and acted for balance and order in his society. Here we see the seeming paradox of an innovator acting to ensure stability. The situation is not as contradictory as it appears since the Meiji period represents a blending of traditional and modern forces, and Shibusawa clearly demonstrates this trend. Rather than allow his traditional Confucian heritage to stifle development, he successfully combined it with progressive ideas and actions to help generate the new Japan.

Conflict, Compromise, and Tragedy

Konoe Fumimaro and Tôjô Hideki

by

GORDON M. BERGER

In the early hours of morning of December 16, 1945, Konoe Fumimaro drank a fatal dosage of potassium cyanide and sunk into sleep for the final time in his fifty-four years of life. Three years later, shortly after midnight on December 23, 1948, Tôjô Hideki was hanged on the gallows of Sugamo Prison, one week prior to his sixty-fourth birthday. One man died by his own hand, the other by order of a foreign occupying army; but both were finally victims of their own unique ability to rise to positions of consummate political responsibility as Japan followed her tragic course towards catastrophe in the late 1930s and early 1940s.

Between them, Prince Konoe and General Tôjô monopolized the premiership of Japan for all but eighteen months of the critical period from June 1937 to July 1944. For both men, leadership proved a challenging and difficult task. In July 1937, Japan became enmeshed in a war with China from which she could not extricate herself. Abandoning her tenuous ties with the world order defined during the 1920s at the Versailles and Washington Conferences, she then set out to construct a New Order in East Asia. Subsequently, she moved to establish her independence of the Anglo-American powers through the creation of the Greater East Asian Co-Prosperity Sphere and membership in the Axis Alliance with Germany and Italy. In 1941, she declared war on the Anglo-American powers and swept through Southeast Asia and the South Pacific in a dramatic but short-lived series of daring military campaigns. And finally, after failing to consolidate her new position of strength in East and Southeast Asia, her empire began to collapse under the withering counter-attacks of the Allied military offensives of 1943 and 1944. Throughout the 1937-1944 period, as successive Konoe and Tôjô govern-

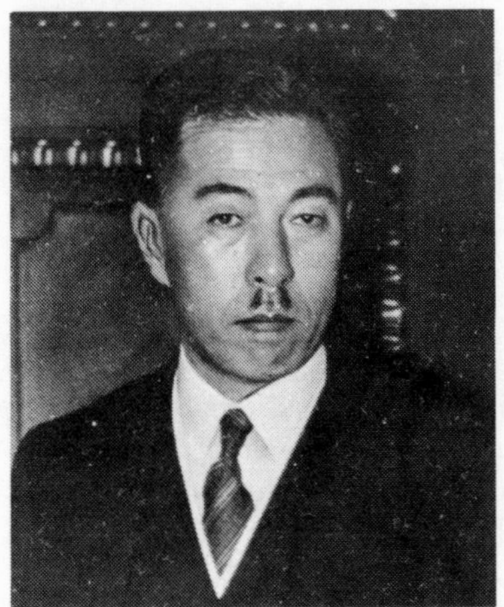

Konoe Fumimaro (left) and Tôjô Hideki (photos; Mainichi Shinbunsha, Tokyo)

ments guided the nation closer to war, into war, and through the war, the two men struggled to maintain control over the diverse ruling elite groups comprising Japan's political establishment, and sought to mobilize the total energy and resources of the empire on behalf of the ambitious foreign and military policies their cabinets had endorsed. Nevertheless, by the time Tôjô stepped down from office, Japan's defeat had become a mere matter of time; and the death of the Japanese Empire was followed shortly thereafter by the deaths of its two most important wartime leaders.

While Konoe and Tôjô thus shared a common final destiny, no two men could have been more different in life. Konoe was a high-born scion of the nobility, destined by birthright to assume a prominent role in Japanese politics. Tôjô was the eldest son of a professional military man, and was thrust into a position of political leadership only because Japan's army became the most powerful political elite group governing the country. Konoe was polished and urbane; Tôjô was blunt and direct. Konoe was flexible – some said even to the point of spinelessness; Tôjô was principled and firm – some said even to the point of rigidity. The prince was acclaimed for his breadth of political vision, and criticized for his lack of interest in implementing the ideas he conceived; the general was lauded for his attention to administrative minutiae, and castigated for his narrowness of perspective. It is doubtful that either man liked the other, although for the sake of the nation and Emperor they both served, they attempted to cooperate with each other. As Tôjô was a principal actor in the drama that unseated Konoe from power in October 1941, Konoe returned to an important behind-the-scenes role in the political maneuvers that toppled Tôjô in mid-1944.

Given their personality differences, it is hardly surprising that Konoe and Tôjô faced the tasks of political leadership in markedly different fashions. Yet, the difference in their political styles tells us much more than the fact that they were dissimilar in nature. An examination of their careers in power, and the ways in which each approached the same problems of government, tells us a great deal about the political environment and constraints on leadership to which each had to adjust in order to lead the nation. Moreover, the careers of Konoe and Tôjô highlight the nature and extent of the important transition taking place in Japan from a society where inherited status had primacy to one in which talent – defined in terms of administrative ability – became the criterion for the allocation of political power and prestige. That this transition was well underway by the early Shôwa period was demonstrated in Tôjô Hideki's rise to prominence; that it was not complete becomes clear in an analysis of the sources of Konoe Fumimaro's lasting political influence.

Konoe Fumimaro was born on October 12, 1891, and at the death of his father in 1904, he became the head of the most prestigious noble house in Japan (excluding, of course, the imperial family itself). Such a position conferred on him considerable public obligations. Not only was he required to fulfill a variety of duties at Court, but as the foremost noble of the realm he was also responsible for defending the Throne and assisting the Emperor in the governance of the realm. Despite personal inclinations to avoid the hurly-burly of public life, Konoe accepted his fate with resignation, and upon his graduation from Kyoto Imperial University, he embarked on a long and active career as one of Japan's foremost political leaders. Apart from a brief period of training in the Home Ministry, however, Konoe never held a position of administrative responsibility prior to assuming the premiership in 1937. Instead, his career was spent in the House of Peers and behind the scenes, where he campaigned vigorously for preserving a modicum of the hereditary nobility's political influence and served as an intermediary to smooth the competition and rivalries which characterized Japanese politics under the Meiji Constitutional system.

Political mediation of the type provided by Konoe was highly necessary under Japan's prewar political system. In order to prevent a situation where the Emperor would become enmeshed in political controversy by choosing to support one group of his ministers over another, Japan's leaders developed a style of cabinet decision-making early in the twentieth century which required the unanimous consent of all ministers before policies were recommended to the throne for ritual ratification. Primary responsibility for resolving disagreements within the cabinet lay with the premier, but while he was responsible for the original recommendation of the cabinet roster of ministers to the throne, he had little leverage vis-à-vis his ministers once they were formally appointed, and he could not force any of them to resign without tendering a general resignation of his entire cabinet. To secure the prerequisite consensus of ministerial views for a formal imperial decision on national policy, a great deal of extra-cabinet political mediation among rival elite factions was essential. Konoe's mediatory role thus both provided important protection of the Emperor's untarnished prestige, and eased the way for successive cabinet coalitions to function effectively.

Konoe had several attributes which made him uniquely suited to a mediator's role. On most issues, he assumed a non-partisan position. He was suave, intelligent, and cordially sympathetic to the viewpoints of all who chose to press their opinions on him. Above all, however, even in the milieu of "Taishô democracy" during the 1920s, it was Konoe's status as a high-ranking courtier with close blood ties to the imperial family that induced otherwise contentious politicians to yield to his mediatory efforts in the hopes of winning his political favor. By the early 1930s, he was regarded as a rising star in the Japanese political firmament, sedulously courted by a wide range of ambitious leaders seeking the advantage of his excellent connections at Court and the prestige he enjoyed by virtue of his impeccable lineage.

In many ways, Konoe's personal career appeared somewhat anomalous in light of the growing proclivity in Japan to allocate power to those with administrative talent, rather than those whose primary qualifications for leadership lay in their inherited status. The muffled ideological tensions between the hereditary principle of power transfer and the Confucian concept of "rule by those with demonstrated talent" erupted with a fury late in the Edo period, and the leaders of the Meiji Restoration carried the nation forward towards modernization with a firm belief in the rectitude of the principle of talent. Not only did the Meiji oligarchs aggressively seek out talented young men and recruit them into their personal political factions, but collectively, they established institutions of higher learning (Tokyo Imperial University, the Army and Navy War Colleges, etc.) to endow the talented young men of the day with the specialized expertise believed necessary to govern Japan in the future. By 1910, these institutions had become the predominant recruiting grounds for the civilian and military administrative leadership of the country.

Nevertheless, the Meiji legacy of political thought on the question of heredity versus talent was not unambivalent. The hereditary nobility of the Court (including the Konoe house) and various daimyo houses were given new patents of nobility in the 1880s, and thereafter enjoyed considerable political power under the Meiji Constitutional system through the hereditary rights of their families to hold positions in the House of Peers. The legitimacy of the entire political structure, moreover, rested on the inherited authority of the Emperor; and the hereditary political duty of nobles was defined in terms of defending the throne through their service in the House of Peers. On the basis of this mission, Japan's modern nobility played an active role in national politics down through the 1920s, and survived severe attacks on its inherited prerogatives during the Taishô period (1912-26) with only a minimum curtailment of its powers.

However, the influence of the hereditary nobility declined seriously during the 1930s, as both the House of Peers and Lower House elite groups became less vital forces in determining national policy. On May 15, 1932, imperial Japan's last parliamentary-based government fell under the hail of assassins' bullets. From this time onwards, the country began to allocate more and more power to those who presumably had the talent to deal with the series of national emergencies emanating from several international crises in East Asia and severe political instability at home. In short, the years from 1933 to 1945 saw a marked increase in the national political influence of the graduates of Tokyo Imperial University and the products of the Army and Navy War Colleges.

While the "men of talent" in the civilian and military bureaucracies demonstrated admirable expertise in their individual areas of specialization and sought aggressively to capitalize on their new-found influence to broaden their political power and prestige, they were narrowly educated and narrowly trained technocrats who lacked the breadth of vision which had so dramatically characterized the Meiji leadership. Repeatedly, each technocratically-oriented elite group in the 1930s insisted that its own vision of the future be adopted as the officially designated road to national survival and greatness. Within the military, conflicting visions of national defense and national mobilization rent the solidarity of the Army, and placed the two services at odds with one another. Similar conflicts grew within and among the civilian ministries of government, and the attainment of consensus in the "national unity" cabinets governing Japan after 1932 became increasingly difficult.

As competition among Japan's political elite groups intensified the political instability of the nation, the empire's foreign policies simultaneously brought the nation to the brink of war in East Asia and alienation from the system of cooperative diplomacy with the Western powers. By 1937, it was clear that the principal challenge to the institutions of government was the task of finding some method for controlling the rampant competitive instincts of the political elites and mobilizing the total energy and resources of the people to provide material support for Japan's foreign and military policies. In light of the failure of Japan's system of leadership recruitment to produce men who combined administrative ability with broad vision and mass popularity, the country was obliged to install as premier a man whose forte was political mediation and whose inherited social prestige made him the object of public respect. On June 1, 1937, Konoe Fumimaro was given the imperial mandate to form a new cabinet.

Konoe served as Japan's prime minister from June 1937 to January 1939, and again from July 1940 to October 1941. During this period, he repeatedly demonstrated an ability to cajole the elite groups into reaching consensus on important national policies. By the same token, however, Konoe's mediatory efforts took place within the fragile structure of the cabinet, and he was obliged for the sake of maintaining cabinet unity to abjure any positive policy leadership in order to mediate among his ministers effectively. Policy trade-offs among the elite groups represented in Konoe's government made the establishment of national priorities almost impossible. Hence, by 1940, the prince had conceived of a new plan to reform the political structure of the nation so that he could exercise effective political leadership independent of the consensus-oriented cabinet system. Konoe's plan, which was labelled Japan's "new political order," would place him at the head of a large mass-based political organization which could generate sufficient political power for him to employ additional leverage against other elite groups in the process of defining national policy. A second objective of Konoe's plan was to establish the institutional context in which the entire nation might be mobilized to meet the demands placed upon it by Japan's foreign policies.

As Japan entered her fourth year of fighting in China, and declared her intention to establish her autonomy and preeminence in East and Southeast Asia through the Greater East Asian Co-Prosperity Sphere, the national controversy over Konoe's "new political order" threw the political elite groups of the country into turmoil. Between July 1940 and March 1941, each group sought to enhance its own power position in the new order, while attempting to block the success of similar efforts by its competitors. Konoe, who was able to diagnose the political ailments of his nation quite clearly, nonetheless proved incapable of treating them. In the midst of controversy, he quickly abandoned the fight over specific aspects of his reform program, and reverted to a mediatory posture. Within a few months, the "new political order" as a vehicle for strengthening the premier's hand vis-à-vis his ministers and the competing elite groups had been entirely eviscerated by political compromise. The only lasting product of Konoe's "new political order" was the Imperial Rule Assistance Association, an organization which embraced all Japanese citizens in a network of mobilization structures, but proved unsuited for partisan political activity on behalf of Konoe's personal policy preferences.

The prince's inability to deal with the nuts-and-bolts of political reform was parallelled by his remarkable failure to gauge the international situation accurately. On several occasions, he attempted to initiate peace negotiations with China without substantially modifying Japan's original peace terms. In 1940 and 1941, he allowed his government to make crucial decisions supporting Japan's southern expansion and alliance with the fascist powers of Europe without fully appreciating the disasterous impact of those policies on Japanese-American relations. When Konoe finally concluded in mid-1941 that negotiations with the United States were essential to preclude a war Japan could not win, he lacked the leverage to override other elite groups' objections to a policy of indefinite negotiation, and was obliged to resign from the premiership in favor of General Tôjô.

Tôjô's rise to political eminence parallelled the rise of the Imperial Army as the nation's leading political force in the late 1930s. Gaining a reputation even as a cadet for working long grueling hours and carrying out his duties fastidiously, Tôjô rose as a talented and dedicated military administrator to the post of commander of the military police of the Kwantung Army in September 1935, Chief-of-Staff of the Kwantung Army in March 1937, and Vice-Minister of the Army in May 1938. In these and other posts, he proved to be so meticulous in his attention to administrative detail that he acquired the sobriquet "*Kamisori*" ("The Razor"). By the same token, however, his perceptions and analyses of Japan's international power position often left much to be desired. He was an outspoken advocate of a firm line against China in 1937, and even suggested unwisely a month prior to the inception of hostilities on the continent that a war against China could be successfully waged with little loss of time or effort in the larger army program of mobilizing against the Soviet Union. Later, as Army Minister in 1941, he preferred to uphold the army's prestige and "leap blindly from Kiyomizu" into war with the Anglo-American powers, rather than consent to an embarrassing but prudent withdrawal of forces from China in compliance with America's diplomatic pressures. The morality and justice of Tôjô's policy views were hotly debated by the prosecution and defense at the International Military Tribunal for the Far East after World War II had ended, and even today, historians engage in lively debates over whether Japan's intentions in Asia were primarily aggressive in nature or essentially a response to international pressures imposed upon her. But it is nevertheless beyond question that insofar as Tôjô was able to influence the course of Japan's foreign and military policies, his leadership, like Konoe's contributed to the formulation of policies which brought disaster down upon the Japanese Empire between 1937 and 1945.

Tôjô became Army Minister in Konoe's second government (July 1940), and in a unique departure from precedent, he was appointed premier on October 18, 1941 while still holding his commission as a military officer. Indeed, the new premier controlled not only the Army Ministry portfolio so vital to military mobilization, but also the key civilian mobilization position of Home Minister for three months as well. In short, Tôjô attempted to enhance the premier's ability to generate cabinet consensus and control potentially disruptive elite competition within the cabinet at this critical juncture by monopolizing three of the four most important seats in the cabinet council (the fourth seat was occupied by the Navy Minister). Later in the war, while serving concurrently as premier and Army Minister, he also assumed the position of Munitions Minister and Army Chief of Staff with the same goal in mind of coordinating the work of various governmental institutions by becoming the administrative head of the agencies in question. Tôjô the consummate military bureaucrat thus assumed greater administrative responsibilities in the Japanese government than any premier before him had ever done.

Tôjô took on these superhuman burdens of personal policy coordination not from any lust for political power but rather from a desire to overcome the same institutional weaknesses of the premier that Konoe had hoped to resolve with the "new political order." The national emergency created by the Pacific War transformed the attitudes of Japan's other elite groups to some extent, and those working under Tôjô and his closest associates in the government subsumed their political rivalries for the sake of the war effort. (Tôjô was never able to establish full control over the navy, and inter-service coordination in military campaigns and policy-making suffered as a consequence.) Despite his impressive record as a wartime administrator, however, Tôjô's ability to analyze the changing international situation correctly remained tragically limited. Riveted to a determined policy of fighting to the finish in the Pacific, he watched the fortunes of battle turn against his country in 1943 and presided over a series of military defeats which culminated in the fall of Saipan in July 1944, without the slightest sign of adjusting his government's policies to the realities of Japan's declining power position vis-à-vis the Allied Powers. A coalition of diverse senior officials – including Konoe – thus formed clandestinely with the intention of removing the general from power before his policies led Japan to total destruction, and on July 18, 1944 he was forced to submit his cabinet's resignation to the Emperor.

Shortly after Japan's defeat and surrender in 1945, both Tôjô and Konoe were informed that the Allied Occupation forces intended to place them on trial for their responsibilities as leaders of a nation which had violated the international peace covenants of the 1920s and had waged aggressive war against the peace of mankind. The legitimacy of the International Military Tribunal which eventually tried Japan's political leaders can now be seen in historical retrospect to have been highly questionable; but at the time, it was a foregone conclusion that both Tôjô and Konoe would be found guilty and executed. On September 11, 1945, as military police arrived at the Tôjô residence to arrest him, the general shot himself in the chest in an attempted suicide. His wound did not prove fatal, however, and he was taken into custody and eventually tried. Konoe was given more time. On December 6, he was notified that he was to report to Sugamo Prison for confinement within ten days. Following a farewell party for his many political associates on the evening of December 15, Konoe had a brief talk with his youngest son shortly after midnight, and then took his own life.

Obliged to stand trial, Tôjô comported himself with immense dignity as a defendant. He openly acknowledged his responsibilities as a wartime leader, but insisted that Japan's policies had been morally and politically legitimate responses to pressures and constraints imposed upon Japan by other powers. The Tribunal, comprised of justices from the victorious Allied nations, was unprepared to accept that defense, and he was convicted with a sentence of death. Until his final hour, Tôjô never ceased paying close attention to minute administrative problems. Exhibiting a commendable regard for other prisoners, he petitioned relentlessly throughout his captivity for an improvement of prison conditions at Sugamo, and immediately prior to his execution, was still imploring his captors to extend assistance to the impoverished families of his fellow inmates. Then, chanting the *nenbutsu,* he was led to the gallows and relieved at last of the onerous life of responsibility he had chosen to lead.

The careers of Konoe and Tôjô, and the catastrophe of Japan's involvement in the China and Pacific Wars, were equally the consequence of the tragic failure of the Japanese system of leadership recruitment to produce policymakers of sound judgement and broad vision to lead the nation in the early Shôwa period. Trapped by its own commitment to professional expertise and specialized training, the nation's leadership turned desperately to Konoe between 1937 and 1941 to mediate the conflicting narrowly-defined policy positions of the major political elite groups in power. Konoe was remarkably gifted as a mediator, but poorly trained as an administrator. Between 1941 and 1944, Tôjô proved to be an able administrator as premier, but never having transcended his limited policy perspectives as an army officer, he was unable to perceive the dire consequences of his policy preferences, and ill-suited to mediate among other elite groups in any fashion other than by assuming direct administrative control over them. Neither man was able to see in time that the Meiji leadership's attainment of the goals of national independence and *fukoku kyôhei* – "wealthy nation, strong military" – could not be indefinitely extended in a later era of international interdependence and limited national resources to the implementation by force of a grand design for a huge Japanese empire in East and Southeast Asia.

Nobel Prize-Winning Novelist

Kawabata Yasunari

by

MAKOTO UEDA

If modern Japanese culture is a singular mixture of the East and the West, the works of Kawabata Yasunari (1899-1972) exemplify that fact in a brilliant and highly individual manner. He was well versed in Western literature: an admirer of James Joyce and Marcel Proust in his youth, he was one of the first Japanese novelists to experiment with the "stream of consciousness" technique. His books on the art of writing, like *An Introduction to the Novel* (*Shôsetsu nyûmon*), are greatly indebted to the literary aesthetics of Western writers such as Virginia Woolf and E. M. Forster. On the other hand, he was keenly aware of the Japanese cultural tradition and took pains to demonstrate its beauty through his novels. Indeed, it was primarily for that reason that he was awarded the Nobel Prize for Literature in 1968. In accepting the honor, he reconfirmed his deep attachment to the beauty of his native culture, as the title of his acceptance speech, "Japan the Beautiful and Myself" (*Utsukushii Nippon no watakushi*), suggests. In this sense Kawabata's works can be said to embody an aesthetic ideal of the twentieth-century Japanese who dream of combining the best of Eastern and Western cultures. His major novels, such as *Snow Country* (*Yukiguni*), *Thousand Cranes* (*Senbazuru*), and *Sound of the Mountain* (*Yama no oto*), represent a modern man's search into traditional cultural values, a search for a possible scheme whereby old Japanese values can be given a new meaning in the context of Westernized life.

Lonely Childhood

Kawabata was born in Osaka on June 14, 1899. His early life was ridden by misfortunes, beginning at birth. He was a premature child born

Kawabata Yasunari

after only seven months' pregnancy. His father, a physician, had a weak constitution and died of tuberculosis less than two years after his birth. The same illness took his mother's life the following year, thereby leaving the three-year-old Kawabata an orphan. He was reared by his grandparents, but death continued to rob him of his kin. He lost his grandmother when he was seven, his only sister when he was ten, and his last surviving relative, his grandfather, when he was fourteen. He attended so many funerals that he nicknamed himself the "undertaker."

The fact that he had an unhappy childhood helps to explain two characteristics of Kawabata as a writer of prose fiction. One is his expertise in the art of short stories. A sickly child of small stature, he knew from early days that he had inherited a delicate body from his parents. Consciously or subconsciously the physique affected his literary form, even after he outgrew his childhood and became a writer. He always seemed more at ease with a short story than with a full-length novel, apparently feeling that he did not have the physical strength to complete a massive work. He was especially fond of composing stories of extremely short length, the kind he called "palm-sized stories." He did write novels, but many of them had initially been written – and published – as short stories. *Thousand Cranes,* for example, was originally five separate stories published in three different magazines on five different occasions.

The second characteristic of Kawabata's writings related to his childhood is the presence of what he called "the eyes of a dying man." Losing his parents and relatives in succession, he felt he was the last member of a dynasty that was dying out. "My family line is about to perish," he once wrote. "Perhaps I am a flower that resembles the last ray of the moon."[1] Here the flower is a metaphor for the artist. In Kawabata's view, a true artist came from a family line that was about to vanish; genuine art was to be created by a man who knew his days were numbered. It is for this reason that Kawabata's world of fiction is often inhabited by an ailing or dying man. Nature looks exquisitely beautiful to a person who knows he is dying. Thus the hero of *Sound of the Mountain,* who can hear the sound of approaching death, discovers unearthly beauty in his young daughter-in-law, while her husband, a healthy man, is quite blind to it. Kawabata who as a child acquired "the eyes of a dying man" grew up to become a seeker of beauty.

Youthful Love Affairs

Kawabata received elementary and secondary education at schools in the vicinity of Osaka. An outstanding student, he was then admitted to the First Higher School in Tokyo, a school where many bright young men gathered from all over the country. He moved to the Asakusa district of Tokyo in 1917. The new, more Westernized environment gave fresh stimulation to the impressionable youth. In 1920 he entered Tokyo Imperial University and majored in English. A few months later, however, he changed his major to Japanese literature. His bachelor's thesis was an ambitious study in which he tried to see premodern Japanese fiction in the light of Western literary criticism. He was graduated in 1924.

Two aspects of his adolescence are worth noting since they relate to his later works as a novelist. One has to do with the manner in which his sexual awakening happened. It took the form of homosexual love. At a dormitory of his middle school in Osaka, young Kawabata became emotionally involved with a male schoolmate of his. The experience later resulted in a short story, "A Boy" (*Shônen*). In the story Kawabata reflected that as a young boy he might have been a bit abnormal sexually because he had no one of the opposite sex to talk to in his family (his sister had been living away from home for years). But in the same story he also asserted that there was nothing physical about his relationship with the schoolmate; it was platonic love from beginning to end. Subsequently, when he was a university student in Tokyo, he fell in love with a young waitress at a coffee shop. He was quite serious and even became engaged to her, but his fiancée eventually broke the engagement for some unknown reason. Kawabata was heartbroken. Again, the affair had ended without physical intimacy.

Those two incidents seem to have contributed to the making of Kawabata's concept of love, which was later to provide a major theme for his novels. He cherished pure, romantic, non-physical love. That is why there are so many maidens appearing in his works: a maiden's love is innocent, idealistic, devoid of lust. Even when he presents a geisha for a main character, she is usually of a clean, fastidious type. The geisha heroine of *Snow Country,* for instance, looks "clean to the hollows under her toes."[2]

Of course, no human being could be completely free of lust and bestiality. The purest type of love is more likely to exist only in one's imagination. This leads to the second distinctive aspect of Kawabata's adolescence: a penchant for imaginative literature. His earliest piece of literary composition dates back to 1914, when he was still in middle school. It is "The Diary of a Sixteen-Year-Old" (*Jûrokusai no nikki*),[3] a largely factual account of his days with his aged grandfather. His adolescent love affairs resulted in several early stories, such as "A Boy," "Chiyo," and "Fire in the South" (*Nanpô no hi*). His creative impulse was also cultivated through his associations with established men of letters in Tokyo. Through his friends at the university he became acquainted with writers like Akutagawa Ryûnosuke (1892-1927), Kikuchi Kan (1888-1948), and Yokomitsu Riichi (1898-1947). He joined these and other men in founding several literary magazines, to which he contributed stories from time to time. Before his senior year was over at Tokyo Imperial University, he had decided to take up writing for his career.

Young Critic and Experimentalist

Kawabata received a B. Litt. degree from the university in the spring of 1924, a few months after the great Tokyo earthquake devastated the area. Shortly after graduation, one of his former professors called him and asked if he was interested in a teaching position at a certain college in western Japan. He answered he was not. Although he was an orphan and was by no means well off financially, he seems to have been confident of his ability to support himself by his pen already at that time. Fortunately for him, Tokyo was rapidly rebuilding itself into a modern city, and cultural activities were even more lively than before the earthquake. Kikuchi, who was to patronize him in literary circles for many years to come, had founded the magazine *Literature Spring and Autumn* (*Bungei shunjû*) the previous year, and it was selling tens of thousands of copies. To be sure, writers of fiction – including popular fiction – who could boast financial success were not many, but society seemed to be becoming more hospitable to men of letters in general. Young writers like Kawabata had good reason to believe that they could sell their writings and make a modest living by them. In Kawabata's case he had more reason to be optimistic in this regard, because still as an undergraduate he had published literary reviews and established connections with the publishing world.

Kawabata's activities as a literary critic proliferated after his graduation; all the more so after his marriage in 1926. Not only did he write reviews, but he participated in informal symposia sponsored by literary magazines and went on tours to give talks on his own writing, too. He also served on committees responsible for editing the works of various writers. Even after he became a full-fledged novelist, he never ceased activities of this kind. The latest edition of his collected works includes four thick volumes of his critical writings.[4] And there are many more essays that remain uncollected. It must be said that he was a major critic of his generation.

As a literary critic Kawabata was perceptive, independent, and kind toward obscure writers. Characteristically his reviews focused more on individual works than on their authors. When he found a story mediocre, he never hesitated to condemn it in writing even when it was a famous author's work. When he found a story good, he praised it warmly no matter how obscure the author was at the time. Always seeking a new source of inspiration, he read a good deal of writing by amateur writers, never begrudging the time it took him to do so. Eventually Kawabata came to be considered the foremost discoverer of new literary talents in contemporary Japan. Novelists whose careers he helped include prominent names like Okamoto Kanoko (1889-1939), Ibuse Masuji (b. 1898), Kajii Motojirô (1901-32), Hôjô Tamio (1914-37), Toyoda Masako (b. 1922), and Mishima Yukio (1925-70).

From a similar motive Kawabata took a profound interest in children's composition. He helped to promote nationwide contests in creative writing among grade school children, and sometimes served on the screening committees himself. He also took part in compiling *A Compendium of Model Composition* (*Mohan tsuzurikata zenshû*) and contributed a preface to it in 1939. In the opening paragraph of that preface he stated, "A child's composition is the truest of all creative writings. It shows us literature's starting point no less than its destination."[5] He went on to urge that the collection be read not only by students and teachers but by adults who were neither.

Gradually Kawabata was becoming known for his short stories, too. He

was considered a very Westernized, experimentalist writer in those early days of his career. Together with Yokomitsu, he was a co-leader of what is known as the Neo-Sensualist Movement, a movement which had its origins in various European avant-garde theories of art like Futurism, Cubism, Expressionism, Dadaism, Symbolism, Formalism, etc. The Neo-Sensualists especially admired Paul Morand, whose *Open All Night* and *Closed All Night* had appeared in Japanese translation in 1924 and 1925 respectively. In its emphasis on the importance of sensory perception, the movement was a reaction to the autobiographical type of realism that had dominated modern Japanese fiction, as well as to the leftist type of didacticism that was rapidly gaining popularity in the 1920s. Kawabata defended the Neo-Sensualist stand in his essays on the one hand, and wrote short stories to demonstrate the principles on the other. Those early stories are characterized by their extreme brevity, dazzling symbolism, and a terse, cryptic style. His friend Yokomitsu called them "flowers made of razor blades." Other critics called their author a "juggler," sometimes in a complimentary sense and sometimes in a derogatory sense.

To the general reading public, however, Kawabata was known less as a Neo-Sensualist than as a writer of "Asakusa stories" and "Izu stories." The Asakusa district of Tokyo was famous for its vaudeville houses, amusement parks, and other popular recreational facilities. Kawabata, who lived in the district during his early days in Tokyo, often went there to see dances and revues performed by young girls. The visits resulted in stories depicting the lives of those teenage showgirls, many of whom had come from less affluent families. The longest of the stories was *The Red Gang of Asakusa* (*Asakusa kurenai-dan*), which presented a group of young outcasts led by a beautiful girl. The novel, serialized in a large newspaper in 1929-30, brought popular recognition to both the novelist and the locale.

The "Izu stories" were the products of Kawabata's frequent sojourns in Izu Peninsula, a rustic resort area located to the southwest of Tokyo. His visits there obviously served as a means of escape from the bustle of the metropolis, but they also brought him opportunities to get acquainted with other groups of socially underprivileged girls working in rural areas. He became especially interested in the lives of travelling vaudeville dancers and hot-spring geisha. One of the most popular stories by Kawabata , "The Izu Dancer" (*Izu no odoriko*), was written from such experiences. In a beautifully lyrical tone the story narrates how a young student, orphaned and friendless, encounters a dancing girl in Izu and regains confidence in the goodness and warmth of the human heart. Another major theme of Kawabata's works had emerged.

The War Years

The late 1930s and early 1940s were difficult years for Japanese writers, as they were under intense pressure from the government to cooperate with its war policies. Some novelists did cooperate, producing works with ultranationalistic implications. At another extreme, writers either resolutely refused to write or openly disagreed with the government and were jailed as a result. A large majority of active authors were between the two extremes, taking an attitude of passive cooperation. Kawabata belonged to the third group. Never a politically-minded author, he watched the trend of the times largely from the sidelines. In 1935 he moved his residence from busy Tokyo to the quiet seaside town of Kamakura, where he devoted his time to reading and writing. He read a good deal of children's composition; it is reported that he read through fifteen thousand pieces in 1939 alone. He also spent time in reading or re-reading Japanese classics like *The Tale of Genji* (*Genji monogatari*). In 1941, however, even he was pressured to come out of his hideout. With other writers and journalists he twice traveled to northern China which was then under Japanese military control.

At all events, the war made hardly any mark on the two masterpieces of fiction Kawabata worked on during those years. The one was *Snow Country,* written and published in twelve segments between 1935 and 1947. It was an extension of the "Izu stories" in the sense that its central character was a geisha working at a hot-spring resort. Also like "The Izu Dancer," the main male character experiences spiritual catharsis through a young woman's help. But the novel is more complex than the short story: whereas the dancer of Izu is a pure maiden and has an innate purifying power, the geisha of the snow country is a mature woman who is all too familiar with the bestial aspect of human nature. It is only through her strong desire for cleanliness that she purifies herself and her male companion. The novel's underlying moral theme, however, is presented through beautiful symbols and in a lyrical style, and that appealed to the reading public. There is evidence to believe that Kawabata himself felt the deepest affection toward *Snow Country* among all his writings.

The other major novel he worked on in this period was *The Master of Go* (*Meijin*), which was published piecemeal between 1942 and 1953. It was based on an actual game of *go* played by two leading experts in 1938-39. The novel is unique in the Kawabata canon in that it has no major female character. Yet the basic ingredient of a Kawabata novel is present, because the protagonist is a *go* player who loves the game with a maiden's purity of heart, and his singleminded devotion to the art of

go deeply impresses the reader. The novel is interesting also for its presentation of conflicts between generations. The aged hero represents old Japan, and it is he who loses the game in the end – indeed, he dies shortly after the game. In that sense the novel can be said to be a eulogy of old Japan, of old Japanese values which Kawabata saw being shattered at the end of World War II.

The Postwar Period

Kawabata was a eulogist in a more literal sense, too. Many writers and artists, including several close friends of his, died in the difficult years during and after the war. An "undertaker" in his younger days, he now wrote a number of eulogies and obituary essays. The eulogy he delivered at Yokomitsu's funeral in 1947 is one of the most famous in modern Japan. Many of his obituary essays were also solid pieces of literary criticism that contained insightful comments on the works of the dead. His critical judgment on the late authors varied, yet he never failed to compliment each subject's sincere devotion to literature and art. In every writer's life he seemed to seek out a longing for perfect art which, in his mind, was like a maiden's longing for a perfect lover.

Kawabata himself was in good health and had one of the most productive periods of his career at this time. He wrote two major novels simultaneously, *Thousand Cranes* (1949-51) and *Sound of the Mountain* (1949-54), each of which was published piecemeal in different magazines. Both novels received high critical acclaim, the former being honored with the Academy of Arts Prize in 1952 and the latter with the Noma Literary Prize in 1954.

Thousand Cranes is a story of a young man trying to escape from a dark feeling of guilt bequeathed to him by his father and his father's mistresses. He tries to dispel his guilt through the help of a maiden whose beauty gives an impression of soaring white cranes. His absolution, however, does not come easily, for he must himself experience the darkness of the soul first. The novel is short in length but has one of the most dextrous plots Kawabata ever devised. The tea ceremony, which provides its backdrop, adds another layer of meaning to the novel.

Sound of the Mountain deals with the plight of a young woman who, though married, instinctively wants to retain her virginal beauty. Unfortunately that type of beauty is not appreciated by her husband, who seeks in her more a wife than a maiden. Her only ally is her aged father-in-law who, because of his awareness of approaching death, has become exceedingly appreciative of pure beauty on earth. The novel is not

very dramatic in terms of story development, but it is rich in images, metaphors, symbols, and associations. With a plot that progresses less through action than through symbolism, *Sound of the Mountain* is perhaps the most sophisticated of all Kawabata's novels.

Kawabata's energetic activities in the postwar period included more mundane ventures, too. Immediately after the end of the war in 1945, he helped to found a new publishing company and himself became one of its executives. Because of his interest in amateur writers, the company published a number of stories by fledgling authors little known to the public then. In 1948 he was elected president of the Japan PEN Club. The following year he became a member of the committee that selected the Akutagawa Prize, a prestigious literary prize awarded biannually honoring the best story written by an unestablished writer. In 1953 he was initiated into the Academy of Arts. As both a novelist and a critic, Kawabata was now a leading figure in contemporary Japan.

Dean of Japanese Writers

Not a man of practical bent, Kawabata was nevertheless a very conscientious person and performed his administrative duties admirably well once he accepted a position in an organization. He was, for instance, the most dynamic president the Japan PEN Club had ever known. He provided the prime moving force in inviting the International PEN Club to hold its twenty-ninth Congress in Tokyo, the first such event in Japan. He was a principal fund raiser for this and other similar undertakings. But such activities inevitably drained his creative energy and affected his health. From around 1954 he suffered from insomnia and began using sleeping pills habitually.

Some of Kawabata's prose fiction in the 1950s and 1960s seem to reflect his subconscious desire to escape into fantasies. *The Lake* (*Mizuumi*, 1954), for example, lacks a story line in the conventional sense. It consists of various sets of memories, reveries, and associations loosely strung together. The reader never knows for sure where the novel ends, and there is reason to believe that Kawabata himself did not know. *House of the Sleeping Beauties* (*Nemureru bijo,* 1960-61) was admittedly written under the influence of sleeping pills, and that shows in the novel. The story is about a strange house operated for a secret club of old, sexually impotent men, whose membership privilege is to spend a night there with drugged maidens sleeping in the nude. Again the novel consists almost entirely of recollections, dreams, and illusions. "One Arm" (*Kataude,* 1963-64) is even more purely a fantasy, as it presents a young

girl who takes off one of her arms and lends it to a man overnight.

Kyoto (*Koto,* 1961-62) and *Beauty and Sadness* (*Utsukushisa to kanashimi to,* 1961-63) include fewer fantasies, but they are far from being realistic novels. The former work features twin girls separated in infancy and reared in dissimilar environments. It is only after they reach adolescence that they discover each other's existence, but once they meet a tender affection starts to grow between them. The latter novel has for its central character a novelist who many years earlier seduced a maiden, made her pregnant, and then abandoned her. He is revenged on, when his own son is lured away by an uncommonly attractive girl who turns out to be a lesbian partner of his former victim. Both novels clearly show the mark of Kawabata in that they present maidenly love which burns intensely but goes unfulfilled – love which is beautiful because of its intensity, love which is sad because of its non-fulfillment. For that matter, most of Kawabata's novels could be retitled *Beauty and Sadness.*

Kawabata's reputation began to be known outside Japan, too, as translations of his works appeared one after another from the 1950s on. *The Atlantic Monthly* published "The Izu Dancer" in 1955, superbly translated by Edward G. Seidensticker who was to render many Kawabata novels into English later. The following two decades saw several of Kawabata's major works made available in one or more European languages. *Snow Country* was translated into English (1956), German (1957), Swedish (1957), Finish (1958), Italian (1959), French (1960), Croatian (1961), Spanish (1962), Dutch (1963), Polish (1964), Greek (1969), and Hungarian (1969). *Thousand Cranes* was published in German (1956), English (1958), French (1960), Dutch (1961), Croatian (1961), Spanish (1962), Italian (1965), Czech (1965), Danish (1966), Swedish (1966), and Finish (1969). Other novels available in Western languages include *The Master of Go*, *Sound of the Mountain*, *The Lake*, *House of the Sleeping Beauties*, *Kyoto*, and *Beauty and Sadness.*[6]

Kawabata himself began to travel to Western countries, partly in connection with his duties as president of the Japan PEN Club. His first European trip took place in 1957, when he went to London to participate in an executive committee meeting of the International PEN Club. He visited other European cities, too, and met some of the leading literary figures like T. S. Eliot and François Mauriac. In 1960 he toured the United States under the auspices of the State Department. Later the same year he visited South America to take part in another PEN Club meeting. He was in Europe for the second time in 1964. And, of course, he traveled to Sweden in 1968 to receive his Nobel Prize. The following year he was a

visiting professor at the University of Hawaii, which subsequently conferred an honorary doctorate upon him. Clearly he had become a novelist of international stature.

Death and Posthumous Fame

For Kawabata 1969 was an extremely busy year that saw him returning from Sweden, making a trip to Hawaii, and participating in various celebrations for his Nobel honor abroad and back home. It was one of the rare years in his career in which he did not produce a single story. He had begun a new novel called *Dandelions* (*Tanpopo*) the previous year, but he lost the momentum to carry on. The frantic pace of life continued into 1970, too, when he traveled to Taiwan and then to Korea for conferences. Later that year his friend and former protégé Mishima committed ritual suicide and, as might be expected, Kawabata presided at the funeral. In 1971 he surprised everyone by actively campaigning for a candidate in the Tokyo gubernatorial election. His sudden interest in politics also led to his joining the Committee of Seven for Peace and appealing for normalization of relations between Japan and the People's Republic of China.

No one knows whether those extra-literary involvements, and the resulting demands on his time and energy, had anything to do with his decision to take his own life. He died on April 16, 1972, by inhaling gas from a bathroom water heater. He had left no suicide note, nor had he shown signs of severe despondency. Speculations have been made as to the motive: some mentioned his failing health, others made much of the effect Mishima's death had on him, and still others tried to attribute it to his failure to be with a young women he had been fond of. None of the explanations is conclusive. The motive for his suicide still remains a mystery.

For whatever reason he died, it must be said that he was a writer who attained both national and international fame in his lifetime. His reputation has not waned after his death, either, and will no doubt remain that way for many years to come. There is no mystery about that, for he made lasting contributions to Japanese literature. He was a typically modern, Western-type writer in that he was acutely aware of the problems of a modern man living in the vast wasteland of contemporary society. And yet he was not a nihilist, not in the Western sense anyway. He saw a possibility of escape from sterile modern life, and that escape was to come in the form of beauty, the purest type of beauty best symbolized in the person of a maiden. In his view, a man suffering from the impurities of everyday life could be cleansed through the love of a maiden who knows no impurity. This kind of romanticism can be traced back to ancient

Japanese classics such as *The Tale of a Bamboo Cutter* (*Taketori monogatari*) and *The Tale of Genji,* as Kawabata himself once noted, and in that sense it can be considered a traditional Japanese scheme of salvation. Kawabata was a seeker of beauty, of salvation through beauty. The finest of his prose fiction shows us what is best and most beautiful in traditional Japanese culture as seen from a modern point of view. His works are sometimes not easy to read because of their complex symbolism, but a reader patient enough to study them carefully will harvest a rich reward.

[NOTES]

1. "Uso to gyaku," *Kawabata Yasunari zenshû* (Tokyo: Shinchô-sha, 1969-74). Vol. 17, p.152.
2. *Zenshû.* Vol. 5, p.274.
3. Kawabata was sixteen years old in 1914, according to the old Japanese method of calculating one's age.
4. The edition is *Kawabata Yasunari zenshû* mentioned above.
5. "Tsuzurikata ni tsuite," *Zenshû.* Vol. 13, p.331.
6. The information is from Takeda Katsuhiko, "Hi Nihongo ni yakusareta Kawabata sakuhin," *Kawabata Yasunari no ningen to geijutsu* (Tokyo: Kyôiku Shuppan Center, 1971), pp.515-23.

CHRONOLOGICAL TABLES

JAPAN		WORLD	
		476	Destruction of the Western Roman Empire
538 (552)	Official introduction of Buddhism		
		589	Unification of China by Sui Dynasty
593	Commencement of Prince Shôtoku's Regency		
607	First official embassy to Sui China		
		610	Propagation of Islam
		618	Unification of China by T'ang Dynasty
630	Embassy to T'ang China		
		642	Destruction of Sassanid Persia
645	Taika Reform		
		661	Saracen Empire founded
672	Jinshin War		
		676	Unification of the Korean peninsula by Silla
710	Location of capital at Nara (Heijô-kyô)		
		711	Conquest of Spain by the Arabs
712	Compilation of *Kojiki*		
720	Compilation of *Nihon shoki*		
		751	Paper introduced to Saracens from T'ang China
ca. 759	Compilation of *Man'yôshû*		
794	Transfer of capital to Kyoto (Heian-kyô)		
		800	Coronation of Charlemagne
805	Tendai sect introduced by Saichô		
806	Shingon sect introduced by Kûkai	806	Establishment of "Ecole de Palais"
894	Abolishment of embassies to T'ang China		
		962	Holy Roman Empire founded
ca. 1000	*Makura no sôshi* by Sei Shônagon		
ca. 1008	*Genji monogatari* by Murasaki Shikibu		
1016	Fujiwara no Michinaga becomes Regent		

		1054	Separation of Roman Catholic Church and Greek Orthodox Church
		1066	Conquest of England by the Normans
		1099	Capture of Jerusalem by the Crusaders
1156	Civil War of Hôgen		
1159	Civil War of Heiji		
1167	Taira no Kiyomori takes the title of Prime Minister		
1185	Final defeat of the Heike in the battle of Dan no Ura		
1192	Kamakura Bakufu founded by Minamoto no Yoritomo		
1199	Death of Yoritomo; rise of the Hôjô family		
		1215	*Magna Carta*
1221	Shôkyû Disturbance		
1224	True Pure Land sect founded by Shinran		
1253	Nichiren sect founded by Nichiren	1253	Founding of the Sorbonne in Paris
		1271 -95	Marco Polo travels to the East
1274	First Mongol invasion		
1281	Second Mongol invasion		
1336	Conflict between Northern and Southern Courts		
1338	Ashikaga Takauji becomes Shogun		
		1339	Commencement of the Hundred Years' War
1368	Ashikaga Yoshimitsu becomes Shogun	1368	Ming Dynasty of China founded
1392	Unification of the Courts	1392	Yi Dynasty of Korea founded
		ca. 1400	Height of the European an Renaissance
		1433	Invention of printing
1443	Ashikaga Yoshimasa becomes Shogun		
		1453	Destruction of the Eastern Roman Empire End of the Hundred Years' War
1467 -77	Ônin War		
1488	Riots led by the Ikkô Church in Kaga Province		
		1492	Columbus sails to the West Indies
		1541	Beginning of Calvin's Reformation

1543	Introduction of firearms by the Portuguese		
1549	Arrival of the Jesuit St. Francis Xavier		
		1555	Augsburg Religious Negotiation
1561	Fourth battle of Kawanakajima		
1568	Seizure of Kyoto by Oda Nobunaga		
1582	Death of Nobunaga at the Honnôji temple		
1587	Great Kitano Tea Gathering		
		1588	Defeat of the Invincible Armada
1592	First Korean expedition		
1597	Second Korean expedition Death of the twenty-six martyrs		
		1598	Edict of Nantes
1600	Battle of Sekigahara	1600	East India Company established by the English
1603	Founding of the Tokugawa Shogunate in Edo	1603	Shakespeare's *Hamlet* first performed
		1618-48	Thirty Years' War
		1636	Founding of Harvard University
1639	Final "seclusion edict"		
		1644	Ch'ing Dynasty of China founded
1682	*Kôshoku ichidai otoko* by Ihara Saikaku		
		1688	Glorious Revolution
1694	*Oku no hosomichi* by Matsuo Bashô		
		1701	War of Spanish Succession
		1707	Legislative Union of England and Scotland
1709	*Seiyô kibun* by Arai Hakuseki		
1720	*Shinjû ten no Amijima* by Chikamatsu Monzaemon		
		1762	*Du contrat social, ou principes du droit politique* by Jean-Jacques Rousseau
		ca. 1770	Beginning of Industrial Revolution
1772	Tanuma Okitsugu becomes Senior Councilor		
		1776	Declaration of Independence
		1789	French Revolution
1798	*Kojiki-den* by Motoori Norinaga		

		1806	Destruction of Holy Roman Empire
		1823	Monroe Doctrine
1827	*Nihon gaishi* by Rai San'yo		
		1840	Opium War
		1850 -64	Taiping Rebellion
1853	Arrival of Commodore Perry at Uraga		
		1854	Crimean War
1858	Commercial Treaty with five nations		
		1861	American Civil War
1863	Bombardment of Kagoshima by the British fleet		
1866	Tokugawa Yoshinobu becomes Shogun		
		1867	*Das Kapital* by Karl Marx
1868	Meiji Restoration		
		1869	Opening of Suez Canal
1871	Departure of Iwakura Mission for America and Europe		
1873	Founding of the First National Bank of Japan		
1877	Satsuma Rebellion	1877	Invention of phonograph
1889	Promulgation of Meiji Constitution		
1894	Sino-Japanese War		
1904	Russo-Japanese War		
1914	Declaration of War with Germany	1914	World War I
		1917	Russian Revolution
		1920	League of Nations established
1923	Great Kantô Earthquake		
		1929	Worldwide Depression
1931	Manchurian Incident		
1937	Marco Polo Bridge Incident		
1941	Pacific War	1941	German invasion of U.S.S.R.
1945	Unconditional surrender	1945	Unconditional surrender of Germany United Nations established
1946	Promulgation of New Constitution		
		1950	Korean Conflict
1951	San Francisco Peace Treaty signed		
		1957	Artificial satellite launched (U.S.S.R.)
1964	Tokyo Olympiad		

Year	Japan	Year	World
		1966	Great Cultural Revolution (The People's Republic of China)
1968	Kawabata wins the Nobel Prize	1969	First landing on the moon (U.S.A.)
1972	Return of Okinawa to Japan		

Map of Japan

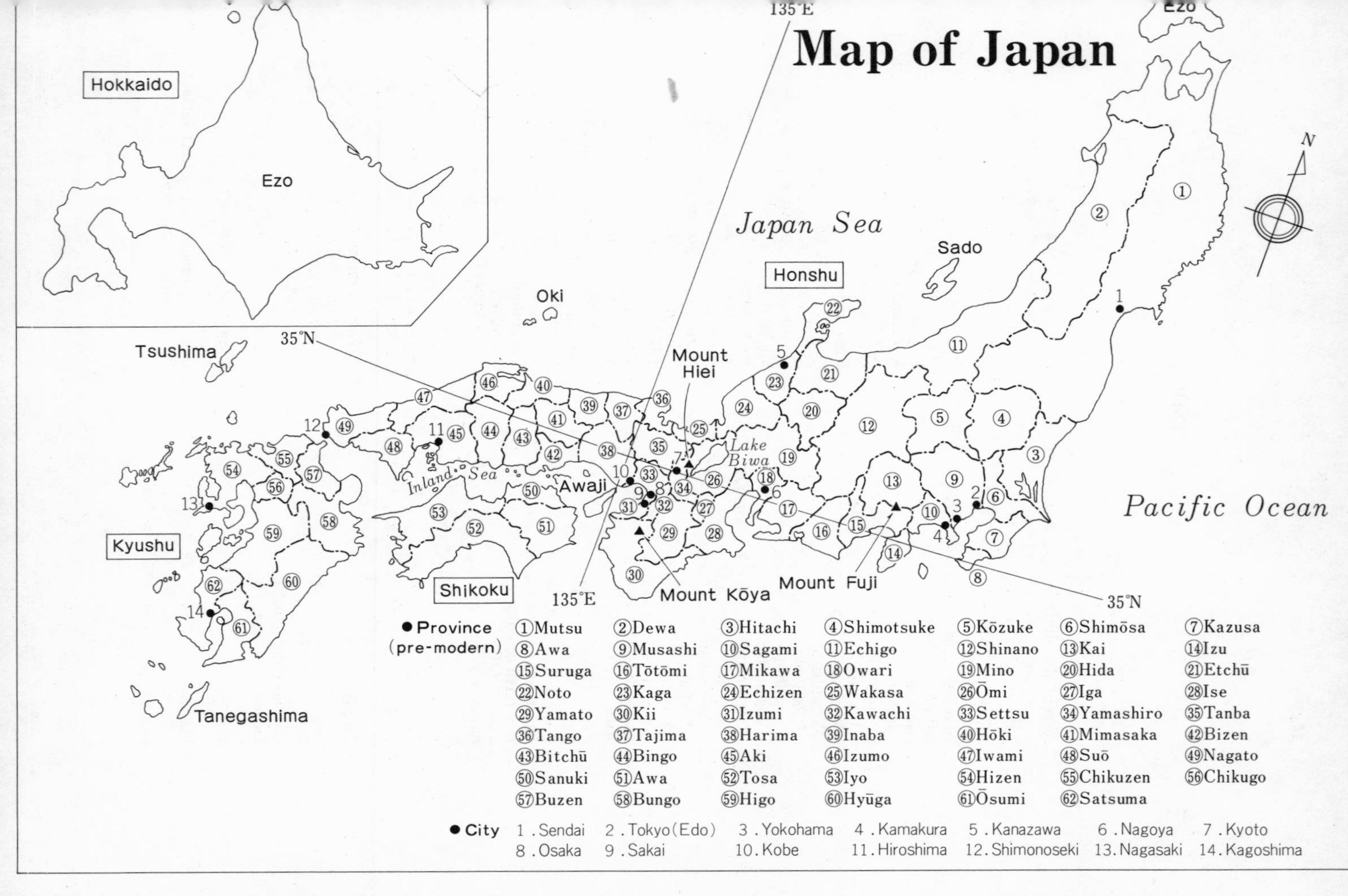
Hokkaido
Ezo
Japan Sea
Honshu
Sado
Oki
Tsushima
Kyushu
Shikoku
Tanegashima
Awaji
Inland Sea
Lake Biwa
Mount Hiei
Mount Kōya
Mount Fuji
Pacific Ocean
135°E
35°N
N
● Province (pre-modern)
①Mutsu ②Dewa ③Hitachi ④Shimotsuke ⑤Kōzuke ⑥Shimōsa ⑦Kazusa
⑧Awa ⑨Musashi ⑩Sagami ⑪Echigo ⑫Shinano ⑬Kai ⑭Izu
⑮Suruga ⑯Tōtōmi ⑰Mikawa ⑱Owari ⑲Mino ⑳Hida ㉑Etchū
㉒Noto ㉓Kaga ㉔Echizen ㉕Wakasa ㉖Ōmi ㉗Iga ㉘Ise
㉙Yamato ㉚Kii ㉛Izumi ㉜Kawachi ㉝Settsu ㉞Yamashiro ㉟Tanba
㊱Tango ㊲Tajima ㊳Harima ㊴Inaba ㊵Hōki ㊶Mimasaka ㊷Bizen
㊸Bitchū ㊹Bingo ㊺Aki ㊻Izumo ㊼Iwami ㊽Suō ㊾Nagato
㊿Sanuki 51 Awa 52 Tosa 53 Iyo 54 Hizen 55 Chikuzen 56 Chikugo
57 Buzen 58 Bungo 59 Higo 60 Hyūga 61 Ōsumi 62 Satsuma
● City 1. Sendai 2. Tokyo (Edo) 3. Yokohama 4. Kamakura 5. Kanazawa 6. Nagoya 7. Kyoto
8. Osaka 9. Sakai 10. Kobe 11. Hiroshima 12. Shimonoseki 13. Nagasaki 14. Kagoshima

INDEX